TOTALLY INCORRECT

TOTALLY INCORRECT
Conversations with Doug Casey

Wherein Mr. Casey's unwillingness
to compromise the truth disqualifies him
from any hope of membership in polite society
(or even acceptance by a decent Upper West Side condo association).

DOUG CASEY

Doug Casey is a highly respected author, publisher and professional investor.

Doug literally wrote the book on profiting from periods of economic turmoil: his book *Crisis Investing* spent multiple weeks as #1 on the *New York Times* bestseller list and became the best-selling financial book of 1980 with 438,640 copies sold; surpassing big-caliber names, like *Free to Choose* by Milton Friedman, *The Real War* by Richard Nixon, and *Cosmos* by Carl Sagan.

Doug broke the record with his next book, *Strategic Investing*, by receiving the largest advance ever paid for a financial book at the time. Interestingly enough, Doug's book *The International Man* was the most sold book in the history of Rhodesia.

He has been a featured guest on hundreds of radio and TV shows, including David Letterman, Merv Griffin, Charlie Rose, Phil Donahue, Regis Philbin, Maury Povich, NBC News and CNN; and has been the topic of numerous features in periodicals such as *Time, Forbes, People,* and the *Washington Post.*

Doug is the founding Chairman of Casey Research, an investment research publisher that helps self-directed investors earn superior returns by taking advantage of market dislocations.

Louis James, *Senior Editor*, Metals Division, Casey Research

Louis travels the world, visiting highly prospective geological targets, grilling management and company geologists, and interviewing natives. His background in physics, economics, and technical writing prepared him well for his role as senior editor of the *International Speculator* and *Casey Investment Alert.* Wherever he is, Louis is on the lookout for the next double-your-money winner.

Terry Coxon, President Passport Financial

Terry Coxon is the author of *Keep What You Earn* and *Using Warrants* and the co-author (with Harry Browne) of *Inflation-Proofing Your Investments.* He edited *Harry Browne's Special Reports* for its 23 years of publication and all of Harry Browne's investment books since 1974.

Terry was the founder and for 22 years the president of the Permanent Portfolio Fund, a mutual fund that invests in precious metals as well as stocks and bonds.

Copyright © 2013—Casey Research
All rights reserved.
Printed in the United States of America.

Co-Publishers:
Laissez Faire Books
808 St. Paul Street
Baltimore, MD 21202
LFB.org

Casey Research, LLC
PO Box 1427
Stowe, VT 05672
caseyresearch.com

ISBN: 978-0-9882851-3-2

18 17 16 15 14 13   3 4 5 6 7 8 9

One more Doug story. Back when Dick Cheney was candidate Cheney, he was making the rounds, shaking hands and kissing babies. He went to press the flesh at a large investment conference where Doug was a keynote speaker. When Cheney entered the room where speakers go to relax in between sessions, the conference organizer introduced him to Doug. Cheney stuck out his hand, saying something about how pleased he was.

Doug looked him in the eye, lifted his hand, slowly folded it behind his back, and says: "I'm not going to shake your hand. I hold you and everything you stand for in contempt." Cheney's answer was that Doug must be a Democrat, so Doug spent the next minute explaining exactly why he despised him. I heard that the following week at another conference, Cheney had still not gotten over it.

Note to Republicans: Doug is an equal-opportunity politician basher and has just as much contempt for left-leaning professional liars as he does for any other variety.

Whether one agrees with Doug's politics or not, there is value to society in people like him who speak their minds regardless of consequences. Personally, I find this sort of fearlessness inspiring.

I hope you will find this collection of interviews equally inspiring. They are derived from the decades of experience Doug has traveling the world, meeting people, investing, buying art, and generally tasting all that life has to offer. But these conversations are not just for your entertainment and enlightenment; they are full of ideas, facts, suggestions, and practical advice that can completely change one's life for the better.

I hope they will benefit you as they have me—or at least that you'll find them as much fun to read as Doug and I had making them.

Sincerely,

Louis James

it through the X-Ray machine. "No, I don't," said Doug, "the machine says it's safe." The guard insisted, which only made Doug more stubborn. "Look," said Doug, dancing back and forth through the machine, "it's not going off, so there's no problem with my belt!"

That's Doug—me, I want to make my flight and not spend the afternoon having tea with border guards. Now I always go through security *before* Doug does.

But there's more to this than fearlessness. Doug can afford to miss planes and meetings and so forth—so he does. I have seen Doug do exactly as he pleases, time after time, and simply pay the consequences if someone doesn't like it. Easier to apologize than to ask for permission—especially if it pertains to something one believes, as a matter of principle, one should not have to ask for permission to do.

I understood this clearly the first time I met Doug in person. It was at a large conference put on by a more conservative than libertarian organization, after the September 11 attacks. Doug was comparing the US to the Roman Empire, a theme that went down even less well than usual, given the patriotic fervor of the time. People were booing and hissing, and Doug just kept right on exploring his theme.

At some point, and I don't remember the logic that took him there, Doug commented that from the Roman perspective, it made sense to feed the Christians to the lions. Doug did *not* say he approved, just that Christians were subversives at the time, and given the morals of the day, feeding the problem to the lions was a predictable and legal way to try to get rid of it.

About half the room—and it was a large room with more than 500 people in it—shouted and gesticulated at Doug, got up, and stormed out.

Here's the part I'll never forget: Doug chuckled, took a sip of water from his glass, leaned closer to the microphone, and said, "Good. I didn't think they were paying attention." Then he went right on exploring his theme.

That was when I understood the concept of "drop dead money"—an expression I'd heard but not fully grasped. When you have enough money that there isn't anyone in the world you can't tell to drop dead, you achieve a real freedom few people attain or even understand.

Now, I'm not suggesting that outraging half your audience is a great move we should all emulate, but there is something to be said for the lack of fear that comes with accumulating a serious amount of capital, which is what we're all about helping people do, here at Casey Research.

I learned a valuable lesson that day, and it changed my life.

Introduction

By Louis James

When I first met Doug Casey, more than 15 years ago, it was in an interview setting. I asked him questions for 45 minutes, and his answers were, if not exactly the words I would say, almost entirely based on the same ideas and values. By the end of the interview, I felt as though I'd just met my long-lost twin.

We're not, of course. The biggest difference between us is probably Doug's well-known lack of fear, which gives rise to semi-famous stories, such as the way he likes to ski straight down the mountain, mogul fields be damned, until he hits something—and then gets up and does it again. It's like the "Jaws" character in the Roger Moore-era James Bond movies, who gets hit by cars, driven off cliffs, tossed in with sharks, etc., only to shrug it all off and keep going.

I think Doug's tombstone will bear the inscription: "Well, it seemed like a good idea at the time."

This is, of course, admirable in certain ways. A fearless man who stands on sound principles can and will do amazing things, including walk away from a *lot* of money left on the table when taking it would compromise his integrity.

But it can also be a pain. Frequently.

Doug, for example, never worries about missing flights or speeches or weddings—everything eventually gets folded back into the Earth's mantle, he likes to say, so why get upset? This is not a convenient trait in a travel companion. Doug also hates bureaucracy, loathes stupidity, and has absolutely no patience for the combination. This is a very bad trait in a travel companion.

One time, we were on a tight schedule going through airport security, so Doug dutifully put his carry-on, jacket, watch, etc. on the X-Ray conveyor and stepped through the metal detector. It did *not* go off. However, the guard saw that Doug was still wearing his belt and told him he had to take it off and run

Contents

Acknowledgments

There are always more people to thank at the birth of a new book than can be named, so let me start by thanking everyone who contributed. To start at the beginning, however, I have to give special thanks to my friend Porter Stansberry, whose idea it was for me to publish the weekly conversations now collected in this book—and the coming sequel collection on more specifically investment-related topics. And Bill Bonner, for a bit of inspiration.

Special thanks go to my wife, Ancha Casey, for suggesting, guiding, correcting, prodding and motivating me on these conversations, throughout the years of their creation. My partners David Galland and Olivier Garret also deserve special thanks, for suggesting this book form, and for their work and support making it happen.

Terry Coxon, economist and editor extraordinaire—also former editor of Harry Browne, whose books contributed so much to my development as a person and as an investor—I thank profusely for jumping on this project and getting it done in record time. The production staff at Casey Research deserve great thanks as well, for all their work proofing, tweaking, posting, fixing, etc., over the years that went into these conversations: Shannara, Dody, Jackie, Jo-Anne, Pam, Veronica, Doug, and Erik.

Finally, I'm not sure how to thank my friend and brother in arms, Lobo Tiggre (Louis James), whose uncanny ability to almost read my mind made these conversations what they are. It is he, the indefatigable "L", who saddled up with me every week for our intellectual excursions and made sure they got published on time for our readers.

I do hope you enjoy reading about the ideas as much as we enjoyed conversing about them.

Sincerely,
DRC

Doug Casey on the TSA

Nov 24, 2010

L: Doug, your favorite group of people, the Transportation Security Agency, have been in the news a lot lately, with their chief being summoned to Capitol Hill to answer for the excesses of his underlings. Today is National Opt Out Day, when Americans are encouraged to refuse the full-body "porno" scans and the alternative pat-downs. And yet, the TSA is said to have very high approval ratings—as high as 81% in one <u>CBS poll</u>. [1] As straws in the wind go, that does not bode well. What do you make of this?

Doug: They're certainly the face of government that one encounters most often these days. Some newer polls and news stories suggest that support for what they do may be waning, but in general, it's another sign of the accelerating decline of the American Empire. As Tacitus pointed out in the second century, the more numerous the laws, the more corrupt the state. Although it's also true that the more corrupt the state, the more numerous the laws…

All bureaucracies inevitably become sodden, counterproductive, and centered mainly on their own agendas. But the TSA is on an extraordinarily steep downward trajectory. I suspect that is for several reasons. One is that the TSA is on the "front line," as they pathetically describe it, of an unnecessary and illusory war on terror, so they're very sensitive about somehow justifying their existence. Another is that they're dressed up in uniforms and organized in a paramilitary manner; once you put people in costumes, they become much more obedient chimpanzees. Another is that their employees are actually the dregs of US society. It amazes me that when Congress created it, they found 50,000 people, practically overnight, who thought that

---

1. Doug references many links throughout this book. We have included short links to redirect you to the original webpage. For this link, see www.totallyincorrectbook.com/go/1. For a complete list of links, see www.totallyincorrectbook.com/links.

getting paid to go through fellow citizens' dirty underwear at airports was a good deal.

This is unskilled labor of the most menial sort. But these are not, by and large, teenagers with no skills; rather, they are middle-aged people who should be able to find *some* more productive—or at least higher-paying—use for their time. I suppose it was perceived as a step up for those who were Walmart greeters or packing bags at Safeway—although that's incorrect, because although those are low-paid, unskilled, and unchallenging occupations, they are at least honorable work.

And they've now expanded the force to 65,000, and they are still hiring—they've placed <u>ads on the backs of pizza boxes</u>.[2] These people are truly the bottom of the barrel.

L: I've just looked it up, and the TSA screener gets paid $10.91–$15.59 per hour. Overtime is up to $23.23, and there are bonuses. I wonder what those are for…

Doug: I doubt the bonuses are based on "customer satisfaction." Though I bet the government benefits are significant, and the fringe benefits are commensurate with government employment. At this point, the average government employee makes about 50% more than a civilian worker. It's appealing to those who have not bothered to learn a useful trade.

But the real problem is psychological. Certain types of people are drawn to certain types of jobs. Only a certain type of person would, for example, become a prison guard. It's bad enough being sent to prison involuntarily, so what does it say about a person who'll spend his or her days there, just to be the one with the baton? Many are really bad apples, and the power has, quite predictably, gone to their heads.

L: You don't think any of them think they are actually making people safe—saving lives?

Doug: There might be a few who actually believe that, but that doesn't mean they are not still, on average, the sort of person who enjoys bullying other people. Actually, the people who are even more contemptible are the members of the chattering classes—you can read their <u>editorials in the Washington Post</u>[3] and <u>here</u>[4]—who cheerlead for the TSA, by saying "Yes, some mistakes are made, some officers are overzealous, or lack common sense, but it's good and necessary in principle." That's totally pernicious nonsense on all levels. It's a matter of principle that's in question, something to which they're completely oblivious.

---

2. www.totallyincorrectbook.com/go/2
3. www.totallyincorrectbook.com/go/3
4. www.totallyincorrectbook.com/go/4

There are many, many recent examples of just how arrogant and abusive these thugs have gotten recently. I just read today about a cancer victim that had a bladder bag...

L: Can't take any liquids through security!

Doug: Yes. So they pawed the thing and spilled urine all over the fellow, and he had to travel that way. Another story I read recently was of a woman who had pierced nipples and the TSA removed the rings with some pliers they had lying around, even after the things were identified and were obviously no threat. And there was a six-year-old child who couldn't walk without a leg brace, but they made him take it off to go through the metal detector.

And you better not back-sass your betters today, either...

Actually, the TSA serves absolutely no useful purpose. On the one hand, it's playing into the bad guys' hands by helping bankrupt the US, by death through a thousand cuts. On the other hand, if a bad guy really wanted to do some damage, he'll just stand in a line with hundreds of others waiting to go through screening, and detonate his carry-on bag there. That will certainly happen.

L: I've just looked up some sample news reports, including the <u>screaming three-year-old</u>[5] and that guy's <u>"don't touch my junk" cell-phone recording</u>[6] that's going around, for people who haven't seen them.

Doug: This is, in my view, criminal malfeasance. These people are completely out of control. But, more importantly, it's a sign of the times. An atmosphere of suspicion, antagonism, envy, and fear is becoming more pervasive every day in the US and Europe. With every real or imagined "terrorist" event, it gets ramped up more. The TSA now has goons patrolling trains and bus stations. A clever bad guy will attack one of those, so that all public travel in the US would be as bad as it is in the airports. Then, a couple incidents using cars and trucks, which would "prove" the necessity for 100,000 more TSA people. Eventually, you'd be unable to travel anywhere, in any way, without the prospect of inspection and detention.

L: People do seem to be realizing this danger. The outrage has become great fodder for comedians. There are some Internet spoofs of the TSA pat-downs going around, including <u>one from Saturday Night Live</u>[7] I just dug up.

Speaking of spoofs, do you remember the *Airplane* movies made back in the 1970s to spoof the *Airport* dramas? In the second one, there's a scene in which two main characters are talking in the foreground, and in the background, people are trooping through the magnetometer with guns, bandoliers,

5. www.totallyincorrectbook.com/go/5
6. www.totallyincorrectbook.com/go/6
7. www.totallyincorrectbook.com/go/7

and bazookas, while a little old lady is thrown against a wall and frisked. These movies are totally slapstick, intended to be utterly ridiculous, and now life is imitating fiction.

Doug: I know; Americans are now the laughingstock of the world. Life is clearly imitating art at this point. There's no question about it. I just wish it would get to the point it did in _V for Vendetta_[8], towards the end of the movie—and sooner rather than later. But I fear that whatever replaces the current system—at least for a while—will be even worse, before it eventually gets better. The French Revolution may offer a precedent. It was great to get rid of Louis XVI—but then came Robespierre.

L: It certainly seems to be a sign of our times—evidence of the decay of the empire, as you say; the roaches are coming out of the woodwork and marching about in the light of day with arrogance and disdain for their inferiors. On the other hand, the head TSA roach did get called out on the mat. The Internet is buzzing with praise for <u>Ron Paul's efforts to put them in their place</u>.[9] Do you think there's any hope Americans will put their collective foot down and stop the airport grope-fest?

Doug: No. Some polls show citizens are outraged, but most others suggest that they are cheering the TSA on. The fact is that when you deal with almost anybody, as an individual, they are generally affable and sensible. But we're dealing here with mob psychology and governments. Therefore you're dealing with the lowest common denominator and the basest motives and emotions. At this point, the whole system is in a self-reinforcing downward spiral. It needs to be flushed.

L: Hmmm. There was a recent comedy about an improbable romance between a "nobody" and a girl who's totally "<u>out of his league</u>".[10] What job did they give the guy to epitomize the insignificance of his life? He was a TSA goon. But it was a Hollywood fantasy, so he was, of course, an under-appreciated nice guy.

Doug: That's classic. But in real life, even people who would ordinarily be nice tend to let the demons within out, once they're sucked into power within an abusive system. It's like the <u>Milgram Experiment</u>.[11] You can put an ordinary person into an authoritarian system, and he starts acting as he's told to. And the public starts acting like sheep. This is why it only takes one guard to intimidate 100 prisoners.

---

8. www.totallyincorrectbook.com/go/8
9. www.totallyincorrectbook.com/go/9
10. www.totallyincorrectbook.com/go/10
11. www.totallyincorrectbook.com/go/11

Take the example of Germany. It was a civilized country in the 1920s, but when the wrong people got in power, the 20 percent of the 20 percent who are the worst people came out of the woodwork and joined the SS and the Gestapo. They were mostly pretty average nothing/nobody people who let power go to their heads—just like the people who work for the TSA today.

The Black Riders have come out from Mordor, and their minions are swarming over the land.

L: Someone replicated the Milgram Experiment[12] recently. I'm amazed they got it past an ethics committee. As for the TSA, here's a collection of horror stories[13] to back you up.

What's really scary is all the preparation our tireless public servants have done, setting up systems that seem benign—or at least mostly harmless—now, but pave the way for serious abuse. The suspension of *posse comitatus* for the drug war, the declaration of US citizens to be "enemy combatants" (a term not mentioned in the US Constitution) and therefore without the rights guaranteed by the Constitution, the stories about the FEMA camps already built, wiretaps without warrants, the erosion of the Second Amendment (the right to keep and bear arms), "free speech zones" where free speech is *allowed*... All of these things are police-state tools.

Right now, the US still feels relatively free. You and I can have this conversation without being sent to the gulag. But make a joke in a TSA screening checkpoint, and see how free you feel. Or make a politically incorrect statement on a college campus. What happens when these insects, with real or manufactured approval from the masses clamoring for security, feel truly free to do whatever they please?

Doug: The cat's totally out of the bag now. It's become Kafkaesque. It's gotten so bad, many people I know go out of their way not to fly through the US. Even if you're not leaving the airport but are just making a flight connection, you have to go through the indignities of customs and immigration—and then you have to deal with these lowlifes at the TSA. And it's just going to get worse.

I'm interested in—but not looking forward to—seeing what happens on my next trip to the US. Flying in most parts of the world is still fairly mellow, unless it's a flight to the US. I plan on opting out next time and not using the back-scatter device. I just have to keep my cool. These people can sense I have an attitude about these things—and frankly, I have only contempt for people who don't have an attitude. They either have no self-respect or no intelligence.

---

12. www.totallyincorrectbook.com/go/12
13. www.totallyincorrectbook.com/go/13

But it's pointless to lose your temper, since you're dealing with robots. Raging against the machine just depletes your own resources, and it can actually strengthen the machine.

The wisest course is to minimize your flying, and soon other travel, in the US. That means spending a minimum of time in the US, but since there is relatively much less wealth and opportunity in the US with each passing day, that's less and less of an inconvenience. I fear it's going to get much worse, at an accelerating rate.

L: And to add insult to injury, none of this makes anyone one bit safer, while there are systems that apparently do. They don't pat people down in Israeli airports, for example, and yet they've not had a breach of security for years. Here's a video[14] I found that makes that point.

Doug: I suppose. The Israelis have gone out of their way to hire street-smart operators, which won't ever happen in the US. And they can be very politically incorrect, looking for a certain type—basically a young Muslim male; that will never happen in the US either. And they've been lucky; only a complete idiot will hit such a hard target. But Israel is a theocratic, ethnically exclusive police state—hardly a model to follow. And I don't like being interrogated by some fool in a uniform, either.

On the bright side, this gross violation of people's rights by the TSA is so personal, it could be the thing that actually pushes the US over a psychological tipping point, and gets Americans to act like Americans and say, "I'm not going to take anymore!" At some point, even a cowering dog will stop cowering and bite. At least in theory.

The would be good for the country but could make things turn pretty ugly in the interim, which is one reason I'm glad I don't have to—and don't—spend much time in the US anymore.

L: But you've said before that the Land of the Free and the Home of the Brave has been turned into the Land of the Lapdogs and the Home of the Whipped Dogs. Do you actually think there's a line beyond which US citizens can't be pushed and will develop the spine to act like Americans?

Doug: Well, one can hope. With millions and millions of people losing their houses and almost 40 million people receiving food stamps,[15] while corporate execs loot their publicly traded and government-subsidized employers for billions in bonuses, and inflation set to take off in the not-too-distant future, these sorts of indignities could push people over the edge.

---

14. www.totallyincorrectbook.com/go/14
15. www.totallyincorrectbook.com/go/15

Sometimes, it amazes me to see the stock market going up in the face of all this volatility, but I believe it's doing so because of the creation of all these trillions and trillions of currency units. Not because of any fundamental soundness in the economy. This has me thinking of the ideal speculations for the next little while.

L: Okay, but generally, investment implications would be as with other straws in the wind spelling out trouble and volatility: liquidate, consolidate, create, and speculate.[16]

Doug: And diversify your political risk.[17] As you know, I always like to look at the bright side of things. In this case, it will be interesting to see if the looming complete bankruptcy of the US government will force a deconstruction of the "national security" state, including disbanding of the TSA, which may well grow to 150,000 employees in the near future. Or whether it will turbocharge its growth for a while thereafter.

L: Okay then, no need to repeat that—but readers who have not read what you have to say on those subjects should follow the links.

Doug: Right.

L: Very well then. Thanks for your input on the TSA today. I hope lots of people opt out!

Doug: You're welcome. Until next time...

---

16. www.totallyincorrectbook.com/go/16
17. www.totallyincorrectbook.com/go/17

Doug Casey on Charities

Nov 4, 2009

L: Doug, our readers are hoping to live well for the rest of their lives. If they are successful, they'll have some money left over at the end. Some have wondered, given your low opinion of trying to use the state to improve the human condition, if there's a private charity you think might be a good place to direct funds when they'll no longer be needing them.

Doug: No.

L: That's it? No?

Doug: Most charities aren't worth the cost of the gunpowder it would take to blow them to hell.

L: And the permitting for the demolition—fuhgeddaboudit. But can you explain why?

Doug: Sure. Charities are largely counterproductive. Their main beneficiaries are not the intended recipients but the givers. They get some tax benefits, but mainly they get the holy high of do-goodism. Frankly, the idea of charity itself is corrupting to both parties in the transaction.

For instance, take Bill Gates and Warren Buffett. Both are geniuses at their businesses. But they're the type of geniuses I consider to be idiot savants. If they really wanted to improve the state of the world, they should continue doing what they do best, which is accumulating wealth. Or, actually, creating it—as opposed to dissipating it by giving it away. Giving money away breaks up a capital pool that could have been used productively by those who build it for making new wealth (which increases the amount of wealth that exists in the world).

Worse, giving money away usually delivers it into the hands of people who don't deserve it. That sends the wrong moral message. People should have, or get, things because they deserve them. And you deserve things because you earn them. In other words, wealth should be a consequence of doing things that improve the state of the world. Endowing groups, or individuals, because they happen to have had some bad luck, or are perpetual losers, is actually immoral.

When money is given away, it's almost as bad as government welfare. It makes it unnecessary for the recipient to produce, and that tends to cement him to his current station in life. The very act of making an urgent situation non-urgent takes away the incentive, the urgency, to improve.

Morally speaking, charity is not a virtue, it's a vice.

L: The giver gets to feel good at the expense of the people whose independent drive they undermine. But what about the programs that are specifically designed to teach an individual to fish, rather than to just hand out fish—those that teach job skills, for example—do you see them the same way?

Doug: I'm not saying that programs like that can have no positive effect. There are people who genuinely want to improve themselves, but, for whatever reason, just can't manage it on their own. But charity is not the best way to approach the issue.

Look, the basic point I'm making is that the best way to reduce the amount of poverty in the world is to create more wealth—as much as possible, as quickly as possible.

The essence of a charity transaction is to transfer wealth from those who have shown they can create it to those who have not shown they can. I mean, if a man doesn't know how to "fish," which isn't exactly rocket science, after all, you have to wonder why—something we discussed in our chat about education. Money is best left in the hands of the most competent and productive people, and the best way to tell who's the most competent and productive is generally to look at who's created the most wealth.

L: And the more wealth there is in the world, the better off everyone is— even those who end up working for the creators.

Doug: Right. And those employees are creating and earning their own wealth as well. It sure has a lot more dignity than being a welfare bum. Besides, if they are competent and creative, there's no reason for them not to rise to the top.

L: And as we discussed in our conversation on technology, you need large pools of capital to develop new technologies—and new technologies tend, on average, to improve the lot of the little guy proportionally more than the guy at the top of the social pyramid.

Doug: Yes. Charity exists, mostly, to make the donor feel good. It assuages guilt people accrue over a lifetime, for real or imaginary reasons.

L: I remember that interview John Stossel did with Ted Turner, in which he asked him to explain why he gave a billion dollars to the UN. Turner looked pole-axed for a minute, then got up and walked out of the interview.

Doug: [Laughs] That's a polar opposite to charity. That was giving money to an organization that is itself destructive. Counterproductive in the extreme. The UN, which is just a corrupt club for governments, should be abolished, not subsidized. And here's this fool *actually feeding the beast.*

It's a perfect example of what most so-called charitable giving is about. It's an excuse for people to display their fine philanthropist plumage. It's a never-ending contest of one-upmanship, to see who can be the king of the hill of fools for a day, by giving the most. In most cases, it's not about what the money is going to, it's about being a big shot among peers and getting invited to all the most fashionable parties. They get to socialize with celebrities and others who, in our corrupt society, buy fame by giving away money—which in many cases was either easily earned or unearned.

In most cases, philanthropy doesn't arise from a love for one's fellow man, but from a need to assuage guilt, a need to show off, and a lack of imagination.

L: So, your basic argument is that it's better (and cheaper) to put a fence at the top of a cliff than to put an ambulance at the bottom. That is, rather than putting Band-Aids on the poverty-stricken, it's better not to *have* any poverty-stricken. Therefore, it's better to allow wealth to continue accumulating and creating more wealth. And that means that any effort to take wealth away from the wealthy—the productive—and give it to the non-productive, is... counterproductive.

Doug: That's basically the argument. Yes. And it's true for both practical and ethical reasons.

L: Okay. So what happens when you run into literally starving orphan babies in Haiti, the way you did? Even if you allow wealth to accumulate, and society becomes 50 or 100 times wealthier, and that decreases poverty by 50 or 100 times—or maybe 1,000 times. There will still be some cases of people who, through genuinely no fault of their own, truly need a helping hand—and the consequences would be dire if they don't get it. What would you advocate in those situations?

Doug: Well, in the first place, though I'm not a Christian, let me quote Jesus of Nazareth. He said, "The poor you will always have with you." He had a different context in mind, but he was quite correct. That's because in most cases, poverty is not a function of bad luck.

It can be, sometimes, of course. Perhaps if you're born in a country with a brutal and repressive regime, or if you're born with mental handicaps—there are all kinds of things that can happen. But generally, with a few such exceptions, poverty is simply a sign of bad habits. In a relatively free country, it's a sign of an inability or unwillingness to save, which is to say, to produce more than you consume. It's a sign of a lack of self-discipline. Sloth that afflicts those not willing to learn skills they can sell to other people. It can be a sign of having no self-respect, as among those who spend all their money on drugs and alcohol, which are debilitating, rather than strengthening.

In the vast majority of cases, those who suffer from poverty are not victims of anything other than their own bad habits.

L: Wow. Tough words.

Doug: It's even worse than that. Think about it. Let's say we're looking at some place where there's been a drought or some other serious natural disaster, and then organizations like the UN ship in thousands of tons of food. What happens when that food hits the local market?

L: Does it even get there? Doesn't the local dictator usually take it and sell it in some other country where people can pay for it, and then stash the cash in a Swiss bank account?

Doug: Well, that's the first thing that happens, of course. But even when it gets through to the intended recipients, such aid rarely helps them. In fact, it usually hurts them because, as I was saying, when all that free food hits the local market, it drives the price of food down so low, the local farmers can't produce profitably.

What happens when you drive the local farmers out of business? They stop planting, there's no crop the next year, and the shortage of food becomes even worse. The very acts of these charities trying to help people in famine-stricken areas prolong the famines.

Now, I'm not saying that if you know someone who needs a helping hand, and you feel good about helping—which is different from feeling guilty about not helping—that you shouldn't do it. It can be a good-karma thing to do—and I do believe in karma, incidentally.

But when these things are institutionalized, they create distortions in the marketplace.

L: People may think it strange to hear you talking about markets in famine-stricken places or regions devastated by earthquakes, etc. But markets are everywhere. They are not physical places in New York and London but are aspects of human psychology. They are patterns of human behavior created by people when they enter into voluntary transactions—as distinct from government action, which is always based on coercion. In today's world, famine can still be caused by storms, drought, and other natural events. But it's more often caused, and always aggravated, by distortions in the market: taxes, wars, idiotic regulation, runaway inflation, and the like.

Doug: And when a big charity intrudes on one of these weakened, distorted markets, it usually adds even more distortions, prolonging the problem.

Consider these charitable organizations going around the world treating diseases. The reason these countries have these terrible diseases that kill so many people is because they are economically undeveloped. Keeping people alive via extraordinary measures in such a place only results in more people competing for the same scarce resources. The answer to the problem is not to send in teams of doctors, so that you'll have even more destitute people producing no wealth, but to free the local market so the people can become wealthy. The disease will go away as a consequence—this is the only permanent cure. What they are doing is the exact opposite of what they should be doing; they are making things worse.

L: Sounds pretty cold, Doug, to say, "Don't send doctors—"

Doug: Well, don't forget that a lot of people have supported the likes of Mugabe and deserve the economic ruin they are getting—and the diseases that are going to follow. Send doctors in if it makes you feel good, but it's putting Band-Aids on smallpox. Don't imagine that you're actually helping solve the problem. People who do this kind of thing, I believe, do it because of feelings of guilt and shame they carry around inside. I understand them, but I don't agree with them.

It does sound cold-blooded, and I'm sorry. I like kids and dogs and the same things most people like. But I'm not talking about whatever I or others might imagine is nice. I'm talking about the only real way to solve such a problem.

It's disgusting to see hot-shot yuppies self-righteously driving around the African bush in new Land Rovers, pretending they're eliminating poverty. That's where most of the money goes, in fact. High living and "administration."

L: You didn't let me finish. I was saying that it sounds cold-blooded, but who's really more cold-blooded: the one who knowingly spends precious resources on measures they know won't be effective and will lead to greater sorrow, or the one who has the courage to make the hard decision and reach for the real, long-term solution?

Doug: Yes. That's the way I see it.

L: It occurs to me, reacting to the distinction you made earlier between individual charity and institutional charity, that perhaps it's like religion. Whether we agree with their beliefs or not, it's clear that many people derive value from those beliefs. But when religions become organizations and dogma sets in, they can get really destructive.

Doug: Well, as an individual, if I come across a person who I have reason to believe is worthy of my charity and my trust, I might act individually. But yes, when things get organized, they get bureaucratized. It's just the natural course of things; it seems almost universal that as organizations get older and more structured, they become counterproductive to their intended purposes.

Charity is especially prone to this problem because of the phony ethical notions that now pervade Western society. It's gotten worse over the last 100 years. People have come to believe that an instrument of coercion, the state, has to take care of them. Perversely, when the state engages in charity—which isn't charity, because tax-supported giving is not voluntary—it discourages true charity. People who have money taken from them by the taxman have less of it to give to those they might know who genuinely need help.

L: *The Tragedy of American Compassion*. Marvin Olasky.

Doug: Great book. I think the Chinese are much more intelligent than Westerners in this regard. The only charity you find in most oriental societies is organized by beneficial societies that seem less pervious to squandering. Peer pressure and moral approbation keep them in line, unlike governments, which exist primarily to serve themselves. And taxes tend to be a lot lower in the Orient, so people have more money to give, if that's their inclination.

In fact, one of the horrible aspects of this issue, in the United States, is that large amounts of money are stolen from estates in the form of death taxes. The idea seems to be that the government will deploy wealth more wisely than the children of its creators. But this is ridiculous. It's part of the whole ethical morass that charity and taxation are tied up in, in the US.

Suppose you have a Chinese and an American, of equal intelligence, work ethic, education, skills, etc.—and an equal amount of starting capital. The American who starts with a dollar might end up with a million. But the Chinese guy in the same circumstances will end up with 50 million. All because of the difference in taxes and regulations.

But it's worse than that, because whatever amount of money the American is going to leave to his kids, half of it is going to disappear down the tax rat hole, while 100% of the money the oriental guy leaves will go exactly where he wants it to go.

That has major implications for wealth accumulation. It's another reason for the diversification of political risk we keep reminding people is so important.

But sadly, even if an American ends up with $100 million, odds are he won't leave the bulk of it intact as an effective capital pool, to be expanded upon by his chosen heir. He'll give it to some charity that will be run for the benefit of its board of directors. They get to be big shots with other people's money—corrupting both themselves and the intended recipients.

L: So, the bottom line is that if you had a magic wand and could abolish all charitable institutions with a wave of it, you'd do it. And you would not replace them with anything. You'd use the wand to reduce taxes and regulations everywhere, to allow for more wealth creation. And for those few desperate cases clinging to the bottom rungs of the social ladder, you think individual conscience would suffice.

Doug: Exactly. To me, charity should be strictly an individual, one-on-one thing. That's the only way you can know that it can really help, and even then it doesn't always work. Once you have to hire somebody to run a charitable organization and have secretaries and assistant vice-presidents in charge of light-bulb changing, it's just another bureaucracy headed for disaster, dissipating wealth as it goes, and doing more harm than good even among the intended recipients of the charity.

L: I don't see a lot of immediate investment implications here, but there's certainly a lot of food for thought for those intent on wealth accumulation.

Doug: Let's just say that your moral obligation to the rest of humanity—insofar as you have such an obligation—is to keep your capital intact. First, that means to deny it to the state, which will very likely use it in a destructive way. Second, to direct it to those who will use it to produce more—not to unproductive consumers. Third, to take some personal responsibility, and do it yourself—don't devolve it upon some unknown board of worthies who will have their own ideas about what to do with your money.

L: Got it. Thanks.

Doug: You're welcome. Till next week.

Doug Casey on the Echoes of War

July 8, 2009

L: Doug, I hear you've been reading the obits recently—what's on your mind?

Doug: Yes, I couldn't help but note the long and generally favorable obits on Robert "the Strange" McNamara, at age 93. The obituaries ranged from glowingly positive to, at worst that I read, neutral. I was shocked and disgusted by these things. I considered the man to be a classic sociopath and a war criminal, among other things. He was possibly one of the worst human beings ever to have lived.

L: Don't pull your punches, Doug…

Doug: Well, I have to say that I take his death a little personally. In life, I find the things I regret most are not the things I've done—although there are some of those—but more, it's the things I haven't done. And one of the things I regret having not done was back in about 1995, when McNamara gave a speech at the Aspen Institute, promoting his book. I wanted very much to ask him a question. Usually, I'm pretty bold about these things, but this time, I just didn't do it.

The question I wanted to ask him was this: "Mr. McNamara, after nearly destroying the Ford Motor Corporation, then destroying Vietnam and almost destroying the United States, and then going on to be the president of the World Bank, where you made great strides towards destroying the world economy— how is it possible that today you can be held in high regard and stand up in front of this audience without being pelted with rotten fruit and vegetables?"

L: So what happened? Did he leave before anyone could ask questions?

Doug: One of the few things I can say in McNamara's favor is that he actually took questions. I believe I could have gotten a chance to ask my question. I honestly don't remember why I didn't do it. It was just one of those moments in which I didn't do what I almost always do, which is to confront these people whenever I have the opportunity.

McNamara was actually an anti-libertarian in many ways. You know, he started his career as a statistical analyst evaluating the success of bombing raids in Germany and especially in Japan. He was a big promoter of raids on civilian population centers, like the carpet-bombing of Tokyo that killed 100,000 people in one night and served no useful purpose at all.

L: Do you know why he advocated that?

Doug: It's a good question, because he later said that he had a conversation with Curtis LeMay, his immediate superior, in which they discussed the fact that if the US had lost the war, it would be Americans who would have been tried as war criminals, not Tojo, Göring, and those guys.

So, apparently, he considered the moral implications of his criminality, but... he didn't learn a thing. He advocated the same thing in Vietnam—but the start of his war crimes was in World War II.

He then went to the Ford Motor Company. It's often said, especially if you read the recent obituaries, that he "saved" Ford, along with eight other wiz-kids that were in the Air Force with him. But I don't think that was true at all. The fact that McNamara and these other number crunchers were hired by Ford is, to me, indicative of the start of the collapse of the American auto industry. Previously, American cars were generally very good. The founders were car guys. They understood the way engines work and suspensions work, etc. They liked driving them, and liked racing them, and enjoyed them as products. That's when cars were good. But McNamara was a bean-counter.

Look at it this way: he was directly responsible for the Edsel, which even today, fifty years later, is still known as the biggest disaster in American automotive history. It was his personal baby.

The only reason earnings went up while he was at Ford was that he was the first of these guys to pinch pennies, fire people who weren't efficient enough in the short term, and do accounting tricks. That sort of thing. He was a non-car guy running a car company, which is a big mistake. Generally, I don't like to own companies where the founding entrepreneurs have gone and been replaced by suits with little interest in the business except fat salaries, bonuses, and stock options. It's always been an issue, but it's a vastly bigger problem now than it was in the '50s. But that's something for another day...

It's shameful, the way people credit him with saving Ford.

And then they go on to talk about Vietnam, where he was directly responsible for the way the US conducted that war. But there were other things before that. He was behind the Bay of Pigs invasion, and he was primarily responsible for the arms race between the US and the Soviet Union. He's the one who came up with MIRV missiles, which made the Soviets believe that the US was planning a first strike against them.

But his record in Vietnam, of course, was a total and complete disaster.

L: Surely the obits aren't absolving him of that? Almost no one views the Vietnam War positively these days.

Doug: Well, they all seem to point out that he had moral qualms about it. But my guess is that they weren't moral qualms at all. Here he was, attacking a simple peasant army that was living on dried rice and had basically nothing but hand-carried weapons, mounting B-52 raids, using the highest-tech weaponry of the day, and spending gigantic amounts of money, just to kill peasants. So it doesn't seem to me that he had any moral qualms. In the end, I think he wanted to get out of Vietnam not because it was wrong, but because he finally came to see how hopelessly stupid it was.

Talk about stupid. Here's a man that was highly intelligent—he was very, very smart—but he was totally lacking in wisdom. He had no common sense at all. He was a very intelligent fool, the type of guy that I would have loved to see confronted by Mr. T, saying, "I pity the fool!"

L: So of course they made him the head of the World Bank.

Doug: Yes, and when he was there, he quadrupled its size. He was more responsible than anyone else for the fetish they developed for building steel mills in parts of Africa that were on opposite sides of the continent from coal supplies, etc. It was another disaster.

His career was a series of unmitigated disasters, and still, he's held in some kind of regard today. To me, this is a sign of how totally dishonest society has become. These obituaries should show that the guy was a sociopath, a criminal, and a loser, but instead they maintain a united front in speaking no ill of the dead.

L: Do you really think it's about respecting the dead, or is it that the journalists of today, being largely products of the US public education system, are simply too ignorant or too biased to see the man for what he was?

Doug: That's a very good question. It could be that the average person writing these editorials—and they are the establishment now—basically agrees with his views and methodology. Therefore they only nit-pick technical issues around the edges, while they should be attacking the very core of what he stood for. But they agree with his core, rotten as it was.

Anyway, I'm sorry he died... before I had a chance to ask him that question. I consider it an unfortunate omission.

L: Maybe you'll have a chance if there's such a thing as reincarnation.

Doug: Yes, perhaps. He'd likely come back as a cockroach, and I might have a chance to squash him.

L: Just so.

Doug: So, we've lost one warmonger, but there are plenty more. The US is making exactly the same mistakes in Iraq and Afghanistan as it did in Vietnam. It's almost a cookie-cutter copy. We're using all this high-tech junk—$200 million fighter planes, $2 billion bombers, etc.—to fight a primitive peasant army on their own ground. I don't see any significant differences at all.

And just as Vietnam was a major step closer to bankruptcy for the US back then, what's happening in Afghanistan and Iraq is the same—but on steroids, because the junk we're using is much more expensive than it was back then.

L: So, you don't believe our savior Obama is going to pull the soldiers out?

Doug: There's not a chance in hell.

Think about the gigantic bases they've built in Iraq. I mean outside the Green Zone. They're huge and can only signal an intention to stay for good. And the same thing is happening in Afghanistan. This is all going to end badly.

I hesitate to call myself a political handicapper, though I did predict that Obama would win, but I do think he's going to be a one-term president. Things are going to be quite bad by the time the next election comes around.

[**Editor's Note**: As of the time we go to press, Obama did pull the bulk of US troops out of Iraq, but not Afghanistan.]

L: Can you describe "end badly" for us?

Doug: The war with Islam is going to heat up for the same reason the Cold War with the Soviet Union escalated under McNamara. The more the US attacks them, the more they feel threatened and feel they have to counterattack. And when they do, the fearmongers in this country feel threatened in turn, and so it keeps escalating.

I don't see any reason for it to de-escalate at this point, though I've got to say that in this respect, Obama is at least marginally better than Bush. At least he doesn't talk in such a hostile and antagonistic way.

L: And he speaks English—he can even pronounce the word "nuclear."

Doug: Yes, that's right. But I don't see things turning around at all. In other words, all these secretaries of defense and such will be taking lessons from McNamara, not learning from his mistakes.

L: When do you think this might really heat up?

Doug: Well, for one thing, forget about Obama and his promise to win this war. The threat has metastasized; it's not just al-Qaeda anymore, but now it's thousands of people all around the world. It only takes two or three guys to get together to hatch a plan. It's "open source" warfare. They don't need a commander in chief in Redmond, Washington, telling them how to design their war ware; there are thousands of war entrepreneurs out there now, making their own designs, driven by what the US is doing.

L: That makes sense, but again, the timing is critical. In our business, being too early is the same as being wrong.

Doug: That's correct, but at the same time, you have to diagnose the trend correctly, which I think we're doing. That said, I think people likely to be plotting against the US have a longer time frame than Americans do. Americans want things done now. Instant gratification. Those on the other side are willing to plan and take their time ensuring their revenge. And they understand that the longer the US keeps spending, the more it's going to be bled to death.

At some point, somebody is going to get hold of one or more nuclear devices, or maybe a biological weapon, from one source or another. There are many possible ways that could happen. Then they fly it into the US on a commercial airliner and detonate on landing, or load it in a perfectly harmless-looking commercial boat and set it off as soon as the boat docks. I think that's the way it's likely to happen; they don't need ICBMs or cruise missiles to mount an effective nuclear attack. But the time, place, and means are impossible to predict. There are millions of people out there now with chips on their shoulders. A lot of them are going to be plotting stuff for all kinds of reasons. So, you can't realistically say what will happen; all you can say is that it's inevitable that something will happen.

L: Investment implications?

Doug: Things haven't changed much: buy gold, buy silver, and diversify your assets internationally. That's the basic step. After you have a firm foundation with those things, you can start looking at speculations. Use the chaos to your advantage.

L: Given how Vietnam-like wars tend to push the states that wage them towards bankruptcy (this happened to the Soviets in Afghanistan as well), is there a particularly leveraged way to short the government's solvency?

Doug: Shorting the dollar and shorting long-term Treasury bonds are fantastic long-term bets. That's especially so for shorting long-term Treasury bonds, as interest rates are still very close to their all-time lows, being artificially suppressed by Federal Reserve buying. That's a one-way street where you can get huge leverage on your money if you have a time frame of a couple years. That's the best single bet I can think of.

L: Makes sense—thanks for your time, Doug.

Doug: Always a pleasure. Till next week.

Doug Casey on Earth Day

April 27, 2011

L: Doug, people around the world just celebrated Earth Day, and I know you have ideas on the subject. Did you ride a bike instead of driving a car that day?

Doug: Well, as you know, I love to drive high-performance cars, but I'm in downtown Buenos Aires now. I don't keep a car here because the taxis are so cheap and convenient. So I used taxis on Earth Day, just like any other day. I don't bicycle and recycle to save the planet. But I did notice, with a sort of morbid fascination, the observation of Earth Day by many people around me.

It's amazing to me—though maybe it shouldn't be—the way Earth Day has caught on among idiots in general. It's on its way to becoming just as bad news as May Day, which is the creation of the same sort of people. May Day—May 1—is Labor Day in of most of the world. It's basically a Marxist holiday. April 22 is Earth Day. So you have a green Earth Day, followed by a red May Day. They ought to call this time of year "Watermelon Week," because the so-called Greens are only green on the outside and red through and through.

L: Can you substantiate that?

Doug: Apart from the fact that it seems there's a very high correlation between Reds and Greens everywhere in the world? Sure: just look at their policy proposals. Mainstream environmentalists never propose any market approaches to improving the environment; they only propose more socialist regulations and government controls. There are a few free-market environmentalists out there, but they are very few and far between. If the movement were all about the environment, there would at least be a mix of policies, constructively looking for whatever works best. But it's not. In my opinion, concern for the environment is just the latest excuse for the same tired old power-hungry collectivist/statist thinking that's been such a disaster for the last hundred years.

Earth Day is nonsense and a bad idea. People of good will should ignore it and work against government efforts to enshrine it.

L: Okay, but wait a minute. You know I agree that real environmentalism should be about the environment, not advancing a leftist agenda without regard for environmental consequences. But we do live on this one planet, and I don't like breathing polluted air—and I doubt you like it any better than I do. What's wrong with celebrating the planet we live on, as well as honest—and voluntary—efforts to keep it clean?

Doug: There's nothing wrong with that, of course. I like green trees, blue skies, the birds and bunnies and so forth, as much as the next person. But that's not really what's going on here. First, we have to put all of this in perspective...

L: What perspective would that be?

Doug: You have to realize that the Earth is just a ball of dirt, circling an insignificant star, lost in an insignificant galaxy among a hundred billion other stars—and our galaxy is itself only one of a hundred billion galaxies, and maybe more, in the known universe. Further, there's increasing conjecture that our universe is just one out of an infinite number of parallel universes, which may include any number just like ours. So on a cosmic scale, anything we do or don't do to this planet is completely and absolutely insignificant. Making a religion out of worshiping the planet, and fomenting hysteria about it, strikes me as being cosmically stupid.

L: Literally.

Doug: Yes, literally. The Earth has an evolution of its own and is constantly in the process of changing, regardless of the activities of men—the ice ages, as one tiny example, show how drastic those changes can be. Incidentally, we're probably just in an interim period between glaciations, from the perspective of geological time. And periodically, other things happen that make human activities pale in significance. The next super volcano, as we talked about in our conversation on global warming, will change the earth's surface environment tremendously. But maybe the environmental extremists will like that, because it could wipe out most of the human race. And though humans evolved on this planet just like all the other species, these people have it in their heads that humans and everything to do with them is somehow unnatural.

L: Well, maybe some would, but many would not, because such a volcanic event would also wipe out countless entire species of plants and animals.

Doug: You're right, but some of these people are so virulently anti-human, they might rejoice anyway and see it as just being a few eggs you have to break to make an omelet.

A big asteroid strike could change everything as well. There are plenty of other things that could sweep all these insane—and unnatural—efforts to freeze nature in its present state aside like piles of leaves in a hurricane. My attitude about all this was summed up perfectly by George Carlin in this video[1]. It's a work of both comic and philosophical genius. I suggest everyone watch it at least once a week, until it sinks in and is grokked[2] in its fullness.

L: Even if there's no such cataclysm, as you like to say, everything gets folded into the Earth's mantle eventually anyway.

Doug: [Chuckles] That's right. That is absolutely inevitable—and natural. The eventual destruction of everything on the surface of the Earth through plate tectonics should appeal to Greens, if only because it's natural—but they're mostly innocent of any knowledge of science in general, and geology in particular. Most places won't be folded into the mantle for many millions of years, of course—or at all, if the sun goes nova first. But that's several billion years in the future. Meanwhile, if you value human life—which many of these people consciously and explicitly do not—this planet is here strictly for our pleasure. At least until we can find something better.

Save the trees, save the bees. Save the whales, save those snails…. What about people? The arrogance of the Greens is at once breathtaking and pitiful. And many come right out and say that they would eliminate all humans if they could, because humans are a disease on the face of Mother Earth—or Gaia, as they call it.

L: I met a young man who said exactly that, once, in Peru. I asked why termites—which can destroy every other living thing in an expanding circle around their nests—are superior to humans. And he's not the only one I've met. Somehow, when I suggest that if they think the Earth would be better off without humans, they could start helping by removing themselves, none of them ever take action. No, no, it's other people whose choices they do not approve of who should go first.

Doug: Yes. They are perfectly horrible people who are polluting the intellectual environment on this planet with their new religion. And it is a religion. It has almost no basis in real science, though they like to doll it up in scientific terminology. Greenism is rife with politically motivated pseudoscientific gobbledygook masquerading as scientific research. Rather like Marxism, again—and not coincidentally, in my opinion.

Lots of fundamentalist Christians can't seem to wait for the world to come to an end with the Rapture. Yahweh, or perhaps Jesus, or maybe the Holy Ghost

---

1. www.totallyincorrectbook.com/go/18
2. www.totallyincorrectbook.com/go/19

only know how many other apocalyptically scary memes cycle through the heads of true believers. And hardcore Muslims, following the dictates of Allah, are at least as anti-life and fanatical. It seems that everywhere one turns, there's somebody with plans to improve the world—or improve you. Anyone with any sense should want to get off this ball of dirt populated by so many busybody lunatics and find some place with better vibes.

But I fear religion is almost a genetic impulse in mankind; I certainly prefer the company of those who lack that gene. Of course, any time you turn anything into a religion, you automatically, and perhaps necessarily, require dogma. Then you get heretics. Then, religious wars.

L: Well, religion has existed for an evolutionarily significant period of time, so in spite of the religious wars and whatnot, I figure it must have some value for its believers. However, having tried to reason with a number of such environmental extremists, I'm inclined to agree with you about them. And the worst part of it is that this intellectual pollution—this Gaia religion dressed up as science—is being deliberately targeted at children in schools, in cartoons, everywhere. It's bad enough to fill young minds with errors and faulty logic, but they are *scaring* children, telling them they are doomed because the evil corporations control the governments and will never stop polluting the planet until we're all dead, and so forth.

Doug: That's exactly why it's important to stand up and be counted as being against things like Earth Day, in no uncertain terms. This garbage needs debunking. It's not enough to say, "Well, it's a good idea, but it's misguided in application." That's what people said about Marxism. They said it was a nice idea meant to help poor people, when in fact it was one of the most destructive ideas ever hatched for poor people. Especially for poor people. It's important to look these people right in the eye and tell them they are wrong and doing great harm—don't give 'em an inch of moral high ground.

Call a spade a spade. If they are going to talk about treating the human race as a disease and eliminating it, they are talking about mass murder—genocide. That's the plain truth. These people are psychologically damaged and dangerous. They should be opposed, unabashedly and at every opportunity. But that's the moral argument. Entirely apart from that, I despise them on a visceral level and find their company revolting. And boring.

L: I've run into that argument about Marxism as well. A lot of leftist apologists will say that Marxism was a good idea—or at least a noble one, but that it was not practical, or never had a real chance, because the evil capitalists never gave it one. But that's a lie; it wasn't a good idea. Marxism might work for ants, but not for humans. Leftist governments of every stripe tried very hard to implement Marxist ideas for many decades, and all we got was a body count in the tens of millions. There is nothing noble about trying to organize a society in a way that's inconsistent with human nature—and there *is* such a thing as human nature.

We're up against something very similar with this earth-worship meme going around. For the true believers, it seems to be much more about being anti-human than about being pro-clean-environment. That's why you see all sorts of environmental proposals that pay scant heed to large and painful human costs in pursuit of the benefit of every other species on the planet.

Doug: Just so. Mother Earth doesn't exist, and if she did, you'd find her a bad-tempered bitch who couldn't care less for the carbon-based biological units covering her skin. She's not a conscious, thinking being. Our planet is just a ball of silicon, carbon, iron, nitrogen, and such. I can hear the Greens now. "Save the beryllium! Save the hydrogen! Don't save the uranium! We're not sure about saving the nitrogen. But get rid of that evil carbon… "

In any event, the planet itself has no rights.

Incidentally, I happen to really like most other living things and want them to live long, happy, and peaceful lives—just on general principles. And I do what I can to see that that happens. But the Greens want to turn the Earth into a political issue—which is to say an issue where they can use coercion to boss around their fellow humans. Like all true believers, they suffer from either stupidity—defined as an unwitting tendency to self-destruction—or a psychological aberration.

L: Good point. Rights are a human construct that has meaning only among people. Actually, if you observe nature, concern for other species is *unnatural*. To a wolf or a worm or a germ, other things are either food or not food, threats or not threats. Any animal, plant, or microorganism on Earth—any and every living thing besides humans—will expand as fast and as far as food supply and space allow, without any regard to the consequences for other species.

Humans do consider the well-being of other species, and this is a noble thing unique to us on this planet—but it should be a matter of aesthetics, not ethics, because ethics has no meaning beyond an intelligent species like ours. Giving hikers and bears equal rights only increases the number of hikers who end up inside of bears. Giving the planet rights would make it impossible for any species, from humans to termites, to live at all; we'd never get permission to build houses or nests, because Mother Earth does not speak.

Doug: Agreed. So, even assuming you want to look at it from the perspective of Mother Earth, the only way for things to get better is to let people get wealthier. Humans are not just going to go away. Relatively few of the six billion people here will agree to drink the environmentalist extremists' Kool-Aid. (Most of the most prominent environmentalists are rich hypocrites, driving around in limos, and flying around in private jets—people like Al Gore.) And, as you've pointed out, people are a natural part of this planet as well. That means you've got to find solutions that include humans and motivate them in the right way.

The fact is that the most destructive societies and individuals for the environment are the poorest ones. Rich people don't generally throw trash on the ground—many poor people do it all the time. The amount of trash blowing in the wind is one obvious way you can see whether a neighborhood is rich or not. The same thing applies to entire societies. From Canada to China, from Germany to Guatemala, the higher the per-capita GDP of any society, the less polluted the country. Poor people are not bad, they just don't have time to care about such niceties—they are struggling to survive. Wealthier people have the time and the means to clean up their environments, so they do.

L: I see this all the time, as I travel the world looking for potentially profitable mining projects. To me, it seems to be clear evidence for your watermelon hypothesis that so-called environmentalists often accept "artisan" miners—generally poor indigenous people—but go apoplectic at the mention of an international mining company. But these evil companies have to live up to international standards of environmental protection, remediation, and reclamation—and, with a few criminal exceptions, they do. They often go above and beyond the legal requirements, because the people working for the companies actually do care and don't want to dump toxic substances into rivers, etc.

But the artisan miners, they are worse than termites. They strip all the vegetation in the area for fuel or building material; they dig without regard for worker safety; they use cyanide and mercury to process gold and dump the residues in the creeks and rivers; and they make no effort whatsoever to protect the environment they work in, remedy any harm they do, or reclaim their work sites to a more natural state when they are done. But somehow, this is better to environmental extremists than letting an evil multinational company put a clean, modern mine in.

Doug: It's true, I've seen it too—like that time we went to Bolivia and saw little boys working in the artisan mining camps… In a wealthier society, that wouldn't happen. Not because of laws, but because kids don't need to do it just in order to survive. And how do you make a society wealthier? Cut taxes, repeal regulations, and get the government out of the way of entrepreneurs. In short, you don't actually have to *do* anything. Just let people create wealth and keep what they create. That will mend more harm than anything else, over time. And building lots of new mines would be an excellent thing.

L: Okay, so wealth is a great antidote to environmental poison; what else?

Doug: Technology. Pollution can be defined as a waste of resources. It is an economic phenomenon and lends itself to economic solutions. The more modern and high-tech the industry, the less pollution there tends to be. Looking ahead, micro-manufacturing will eliminate the great industrial slag heaps of the past. Ultimately, when practical nanotechnology arrives, there will be *no* pollution, because things will be assembled one atom at a time, precisely and with no waste. And anything that does get discarded, or becomes trash, is just more atoms someone can use as raw material for making something new. If you love the Earth, but don't hate humans, there is only one way forward: push for the fastest advance in technology possible.

L: Makes sense to me… anything else people can do if they want a cleaner environment?

Doug: Embrace reason. So much of what people believe about the environment simply ain't so, and much of it is pure hysteria—or outright scams. Anthropogenic global warming, as we've discussed in the past, is certainly a gigantic scam.

Incidentally, one of the worst things about the global-warming scare is its effect on science. After it has been thoroughly debunked—which I'm confident will happen, and sooner rather than later—it may actually serve to discredit science itself. That's because most people believe the lie that science has shown that anthropogenic global warming is real. I fear people will come to regard scientists as unreliable and throw the baby out with the bath water.

But there are lots of other nasty aspects of the ongoing Green hysteria. A big one is how it actually wastes resources, even while it's telling people to conserve them. For instance, the mandate for so-called "green jobs." Or the drive for biofuels, which is moving a lot of corn production from food to fuel, which is raising food prices, destroying capital, and increasing hunger around the world. Carbon! Carbon, one of the basic elements in all living things, has become an environmental bogeyman. Children are being taught to feel guilty about their "carbon footprints." All of these things misallocate resources, which is destructive of wealth.

L: I've seen that too. Okay, what about investment implications?

Doug: Well, even though I advocate resisting this eco-religion whenever and however possible, I do recognize its arrival as a *fait accompli*. I recognize that

I'm swimming against the tide, just as I am with my libertarian social, political, and economic views. But, frankly, I don't give a damn. I believe in doing the right thing. Also, I find it diverting and amusing.

Be that as it may, greenism has been codified into law in many ways already. This creates distortions, which are necessary for profitable speculation. One of these is the emphasis on green energy—there is big, big money involved in that, and it's something our readers are positioned to take advantage of.

L: Anything else?

Doug: Technology again. There will be research money poured into green technologies, including forms of solar and wind power that are currently uneconomic but may not be in the future.

L: And, of course, I need to watch out for changes in environmental regulations as they affect mining for m etals. It's an industry people love to hate, without realizing just how much metal they use every day in their lives. That means that if you don't want to lose your shirt investing in metals projects—even good ones—you have to watch out for political risk.

Doug: Indeed. Without metals, 100% of which are brutally extracted from Mother Earth, we would all be using stone tools and dressed in animal skins. More important, those metals will enable us to reach out for the stars. And provide us with the wealth to do so. My motto is Earth First: We'll mine the other planets later!

L: You *are* an optimist. Okay then. I'll see you at our conference in Boca Raton shortly—I'm sure we'll find more to converse about then.

Doug: I'm sure we will. Next week then.

Doug Casey on Technology

Oct 28, 2009

L: Doug, people have written in saying you're a "doom-and-gloomer" and a "permabear"—but I know you're an optimist. Why do you suppose that's so?

Doug: Perhaps it's because I've long said that the Greater Depression is going to be worse than even *I* think it will be. But looking forward with a long view, I think the future is not only going to be better than I imagine, it's going to be better than I *can* imagine.

The coming Greater Depression will be serious, but I don't think it's going to change the fundamental long-term trend of human history. I believe Jacob Bronowski was right: the Ascent of Man will continue. Mankind started out grubbing for roots and berries in the mud, but our descendants—not so far in the future—will be colonizing the stars.

L: That was the guy who wrote the BBC series back in the '70s called *The Ascent of Man*? I didn't remember his name, but I remember watching the series… even though I was only eight. So, when you talk about the long term, you're not talking years, decades, or even centuries, but the grand sweep of human history and beyond.

Doug: Yes, exactly. An interesting thing about investing, and life in general, is that there are long-term trends, medium-term trends, and short-term trends. You have to figure out which ones are important, and then if and how to capitalize on any of them. And it seems to me that one of the longest-term human trends in existence is the 10,000-year-long bear market in commodities.

In real terms, metals were extremely expensive and rare in Neolithic times.

L: Iron was so rare, it didn't exist. And I'd guess that a polished copper mirror would have taken the equivalent of many human lives to make.

Doug: Right. What metals there were came from what people could find in those metals' native forms. That meant primarily gold, for the reasons we talked about in our <u>conversation on gold</u>[1]. There would have been some copper and some silver, but that would have been about it. And even the equivalent of kings back then would have had very little of it.

Then civilization developed in the Middle East, and we entered the Bronze Age, which gave way to the Iron Age—and now we're in the Silicon Age. Each one of these things is progressively less rare. Silicon makes up the computer chips that drive modern life, but it's basically just sand. On a scale of millennia, commodities have collapsed in price. Eventually, they'll go to near zero in cost. Commodities will drop to no more than the royalties on the software that runs the nanotechnology that extracts them. The future, at least given a free market, should produce mind-boggling abundance.

L: Let's come back to nanotechnology in a moment. The overall trend you're describing doesn't depend on it. Even without nanotech, cheap and abundant energy would drop the prices of most commodities to near zero. Sea water is full of dissolved metals, for example; you could have all you wanted if you just had the energy to process all that water. Cheap enough energy makes the lowest-grade concentration of anything economical.

Doug: Yes. We already know how to extract those metals or make artificial oil; it's strictly a matter of having enough energy to drive the engineering. And, of course, the economics. This is why I find it so frustrating when people talk about running out of natural resources. There's no danger whatsoever of that. Not only are the resources of the world adequate, they are essentially infinite. It's a question of technology—know-how—and capital, enough wealth to implement the know-how, that is, to build the machines.

Look, every material thing in the universe is constructed out of the 92 naturally occurring elements in the periodic table. Having anything we want, from a slice of bread, to a new car, to perhaps a new life form, is simply a matter of rearranging atoms into the correct combinations at an acceptable cost.

L: My friend Jim Von Ehr, CEO of Zyvex, a nanotech instrument company, once told me that some of the most valuable land in the future would be the sites of old landfills, because they are basically mountains of purified materials. Once you can reduce matter into its component atoms and make new things with it, such places, packed with high concentrations of useful atoms, will command a premium. In the future, there will be no such thing as trash. So, this bearish trend in commodities you speak of isn't really a bearish trend at all; it's a bullish trend in technology.

---

1. www.totallyincorrectbook.com/go/20

Doug: And that includes nuclear waste. Greens, who generally have little background in science, are completely unaware that spent reactor fuel is a potentially valuable future resource—in addition to being a trivial storage problem in the interim. The storage problems are almost entirely political. Technology—it's the most bullish thing possible for the standard of living of the average human being. Many people living below the poverty line in the US have televisions, refrigerators, medicines, and luxuries that even kings and queens of only a hundred years ago couldn't have dreamed of. That trend is going to continue—and accelerate. It's hard to overstate how favorable this is.

Among other consequences, advancing technology makes it cheaper and easier to extract, purify, and utilize commodities. As we've discussed before, in pre-industrial times, a gold mine needed to grade an ounce or more of gold per ton in order to be worth bothering with. Now you can make money mining deposits that grade a hundredth of that. Simultaneously, our use of these commodities has become more efficient. You can see that clearly in automobiles; the average car in the 1950s might have gotten 10 miles per gallon, now it gets closer to 30 miles per gallon—and goes much faster in the process.

L: And has safer glass, better headlights, movie screens to entertain children on long trips, anti-theft technology, and performs *much* better in collisions.

Doug: Yes, and that's how it is with all technology. Just think about computers. Moore's Law. They double in capacity every 18 months.

Incidentally, that's the solution to one of the bugaboos of our age: pollution. The better the technology, the less pollution there is.

L: So, would you say you're a techno-optimist as a matter of general principle—because that's the way you'd bet on the multi-millennia trend— or because there are specific technologies you see developing that lead you to this conclusion?

Doug: Both.

A key fact is that there are more engineers and scientists alive today than there have been in all of the rest of human history combined. And all of these people want to become the next Steve Jobs or Albert Einstein—they all want to become immensely wealthy or make major breakthroughs. The path to the former is by inventing better technologies, and the path to the latter adds to the understanding that allows us to do the same. These people are as motivated as any alive, and I expect a good number of them will succeed.

There is a countertrend, however: government. States all around the world are becoming increasingly virulent, both in terms of seizing capital and in terms of making capital accumulation more and more difficult.

Further, they're constantly creating new regulations on what can and can't be done. And remember what I said before: technology isn't enough—you have to have the wealth to implement the new technology. Governments, however, are actively destroying the capital we need to advance, and slowing its accumulation, through power-hungry myopia, bureaucratic stupidity, and ideological insanity.

Back on the positive side, I'm a huge believer in nanotechnology. I believe it is likely—even in the span of the next generation—to change the nature of life on this planet totally, unrecognizably, and irrevocably. It's the single biggest thing on the horizon.

L: Want to take a moment to define the term, in case any readers are not familiar with it?

Doug: Sure, it's the creation of computers and machines on the sub-microscopic level—the atomic level, really.

L: There are lots of definitions, but that's as good as any I've heard. Why should anyone care about machines the size of a molecule? Well, for one thing—it carries what you said about better technology and pollution to the ultimate level. If you use molecular machines to build things one atom at a time, there is literally *no* waste. Zero. Every atom is used and put exactly where it is needed. No byproducts, no pollution.

Doug: Yes. And it enables you to build perfect machines—perfect in the sense of them having no mechanical imperfections—which vastly increases their efficiency and reduces the need for energy.

L: A good example of this I've read about is the creation of rocket engines that deliver perfectly linear thrust. Rocket motors now spew out all sorts of stuff, roughly in the right direction, but also including a lot of noise and light, which don't really help them move. If you could build rocket motors that eject perfectly linear exhaust, you might be able to lift the same payload one of those monstrous Saturn V rockets lifted, with a motor the size of a toaster.

Doug: There are many applications. Medical applications are among the ones I'm most interested in. Once you have machines the size of an enzyme—which is really just a natural molecular machine—you can program them to spread through a patient like a "doctor virus," one that repairs cellular damage from within each and every single cell in a human body. That doesn't just mean fixing malfunctioning cells as in the case of cancer, though that would be trivial for such machines, but also fine-tuning all sorts of tissues for optimal health—which basically means preventing (and repairing) aging.

L: A fountain of youth—sounds like science fiction.

Doug: It does, but it isn't. This is hard science. One person I have great respect for is Ray Kurzweil, an inventor and thinker about the future who's written about a coming "technology singularity"—a point at which technology doesn't just get better, it all but instantly leaps to its full potential. Everything that is possible to do, we'll know how to do. After this happens, people will look at this event as the single most important thing to happen—*ever*. We date things now BC and AD; in the future everything will be pre- and post-singularity. And this could happen within the next 20 or 30 years.

L: Sounds even more like science fiction.

Doug: Well, if you look at a graph of the rate of change in technology, it's basically flat for a long, long time, then slopes upward gently until about the 1750s. Then the Great Enlightenment and the Industrial Revolution hit, and the curve rises more and more steeply. If you look at it now, it looks poised to basically go vertical. Short of a global catastrophe that knocks us back to the Stone Age or wipes our species clean off the planet, there's no stopping it. The rate of change *is* accelerating. If it's not stopped, you get to the point at which the lifespan of your body—or a better one you make— has no natural limit, and your control over everything in the universe that can be controlled is complete.

[**Editor's Note**: Here is a chart on this subject from Doug's book, *Crisis Investing for the Rest of the 90s*.]

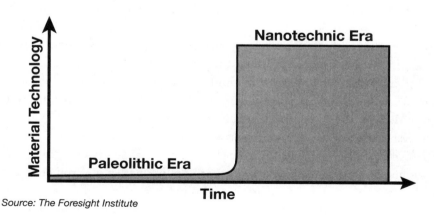

Source: The Foresight Institute

The expected abrupt transition from the paleolithic to nanotechnic eras (a long-term perspective). Stone Age agriculture and Moon landings lie in the transitional zone.

L: Do you really believe that's possible? Can atomic-scale machines really be built by human beings? Dick Feynman first introduced the concept we now call nanotechnology in his mind-bending paper, "There's Plenty of Room at the Bottom[2]" back in 1959. He opened with the idea of recording the entire (then) 24 volumes of the *Encyclopedia Britannica* on the head of a pin. But then nothing much happened with the idea, or so it seemed, until the 1980s, when K. Eric Drexler started promoting and popularizing nanotech, particularly in his seminal book, *Engines of Creation: The Coming Era of Nanotechnology*. Now there's a lot of talk about it, and the non-profit Foresight Institute[3] continues Drexler's promotional work, but nobody has built an atomic-scale assembler robot—nor even knows how to do it.

Doug: The way Drexler explained it, if you extend Moore's Law, not only are computers getting twice as powerful every 18 months, their components are getting twice as small at the same time. Don't forget that Moore's Law describes an exponential curve. So, we're approaching the point at which we'll have molecular-scale super-computers. And there's no reason not to suppose those computers couldn't give instructions to molecular robots, which he called assemblers. Assemblers could take apart anything at all, one atom at a time, and reassemble those atoms into anything you like. That's where I think we're headed.

But even without getting to that level, there are so many other technologies advancing, I think great optimism is warranted. Great optimism in everything except politics and ethics, which continue to be very degraded.

L: What other technologies, besides nanotech, do you see ripening?

Doug: I'm very bullish on space flight—as long as it's not left to the likes of NASA. I'd draw your attention in particular to what Burt Rutan is doing at Scaled Composites[4] on the latest developments) but that's not a stock pick. There are several private rocket companies, but this, too, is a field that's still mostly in the R&D phase. But their time will come.

As an aside, I have to say that I think the space cat is out of the bag. NASA may not like private space companies, but that won't stop other countries from hiring those companies to build space vehicles for them.

Ever since my friend Erwin Straus wrote a book called *Basement Nukes* in the 1970s, in which he argued that the average upper-middle-class American family could build a small nuclear device, I've been optimistic that government will not be able to stop progress. And that's a good thing, because technological advances have always been to the greater benefit of the average man over those in power.

---

2. www.totallyincorrectbook.com/go/21

3. www.totallyincorrectbook.com/go/22

4. www.totallyincorrectbook.com/go/23

The greatest example of this is the invention of gunpowder, which made it possible for the average peasant to kill the heavily armored thugs—knights—who were dominating them.

L: The great equalizer.

Doug: Exactly. The state did try to appropriate that technology for itself, but it didn't work. Just as the gunpowder cat got out of the bag, newer technologies will as well. That's especially true as there are many more new technologies in development now than there were at the time gunpowder and the printing press were being developed. By the time government committees are done drafting proposals to study possible frameworks for regulating new technologies, the bureaucrats' plans will be obsolete.

So, yes, I'm an optimist—and the greatest single reason for that is technology.

L: Well, I'm feeling upbeat. Thanks for your insights, Doug.

Doug: You're welcome. Talk to you next week.

Doug Casey on Rome

Dec 9, 2009

L: Doug, it seems that in almost every conversation we have, you mention something about ancient history, particularly Roman history. In our conversation on speculative fiction, you mentioned that it and ancient history and philosophy are your favorite kinds of reading. So let's talk about Rome—why the fascination, and is it really that relevant to investors struggling to understand the 21st century?

Doug: Well, there's actually a bit of a cottage industry that's developed, comparing ancient times to modern times, since Gibbon wrote the *Decline and Fall of the Roman Empire*[1], the first volume of which was published in 1776. I'm a big fan of his work, not only as a history but as very elegant and readable literature. And it's actually a laugh riot; Gibbon had a very subtle and acerbic wit. But since then there have been huge advances in our understanding of Rome, driven by archeological discoveries. There were many things Gibbon just didn't know, because he was basically a philologist and based his synthesis on what the ancients said about themselves.

L: There was no real science of archeology back then, so Gibbon was a collector of hearsay.

Doug: That's why the study of history is so tendentious; so much of it is "he said/she said," so to speak. But in Gibbon's day, there wasn't even yet much done to correlate what was written with what was on the monuments—even the well-known monuments—and on the coins. Forget about people actually getting their hands dirty, digging around in the provinces for what was left of Roman villas, battle sites, and that sort of thing. A great deal of work has been done on this in the last generation especially, so we know a lot more about what probably really happened now.

---

1. www.totallyincorrectbook.com/go/24

The thing that interests me the most about it is what you can learn following the history of Rome, from its semi-mythical founding by Romulus and Remus to what's generally designated as its end in 476 AD, when the child-emperor Romulus Augustus was deposed by Odoacer (a Germanic general who was in charge of what passed for the Roman army—but by then the army was almost entirely Germanic mercenaries who had no loyalty to the idea of Rome). It looks a lot like the American experience over the last couple hundred years. It starts with conquest and expansion, leads to global dominance, and then slips into decline.

L: Wait, wasn't Rome overrun by Goths?

Doug: At that time, basically the beginning of the 5th century, the capital had long since left Rome, even in the western empire, so it wasn't really a question of the city being overrun by Goths in one final bloody orgy. Rome was sacked several times in the 5th and 6th centuries. These were very costly in terms of accumulated capital, but all that capital apparently couldn't motivate the Romans to defend themselves. The sacks were actually more of a shake-down, or a mugging, than a conquest.

The first big sack was courtesy of the Visigoths under Alaric in 410 AD. But Alaric had worked with the Romans as a mercenary, and he was a convert to Christianity. The sack was relatively sedate, lasting three days by agreement. What happened under the Vandals under Geiseric in 455 lasted two weeks, but still didn't result in the burning of the city and wholesale murder of the populace. Like the sack of 410, it was basically just a time when, by agreement, the Vandals were allowed to come and haul off whatever they could move, because it seemed better than the alternative. What's interesting to me is that the Vandals arrived by ship, from North Africa. In other words, by then Spain, Gaul, and North Africa were already independent, feudal-style kingdoms.

But Rome was still a giant city then, with several hundred thousand inhabitants, although down from perhaps a million at its peak in Caesar's time. The actual collapse—the depopulation—of the city only really occurred starting in the mid-6th century, when the eastern emperor Justinian tried to recapture the west and wound up destroying what was left of it, while bankrupting the east. So many wars, then and now, are nothing more than rulers demonstrating their unbalanced mental state, played out at the expense of their subjects...

L: Back up a second, how about an overview before we get into the details?

Doug: Sure. Rome went through at least three stages. It started out as a yeoman republic, just a village on the Tiber river. Whether it was the Romans, or the Sabines, or any of the other numerous tribes of the times that became dominant was really simply the luck of the draw. Anyway, Rome started out as a republic of farmers, each of whom had his own plot of land on which he grew his grain and raised cattle. It's a bit of a paradox, in some ways resembling what's happened with America, because they fought these wars against their neighbors, which made them bigger and brought them wealth, but that also sowed the seeds of their own destruction. That was especially true of the big wars, like the three against Carthage, each of which lasted a long time.

You see, in order to fight in the Roman army, you had to be a landowner. They wouldn't take the riff-raff; it was a great honor to be in the Roman army. So, you had to be a landowner to join, but if you did join, you had to leave for five, ten years, maybe more. Your wife and maybe a young son you left behind often couldn't handle things. They'd borrow money and then couldn't pay it back. So, the soldiers' farms would go back to bush or get taken over by creditors. And by the time he was done fighting in the wars, if he survived, the typical legionary was not so interested in being a farmer anymore. They'd looted and plundered, perhaps gained some slaves, and wanted to live the high life in the city. So, like America, Rome became more urban and less agrarian.

Things started coming apart in the second century BC, with civil wars and generals like Marius and Sulla appearing on the scene, finally reaching a crisis with Julius Caesar—which, incidentally, is the portion of Roman history that's been best recorded, with the most written documents that have survived...

L: Hold on a minute. You're saying that Julius Caesar was the beginning of the end? Most people think of him as the beginning of the beginning—the man who forged the empire.

Doug: By the time of Caesar, the Romans had already conquered Greece. Pompey the Great had conquered the Near East. Spain and North Africa had been provinces since the Punic wars. Most of the empire had already been conquered—except for Gaul, Egypt, and Dacia, which is today's Romania. Gaul, today's France, was the big one. Incidentally, the HBO series _Rome_[2] is quite historically accurate, with relatively minor flights of poetic license. It covers the time from the rise of Caesar to the ascension of Augustus, with great attention to the detail of daily life back then. I also recommend _Gladiator_[3] especially for the opening battle scene.

The interesting thing is that in the early days, war was actually quite profitable. You conquered a place and stole all the gold, cattle, and... people who were eligible to be enslaved. That was a lot of wealth you could bring home—and then you could milk the area for many years to come with taxes.

---

2. www.totallyincorrectbook.com/go/25
3. www.totallyincorrectbook.com/go/26

L: And you gave the people bread and circuses once a year, so they'd decide you weren't such bad guys and weren't worth rebelling against.

Doug: Yes. It was a very profitable enterprise. The problem was that as they pushed their borders out, after they looted and pillaged, they had to defend those borders—especially against those people not worth conquering, like the Germans across the Rhine and Danube. The Goths, Huns, and Vandals, and so forth. They didn't have anything worth plundering in their endless forests, but they had to be defended against. And on the other side of the empire, the Persians were a military power to contend with. This became increasingly, impossibly costly. So the wars were what made Rome great but were also a big part of its undoing. Both because they helped destroy the essential social fabric of Rome by wiping out its agrarian roots and by corrupting everyone with a constant influx of cheap slave labor and free food—and by actually drawing in potential invaders.

Anyway, after Caesar, Rome changed from the Republic into what's called the Principate, starting with Augustus, the first emperor, although he pretended to be just the first man of the senate. Pretenses increasingly fell off over time. After the third century, which was a disastrous period of one civil war after another, with the legions fighting each other and the currency getting debased to nothing, the Principate changed into what's known as the Dominate, with the ascension of Diocletian and then Constantine. From that point forward, the emperor no longer even pretended to be the first among equals but was treated more like an oriental prince.

L: By saying "oriental prince," you're saying there was an element of divinity in that?

Doug: Yes, although even early western emperors liked to think they were related to the gods and would become one after death. When the capital moved from Rome to Constantinople, in the early 4th century, that brought in a lot of oriental influence, including habits like bowing and scraping before the emperor. That was previously unheard of. The senate, which had been run under something of an ethos of noblesse oblige among the powerful, turned into a bureaucracy. The official language changed from Latin to Greek, at least in the east.

By the time Odoacer overthrew Romulus Augustus, no one even cared that it happened—it was a minor event. Even Odoacer himself didn't care, because he didn't bother making himself emperor. Nothing changed because of it. Archeologists have found that even in places overrun by Goths and Vandals, life in the villas went on more or less as it had; the "barbarians" had been at least partially Romanized for a hundred years or so. It was more a change of management than a bloody invasion. In terms of raw numbers, there weren't more than a couple hundred thousand barbarians, in an empire of perhaps 70 million.

Perhaps it might be as if your worthless and ineffectual town council, which serves no useful purpose but bedevils you with taxes and regulations, were kicked out and replaced by an out-of-town motorcycle gang. They might actually be better in some ways, because at least they'd probably be practical and realistic people. The decay was a gradual thing.

L: The Dark Ages didn't start with a crash, then, but with a loss of knowledge over centuries?

Doug: Actually, the Dark Ages didn't really start until the Muslims closed off commerce on the Mediterranean. Islam comes out of what's now Saudi Arabia in 630-something AD, and as the Muslim Empire grew, it cut off commerce east and west, and especially on the Mediterranean.

L: So, you're saying that the final obliteration of what had been Roman civilization was the result of… an economic embargo?

Doug: That's partially it. Lists have been compiled of at least 180 reasons why Rome fell. They range from lead in the pipes and cookware, Christianity, climate change, population decline, to barbarian invasions. And many, many others—many of them closely related, generally centering on political and military devolution. It seems to me that one of the major reasons was basic economics.

The bureaucracy became stifling, the taxes became unbearable, the money was completely debased. Diocletian put on wage and price controls—the first time recorded in the West. People became tied to their land, which became the start of feudalism. Trade came grinding to a halt. In those days there was very little surplus; the Industrial Revolution wasn't there to magically make food and material appear. There's some evidence that many residents of the empire were glad to see the overthrow of a system that made production and saving impossible. Many Roman citizens escaped to barbarian lands to increase their freedom—much the way many Americans today are leaving the US. The empire in 400 AD was sociologically, politically, and militarily very different from the one of, say, Marcus Aurelius in around 180, when the decline began in earnest—even though it still had the same borders.

Rome brought some fantastic benefits to the world, and by the time things really came unglued after the battle of Adrianople in 376, the roads, cities, baths, and aqueducts were everywhere. But the political system had hollowed out the economic system, and a lot of people were living in buildings they could no longer afford to maintain. Some similarities to modern times come to mind…

L: You mean it wasn't Obelix and his mass production of menhirs that bankrupted Rome?

Doug: When it comes to <u>Obelix and Asterix</u>[4], I've got to say I'm firmly on the side of the Gauls. The emperors were always interested in amassing wealth and glory, but this always came at the expense of the conquered peoples, like the Gauls—who had quite an advanced civilization themselves. People think of the Romans as being a great civilizing force, but they were really just looting and pillaging their weaker neighbors.

L: How did it all get started? The Roman legions became famous for their advances in warfare, their "turtle" formations, etc., but that must have taken centuries to develop. Did they start with some advantage that allowed them to take over the Sabines and what-not?

Doug: It could just have been luck. I'm not sure anyone has come up with a credible explanation as to why it was Rome and not one of the other early tribes in the area that became dominant.

L: How about later? Were those military advances that decisive, or was it just a matter of having more and more wealth to put into the war effort with each conquest?

Doug: The technology the Romans developed was very important. For instance, the legion, with its flexible centuries and cohorts, proved superior to the Greek phalanx; its short swords were superior for formation fighting to the long swords of the Celts. Its throwing *pilum* were much superior to the long spears others used. Of course, against generals like Hannibal, Rome suffered some of its greatest military defeats. In the famous battle of Cannae, some 50,000 Romans were slaughtered in spite of their supposedly better training and equipment. The Romans' main advantage was their organization. The Celts and Germanic tribes fought as individual warriors. Even in large numbers, they couldn't cope with well-trained and well-organized soldiers fighting out well-planned battles. And the Romans were masters of engineering, as the Gauls discovered at Alesia and the Jews at Masada.

L: Okay… Hm. So, is this fascination of yours with Rome a quirk of your personality, or is there some reason it should matter to investors today?

Doug: Along with the Greeks, the Romans form the base of Western civilization. We know a lot about Rome now, and they were people exactly like us. And the rise of Rome does in many ways parallel the rise of America. Its rise, its peak—and at this point, I think you can even see its decline reflected in the distant mirror

---

4. www.totallyincorrectbook.com/go/27

of Rome. We see the same change from a republic to a highly bureaucratized state with tentacles all over the world and great importance placed on the military. The population relying on welfare (after the time of the conquest of Egypt by Caesar, most of the grain and olive oil, the two big commodities of the ancient world, were no longer grown in Italy; they were imported from Africa and given for free, or nearly free, to the people in Rome). Even what went on in the Circus Maximus, the Coliseum, and their many copies in smaller cities, has its parallel in today's massive football events—not to mention cage fighting and extreme sports. The big one, of course, is the gradual destruction of the currency.

Quite interesting to me is that in the days of the republic, Roman coins portrayed mythical figures, like gods and goddesses, and ideal concepts. They changed to portraits of the emperor after Caesar. In the US, 1913—a pretty bad year overall, with the initiation of both the income tax and the Federal Reserve—was the year the first coin with a dead president's head on it was introduced, the Lincoln penny. Before then, we only had things like Liberty, Indians, buffaloes, etc. on our coins. Since then, all our coins have had dead emperors on them. We started out with semi-mythic figures like Washington and Jefferson. But now we do the recently dead—Roosevelt, Kennedy, Eisenhower. It's simply wrong to put the features of your rulers on the coinage. The Romans, before Augustus, agreed. And, of course, gold was taken out of daily circulation in 1933, silver in 1965, and copper from the penny in 1982. Nothing new.

L: So, if the US is in Roman-style decline now, what would you say is the cause?

Doug: The same thing as in Rome: the currency has been debased, taxes have soared, regulation has become extremely onerous. But these things have political causes. Many, if not all, of those 180 reasons why Rome fell apply to the US. The empire has grown large, and it's bankrupting the country to defend itself against barbarian incursions. Even the lead in the water might have its counterpart in industrial food production.

I think there's a good chance the US government will disappear at some point, consumed by pure ineffectiveness, and be replaced with *nothing*. As we discussed in our <u>conversation on anarchy</u>[5], the very concept of the nation-state as we know it is an innovation of recent centuries and not something written in the bedrock of the universe. Its time is up. Good riddance.

L: So, back to my previous question, do you just like ancient history, or do you think it's worth studying because those who don't learn from history are doomed to repeat it?

---

5. www.totallyincorrectbook.com/go/28

Doug: It's also been said that the only thing we learn from history is that we don't learn anything from history.

L: Or that it doesn't repeat, but it rhymes…

Doug: Yes, or simply that "history is bunk."

But I do think it's worth knowing and understanding history, for its perspective on the big picture, which is something we try to keep in mind while looking for trends to invest in. Like all the reasons we see for energy—especially oil—prices to go higher.

Before Rome, there was Athens. With the conquest of the New World, the Spanish Empire rose to a great height before disappearing completely. Most recently, there was the Soviet Empire, now consigned to the dustbin of history. All of these and many more have come and gone. Nothing lasts forever, and everyone knows it—if they'll be honest for a moment. So it impresses me as being very jingoistic for Americans to carry on as though the US can, should, and will dominate the world forever.

And, as we've discussed before, I don't even like to call them Americans anymore, since the idea of America—which was excellent and unique—is dead, replaced by the United States.

L: The now forcibly United State.

Doug: Yes. I think it's important for people to realize that what's happening to the US Empire is not the first time it's ever happened to anyone. If history is any guide, it's very unlikely that the US will exist for much longer as the semi-coherent entity it is now, whether it takes 50 years, 100, or 150. The colors of the maps on the walls are always running. None of today's borders, or politics, are part of the cosmic firmament.

The question is whether we're more like Rome in 200 AD, 300 AD, or 400 AD? We're definitely in severe decline.

It seems clear to me that once a power goes into decline, it never really makes a comeback. At least not for centuries. Greece and Rome never came back. Spain, Portugal, France, and Britain are still in decline, with Britain edging near the precipice. So is Russia. The Chinese and the Indians now seem well on their way to their day in the sun, however.

L: Has there ever been a time when your study of Roman history has given you understanding you've used directly, as a speculator?

Doug: Good question. Well, the clipping of the coins has a direct bearing on what's going on now, with the same endgame looking very likely. It's actually almost funny: one of the reasons the eastern Roman Empire lasted as long as it did was that for some reason—maybe they learned something from the fall of the western empire—their gold solidus remained a stable and sound money for almost a thousand years after the western Roman Empire dried up and blew away. Looking at the history of Rome and other empires helps you keep things in perspective. We're just another part of the passing parade. Regrettably, no longer different or special.

So, I do think about these things as an investor and speculator. The root cause of the fall of Rome was not just political, social and military, but also economic—so it matters when I see the same patterns today. It's a perspective that helps us define trends like the long-term bets on higher energy prices and precious metals we track at Casey Research.

L: Well, I can't say I've thought much about Augustus while out kicking rocks, looking for gold deposits, but I have been on sites mined by Romans, as well as other empires over the centuries. Maybe I should give it more thought—when the facts today are obscured by fearful governments, history may provide the only reliable data for us to consider.

Doug: Maybe you should. 'Til next time.

Doug Casey on the Nanny State

March 14, 2012

L: Doug, you're going to love this; there's a new study out, purporting to show that eating any amount of any kind of red meat is bad for you[1]—making you 13% more likely to die, in fact. So, with your growing herd of cattle in Argentina, you're close to becoming a mass murderer.

Doug: I saw that. I wonder what you have to do to make it 26% more likely to die? If I go back to skydiving, does that mean I'm 1,000% more likely to die? It's rather strange, in that I always thought we're all basically 100% likely to die.

It's yet another sign of how degraded US society has become, that something so ridiculous can be passed off as news. According to the _LA Times_ article[2] I read, the "study" was just a survey of people's reported eating habits. So, at best—assuming people responded accurately and honestly—the survey might show us a correlation. But even a high-school student should be able to tell you that correlation does not establish causality. The typical science journalist may be even more ignorant and misinformed than the typical financial journalist, which is saying something. It's why I read the papers mostly for entertainment.

L: The study failed to consider, for example, if those who reported eating more meat happen to include more people who ride motorcycles, party hardy, or engage in other higher-risk behaviors—which could easily be true of steak lovers. This survey wouldn't catch such patterns. And yet I read one of the authors claiming:

> This study provides clear evidence that regular consumption of red meat, especially processed meat, contributes substantially to premature death... On the other hand, choosing more healthful sources of

---

1. www.totallyincorrectbook.com/go/29
2. www.totallyincorrectbook.com/go/30

protein in place of red meat can confer significant health benefits by reducing chronic disease morbidity and mortality.

Doug: It sounds as if the authors might have a political agenda. But what do you expect from government "science?" Much of it is politically driven, and if you don't arrive at politically correct answers, funding might dry up.

L: But this was a Harvard study...

Doug: Sure it was—but paid for by a branch of the <u>US government health bureaucracy</u>[3], the NIH. These so-called scientists may well be hacks who got paid a lot of money because they were deemed likely to deliver a result that meshes with the agendas of various politically correct groups.

One of those is the anti-meat fanatics, including the animal rights activists at PETA; they're relatively few in number but very strident. Another is the environmentalists who fear the methane cows and sheep produce; because methane—$CH4$—is a "greenhouse gas." They believe it will turn this rock with its thin skin of an atmosphere—floating in the cosmos where the average temperature is a couple degrees above absolute zero—into an inferno. Actually, termites and decomposing vegetable matter emit hundreds of times more methane than domestic animals—not to mention volcanoes.

I'm of the opinion that these greens don't really love animals; what's really going on is that they hate people in particular and life in general. Anyway, these types have taken to using science as a cover. There should be a separation of science and state, for the very same reasons there should be a separation between church and state.

L: What would you say to people who say you're biased because you're in the cattle business?

Doug: Yes, the busybodies have convinced *Boobus americanus* that anyone who actually makes his living dealing with nature shouldn't say anything about it. People who mine minerals, drill for oil, farm, grow animals—people who actually know something about these things, and make them available for use—have largely been intimidated into silence. They're commercial, and to be commercial is bad, QED. Of course that's a completely insane attitude. But the self-righteous busybodies have managed to claim the moral high ground and discredit the producers. They've done this by capturing the government, academia, and the media.

Anyway, I'd say the average "consumer"—which is itself a perverse and degrading way to describe a person—should start using what's left of his own

---

3. www.totallyincorrectbook.com/go/31

brain instead of relying on experts, whether those be government-stooge scientists or… me. Just think about it: humans evolved over millions of years eating meat—and as much of it as they could get, whenever and wherever it was available. The conclusion of the anti-meat study, at least as broadly stated in the press, has serious credibility problems on its face.

L: The study does make a point of saying that processed meats, like hot dogs, are supposed to be much worse for us. That would seem to have some face validity.

Doug: Yes, I can see that. When you're providing mass quantities of stuff for the masses through industrial processes, it seems inevitable that all kinds of additives, chemicals, and preservatives will get into the mix. Indeed, how much pure beef remains in a typical modern hot dog? I think they're mostly cereal and artificial flavoring these days, plus a good measure of the "pink slime[4]" the USDA puts into lunchmeat for school kids' government-mandated meals.

Equally important, in my view, is that almost all meat these days is from cows raised on unnatural diets, pumped full of steroids and antibiotics, eating cardboard and unnatural food, living miserable lives, shoulder to shoulder in feedlots. How many survey respondents would know or care what kind of chemicals and pharmaceuticals went into the meat they are eating? I doubt they could give accurate answers to such questions, if they were even asked—I'd guess the researchers didn't even bother.

Here in Argentina, all my beef cows eat grass on wide open and quite pleasant pampas. No antibiotics, steroids, or cardboard are necessary. I understand that if you're going to provide meat for the masses, that quality may suffer. But that's all the more reason to elevate yourself out of the masses. Entirely apart from the fact "the masses" is a term Marx originated…

Trends in demonized foods are like trends in fashion. For some time, salt was the greatest bogeyman—until some people, particularly an Iranian doctor I once knew named Batmanghelidj, pointed out the obvious, namely that salt is essential to life, and that problems attributed to too much salt are usually problems with not enough water. You need a lot of water washing through your cells. But anything in excess can be a problem, including water. If it's not salt, then it's sugar. If it's not sugar, then it's fat. Red meat has had its turn as demon *du jour* before, and it looks like it coming back into fashion again.

L: I see Dr. Batmanghelidj's book on Amazon: *You're Not Sick, You're Thirsty*[5]. I remember the salt scare—that was a big thing back in the '70s, as I recall. The

4. www.totallyincorrectbook.com/go/32
5. www.totallyincorrectbook.com/go/33

odd thing is that post-scare, salt still seems to have a bad name, but consumption has moved toward gourmet salts. Plain old iodized Morton's salt is not to be found in certain politically correct cupboards, but sea salt or rock salt you grind yourself is acceptable.

Doug: Yes, rich people can't be denied their gourmet designer salts, even though what we generally call "salt" is made of sodium and chlorine—two of the deadliest elements on the periodic table. It's all part of the War on the Periodic Table of the Elements. Plutonium was perhaps the original enemy element, then uranium, then sodium. Gold is considered an evil element by many. Now the most evil element of them all is carbon, which is the essential component of all organic matter, and hence all life on this planet.

L: Hm. Now that you mention it, sodium ends in –ium, like thorium, so it must be bad.

Doug: Yes, and if it weren't for government policy, we'd likely be generating power from thorium instead of uranium; it's a much better fuel[6]. But that's another story. I'm sure that once the Greens discover that it's atomic number 90, it, too, will join the enemies list in their general war on the periodic table.

This reminds me of all the government-funded crash programs to find the cause of AIDS. Lo and behold, they found one and called it the Human Immunodeficiency Virus (HIV). But as I understand it, there are people who have AIDS and no HIV, and there are people who have HIV and never show any symptoms of AIDS. And yet, to question the HIV orthodoxy is to invite accusations of being a "denialist," homophobe, and maybe even a remover of those tags you're not supposed to take off mattresses under penalty of law. Fortunately, the AIDS hysteria, which was supposed to destroy the human race, has pretty much burned itself out.

And then there's the "overwhelming evidence" of anthropogenic global warming that fearmongers proclaim. Again, with a lot of government "science" involved. It's turned into an industry that destroys capital.

If we could get the state and its corrupting influence completely out of the science business, I'd be much more inclined to accept what the majority of scientists believe on "soft" sciences—like climate studies and epidemiology. Those things aren't at all the same as physics and chemistry; they're far above things like psychology and sociology, but hardly in the same class with mathematics. Certainly, as long as there's government money with a political agenda involved, I'm inclined to take so-called consensus views with at least a grain of gourmet sea salt, or even as possible contrary indicators for the truth.

---

6. www.totallyincorrectbook.com/go/34

L: That's a pretty strong statement, Doug.

Doug: It pays to be skeptical—about everything. Most of the reading that I do is either science or history, so I consider myself fairly knowledgeable in those areas, although I'm not a professional in either. But I didn't say I would refuse to believe anything supported by solid evidence just because I didn't like its source. I said that if the data come from what I regard as a corrupt source, I proceed with greater-than-usual caution.

Although the corruption of science is very bad, what's even worse is the continuing and accelerating encroachment of the "nanny state." This meat study—and others like it—can easily be used to manufacture a scare. The scare will then be used to implement more laws and restrictions on people's freedom to live their lives as they see fit... and to destroy another industry. One example of that is the FDA's campaign against farmers who sell unpasteurized milk[7] to those who prefer it.

L: So, whether or not red meat is good for us, we all have a natural or God-given right to eat what we want and go to hell in our own way? Big Brother, step aside, Big Momma is gonna make us eat our veggies.

Doug: Exactly. I'm of the opinion that quality of life trumps quantity of life. That's the exact opposite view from what rulers and would-be rulers hold; they view the rest of our species as milk cows, to be kept alive and milked for as long as possible, no matter how much joy is taken from them. The purpose of life, however, is to enjoy yourself. It's not to be treated like part of a herd and be fed what your master wants for his own purposes.

L: Is that why politicians bother meddling with whether people eat hot dogs or salads?

Doug: That, among many other reasons. They can win brownie points with very vocal activists if they beat up on an unpopular personal choice, like smoking. That's very valuable to them come election time. Politicians, with the possible exceptions of the likes of Ron Paul[8], always want to increase the state's—and thereby their own—power. Any scare is a great tool for manipulating people into handing over more of their freedom, which is to say, increasing their power over people.

L: *Crisis and Leviathan*[9].

Doug: Right. That's an important book everyone should read. The whole trend is very ominous. It's as Martin Niemöller said during WWII[10]: "First they

7. www.totallyincorrectbook.com/go/35
8. www.totallyincorrectbook.com/go/36
9. www.totallyincorrectbook.com/go/37
10. www.totallyincorrectbook.com/go/38

came for the communists, but I didn't speak out, because I was not a communist."

L: "And then they came for the Jews… And then they came for me, and there was no one left to speak out for me."

Doug: Right. I believe in speaking out, even though it probably doesn't do any good. I do it because I have to live with myself. I do it because I believe in karma.

L: If we end up in a totalitarian police state or nanny state, I don't want my children to lift their manacled wrists before my eyes and ask me why I didn't resist while resistance was possible.

Doug: Indeed. In spite of the blatantly obvious and disastrous results of Prohibition[11], politicians have declared open season on drug users, then smokers, then gun owners—All Things Fun. How far can it be from regulating politically incorrect eaters to regulating just about everyone's choices on every subject?

L: Not far.

Doug: And it gets worse. Now that we have socialized medical services in the US (which is not the same as health care), genuine bad health choices that used to be individuals' problems have become everyone's problems, because we all have to pay for them. Socialized medicine is terrible—it's entrusting medical services to the same bankrupt organization that can't even deliver the mail reliably. It's also a powerful excuse for the nanny state to monitor, inspect, interfere with, and control all aspects of our lives, from what we eat and drink all the way down to what we do in the privacy of our bedrooms—because everything can impact our health, which is now society's obligation.

L: But it's all for our own good. "If it saves one child… "

Doug: If it saves one child, how many children does it kill? If you ban Freon over an unproven fear that it contributes to ozone depletion, for example, and require use of a more expensive, less efficient, and incidentally more toxic and corrosive substitute, all because it might save one child, how many babies did you kill with spoiled milk and meat? What other consequences to your intervention are you ignoring?

This reminds me of the time Madeleine Halfbright was told that the sanctions she saw imposed on Iraq had killed about half a million children, and she answered: "Yes, it was costly, but we think it was worth it." These people are hypocrites—and extremely dangerous. Sociopaths. They don't care about saving human lives—they are more than willing to expend any number of them, like pawns on a chessboard, to advance their quest for power.

---

11. www.totallyincorrectbook.com/go/39

L: Bastiat's broken window all over again: "the seen and the unseen[12]". But you've got to have a good cover story, like saving children's lives.

Doug: Of course. If you say you're doing it for the children, you can get away with almost anything.

L: Clearly, you don't subscribe to the precautionary principle—the idea that no new technology or innovation should be implemented until it can be shown to be safe.

Doug: It's a load of horse manure—and you can quote me on that.

L: I will.

Doug: Good! If our ancestors had been stupid enough to adopt such an absolutely paralyzing idea, we'd still be shivering in caves, ravaged by dread diseases, and hunted by animals larger and more powerful than we. No, I misspeak; most likely, we'd have gone extinct.

If the car were invented today, it would never be approved for use. The idea of millions of people racing towards each other at high speeds in vehicles they control themselves, with tanks full of explosive gasoline... it would never make it through OSHA, EPA, or a dozen other agencies. The idea of air travel—forget about it. We're just lucky these things were in common use before the nanny state came into its own.

L: Extinction... another strong statement. That's what you think would happen now if the precautionary principle were adopted and enforced by law?

Doug: 'Fraid so. Life without risk is a patent impossibility. Almost a contradiction in terms. And life without risk, innovation, new horizons, would hardly be worth living. But that's the way the world is headed.

You know, most people hardly pay any attention to such matters these days. Important news hardly gets discussed, while Rush Limbaugh insulting some law student is headline news for a week. (Whether or not the student in question is a slut, as Limbaugh said, is her business, not mine or Limbaugh's—and the whole issue is a matter of manners, not even deserving of a mention in the back of the society section of the papers.)

The issue of the student's call for expanding the US's socialized medical system to include free birth control, however, is a suitable issue for conversation. The costs affect us all—and it's another tightening of the grip of the nanny state on people's lives. All this squabbling over what should be paid for by the state would be eliminated if *nothing* were covered at "public" expense (i.e., using other people's money). But most people don't even think about that possibility.

---

12. www.totallyincorrectbook.com/go/40

We've already beat up on Limbaugh, so we don't really have to go there, but while it's on my mind, I have to point out that he really showed what an ignoramus he is when he defended Joseph Kony[13] and the Lord's Resistance Army[14] last year. He apparently thought they were Christians fighting Muslim tyrants, not the kidnappers and murderers the preponderance of evidence says they are. There's a video about Kony[15] that's gone truly viral on YouTube, with over 75 million views in just one week.

The fact that an ignorant hypocrite like Limbaugh, who wanted to have drug users executed even as he was getting phony prescriptions for his Oxycontin habit, has such a large following is another sad sign of our times. It's not just the socialists advocating the nanny state who are the problem. So-called right-wingers are just as dangerous to personal freedom as left-wingers.

L: Any way to stop this train wreck?

Doug: None. It's like I said to begin with: this is a sign of advanced decay in a society that has lost its élan. It's not something you can fix independently of fixing the whole rotten mess; nanny-state thinking goes hand in hand with the entitlement mentality, which goes with irresponsible and self-destructive behavior. That accelerates the other, "male" side of ever-expanding state power that people like Limbaugh favor: the warfare state, the paternalistic, authoritarian state.

The bottom line is that, with more than half the US population on one form of government dole or another, we've crossed the point of no return. We're going to have to go through the wringer before things can improve. The current situation is unsustainable. It's going to collapse.

Incidentally, as unpleasant and inconvenient as it will be, a collapse and reboot is necessary and will be a good thing. Hopefully it will destroy the nanny state, if only because the nanny state is a dead hand on the development of technology. The most positive thing going on in the world today is the advance of technology. But, just as the car and the airplane likely couldn't be developed today because of the safety-first nanny state, there are lots of other technologies that won't ever come into existence—and we might never know it. Our conversation on technology is an example of what I mean by that. Anyway, we've got to pay the piper first... and the bill is rapidly coming due.

L: [Sighs] Okay, before we go all poetic, are there investment implications to the rise of the nanny state?

---

13. www.totallyincorrectbook.com/go/41
14. www.totallyincorrectbook.com/go/42
15. www.totallyincorrectbook.com/go/43

Doug: Yes. On the wealth-preservation—and health-preservation—side, it's vital to understand that today's wealthy Western countries are increasingly hazardous to the well-being of the people who live there. They have the power and the motive to do harm to any citizen as suits the short-term goals of those in office. That's long been the case financially and is increasingly becoming the case physically, both in terms of health and safety from police brutality. Just as we said last week in our conversation on <u>cashless societies</u>[16], the time is approaching—if not here already—when the wisest course of action is to <u>get out of Dodge</u>[17]... or at least out of countries with powerful governments.

On the investment side, the West's increasingly irrational attitudes about meat may create more buying opportunities in the cattle business. Even if every single person in the US stopped eating meat, those eating more in China and the rest of the developing world would make up the difference before long. At the same time, herds continue to go into liquidation in the West. Cattle have been in a bear market for many, many years, making it one of the best contrarian plays in decades. That's why I'm building my own herd: I'm buying low so I can later sell high. But we've <u>talked about that before</u>[18]. Like any good speculator, I plan on making a lot of money while performing a public service.

Other implications are as we've discussed many times: buy gold and silver, speculate on gold and silver mining stocks, own long-term energy plays and technology plays that will do well in hard economic times, harden your assets, and diversify yourself internationally.

L: Well then, I think our readers know what to do. Thanks for another interesting conversation.

Doug: Any time.

L: Next time.

---

16. www.totallyincorrectbook.com/go/44
17. www.totallyincorrectbook.com/go/45
18. www.totallyincorrectbook.com/go/46

Doug Casey on the Silver Screen

Feb 17, 2010

L: Doug, we've promised to talk about what you call the literature of today's world: movies. So, let's talk about the silver screen.

Doug: Good idea. Some may dismiss this as fluff, but I think it can be very important, as per our conversation on *Avatar* a couple weeks ago. In today's world, movies, not books anymore, are the most important media for transferring memes.

L: Okay, but there's so much to say—we could do a long interview just listing your favorite movies and saying why. But we should also talk about the medium as an art form and a social phenomenon itself. And the movie industry is a kaleidoscope mix of the good, the bad, and the ugly. Where do we start?

Doug: Well, let's start with *The Good, the Bad and the Ugly*[1]. I think it—and almost all of Clint Eastwood's movies—are going to have staying power. That's partially because he's in them. He projects a certain strength of character and a certain attitude towards life that has justifiable appeal. He's also one of the few overt libertarians in Hollywood—along with Kurt Russell and Charles Bronson, who died a few years ago. In addition, Eastwood has almost always selected his roles very well. *The Good, the Bad and the Ugly* is a favorite of mine, and not just because of the great theme song...

L: A theme song we heard played live by an orchestra in Lithuania, conducted by the song's composer.

Doug: We caught that show in Vilnius in 2008.

L: Even jet-lagged, that was fun. But back to *The Good, the Bad and the Ugly*...

Doug: It's not just that movie, but Westerns as a genre, that tend to be the most reliably engaging movies, in my view. As a group, I'd put them absolutely at the top for almost always having the most heroic themes and being philosophically sound. There's a reason for that. They deal—they must deal—with

---

1. www.totallyincorrectbook.com/go/47

the basic stuff of life: Man and woman. Life and death. Earth and sun. Courage and cowardice. Survival against hostile opponents and hostile nature. The one against the many.

L: You know, I never thought of it that way. Of course it would tend to be so; Westerns deal with life on the frontier, and that's what it was like then.

Doug: Exactly. On the frontier, you're forced to be independent and solve problems yourself. There's nobody that's going to bail you out when you live in a solitary little house way out on the prairie. Of course, the cavalry can always save you in the final reel, but that's *deus ex machina* on the part of lazy script-writers. It would have been an exceedingly rare occurrence in real life, and it's not common in good Westerns. On the frontier, you have to solve your own problems and create your own future reality.

That's why I think Westerns are so great—and incidentally, I think that's why the chattering classes, as a group, tend to hold Westerns in low regard. Anything that smacks of individualism, independence, and industry will go against the grain of their values. I intuitively distrust the motives and values of people who dislike Westerns. Could Woody Allen produce a Western? I think not.

L: "Westerns" aren't movies about Western Europe nor Western China, they're about the American West, a place and time that highlighted the virtues of "rugged individualism."

Doug: That's right. It's a uniquely American genre—and I mean American in the best sense of the word, dating to the time when America was *America* and not just the United States.

L: So, let's list some examples. What other Westerns are among your favorite movies?

Doug: Well, there's no question that my favorite Western, and perhaps my favorite movie of all time, is _The Wild Bunch_[2]. I called my polo teams in Palm Beach and New Zealand by that name. Anyway, it's the movie that put Sam Peckinpah on the map. One reason that movie made such a splash—set a trend, really—was that it was the first movie that showed graphically detailed violence. It showed, for example, bullets hitting bodies and going out the other side. It had shock value—but that's not the reason I like the movie.

I like it because it is pure Aristotelian drama. And by that I mean that it has a beginning and an end, joined by a plot line that has a crisis followed by a ca-tharsis, in which the Good Guys wipe out the Bad Guys. Or, in the case of *The Wild Bunch*, in which the Kind-of Good Guys wipe out the Really Bad Guys.

2. www.totallyincorrectbook.com/go/48

It's an excellent film from that perspective. And I think that William Holden and Ernest Borgnine were both truly excellent.

Another thing about it is the era it's set in, 1917, the end of the Long 19th Century (which really went from about 1776 to 1914). It was the end of the Belle Époque and the end of the Wild West. The protagonists, the Wild Bunch led by Holden, are aging outlaws looking to make just one more big score before they have to hang up their spurs. If they hadn't known that it was the end of an era and that they were dinosaurs, they wouldn't have taken on the Mexican army/bandits at the end.

I believe that we're at the end of another epoch now, for what that's worth. That's something to talk about another day…

But there are a lot of other Westerns that fall into the great category. All the Clint Eastwood ones, certainly including _Pale Rider_[3] and _Unforgiven_[4]. _Hombre_[5], with Paul Newman, is fantastic—definitely one of the best ones. It, like _The Wild Bunch_, has great Mexican bandits.

Incidentally, the portrayal of Mexican bandits in movies is almost a subgenre in its own right. _The Professionals_[6] had excellent Mexican bandits. It was an underrated but terrific movie starring Burt Lancaster, also set in 1917. I'd put Burt in the same class with Clint Eastwood; all of his movies are worth seeing, just because he's in them. _The Treasure of the Sierra Madre_[7] also had excellent Mexican bandits. Everybody knows the classic line from it, "Badges? We ain't got no badges. We don't need no stinking badges." A great attitude I'd like to see more of from the general public.

Another characteristic of Westerns is their attitude towards weapons. Everybody is expected to defend himself and, if he's smart, comport himself in a way that simultaneously won't make that necessary but will gain the respect of others. I've got to believe that's another reason statists tend to hate Westerns. A proper Western naturally makes the typical self-loathing liberal very uncomfortable.

But not all good Westerns are confined to the cinema.

L. You mean TV? I don't know of any currently being aired.

Doug: I don't believe there are any at the moment. A sad sign of the times, perhaps. But my favorites are _Have Gun Will Travel (HGWT)_[8] and _Deadwood_[9].

3. www.totallyincorrectbook.com/go/49
4. www.totallyincorrectbook.com/go/50
5. www.totallyincorrectbook.com/go/51
6. www.totallyincorrectbook.com/go/52
7. www.totallyincorrectbook.com/go/53
8. www.totallyincorrectbook.com/go/54
9. www.totallyincorrectbook.com/go/55

HGWT was on TV from about 1957 to 1962. Interestingly, everybody has heard the phrase, but apparently very few who weren't around in those days have seen it. *HGWT* is the original thinking man's Western. Paladin, who's perfectly played by Richard Boone, is, if you will, a professional problem solver. More important, he is a true Renaissance Man. Each 30-minute episode opens with him at his hotel in San Francisco, living the high life, a sophisticated man of the world. He might be outplaying a chess master, or commenting on a rare wine, or returning from the opera with the *prima donna*. Or he might be reading the paper, looking for a situation ripe for him to set right. After the catharsis, when justice is done, Paladin usually offers a quote from one of the Greek or Roman classics, or at least Shakespeare, to enlighten anyone left standing. I have the whole series.

L: Sounds quite a bit different from *Deadwood*…

Doug: Oh yes. *Deadwood* specializes in the gritty reality of the eponymous town in South Dakota, at the time of both Custer's misadventure at Little Big Horn and the discovery of the Homestake mine. It's one of the best series ever done… and I mean ever.

The story revolves around Al Swearengen, the proprietor of a saloon and cathouse. Aside from the well-drawn characters—and I believe they must have somehow channeled Wild Bill Hickok, who was famously killed in a poker game there—I love the use of language in it. Most people will be shocked by it, of course, since it's at least as colorful as any you could hope to hear in the roughest barracks. But that's not the point. Many of the episodes are written in Shakespearean blank verse and are highly poetic. The series is good enough to be worth watching more than once.

One more that was made for TV: <u>*Lonesome Dove*</u>[10]. Larry McMurtry did it, and he's not only an excellent writer but a scholar of the Old West. It's very well-acted by Robert Duval and Tommy Lee Jones as the main characters.

L: Okay, I'll look into getting the ones you mention I haven't already seen. What about beyond Westerns? I know you like SF movies, and I'd guess you like most or all of the ones with Arnold Schwarzenegger in them.

Doug: Yes. I think the first two *Terminator* movies are absolutely fantastic. As I pointed out at the time, I think both <u>*The Terminator*</u>[11] and especially <u>*Terminator 2*</u>[12] showed the direction in which nanotechnology is going, that will make actual terminators possible. I do enjoy watching Arnold on screen; it's a pity he turned out to be such a terrible Governor.

---

10. www.totallyincorrectbook.com/go/56
11. www.totallyincorrectbook.com/go/57
12. www.totallyincorrectbook.com/go/58

The Matrix[13] was even better, and it appealed to my solipsistic tendencies, with all of reality being a shared illusion.

Blade Runner[14] is another fantastic movie that deals with the essentials of life. _Blade Runner_ is in many ways a Western, set in the future. I'd say it makes my Top Ten list, especially the Director's Cut version.

And that reminds me of another Western that can't be overlooked, and that's _High Noon_[15] with Gary Cooper.

L: Ah, yes. Did you see the SF version, called _Outland_[16]?

Doug: With Sean Connery. Yes, it was interesting but not as good as the original, in my opinion. The originals are almost always the best in every genre.

But, you know, there's a similarity between SF movies and Westerns. If Westerns deal with the raw essentials and a related worldview set in the past, SF movies often portray the exact same essentials and worldview and set it in the future. That's why both genres of movies are generally disrespected by the so-called intellectuals of our day. Those people come from a totally different place, psychologically and philosophically.

L: I never thought of it that way before either.

Doug: Those two genres of movies are my favorites. They both take you out of the present and catapult you into a Once and Future reality. As any Zen master will tell you, it's important to live in the present, however sordid and degraded it may be. But stories about a heroic past and a heroic future help frame the present. It's myth, as good as, and in many ways similar to, that of Homer. It helps you keep your eye on the way life should be lived.

L: Well, there's the _Firefly_[17] series and the _Serenity_[18] movie sequel—they make that crossover explicitly. They're basically "cowboys in space."

Doug: Ah, yes. I'm glad you mention that. It was you and another friend of mine who thought enough of it that you both gave me a set of _Firefly_ discs. I would definitely recommend it to our readers—both the TV series, which only lasted one season, and the _Serenity_ movie based on it. They're very worthwhile, entertaining, and philosophically sound. For what it's worth, our partner David Galland looks like, and acts like, the lead character.

L: By the way of philosophically sound—meaning, pro-individual, pro-freedom, laissez-faire, etc.—that draws me back to your mention of _The Matrix_.

---

13. www.totallyincorrectbook.com/go/59
14. www.totallyincorrectbook.com/go/60
15. www.totallyincorrectbook.com/go/61
16. www.totallyincorrectbook.com/go/62
17. www.totallyincorrectbook.com/go/63
18. www.totallyincorrectbook.com/go/64

While not explicitly libertarian, its central theme is choice, which is an essentially libertarian concept. One way of describing a libertarian is to say it's someone who's pro-choice—on everything.

Doug: [Laughs] Yes. And when it comes to the choice, always take the red pill. That's my advice.

L: Right. But while the *Matrix* movies were not explicitly political, the same guys made *V for Vendetta*[19], which is very political. It's so in-your-face political, it's amazing it ever made it through Hollywood.

Doug: Yes, the Wachowski brothers. *V for Vendetta* is another of my all-time favorites. V also, I have to say, uses one of my favorite rock songs of all time for its end-theme music: The Rolling Stones' "Street Fighting Man." It's a fantastic movie—anyone who hasn't seen it should go out and buy it. Right now.

L: One SF movie that didn't have great production values—and totally butchered the books it was based on—but did have interesting socio-political content was *Logan's Run*.

Doug: *Logan's Run* was good. It makes the point that it's worth living past age 30. But could they remake it to show that it's worth living beyond 60?

L: I'm sure they could—and use the same actors. Any others?

Doug: A genre I have mixed feelings about is the war movie. Well done, they can be riveting. Whether they're pro-war (we're the good guys, and the enemy needs killing—the kind John Wayne liked to make) or anti-war (war is a terrible thing, no matter who the good guys are—and good guys engage in wholesale murder).

The problem with either type, philosophically, is that the individual is caught in a hellish situation where he has little control and has to follow orders. That said, *Apocalypse Now Redux*[20] (which has many important scenes that were cut from the movie theater version) offers a surreal thrill ride. *Stalingrad*[21] is horrific, almost putting you in the battle. *Saving Private Ryan*[22] is equally good. *Alien*[23] is SF, but it's actually a well-done war movie as well.

The Lord of the Rings[24] trilogy is a fantasy, of course, but something of a war movie as well. It's as perfect a translation of the books to screen as can be done. I read the books, and it's as if Peter Jackson, the director, reached into my mind and put my own visualization of the books on film. It's a work of genius. And

19. www.totallyincorrectbook.com/go/65
20. www.totallyincorrectbook.com/go/66
21. www.totallyincorrectbook.com/go/67
22. www.totallyincorrectbook.com/go/68
23. www.totallyincorrectbook.com/go/69
24. www.totallyincorrectbook.com/go/70

it demonstrates that a movie can be just as good as the book it was made from, while making the experience accessible to vastly more people.

L: Others?

Doug: One movie that's outside of these genres but is just an excellent, well-done drama is _Casablanca_[25]. It's a classic for the ages, for good reasons.

L: Hm. I saw that a long, long time ago. I don't remember it having any particularly strong ideological content. You like it just for being a good movie?

Doug: That's right. But it does have a sort of philosophical content, in that Rick is a cynical, nihilistic guy who makes a point of looking out only for number one. But he gradually redeems himself in the end, proving to have a heart of gold. There's something to be said for people finding themselves and going off in the right direction. Also, the dialogue in the movie is first class.

L: Are you a fan of Humphrey Bogart in general?

Doug: No question about that; Bogart is one of the greats. I like almost all of his movies.

I'm trying to think of who else is a great actor on that level, whose movies are reliably good.

L: How about Charlie Chaplin? You must have loved his film _The Great Dictator_[26]...

Doug: You sent me that, but I haven't made time to watch it.

L: You still haven't seen _The Great Dictator_?

Doug: No. I'll go watch it when we're done here.

L: I won't twist your arm, but I think you'll really like it. The movie is totally amazing in many ways, not just intellectually. Chaplin was one of the few old movie actors who made the transition to being a "talkie" actor. Not only did he make the transition as an actor, but he uses his voice absolutely brilliantly, speaking pseudo-German via his Hitleresque character that's very, very funny. And special effects too, including an upside-down scene shot 70 years ago! He even wrote the music for the film. He was a true genius.

Hm. What about Mel Gibson? _Braveheart_[27] is a great pro-freedom movie, and _The Patriot_[28] wasn't too bad either.

Doug: Ah, yes... Well, Gibson appears to be a religious fanatic, but _Braveheart_ is a fantastic movie, and _The Patriot_ is both excellent and well done.

---

25. www.totallyincorrectbook.com/go/71
26. www.totallyincorrectbook.com/go/72
27. www.totallyincorrectbook.com/go/73
28. www.totallyincorrectbook.com/go/74

L: I especially like the way the nobles in *Braveheart* are always turning their backs on the people—when they are not actively abusing them. Something to think about, for those who imagine that government attracts any more of the best and the brightest now than it did then.

Doug: Another actor comes to mind who had very few clinkers: Steve McQueen. His movies don't necessarily have a lot of ideological import, but I've enjoyed them. My favorite by him is probably *The Sand Pebbles*[29], in which he plays a China sailor during the Boxer Rebellion. Another Western starring McQueen is *Nevada Smith*[30]. Great movie, very underrated.

Another big movie is *The Aviator*[31], which is about Howard Hughes, before he went off the deep end. The movie presents many important values positively and shows what a creative man Hughes was. That scene where he's testifying before Congress, being interrogated by the scumbag senator, is, alone, worth the price of admission.

L: What about ladies? Any favorite female actresses?

Doug: Well, there was Katherine Hepburn, who played with Bogart in *The African Queen*[32], a super movie.

L: That's right. She also played with John Wayne in at least one movie.

Doug: I think that was *Rooster Cogburn*[33]. I like John Wayne's Westerns, of course. I might put my finger on *Hondo* as one of his best. The thing about Wayne, like Eastwood, Bronson, Bogart, and Lancaster, is that they basically just played themselves. A lot of these guys got into movies by accident, with no acting training at all. Many actors today—I'm thinking Ed Norton, Johnny Depp, and Orlando Bloom, for instance—have better technical skills as actors. But because of that, it's much harder to tell who they are as people.

L: So, who's your favorite femme fatale? *La Femme Nikita*[34]?

Doug: *La Femme Nikita* impresses me as a very anti-government movie. And it's a hell of a good story. And the same director, Luc Besson, did *The Professional*[35] with Jean Reno and Natalie Portman. It's about a very sympathetic and competent but somewhat naïve hit man. He's the good guy, and all the cops and government agents are the bad guys. The movie fires on all

29. www.totallyincorrectbook.com/go/75
30. www.totallyincorrectbook.com/go/76
31. www.totallyincorrectbook.com/go/77
32. www.totallyincorrectbook.com/go/78
33. www.totallyincorrectbook.com/go/79
34. www.totallyincorrectbook.com/go/80
35. www.totallyincorrectbook.com/go/81

cylinders, as does Besson's _The Messenger: Joan of Arc_[36].

L: Who would you say was the most beautiful lady of the silver screen? Marilyn Monroe? Bo Derek?

Doug: Cameron Diaz may the best looking. But she appears, based on what I've heard her say in real life, to be a ditz. Angelina Jolie is much more interesting; her character Laura Croft could have been a Randian heroine. And I understand both she and Brad Pitt, whose stuff I also like, are fans of Rand. Charlize Theron is incredibly beautiful, incredibly talented and, based on what I've read in an interview, very intelligent. But one of the most appealing roles I can remember is that of Naomi Watts in Peter Jackson's _King Kong_[37]. That guy is probably the best director in the business, but Watts was perfect in that role.

L: This may surprise some people, but I found the original _Star Wars_[38] movies uplifting and even philosophically useful. I liked that Han Solo was an unabashed capitalist and black-marketer. George Lukas' first movie was called _THX 1138_[39], which was the name of a man in a dystopian future, in which the totalitarian government kept everyone on drugs all the time to control them. THX-1138 becomes guilty of criminal drug evasion. But in spite of the interesting concepts, the movie was slow and rather boring. I always thought that some older hand must have taken Lukas under his wing and said, "George, that was great—really important stuff. But people won't get it. There were no explosions, no villain in black, no jet fighters. Try throwing in a princess that needs rescuing next time. Maybe some funny robots... "

Doug: Well, as I said, most SF movies, like most Westerns, tend to be sound. It's really too bad they are such underrated genres by the critical powers that be, in most cases. It's really shameful.

L: But does that matter? The movies make money in the box office anyway, so good storytellers like the Wachowski brothers can get powerful ideas out to lots of people, as they did with _V for Vendetta_.

Doug: True enough. But I've noticed that once people rise to a certain level in the world, they tend to disavow those two classes of movies and the values that they tend to represent.

L: Okay. Hm. Investment implications?

Doug: In a way, it's all just good fun. But I'll say again that movies are the literature of our times. Books are wonderful, of course, and until computer

36. www.totallyincorrectbook.com/go/82
37. www.totallyincorrectbook.com/go/83
38. www.totallyincorrectbook.com/go/84
39. www.totallyincorrectbook.com/go/85

graphics came along, there were many things you could describe on paper that you just couldn't show in a movie (except in the case of some really good cartoon animation). But movies shouldn't be put down, as compared to books, as a form of literature.

That's because the amount of information you can take in, in a minute, from a movie is an order of magnitude—maybe two—above what you can take in from a minute of reading a book. That time is often wasted in bad movies, but in well-done films, vastly greater volumes of subtle meaning, sense, emotion, and just straight data about the world being shown can be transmitted. That's a power that can be used to create powerful, meaningful art. Literature.

L: That thought has crossed my mind, particularly in terms of power to persuade the masses. If Thomas Paine were alive today and were of a mind to write a new version of his pamphlet that so inflamed colonial America, *Common Sense*, he wouldn't write a pamphlet. He'd make a movie. That's why movies that are propaganda for destructive ideas, like *Avatar*, as we've discussed, are so dangerous.

Doug: Exactly. Movies engage almost all of the senses today—and eventually they will engage them all, including smell, touch, and taste. That will give them even more power to reach deep into people's emotions and thoughts.

L: This is Big Business. Would you invest in new movie technology? I don't know who did the 3D graphics for *Avatar*, but would you invest in that company? Would you risk venture capital in the first company to introduce smell and other sensory input to movies?

Doug: Well, believe it or not, I've actually invested in several movies. Small indie things. But that's been leading with my heart, not my head. It's a long shot to make any money investing in movies, especially with Hollywood accounting—it's legendary how those people will find some way to screw you, no matter how much money a movie makes in the box office. But still, if there were a great script and good, independent actors, I'd be up for investing in a movie, because you don't need to have a $400 million budget like *Avatar's* to have a good movie. *Casablanca* had a very low budget. I think there's room for something like that out there.

So, I wouldn't recommend investing in movie studios, but if you can get a good script and good actors who will work for nothing, as Harrison Ford did in *Star Wars*—he worked for $50,000, realizing that if he got lucky, it would make his name—taking it on as your own start-up would, if nothing else, be fun. It'd be extremely high-risk, but very high-reward.

I remember Ford also had a bit part in *American Graffiti*[40]. I liked that movie because I had a few nights that seemed like cuts from it. It's a must-watch—but there are so many of those.

L: What about movie technology? If someone came up with an idea for "smell-a-vision," would you invest in it?

Doug: Probably not. The first guy to invent something rarely makes any money from it. But I'm very interested in successful companies in new fields.

So that's how I'd play the movie industry: either taking it head-on, getting involved in an indie project yourself—but for love more than for profit—or through new technologies. But at a minimum, our readers have a whole bunch of movies now that are worth watching.

L: Okay then. Thanks, Doug.

Doug: My pleasure. Talk to you next week.

---

40. www.totallyincorrectbook.com/go/86

Doug Casey on "The Donald" for President

April 20, 2011

Doug: Did you see that interview Donald Trump gave about running for president? Someone needs to debunk him—he's dangerous.

L: No, I didn't. I've never paid any attention to the man. But if not us, who? If not now, when?

Doug: I saw the interview with an important reporter from the *Wall Street Journal*, but it's <u>all over the Net now</u>[1].

L: Wait. An important reporter? I didn't think you believed such a thing was possible.

Doug: What?

L: You said, an "important reporter"—maybe you meant an "important interview?"

Doug: I don't know what I said, but I couldn't have said "important" and "reporter" in the same sentence. That would be ludicrous, like an "important talking head."

L: I know—that's why I asked. I was afraid the "<u>pod people</u>"[2] had grabbed you and left a mannequin in your place.

Doug: No, no, strike that. I couldn't have somehow said "important reporter." Let's go to the tape. [Pause for a replay.] Damn. You're right. I wonder what Freud would have said about that…

Anyway, I truly did misspeak. Back to Trump. I've got to say that, if nothing else, "The Donald" is certainly glib, and a skilled television performer. One of his main characteristics is the extreme certainty he projects about everything—mainly because he says it, and therefore believes it.

It's disturbing that he might actually gain traction this time, for this very

---

1. www.totallyincorrectbook.com/go/87
2. www.totallyincorrectbook.com/go/88

reason. In uncertain times, people want to believe in someone who is certain he knows what's right and what should be done. At such times they also want a strong, aggressive leader, and based on everything he said, Trump would go beyond aggression to being an actively belligerent leader. He wants to be the alpha chimpanzee.

L: I've brought up an ABC interview on YouTube[3]—he certainly sounds like a bully to me. Maybe that's what it's come to in what little is left of America; we need a bully in the White House to make ourselves feel strong again.

Doug: Sure. Jingoism plays well to an unhappy audience. One of the things that came up in the *Wall Street Journal* interview I saw was that the Chinese are taking "unfair advantage" of Americans by selling them inexpensive goods that improve their standard of living.

To Trump, this is ripping us off, and he, as president, would make sure it doesn't happen. He mentioned import tariffs, specifically. He also mentioned Colombia, among others, saying that although he believes in free trade, he also believes in "fair trade." This, of course, is a contradiction; the moment you impose restrictions on trade for political reasons, no matter how "fair" some people think those constraints may be, it ceases to be free. I'm sure The Donald would come up with all manner of cockamamie schemes to make things suit his idea of "fair."

L: It's always astonishing to me the way people who would laugh at a girl who says she's a "little pregnant" will, with a serious face, say that a "little" coercive government intervention makes markets work better.

Doug: That's him; he thinks he's a capitalist because he's been a winner in the marketplace. But cutting deals with his banking and political buddies to make money in real estate, and using borrowed money while the property bubble was still inflating, is not like building a whole new business as Steve Jobs did. And it doesn't make him knowledgeable about economics. He believes in tariffs and quotas and all sorts of government interventions. He's a classic fascist—

L: [Laughs]

Doug: I mean it, literally. Let's clarify a few common words. People always bandy terms around without having more than a vague idea what they really mean.

Fascism is based on the theory that government and business should work together as "partners." Fascism posits that both private goods and essentially all the means of production should be privately owned—but be controlled by the state. Fascism is associated with jackboots and uniforms, because of Hitler, but that's by no means its essence. It's essentially an economic system.

---

3. www.totallyincorrectbook.com/go/89

Idiotically, fascism is often conflated with capitalism, which is also a system where everything is privately owned—but controlled *privately*. A true capitalist country doesn't currently exist anywhere.

Socialism is a system where consumer goods—houses, cars, and the like— are privately owned (albeit regulated), but all of the means of production are state owned.

In communism, everything is state owned.

Anyway, all the countries of the world today are either fascist or socialist. It's a mistake to say the US is a capitalist country; it's fascist, and it gives capitalism a bad name. If The Donald somehow became president, he would make the US economy even more controlled, with an even stronger, more intrusive govern-ment. He'd be a disaster in every way possible.

L: Public-private partnerships. We all know which partner has the guns and calls the shots—but also which one pays the bribes and profits from legally sanitized corruption.

Doug: Right. In practice, that tends to lead to strongmen at the top, but it starts with this economic idea, obscured by large volumes of political rhetoric. The *capite censi,* the booboisie, come to think they can get something for nothing from the magic cornucopia of the state.

In Trump's case, a lot of the things he proposes will sound like good ideas to an economically miseducated population. Some of them may even work, because he does have experience in business—unlike almost everybody in gov-ernment. So it's not out of the question that he would propose a few things that make sense, assuming they cut back state power. But because of his basic worldview and flawed economic premises, he'd be a disaster.

L: For instance…

Doug: He's a huge fan of the military. He'd likely be using it everywhere, spending absurd amounts of money creating more orphans and widows and future enemies.

He said that going into Libya for humanitarian purposes would be okay, but that you'd have to get in and out quickly—a surgical strike to cut out the cancer at the top. But this is ridiculous. If you're going to sanction what amounts to regicide in Libya for the common good, you'd have to do the same in Syria, Bahrain, Saudi Arabia, Yemen, and so forth, and that's just for starters. It would be equally logical to do the same in most of the countries in Africa and Central Asia, plus a few more in the Western Hemisphere. It's as if The Donald watched South Park's movie *Team America: World Police*, and thought it was a documen-tary, not a comedy.

L: Maybe the US should launch multiple surgical strikes on itself to cut off the heads of our home-grown hydra. It could be for the common good.

Doug: Hey, turnabout is fair play. Going to war for humanitarian purposes opens Pandora's box; any government can say any other government is misbehaving and can then launch attacks, surgical or otherwise.

Look, Libya is in the news today, but why is it getting so much more attention than any of the other despotisms in the region? Of course Gaddafi's a criminal—someone the planet would be better off without. But as criminally idiotic kleptocrats go, he's actually one of the better ones, from the point of view of the average man on the street—especially among the tyrants of Africa and the Arab world. But he spoke out, poked at the beast in Washington, and now he's being made out to be the worst *bête noir* since the previous enemy *du jour*. That's the reality.

To his credit, The Donald says his only real interest in Libya is the oil. I thought that was refreshing candor. He says he's got no great interest in Iraq, except that we should keep their oil—this would repay us for freeing them from their tyrant at the cost of the blood of American soldiers. If he had a sense of humor—something he appears to lack totally—he would simply have said, "What's our oil doing under their sand?" This is the sort of fascist populism that's really dangerous. Their blood doesn't matter, but ours is sacred—never mind the lies about Saddam Hussein having weapons of mass destruction that were used to justify the Iraq debacle.

I have sympathy for those soldiers who get maimed, physically and psychologically, actualizing the foolish adventures politicians imagine. But they did volunteer, knowing they would be asked to go and kill people in their homes—people they know nothing about. That's risky, because those people are going to defend themselves and their property. "You pays your money, you takes your chances." US soldiers aren't heroes by virtue of wearing a uniform. They're basically just government employees, a heavily armed version of the post office. Soldiering for a government is basically a job for thoughtless kids who have too much testosterone and not enough other options.

Trump also mentioned "keeping Iran out" as a reason to steal Iraqi oil. Not only is this attitude akin to throwing rocks at a hornet nest, it shows that he doesn't understand that Iran is in a state of flux. The clique of old theocratic criminals who now run the place will soon join the ranks of the departed. Many—if not most—of the young people in Iran are pro-West. They get plenty of Western movies and videos, both on DVD and from the Internet. They're tired of missing out on a good thing. There's living memory in Iran of a more modern lifestyle, something many Iranians want. And because the US hasn't bombed them yet, they are not as anti-American as many Muslims are. Doing the wrong thing, The Donald could turn this around and create a fresh new wave of enemies for the US.

Anyway, the idiocy—and ethical paucity—of Trump's view that we should take other peoples' resources as virtuous plunder, justified by the price the US paid intervening where it was not invited, is staggering. It's essentially the theft of resources, just because you want them and you can. The man appears to have a basically criminal personality. I'd never do business with him if I could avoid it. Fortunately, I can.

He thinks he's a maven in foreign policy, but that's exactly where he'd likely do the most damage.

L: He must have been one of those kids who took other kids' toys away in the sandbox.

Doug: Could be. He certainly seems to have a predilection for consorting with low-life political thugs.

L: I notice the reporter in the video I see going through a list of potential competitors for the White House. I think he was trying to seem knowledgeable and gentlemanly, while still making the case for himself. So he kept saying what nice guys or good people they were, even while pointing out their weaknesses.

Doug: Exactly—he spoke of them all as personal friends. But what kind of person has friends like that? I can't imagine inviting such rabble over for dinner. I'd have to count the silverware afterwards. Maybe even my fingers…

L: Not a great character reference.

Doug: Sure. And it's not just a few odd ducks he might have gotten to know over the years; he consorts with all of these people, as a matter of business policy. The way he was pandering to Sarah Palin, in particular, struck me as a shrewd move. He partially did it to reward her for backing him up about the birth issue with Obama—also because he knows *Boobus americanus* likes Palin. They see her as a salt-of-the-earth type; she's no Boston Brahmin. They figure she must have a lot of common sense because she comes from the lower middle class, espouses conservative values, and so forth. They can relate to her because she has a reality show and the type of family that could do *Jerry Springer*. But she's a dim bulb without any knowledge or experience of consequence. She's like a female George Bush.

L: Ouch! That's a pretty harsh thing to say about a lady…

Doug: Is she a lady, or just some woman who is good-looking? Look, anyone who presumes to rule invites scrutiny and criticism—the harsher the better. Not nearly enough harsh things were said about Bush, who will vie with Obama for being the worst president in US history.

L: Do you think Trump's kind words about Palin were an overture towards a VP invitation?

Doug: During the interview I saw, The Donald very deftly deflected that question. He's definitely a very skilled TV celebrity who knows how to deal with reporters. I liked it, for example, when the reporter asked him a snarky question, and he came back, told the reporter it was a snarky question, and dismissed it. You've got to at least give him points for style—except for his haircut, of course.

L: That was almost painful to watch. Maybe straight on, in the mirror, it looks fine, but in the camera angle I saw, the hair flopped about like a giant piece of French toast on his head.

Doug: I know. It becomes more bizarre as time goes on and he loses more of his hair. I'm not sure what I'd do if I were him, but I'd be embarrassed to be caught on TV looking like that. And he has more hair left than I do. Or appears to. But what amounts to a bouffant comb-over really isn't very flattering. On the other hand, "*De gustibus non est disputandum.*"

L: He could adopt the Yul Brynner look from *The King and I*. Go ageless.

Doug: That'd work. Or, being such a fan of the military, he could get a crew cut. After all, he did go to a military high school.

L: That'd fit—but we're straying into *ad hominem* territory here. What matters is what's between his ears, not what's on top. Do you think this is another case of an idiot savant venturing beyond his field of strength? *He* says he's smart. Do you agree?

Doug: I think he does have a high IQ, but I think he's... how shall I put this? I think he's mildly deranged. He's actually, clinically speaking, a megalomaniac. His arrogance is just overwhelming. This is an extremely dangerous type of person to have running a country with a large military. It'd be "my way or the highway." He's the kind of person who'd be willing to start a war almost anywhere, with almost anyone, if he thought it would be to his advantage. He has no principles that would restrain him, no guiding philosophical principles at all. He's totally unscrupulous. He'd wind up doing whatever seemed like a good idea at the time, as long as it was his idea, because he thinks he's always right. He's a complete pragmatist, but not even a very thoughtful one.

L: For those who may not have made the connection before, "pragmatic" is often used as a compliment—describing someone practical who gets things done. But to be philosophically pragmatic means to adhere to no principles, to shift with the winds of fashion and expedience. That's extremely dangerous when dealing with the chaotic and unpredictable—like human nature and history. The lack of solid principles can lead to adopting horrific policies that may seem practical at the time.

Doug: Yes. One question the reporter asked that I thought was good was why anyone should trust him to run the country when he's filed for bankruptcy. His answer was that he's never personally <u>filed for bankruptcy</u>[4], merely used the law of the land to negotiate business deals. I suppose that's true, but whether or not it's true, it highlights the fact that he may be a billionaire at present, but he's come close to the edge with some frequency over his career. It was unseemly at best. He's promiscuous with money, especially if it's OPM (Other People's Money).

L: And whether or not it's legal, it is without question an ethical problem to default on debt and other promises to employees and business associates. That violates one of the only two laws you say are justified: do all that you say you will do, and don't aggress against other people.

Doug: Yes, and it's hiding behind the skirts of the state when you want to default on people for whom you've taken on obligations. That said, he does have business experience—cutting costs, making layoffs, etc., so it's hard to see how he could be worse than Obama... but then, I didn't see how Obama could be worse than Bush, nor how Bush could be worse than Clinton.

It's as I've always said about the Roman emperors: People thought it couldn't get any worse after Tiberius, but then they got Caligula, then Claudius. They really thought it couldn't get any worse than that—and then they got Nero. And then a civil war. This is exactly the way it's going in the US now. The people who actually want to be president are the worst among us. It's hard to imagine a decent person wanting the job at this point, or at least anyone who's not an egotistical fool, since it's impossible—at least in my opinion—to salvage the current ship of state. Whoever is at the helm when it sinks will be blamed for it, even if he isn't directly at fault. I see Ron Paul's efforts as being only... educational in nature.

L: So, do you think Trump could actually win the Oval Office?

Doug: I'm the worst political handicapper there is, partially because—perpetual optimist that I am—I perennially give the voters much more credit than they deserve. But no, I don't think so. He'll likely end up in bankruptcy again soon, and that will knock him out of the race. Remember, he's in real estate. The losses among real estate speculators in places like Florida are staggering, and I have

---

4. www.totallyincorrectbook.com/go/90

doubts about the posted profits of many real estate companies. The bear market in real estate isn't nearly over, and he'll be a casualty of that, if nothing else.

He claims to have $600 million in spare change he can put into a presidential bid, but he could end up on welfare before he could take office.

L: Maybe that's why he wants to be president. The friends in high places he has now are not high enough to save his bacon.

Doug: Could be. I just wish we could get a real capitalist on stage, more like Uncle Scrooge[5], instead of another Donald.

L: If I could have my wish, I'd wish for US persons to remember that they are Americans, to stop submitting to voluntary servitude, and vote for "None of the Above."

Doug: I'll drink to that.

---

5. www.totallyincorrectbook.com/go/91

Doug Casey: Make Corruption Your Friend, Part 1

Feb 9, 2011

L: Doug, one of the complaints Egyptians have of the rulers they are showing to the door is corruption. It's the same in Tunisia. It seems that more than the lack of freedom or even the secret police, it's government corruption that bothers citizens the most. This fits with your concern that ousting the old bosses will just lead to new bosses who will be every bit as bad; these people don't want to get rid of their governments, they want those governments to *work*. And yet, I've heard you speak of making corruption your friend. Can you tell us what you mean by that?

Doug: Sure. As always, the place to start is with a definition. This is critical, because people use terms like corruption in nebulous ways that enable sloppy thinking. Unless you can define precisely what a word means, you literally can't know what you're talking about. That's one reason why listening to commentators like Hannity, Beck, and O'Reilly is such a frustrating waste of time. These people are constantly conflating concepts—like the idea of America with the reality of the US, or confusing capitalism with fascism, or war with defense— because precise definitions often get in the way of emotive rhetoric.

L: My Webster's says corruption is:

A: Impairment of integrity, virtue, or moral principle. Depravity.
B: Decay, decomposition.
C: Inducement to wrong by improper or unlawful means (bribery).
D: A departure from the original or from what is pure or correct.

Doug: Yes, I looked it up too, and those definitions are accurate as far as they go. But they don't get to the heart of corruption, its essence, and why people hate it, even while it is often a necessary thing. A more meaningful definition—certainly when it comes to political corruption—is: a betrayal of a trust for personal gain.

L: Hmmm… Yes, that makes sense to me. Corruption is not just bribery of officials, though that's the context we started with. It's a bigger idea, and the "personal gain" angle is important.

Doug: Sure. One can find corruption within corporations, as when directors betray their duty to the shareholders for personal gain. Or churches, as when priests, for pleasure, betray the trust of the young people under their guidance. Even a parent can be corrupt, if he fritters away on high living money needed to feed his kids. But those types of corruption stem from personal weakness and personal vices. They're horrible—but corruption in government is much worse.

Only government can impose its will on you by law and back it up with a gun. And with other sources of corruption you can—theoretically at least—go to the government for redress. But when the government is corrupt, it's hard to get the state's right hand to cut off its left. Not only that, but government—partly because its essence is force—concentrates corruption and incubates it. If a company or church is corrupt, one can quit them. But most citizens are stuck with their government—and they'll probably keep paying taxes to it regardless of their feelings toward it. A discussion about corruption is necessarily a discussion about government as an institution.

L: Because government officials have power that can make or break fortunes. And that creates incentives among those on the receiving end of state power to try to sway it to their advantage.

Doug: As Tacitus said in the second century A.D., "The more corrupt the state, the more numerous the laws." It's absolutely predictable that as all these governments around the world—and I mean *all* of them—respond to the ongoing crisis with an ever-accelerating onslaught of new laws, there will be more and more corruption, and frustration with that corruption.

Tacitus was right. But he could just as accurately have said, "The more numerous the laws, the more corrupt the state," because lots of laws engender lots of corruption. In other words, corruption isn't the problem. The state and its laws are the problem, to which corruption is an unsavory and unaesthetic—but necessary—solution. Laws create corruption, and corruption engenders laws.

Every time a legislature convenes, they pass more and more laws. That's all they do, all day long. So the body of laws and the accompanying volumes of administrative regulations and procedures to implement them is constantly growing—the whole world over. Legislatures are horrible and dangerous things that bring out the absolute worst in the people who inhabit them.

Laws and regulations are like barnacles on a ship. They keep growing and growing, weighing the ship down, slowing it down. If they aren't scraped off from time to time, they will threaten the ship's structural integrity.

L: Tacitus also said: "The desire for safety stands against every great and noble enterprise." No matter how many times I see it, it always astounds me how the more things change, the more they remain the same. That's really just another way to say that there is such a thing as human nature.

At any rate, the reason corruption results from the proliferation of laws may not be clear to all our readers. Consider the Internet: it interprets censorship as damage and automatically routes around it. The market interprets government regulation as a hindrance and seeks ways around it. (Private regulation, in contrast, is a selling point, as when electronics have the UL—Underwriters Laboratories—seal of approval.) The proliferation of laws increases the incentive to circumvent the law, and circumventing the law, in this context, is corruption.

Doug: My thoughts exactly. A law is passed because it seems like a good idea at the time, at least for some groups of people who approve of it—anti-pornography laws, for example. But it doesn't seem like a good idea to people who like pornography, or even most normal people these days, who don't think human sexuality is inherently evil. Meanwhile, the people whose preferred choices just got made illegal aren't going to change their views because the government passed a law. So they find ways to work around the law.

Consumers then become small-time outlaws, and providers become "organized crime." What does organized crime do? Generally, they try to bribe the people at the cutting edge of applying the law: the police, prosecutors, judges, inspectors, politicians, etc. It's one reason why vice cops, along with drug cops, are notoriously the most corrupt among police.

L: What about anti-corruption laws?

Doug: Stupid—in the literal sense of the word, meaning unwittingly self-destructive. Those laws *necessarily* have the opposite effect of what's intended. By raising the stakes, they just raise the level of bribery required, resulting in even more severe corruption. Like everything governments do, it's not just the wrong thing to do, but the exact opposite of the right thing to do.

L: Which is… to reduce the number of laws and regulations.

Doug: Exactly. The only way to fight official corruption is to reduce the amount of legal control of officials, particularly their regulatory power over the economy. If there were no government regulators, inspectors, assessors, auditors, and so forth ad nauseam, there'd be no reason for businesses and consumers to bribe them to get the hell out of the way.

L: I can hear some people now crying in horror, "But that would be anarchy!" I know your answer to that is: "Good![1]" But to keep this conversation a little more constructive, let's remind people that government regulation is not the only kind of regulation there is; and, of all forces interacting in the marketplace, it is almost certainly the least efficient and most likely to produce unintended consequences.

Doug: Yes. There are many market forces that regulate business activity— and more broadly, cultural forces that regulate interactions between people. In the marketplace, reputation is a very powerful force. So is competition. And so is liability—it's a powerful negative incentive. More broadly, *culture* is a very powerful regulatory force, which is to say, peer pressure, moral opprobrium, and social approbation restrain people from being naughty far more than fear of police does. And there are also private institutions that have powerful regulatory influences, such as churches, Rotary, Lions Clubs, and the like.

L: Not to mention private companies that *sell* regulatory services, like Underwriters Laboratories for electronics; various rating agencies, like Consumer Reports; or the numerous magazines, news columns, and blogs that comment on every product, practice, and notion under the sun. But people who trust UL to certify that their toaster won't electrocute them can't seem to see a similar agency doing the same thing for meat inspection. And they gasp at the very notion of a private agency regulating, say, pollution.

Doug: I've never heard of an instance of corruption with UL or Consumer Reports. But government agencies are rife with it—plus incompetence as a bonus. People somehow imagine that because government regulations are backed with the iron fist of the law, they work better, especially when the matter is considered vital. This is simply incorrect. It shows ignorance of history and of the state of the world today.

Government regulation usually becomes so corrupt that it ends up doing the opposite of its intended effect. A business that pays officials to look the other way can do even worse things than it would do if there were no officials, because the official seal of approval falsely tells the people that all is well. That's why the SEC should be called the "Swindler's Encouragement Commission"— because it lulls investors, especially the novices, into feeling they're protected.

Even when that doesn't happen, government regulations' inefficiencies and unintended consequences still result in having the opposite of their intended effects. For example, when the Endangered Species Act prompts landowners in

---

1. www.totallyincorrectbook.com/go/92

the US to kill anything endangered they find on their property before anyone can see it, so they don't get their property seized.

It is precisely because some things are so critical that the government should never be trusted with them. Universally—in every country and in every culture—it invites corruption and makes things worse than they would be under private regulatory arrangements and a more vigilant populace.

Strict regulation leads naïve people to think, "Everything is under control." That has two important effects. One, it makes them irresponsible—a belief that they don't have to concern themselves. That general attitude then permeates the society. Two, regulation always creates distortions in the market. It's like a lid on a pressure cooker. Everything looks under control until the whole thing blows up.

That's what lies at the root of the concept of "black swan" type unexpected events in politics and economics. The black swan lands when the amount of corruption necessary to evade laws becomes as onerous as the laws themselves.

Egypt—and the whole Muslim world—are terminally corrupt. Their governments are scams that serve no purpose but to enrich officialdom. Those worthies, though they collect salaries, mainly take bribes for an income.

But if there wasn't corruption to work around the laws, every one of those places would be totally impossible to live in. So it's actually a paradox. Corruption in government is a bad thing in that it unjustly enriches officials who are betraying a trust. But it's also a good and necessary thing, in that without it nothing would happen at all. It's a shaky arrangement that lasts only until the corruption becomes as bad as the laws themselves. It's like the mercury that was once used to treat syphilis—too much, and it will kill you as surely as the syphilis.

L: I think the point of government-sponsored irresponsibility is particularly important, and often overlooked. I've long thought that it was FDR's New Deal that really pushed America over the edge, not so much because of the economic cost, but because it made it very clear to people that they did not need to be responsible for themselves. Big Brother now takes care of them when they get old, or should they fall ill, or lose a job—no need to plan ahead or save… It's no wonder our culture has transformed from one of individualism and self-reliance to one of group-think and reliance on the state, populated by entitlement-minded couch potatoes.

But what do you say to people who point to places like Sweden—a highly government-regulated society that seems to work? Such a nice, clean place—with *lots* of government.

Doug: It's a good point. Sweden is at the low end of the corruption scale, but it's not because they have laws against corruption—everybody has those. It's because of the culture—the peer pressure, moral opprobrium, and social approbation I mentioned earlier. Sweden is a small country where word of misdeeds spreads quickly. It has a highly homogeneous culture based on deep-rooted traditions, and there's a high degree of consensus about how things should be. That makes Swedes cooperate with the large body of law that reflects that consensus, much more than would happen almost anywhere else—or is even possible anywhere else.

Out of a couple hundred countries in the world outside of Scandinavia, I can think of two other places that have a similarly powerful culture that makes a "big-government" approach to managing society seem to work: New Zealand and Uruguay. These places are small, relatively isolated, homogeneous, and with powerful cultural traditions that have—unfortunately—been codified into law. These countries, coincidentally, also have the three oldest socialist governments in the world, all dating back to the turn of the 20th century. Trying to bribe officials in these places—even Uruguay—is pretty much out of the question.

But these places are anomalous. Because of their rare characteristics, they ın't be held up as role models for other places. Almost everywhere else— where there's more diversity of ethnicity, culture, much larger population, and so forth—Scandinavian socialism wouldn't even have the appearance of working. And, I'd argue, it won't work much longer in Scandinavia either; Sweden and these other places will ultimately collapse under the weight of their mass of laws and socialist intervention in their economies.

L: It's interesting: these countries where a high degree of legal regulation seems to work are also highly homogeneous and have very powerful cultures— makes you wonder if the laws are really doing anything at all, or if they are just window dressing on more powerful social systems.

It makes me think of the many experimental societies tried out in the 19th century in the US, when there were still open frontiers to which one could escape with like-minded people and try to do things differently. Most were communes. And most were disasters. Some worked, and a few even still exist in vestigial form today, like the Amana colonies[2]. Those that worked best were religious communes. Just goes to show that if you can go beyond homogeneity and get unanimity, you can create a society that seems to defy all experience to the contrary. When *everyone* buys in, amazing things can happen… at least for a while.

Doug: Almost anything can work for a while. Some monasteries approach an almost perfect state of communism. It's possible because everyone there

---

2. www.totallyincorrectbook.com/go/93

chooses to be there and live according to those rules. Unanimous consent. But that's not possible in an entire country, and even the super-majority buy-in of highly homogeneous cultures like New Zealand and Scandinavia is not possible in 98% of the rest of the countries in the world. If you look at the rest of the world, the more socialistic and regulated the country, the more corrupt it tends to be. And the larger the country, the more disparate the population and divergent the mores, the less effective the government's regulation.

L: That would cover China, Russia… Brazil, Mexico.

Doug: And Argentina, where I am now. The customs inspectors down here, for example, all expect to retire as multimillionaires. That's because they have so many laws on what you can export or import, how, when, why, it's almost impossible to comply with—or even know—all the laws. It's much cheaper and easier to get the inspector to look the other way with a well-placed envelope.

There's good news and bad news in this.

In itself, corruption is a bad thing—it shouldn't have to be necessary. As I touched on earlier, insofar as it's necessary, it's also a good thing. If we can't eliminate the laws that give rise to corruption, it's a good thing that it's possible to circumvent these laws. The worst of all situations is to have a mass of strict, stultifying, economically suicidal laws—and also have strict, *effective* enforcement of those laws. If a culture doesn't allow people to work around stupid laws, that culture's doom is further sealed with every stupid law passed—which is pretty much all of them.

L: Strict laws, strictly enforced, is a recipe for paralysis. I've often said that while Mexico is much less free than the US on paper, it is much more free in fact. People in the US *fear* their government, especially the IRS. In Mexico, people build what they want, eat what they want, sell what they want—tax-evasion is the national pastime.

Doug: Right. This is one of the reasons why, though I've lived in New Zealand quite a bit over the last ten years, I'm not really interested in hanging my spurs there any longer. Although it's gotten vastly better since the reforms of the mid-'80s, it's still a dull, insular place with a lot of ingrained socialist attitudes—but not much corruption to help you obviate them. And I wouldn't want to live in the Scandinavian countries either. They have all these incredibly stupid laws that sheep-like residents obey, enabling great tyranny—but it goes unrecognized because it has such popular support. It suits me much better to live in a place like Argentina, where there's an equal number of stupid laws, but nobody pays any attention to them. And when there is a problem, it can most often be handled—informally.

L: I won't ask you on the record if you've ever actually done that. Interesting comment about Scandinavia—I was just reading Google News yesterday, and one of the top video news stories was a clip about some poor <u>woman in Sweden who's had her twin daughters taken away</u>[3] by the child protection busybodies. The children were taken—without notice—from their school, and the woman didn't even know it was an official abduction until she got a letter a week later. The real horror of it is that there isn't actually any evidence of wrongdoing on the woman's part. The law is preemptive and protective—the bureaucrats are authorized to remove children from their families if there *might* be danger to them. No due process, and forget about "innocent until proven guilty." The breathtaking assumption is that it's better to rip children out of their families than to find out if there's a real problem first. This could only hold sway in a place where the culture is one of great confidence in the wisdom and benevolence of the state.

Doug: Scandinavia is on a slippery slope. I wouldn't be surprised if a very nasty "black swan" the size of a pterodactyl landed there. The US isn't far behind. Big Brother is coming out of the cellar, where he's been chained up, in the US. And I'm afraid he's so strong and nasty that few people will be able to pay him enough to leave them alone.

There have long been local pockets of notorious corruption in the US, of course: building inspectors, people like that. On a national level, the DEA became very corrupt early on—a natural consequence of "regulating" an industry that runs on billions in cash.

Other federal agencies are more subtly corrupt. Generals are paid off by being hired by defense contractors after they're mustered out. FDA types are hired by the drug companies and large agribusinesses—and executives from those companies become high-level bureaucrats in the FDA. Politicians rarely take envelopes of cash anymore. They wait until they are out of office to collect millions in directors' fees, book deals, speaking tours, stock deals, and the like. Bill Clinton is a perfect example of someone who went from near penniless to a net worth of $50 million–plus overnight. The Clintons have made a huge leap from the days when Hillary had to take a $100,000 payoff in the guise of her totally transparent cattle trading scheme.

The problem now, though, is that there are giant police bureaucracies like the TSA and the FBI that have no direct way of getting paid off. So they enforce the idiotic laws like robots. Other bureaucracies like NSA do their damage remotely, too far from the victim to be negotiated with. This is a real source of danger.

L: I'm afraid it does look that way. Okay, now that we've looked at what the beast is, let's talk about making it our friend. Seems like the last thing anyone would want to do...

---

3. www.totallyincorrectbook.com/go/94

Doug Casey: Make Corruption Your Friend, Part 2

Feb 16, 2011

L: Okay, now that we've looked at what the beast [corruption] is, let's talk about making it our friend. Seems like the last thing anyone would want to do…

Doug: It's hard to find a good analogy, but almost everything has a bright side. Let's say corruption is like an African buffalo—stinking, unpredictable, bad-tempered, and powerful—but it can also be a great source of meat and leather. Before we talk about making leather, we should point out that, while these ideas we've been discussing about corruption may seem abstract to some, there's a vast amount of historical evidence in support of what we're saying. Like all serious problems, you must confront it. Trying to tiptoe around it, or pretend it doesn't exist, is only a formula for disaster.

In point of fact, corruption is going to be the biggest of growth industries in the years to come. Why? Because the governments of the world are in growth mode, and history shows that absolutely guarantees a massive growth in all kinds of corruption.

L: The clearest and most powerful example for Americans probably was Prohibition.

Doug: A sorry example of what blue-nosed puritans people can be. The Volstead Act and the 18th Amendment were not repealed in 1933 because Americans suddenly remembered that human rights are individual rights; the light of philosophy rarely penetrates very deeply into the dark recesses of collective psychology. It was not because *Boobus americanus* thought the busybodies' efforts to stop people from drinking alcohol were unethical and un-American. The measures were repealed out of practicality; people saw that they were stupid and inconvenient.

Prohibition turned a large segment of the law-abiding population into criminals and created an illegal free market, which is to say a "black market."

The result of that huge new black market was wholesale corruption of the police and government officials tasked with shutting it down, and gigantic growth of the mafia in the US. Widespread corruption of the so-called pillars of society—plus the undeniable failure of Prohibition to stop the flow of alcohol—was what turned the tide against the temperance movement and made alcohol legal again. The crime wave also prompted the creation and growth of the FBI, which amounts to a national plainclothes police force—not a good thing. The FBI has since expanded into yet another plodding and increasingly corrupt bureaucracy.

L: I wonder why people responded to that failure rationally back then, by discontinuing a counterproductive prohibition, while today we have an equally abject failure and source of corruption in the War on Drugs. But declaring a ceasefire is unthinkable…

Doug: That's a good question; the two prohibitions—alcohol in the '20s and drugs today—are exactly equivalent and are having exactly the same results. Well, same in kind, but the drug prohibition is actually worse in magnitude and consequences. The state has become much larger, much more powerful, and much more draconian this time around.

A few weeks ago, Hillary Clinton said they can't legalize drugs because "there's too much money in it"—an extremely odd statement. Too much money being spent fighting drugs by a bankrupt government? Too much money dealing in them by the *narcotraficantes*, who use a lot of it to pay off the police, the DEA, and other government types? If the stories from the days when Bill was governor of Arkansas—the goings-on in Mena[1] and such—are true, she knows a lot more about the drug business than I do, and from hands-on experience.

The only reason drugs are so profitable, of course, is because they're illegal. If they were legalized, there would be about as much profit in them as any other chemical or agricultural business—maybe less, since marijuana can be grown in useful quantities in a one-bedroom flat. And of course, the more draconian the drug laws, the higher the price drugs command—which draws in more entrepreneurs.

The drug business is problematical—like so many activities—in a number of ways. But it certainly offers giant entrepreneurial profits precisely because it's currently illegal. A drug lord must necessarily make corruption his friend.

L: It's depressing that the grandchildren of the very same people who rebelled against the stupidity, futility, lethality, and corrupting influence of the War on Alcohol are completely acquiescent to this new and more virulent war. Why do you suppose that is?

---

1. www.totallyincorrectbook.com/go/95

Doug: It is strange, in that during the '60s and '70s everybody was toking and snorting. One might have thought the Boomers would have ended the War on Drugs. But, after generations of government-sponsored irresponsibility and government-run schools that spread an entitlement mentality instead of a work ethic, maybe the clock is just winding down. Perhaps Americans have become a nation of whipped dogs, who just do what they're told.

America is an empire in decline, getting old and tired. What makes this particularly dangerous is that it's not only becoming corrupt, like Eastern Europe, Latin America, Africa, the Orient, the Mideast—almost all of the world—but worse, it's got this huge and fairly efficient enforcement mechanism few of the other countries have. The Nazis would have loved the situation in the US. It's become the worst of both worlds: Nordic efficiency and American neo-puritanism. A deadly combination. Only an increasing measure of corruption can keep things going until the whole mess collapses on itself.

L: Made all the worse because a dumbed-down and quiescent population cheers it on and, without acknowledging it, accepts that corruption is normal and nothing can be done about it. Back in the Prohibition era, America had a moral culture that rejected corruption vehemently. Not so now.

Doug: Yes, well, political corruption is certainly a double-edged sword. And you can see that in the counterproductive solutions people propose. They say we should pay our legislators and judges and police more, so they are less tempted by bribes. But that's complete nonsense; today, the average government employee already earns between 50% and 100% more than the average citizen does. These people are already fleecing the taxpayers they supposedly serve. Adding to that will only make the brown envelopes fatter, because they'll feel they need even more. It just adds insult to injury. Would doubling Mubarak's salary have made him less corrupt? I think not.

The solution is not to pay government thugs and stooges more. Remember Tacitus. Nothing has changed in 2,000 years. The only answer now—and the only thing that has ever worked throughout history—is to abolish these laws that force people to work around them.

L: That would mean repealing 99% of all laws.

Doug: Ultimately, it would mean repealing them all. In the end, there are only two laws that are necessary, and, not coincidentally, only two laws that work, because they are the two fundamental laws of human ethics: Do all that you say you'll do, and don't aggress against other people or their property.

We don't need any other laws—and we don't need no stinking badges either.

L: That'll never happen—not voluntarily. The politicians would never derail their own gravy train, and even if they did suddenly develop some moral fiber, fearful people who believe they are entitled to a life of luxury will never allow it. Still, that fits what we've been saying: if you repeal the laws, particularly those that impede industry, you remove the incentive of businessmen to bribe regulators. If you take away the power of vice squads to try to control people's private choices of recreation, you bring those markets into the white and eliminate the incentive to corrupt the police. And so forth…

Doug: How true. I don't know where this is going to end, but it's going to end badly. All of these people who write about how the government should increase its efforts to combat corruption are looking in exactly the wrong place for answers. They think the answers are: more pay for government employees; pass more laws; impose stricter penalties—all the very things that result in more corruption. If stricter penalties worked, there'd be no corruption in China, where corruption is a capital crime—and yet, it's as corrupt as it gets. As always, it's not just the wrong thing, but the exact opposite of the right thing, it's…

L: I can hear it coming—go ahead and say it, Doug…

Doug: Yes, it's… perverse. Totally perverse. This is why I'm increasingly convinced that I've been put on this planet as a punishment for something really bad I must have done in some past life. I must have been quite naughty. But not as naughty as most of those here on this prison planet, judging by the fact that half the people still live on less than $3 a day. At least I'm like a trustee this time—it's not like I'm in the hole, in solitary confinement.

L: Okay, so, getting back to making corruption your friend. I presume you're not talking about practicing the art of passing along envelopes full of cash, but about observing the trends created by the distortion corruption makes in economies, and then investing accordingly.

Doug: Yes, just so. As you know, I always try to look on the bright side of things. The more corruption there is in a society, the more distortions that will create in the market, and therefore, the more opportunities for a speculator—especially when those distortions liquidate. It's as though governments are stretching rubber bands that must eventually break, and when they do, that's when you can make life-altering investments, buying all sorts of things for pennies on the dollar.

You know, I would prefer to live in a world where corruption didn't exist and wasn't necessary, but the only world where that could be the case would be one in which the only laws were the two I mentioned. Since we do live in a world awash in laws and corruption—soon to drown in both—we ought to take advantage of it.

It may seem like taking advantage of misfortune, and perhaps it is—but if someone is going to buy distressed assets, why not you? The people selling them need the cash, and if you've been smart, consuming less than you produce, you'll have the cash they need. If you make a bundle once the market bottoms, you deserve it for taking the risk you did when no one else would.

In my own life, I make the rules. But in the broader world, I don't make the rules, I just play the game.

L: It's worth emphasizing that this is not a quick trading strategy but a long-term plan.

Doug: Absolutely. These huge market liquidations make and break fortunes—or, more accurately, move them from weak hands to strong—but major fluctuations take years to play out.

It's quite interesting, actually, how the culture of corruption has overcome the whole world. These governments around the world are growing like cancers, passing more and more laws as the alleged cure for the very problems they are creating. That means there will be opportunities to take advantage of all over the world.

People have learned absolutely nothing. Like in Egypt. It's wonderful they've gotten rid of Mubarak. But that stooge and his family are going to get away with many billions, stolen from the Egyptian economy. And the poor fools in Tahrir Square think they've won a victory! They've only opened a space at the top for some general—most of them are already multimillionaires, but that's chicken feed when you're running a government—to become a multibillionaire. Meanwhile, stupid, bankrupt Americans keep sending them at least $1.5 billion a year.

But back to making corruption your friend. On a personal level, one prudent thing I would advise readers to do is to move to a country where people already know how to deal with corruption. The US is going to get increasingly unpleasant as it passes ever more draconian laws that will be strictly enforced. Latin America is much more pleasant, because nobody takes their stupid laws seriously, and corruption takes the sting out of those that actually are enforced—reducing them to the level of a nuisance.

From a speculator's point of view—or even an entrepreneur's point of view—I have to say that, as much as I've bashed Africa as being a hopeless basket case, I can see the day coming when there will be a lot of opportunities there. There's no question that Africa is, by far, the most corrupt place on the planet—and that's going to create huge opportunities.

L: Hm. I can see it being, therefore, closer to the bottom, but will the place ever really head back up again?

Doug: I would like to see Africa, with all its abundant resources and struggling people, become the shining city on the hill, an example of health and wealth for all the world to see.

L: Hm. I'm not going to hold my breath. But the untapped potential is certainly there. Any investment implications specific to America?

Doug: Well, a lot of this money the governments are now creating is flowing into the stock market, and it's creating a new equities bubble. A lot is also creating a commodities bubble. That bubble will be caused by paper money. But paper money represents a very profound type of corruption; while it may pump up the stock market in the short run, it will destroy the underlying corporations at some point.

Unbacked paper money is already responsible for much of the corporate corruption so evident today. Directors and high corporate officers are quite susceptible to betraying trust for personal gain—especially if they're not the entrepreneurs who started the company, but are just hired help. Most executives at big companies are good mainly at back-slapping and back-stabbing. In today's highly politicized economy, they have to spend a lot of time dealing with their opposite numbers in government agencies. They're not really businessmen, they're political hacks. And they're like magnets for bad habits and attitudes.

We've seen some of that already in corporate executives who pay themselves huge salaries, bonuses, and option grants, while treating the shareholders as suckers. They themselves rarely pay for a share.

Mainstream stocks are increasingly becoming a speculative vehicle, rather than an investment vehicle. Where we're headed, investing based on Graham-Dodd fundamentals will become less and less valid.

You know I'm a hardcore capitalist; I think you should charge whatever the market will bear. But these huge multimillion-dollar bonuses are in truth not only unwarranted, they're criminal. They amount to theft from the shareholders. As many problems as I think Warren Buffett has, I must say that I do respect the fact that he only pays himself something like $150,000 per year, making his real money on the same capital gains he's supposed to be creating for investors. Though, for the reasons I just gave, I think his method of investing is going to become less and less effective in the years to come, and we'll be left with just his goofy political views.

L: It occurs to me that as corruption accelerates, it's not just equities that are in jeopardy, but all business is in trouble. Any good business can be ruined by a competitor who pays a bribe to an official to give him an advantage. You can't make any sound business decisions when the arbitrary power of the state can upset all your plans with the stroke of a pen.

Doug: That's true. And that will only accelerate the collapse of the old world order. That's the good news: a collapse will wipe many tables clear and allow people who learn from history to start again, on sounder foundations—like, hopefully, limiting laws to the two I mentioned. Until corruption sets in again. So, even though things often have to get worse before they can get better, I'm optimistic that things will get better.

L: Another grim foretelling, Sir Guru. I don't know whether to hope you're right or you're wrong.

Doug: You know I just call 'em like I see 'em. 'Til next week, Sir Wolf.

Doug Casey on Global Warming

Oct 7, 2009

L: What's on your mind this week, Doug?

Doug: Global warming. People like my fanatical neighbors here in Aspen seem perfectly willing to undo centuries of progress because they are completely delusional about global warming. The People's Republic of Aspen is an epicenter of political correctness.

L: Don't hold back, Doug, tell me what you really think.

Doug: Global warming is the most prominent form of mass hysteria raging across the world today. Kids in school these days are almost afraid to breathe, because it will "increase their carbon footprint." The kids have been convinced that a minor gas, carbon dioxide—minor except for being essential to the survival of all plant life on earth—is changing the climate and must be eliminated.

Better they look at deadly dihydrogen monoxide vapor, which is perhaps 20 times more important simply because of the amount in the atmosphere. Of course, that would add water to the growing list of enemy molecules.

The Earth's atmosphere is 0.039% carbon dioxide. Argon, an inert gas nobody but chemists has even heard of, is 0.93%—twenty times as much. It's quite amazing, the way carbon, the element all life is based on, has replaced plutonium as enemy element number one. It's as if the chattering classes are making war on the periodic table of the elements.

Meanwhile, they've been changing the cry from "global warming" to "climate change" because there's so little evidence there's actually any warming going on. I believe that as little as a decade from now, anthropogenic global warming will be recognized as one of the greatest swindles in world history. It has so little scientific basis, it can only rationally be considered a political scam.

L: If that's true, will the scam ever be revealed? There was a silly movie—I believe it was called "The Day After Tomorrow"—in which global warming caused the world to suddenly freeze over. If people are willing to think that's possible, and the only thing certain is that things will change, and any change can be blamed on people, perhaps the con job can be maintained indefinitely. It could become a perpetual guilt trip aimed at the population, just as useful as the one certain churches used for centuries to control people.

Doug: Yes. I think Roseanne Rosannadanna of *Saturday Night Live* said it best: If it's not one damn thing, it's another. It's always something.

There's a professional class of hysterics in the world. They are the same type of people who were walking around in the Middle Ages in sack-cloth, throwing ashes on themselves, saying that the world was going to come to an end. They're the same people who repeatedly believe religious types who predict the end of the world on a specific date.

The world will come to an end, of course, even before the Sun dies in about five billion years. But these people have no perspective at all. They don't realize that the Earth is just an insignificant ball of dirt, in a nothing/nowhere star system, in a nothing/nowhere galaxy—of which there are billions, each containing billions and billions of stars. And that's just in this universe. There's reason to believe that there's an almost infinite number of universes like ours, with the possibility that new ones are being created virtually every second.

And these people are worried about changes in the biosphere of this one, tiny little planet. To me, it makes no sense.

But dropping from the sublime, cosmic scale down to the local level, it's still completely ridiculous.

L: Okay, let's talk about that. What are the facts? How ridiculous is fear of climate change?

Doug: Contrary to the blatantly untrue statements these people make about the science being "settled," if the science indicates anything at all, it indicates that anthropogenic global warming is not significant. Remember, the question is not so much whether there is any warming—which is another question—but whether human activity is a major, or even significant, contributing factor to global warming.

Of course men can have an effect on the planet. We have wiped out numerous species that we know about, just in historic times, like the dodo, and the passenger pigeon. We almost did in the North American bison. Of course we have an impact, and people do make mistakes. It's unfortunate. And because of the butterfly effect (because tiny changes can have huge consequences, such as a butterfly flapping its wings on one side of the world resulting in a hurricane on the other side), humans could have a big effect on climate change—but so could everything else.

The point is that there are other factors that have orders of magnitude greater impacts on the Earth's climate, things that are tens, hundreds, and thousands of times more important to the climate than anything mankind can do—perhaps even including a major nuclear war.

Fear is being used by the political class as an excuse to accumulate more power and self-importance—and collect a lot more taxes to support their agenda.

Instead of being stampeded into the dark fantasy, we should focus on increasing our wealth and our knowledge. Eventually, mankind's fate will depend on our technological advancement. Nature teaches us—not that many environmentalists listen—that we need to colonize the rest of the solar system, and beyond. Mankind must diversify, so all our eggs aren't in one planetary basket.

But as an aside, I have to say I'm not sure I care if mankind is going to survive—I'm not sure why anyone should care, since most of us aren't going to live more than three score and ten years anyway. Perhaps the world ends when we end... Mankind's future seems beyond any individual's concern, at least beyond the lifespan of your immediate friends and family. Too much worrying about things beyond your control can turn you into a busybody.

L: You're speaking as one with no children. Having children, I have a different view on that.

Doug: How about your great-great-grandchildren, whom you'll probably never meet?

L: I'm not so sure about that. Life is already longer than it has ever been in history, and medical technology keeps advancing. And that's not even getting into nanotechnology. I believe my generation may live for centuries, aside from violent death and acute, fatal illnesses.

Doug: Well, I'm sympathetic to that view. But the morality of caring for one's posterity is a philosophical issue we can perhaps discuss another day. For now, I'll say that I don't like to think of myself as a survival machine for my genes—so I don't give a damn what happens to my genes. I have my own plans. The consideration I would have for my children, if I did have any, would be reserved for those who earned it as individuals, not just because they're my children.

L: I recall your Roman attitude about that, but that's also a conversation for another day. Back to global warming... it's been a while since I've researched this, but I seem to recall that the latest actual science is that there has, in fact, been some warming recorded in the Northern Hemisphere over the 20th century, but there's insufficient data on the Southern Hemisphere, and the warming has been less than the global warming models predicted.

Doug: Well, as I understand it, for the last five years or so, it's been getting cooler, not warmer, and that's entirely apart from the fact that back in the 1970s, magazines were showing pictures of glaciers toppling over the buildings of New York, because we were going into a new ice age. Even measuring the temperature is problematical, since many historical sites that were once isolated are now surrounded by civilization, giving an upward bias to readings. It's impossible to cover all the bases in a brief conversation like this, because there have been volumes and volumes and volumes written on this.

But look, the climate on this planet has been changing since Day One. When the solar system was formed, our best guess is about 4.2 billion years ago, things were very, very cold—as cold as deep space. Then, after the sun ignited, things got very, very hot. And, in essence, things have been cooling ever since.

Remember, there have been numerous ice ages, starting with a first period of glaciation thought to have occurred about 2.3 billion years ago. That was during the early Proterozoic eon, after the appearance of oxygen in the Earth's atmosphere. There was one that lasted over 200 million years, from about 850 to 630 million years ago, called the Cryogenian period, in which the ice caps may have met at the Earth's equator, covering the planet completely.

Geologists actually define the Earth as being in an interglacial period of the most recent ice age (the Quaternary glaciation), which started about 2.6 million years ago, during the late Pliocene. Ice sheets have advanced and retreated every 40,000 to 100,000 years or so, with the last glacial period, which covered North America and Europe with glaciers thousands of feet thick, having ended only about 10,000 years ago. It's no surprise that the climate has been generally warming since then.

So, the climate has gotten hotter, then cooler, hotter, cooler… And for the last 10,000 years or so, it's gotten warmer. That's the fact of the matter—and generally, warmer is better. The whole of the Earth's existence is marked by changes in climate. It happens naturally.

L: Why?

Doug: There are lots of reasons. One is cosmic rays, which is to say, radiation coming from billions of stars, light-years away. Cosmic rays have a huge impact on cloud formation. And cloud formation has a huge impact on the climate.

A second reason is changes in the ocean and its currents. The ocean has vastly greater mass than the atmosphere, so it's a far greater heat-sink, and its currents have a major influence on climate.

Another is volcanism. Just in historic times, we've seen major climate impact from volcanism. For example, there was Mt. Tambora, the most powerful volcanic eruption in history, which happened in April of 1815, killing thousands of people directly and tens of thousands indirectly through starvation. The eruption altered global climate so dramatically, 1816 became known as The Year Without a Summer, as crops and livestock around the planet were wiped out. Just one of these big eruptions, by the way, can dump more toxic pollutants into the atmosphere than man has created in the entire industrial age.

Another is the periodic circulation of this solar system around the galaxy, the periodic shift in the Earth's elliptical orbit, and the cyclical precession of the Earth on its axis. All three have different periods, all of them affect the climate, though it's uncertain to what degree.

And that's just scratching the surface; it's quite complex.

L: I happen to have been kicking rocks recently in a caldera in Idaho that was the location of the last eruption of the Yellowstone hot spot, before it blew the current Yellowstone caldera into existence. By way of comparison, Mt. St. Helens blew 0.7 cubic kilometers of rock into the air, covering half of Washington with four inches of ash. The eruption that created the caldera I was standing on blew about 1,000 cubic kilometers of rock into the air. Such an eruption, today, I was told, would kill everything as far away as Chicago.

Doug: Right, and imagine all the gases that would go with that. Sulfur compounds and the like—talk about ecological disasters! And these ninnies are bicycling and recycling to save the planet from our puny little smokestacks. When something like the potential volcano under Long Valley caldera at Mammoth Lake in California or the Yellowstone caldera blows—and that could be two years from now, or two thousand years from now, nobody knows—it's anticipated that these will be among the largest volcanic eruptions *ever*. And that's just picking two in North America.

L: I remember a park ranger in Yellowstone telling my family that, in geological terms, the next Yellowstone eruption is overdue.

Doug: Yes, and there are other situations like that. Consider the near statistical certainty of the Earth encountering a piece of space debris large enough to have an impact on the Earth's climate. The last one we know of was the Tunguska event in 1908, which is thought to have been caused by a meteor only a few tens of meters across—it still leveled almost a thousand square miles of trees.

Worse than sticking their heads in the sand about this, these people are trying to stop science from progressing, ruining everyone's lives in the process. They think they are saving the planet, but in the end, the planet's fate is out of our hands, and their obstruction could keep people from getting off this planet while they can.

But we haven't talked about the main thing—and really, ultimately, the only climate change variable that really matters—which is the Sun. Relative to the Sun, everything else is totally trivial. Which, much as deluded believers in the omnipotence of the state might not believe, is beyond the power of human governments to regulate. To me, this is really the proof that the whole climate change thing is just a scam perpetrated by the ill-informed and ill-intentioned on the ignorant and the credulous.

L: What, specifically, does the Sun do that swamps other effects?

Doug: The Sun has a number of cycles it goes through—the sunspot cycle, for example—that have a huge impact on the Earth's climate. The Sun is essentially all that keeps the Earth from being an ice ball a few degrees above absolute zero, so any change in it has major consequences for the Earth.

The global-warming people forget that within this pattern of warming and cooling, modern man only really came on the scene in the warming period after the last period of glaciation ended 10,000 years ago. Civilization has only been around for less than 5,000 years—which has generally been a period of global warming.

Interestingly enough, the collapse of the Han Dynasty and the Roman Empire coincide with a period of global cooling, possibly acting as a cause of what's commonly called the Dark Ages. And then we had the medieval warm period—when wine was grown in England and crops in Greenland—that ended with the Renaissance. Fortunately, technology had enough momentum by then that we kept advancing through the Little Ice Age, which ended only about 150 years ago. Things have been warming up since then.

Global-warming hysterics generally have limited scientific knowledge, of geology and meteorology in particular. Their belief is not science; it's more akin to religion. The main epicenter of hysteria is not the scientific community but seems to be Hollywood. The charge is being led by actors and celebrities given free access to the pulpit by the talking heads on the various entertainment media—and you're kidding yourself if you don't think news shows are primarily entertainment. Through the intellectual lightweights that populate most of our classrooms, their ideas spread to our kids, and they filter up from the kids to their parents, who end up feeling guilty about something they don't understand.

One of the worst things about all this is that it may in the future discredit science itself in the eyes of the common man. When it becomes clear to everyone that the whole global-warming scare is as silly as the tin-foil hats of the 1970s, people could mistakenly think that science itself is silly, because of all these people claiming science proves that anthropogenic global warming is real.

L: Well, maybe. But people don't believe the Sun revolves around the Earth anymore either. Lots of "scientific" notions change without damaging science itself.

Doug: True enough. But unfortunately, anthropogenic global warming has become *the* scientific issue. And worse, today most funding for science comes through government. That means that you have to be known to be sympathetic to conclusions that are acceptable to the political classes.

It's a shameful thing, and many scientists will deny it, but a lot of today's research is politically biased. Scientists like to think they are unbiased, but they all know what's more and what's less likely to get funded—and what politically incorrect words at conferences and budget meetings can get funding cut. It's only human for such opinions to have an effect—which is why scientists use double-blind experiments when the beliefs of the researchers themselves can sway the outcome of experiments.

If you don't robotically accept and parrot the "fact" of anthropogenic global warming, you're looked upon as the moral equivalent of a Holocaust denier. I've heard members of the chattering class actually come out and say things like this.

L: But this is science. In spite of the peer pressure and such, shouldn't the facts lead to correct conclusions?

Doug: They should, but science is no longer the province of individual researchers. A rich amateur could be, and often was, a scientist back in Ben Franklin's day, simply because it amused him. That afforded a great degree of independence. Today it seems to take billions of dollars to study almost anything, and the state is the center of big money these days. The result is that science is no longer run by scientists; it's run by politicians—or to be more precise, by bureaucratic administrators who dispense money according to their own agendas.

L: So, would you say that in this environment, the peer-review process has become counter-productive, and now, instead of ensuring standards, it ensures desired answers?

Doug: The peer-review process has probably been corrupted. People are afraid to say things, to consider hypotheses unbiased research might support, because it's become such a politically charged atmosphere.

L: They could lose their funding.

Doug: Exactly. So anything and everything you listen to on this subject of climate change—including what I'm saying today—is something you should investigate and analyze for yourself. Draw your own independent conclusions. But if you draw the conclusion that anthropogenic global warming is a fraud, you may find yourself reluctant to say it in public, for fear of being hunted down as a heretic and ridiculed by the hoi polloi.

L: Perish the thought that they might come to the conclusion that a little global warming might be a good thing. Coasts might change a bit, but you'd have longer growing seasons and more food for everyone…

Doug: Right. And—gasp!—people might not need to burn so much fossil fuel to keep warm in the winter, cutting back on pollution. Who knows? Look, no one can predict whether the Earth will be cooler or hotter next year, let alone do anything to change it. If you're afraid of global warming, turn off the lights when you leave the room—but don't participate in the corruption of science, don't scare our kids with unproven cataclysmic theories, and don't try to ban economic energy sources that people living on this planet depend upon today.

Don't try to stop progress; it's the only hope the Earth has of seeing clean industry, short of exterminating mankind.

L: Well, I did ask you to tell us what you really think…

Doug: You know I would have anyway.

Doug Casey on NASA and Space Exploration

Aug 10, 2011

L: Hola, Doug. Care to share?

Doug: Well, the markets have been very interesting lately. Gold shooting up to $1,800 an ounce was a predictable consequence of the US credit-rating downgrade, which was in turn a predictable consequence of out-of-control money printing and spending on the part of the government. And I'm back from my jaunt to the Middle East. But for now I want to bring readers' attention to the recent, barely noticed sunset on the space shuttle program[1]. *Atlantis*—the last of the four space shuttles—has just become a museum piece, and that's rather historic. The US space effort has basically ground to a halt.

L: Are you mourning that or celebrating it?

Doug: A little of both. It's something to mourn because space is the final frontier, and we need that frontier. It'd be wonderful if we could get off this planet. For many reasons—sociological, political, technological, and more—I'm highly enthusiastic about the conquest of space. But it's a mixed bag, because a government program is the worst way possible to go about it. So in a way, I'm glad the government is out of the game, and I'm glad the economic crisis makes it unlikely that the government will get back in it soon, at least not on anything like the scale we've seen in recent years. This is one bright side of the governments of the world going bankrupt.

L: I'm shocked to hear you call it a mixed bag. I'd have thought you—the International Man who never shrinks from strong statements—would have called NASA or any government space program an unalloyed evil. Since we agree that getting the state involved in this or any creative venture is the worst possible approach, what is there to see as "mixed?"

Doug: Perhaps I wasn't clear—I should have fully separated the concepts of space exploration, which I wholeheartedly endorse, and government space

---

1. www.totallyincorrectbook.com/go/96

programs, which I oppose on principle and in practice. Government in space is bad economics. It's unethical to force those not interested in space to pay for its exploration through taxes. And though few people like to think about it, most of what the state now does in space has military intent, and that is very grave, very destructive, on multiple fronts.

L: This is an important distinction, because a lot of people who agree in general with our skepticism of state involvement in any economic activity make an exception as regards space. Their dream of going to the stars is important and exciting to them, and they see only governments active in space exploration, so they forget their principles and endorse government spending on space programs.

Doug: I agree completely. I'm sad to see less space exploration, but I'm very happy to see the government out of it. Even better, now that the government's broke, space exploration will necessarily be privatized. That'll throw it open to entrepreneurs, and they will give access to everyone, not just a few anointed astronauts. Moving space exploration from the government sector to the private sector will change its entire nature. All sorts of entrepreneurs and inventors will get involved, not just a few creative individuals like Burt Rutan[2], who's already shown that access to space can be cheap and effective. It's going to spread all over the planet—I think we'll see rockets heading for orbit from all corners of the world soon. Space exploration will never get anywhere as long as the state is involved.

L: "Space Ship One, Government Zero[3]"—remember that sign? De-funding and entirely scrapping the government space program is the best thing that could happen for space exploration. It would release talent to the private sector. I'd pop a bottle of champagne if they padlocked the doors on NASA's headquarters full of bureaucrats in downtown Washington.

Doug: Yes, I do remember the pilot holding that sign up after *Space Ship One* landed. And not only would shutting NASA down release talent, it would also reduce bureaucratic resistance to private space exploration; if the government's not doing it, the bureaucrats involved won't have turf to defend. So of course NASA should be abolished, and its assets should be auctioned off. Many of those are uneconomic under current ownership but probably would be economic under new management. (Or maybe they shouldn't be auctioned— because I wouldn't want to see the money go to the state.)

One solution would be to put NASA into a corporation and distribute its shares to taxpayers. Then it would be just another aerospace company, competing

2. www.totallyincorrectbook.com/go/97
3. www.totallyincorrectbook.com/go/98

with scores of others around the world. We'd then see if it can create capital, instead of just consuming it. The problem is that current management probably has such a bureaucratic, government-employee mindset that they'd run it into the ground before they could be replaced.

L: An ethically superior idea might be to auction the assets and distribute the proceeds to taxpayers who were plundered to pay for NASA in the first place. A sort of delayed restitution. That would never happen, but getting the government out of space is so important, I'd be willing to encourage them to disband NASA and sell the parts to pay down the national debt. That idea might actually gain some traction in DC, and the proceeds wouldn't be enough to really help the government much.

Doug: Yes. But I fear NASA will never be abolished simply because it's effectively an arm of the military. Anyway, you can never really reduce bureaucracy by trimming it back. It just grows again in subsequent appropriations rounds. The only way is to totally abolish the bureaucracy, cut it out by the roots, and ban the state from getting involved in its former functions.

That would create the space for a phoenix to rise from the ashes. That's important, because a lot of people who should know better are still sympathetic to NASA. When it was a brand-new bureaucracy with a clearly defined and powerful mission, full of young, idealistic hotshots, it actually was an organization that got things done. That was before it became corrupt, stodgy, concrete-bound, and constipated. People remember the glory days and don't see that NASA is just another bureaucracy today. It's not quite like the post office playing with rockets, but it is unfocused and inefficient. I wonder if NASA even could put a man on the Moon today, if it were given the green light to do so. It's not a certainty, even though the technology has taken quantum leaps forward since 1969. Do you realize it's been 39 years since a man last walked on the Moon?

L: Yes—and if the government hadn't been left in charge of space exploration, I think we'd be able to vacation there as easily as Argentina these days. The technology exists.

Doug: We should have colonies on the Moon by now, and more: We should be mining the asteroids and developing real estate on Mars. There should be active homesteading going on out there right now. As you say, the technology for doing it is fairly mature—and would be far more so if the field had been left to the private sector, which always does things faster and more efficiently than the state.

L: Let's talk about that for a moment. You and I see eye to eye on this, but some of our readers may not. At a time when people are worried about basic things like having a job tomorrow and food the week after, why should anyone care about exploring space? Why on Earth—or off it—would anyone want to move out there? And how would one make money off it, justifying the R&D expenses?

Doug: Well, on the most fundamental level, getting out there makes the pie bigger for everyone. If it's done economically, and for economic gain, we're talking about whole new worlds to develop—that's valuable real estate. There are vast new resources to make use of, ranging from metals in the asteroid belt to all that solar energy that's just being radiated off into space right now. There's the ability to manufacture in zero gravity, which has enormous efficiency implications, as well as other technical advantages.

Space access is extremely *valuable*, and those who get there first are going to make fortunes. Mobilizing that wealth could and would create far more work than there are people to do it—not just in America, but even for the hungry masses in Africa and Asia. Simply put, adding to the net wealth in the world is good for everyone.

Just look at what China has done in the last 30 years; it's gone from a backward, peasant economy to a modern, high-tech powerhouse, creating huge amounts of wealth for many people. I see the conquest of space as having similar effects, only orders of magnitude greater.

L: You *are* an optimist.

Doug: I am. The future can be not only better than we imagine, but better than we *can* imagine. But it's critical to get the state out of the way.

L: I hadn't really thought of it before, but opening up the final frontier is just the sort of thing that could revitalize a dispirited people. We'd still need sound money, which I think we'll see after the sham of paper currencies is finally and fully exposed for the fraud it is, but to really get things going again in the global economy, we need the lure of huge profits that will pull frightened capital out of hibernation. The vast riches of new worlds could be just the ticket—maybe even the only thing that could get enough people to forget about their squabbling and fears and start thinking about reaching—literally—for the stars.

Doug: Indeed. I'd find it quite entertaining to see all that potential out there unleashed… What a show it would be to see how millions of entrepreneurs come up with new ways to make use of it! Space opens the possibility of thousands of different societies to live in. And with infinite power from the sun, materials from the asteroid belt, and room, it could provide a standard of living many orders of magnitude above anything on Earth. Forget about space as surviving in a cramped tin can. And forget about the military overtones of *Star Trek* and *Star Wars*—although I'm a fan of Han Solo. Maybe think in terms of the excellent TV series <u>*Firefly*</u>[4], or its movie spinoff *Serenity*.

L: And we don't even have to wipe out beautiful blue aliens to achieve these things.

Doug: Hopefully not. Although it's an excellent bet that we eventually will find aliens. I just hope it's merchant adventurers who discover them, not space Marines; the military isn't into trade, it's into weaponry.

On a different but equally fundamental level, another reason to get out there is the fact that right now humanity has all its eggs in one fragile basket. One big meteor hits the Earth, and that's it for our species. We need to spread out beyond this one little world.

L: That's hard for most people to feel as a pressing need, not when they are two mortgage payments behind and just got laid off, but I agree.

Doug: Well, one thing even those behind on their mortgages should feel, deeply and personally, is the loss of freedom we're all seeing from the cancerous growth of the police state in America and all around the world. When people can be arrested for quietly <u>dancing in the Jefferson Memorial</u>[5], or making a joke at an airport, or for tossing an aluminum can in the trash, or for not handing over half their income to the state, or for any of the myriad other things that can land peaceful, productive people in jail these days, you know this planet has too much government. And you know government is never going to get any smaller by choice. You could try to start a revolution, but that's extremely dangerous and won't make things any better in a society full of people who don't understand the nature of the problem.

It's far better to settle the new frontier, just as Europeans did when abandoning Old World despotisms for New World risks and rewards, or as Americans did, settling the West. We need a new frontier, both for those of us who want to go out there and seek our own freedom and fortune, and as a safety valve for society's discontents, who have had no place to go for the better part of a century.

L: Freedom in space—I like it. We ought to buy the Statue of Liberty when the US government is really desperate for hard money, then strive to be among the first real-estate developers on Mars. We can set it up there and welcome the tired, the poor, the huddled masses yearning to breathe free—they <u>sure aren't welcome</u>[6] in what was America anymore.

Doug: That's right—the Statue of Liberty belongs in a place that respects freedom and has open borders. A place on the frontier. The loss of freedom in the US is going to accelerate hyperbolically, with the next real or imagined terrorist attack—or just on the back of deteriorating economic conditions. This is a clear and present danger that people should be thinking about.

---

5. www.totallyincorrectbook.com/go/100
6. www.totallyincorrectbook.com/go/101

What about you, can you think of other reasons why people should care about colonizing space?

L: I have long said that if you're green, you have to be pro-space. Even if you're of the anti-human persuasion, you have to understand that Earth's hungry billions are not going to lay down and die for your idea of paradise. On the contrary, they'll fight you if your policies make their lives harder. Instead of fueling that conflict, it's far better to move towards exploitation of space ASAP. After all, space is mostly... *nothing*. It's empty—space. You build a factory in a far-off orbit, and nothing is disturbed. You move all heavy manufacturing off planet, where it would be cheaper and better, and you have no pollution to speak of on Earth.

We should mine the asteroids. If they do indeed come from a smashed planet, they should have many, many, many times more metals, more easily available, than have ever been mined on earth—or ever need be.

It's possible to increase prosperity for all of Earth's billions, *and* make the planet greener than it's ever been in history, simply by pushing for economic access to space as fast as possible.

Doug: Good point. You're an optimist too. Most anarcho-capitalists are optimists.

L: Are there space exploration companies to buy? Other actions to take?

Doug: There are a few private space companies out there.

L: But if they are *private* companies, would you really invest in them? It's one thing to be a space enthusiast, it's another to put cash into an illiquid investment in a highly challenged industry. I know you don't invest with your heart...

Doug: I try not to. But sometimes I just can't help myself.

L: I'm glad to hear it's not just me!

Doug: But you're right—I don't like investing in private companies, for many reasons, and that's all that's available in this field right now. I might invest in some of these companies with the sort of money other people give to charity—not because I think I'll profit directly, but because I think their work is worth doing, regardless. That's not an investment strategy I'd recommend to readers, but I am monitoring progress in this field because there will come a day when there's big money to be made in it—just as with nanotechnology, 3D fax, biotech, quantum computers, and other fields that are developing rapidly now.

Space technology is like any of these fields. We're right on the edge of it, and it could advance full-speed in this generation. There will be fortunes made, just as early investors in IBM, Apple, or Microsoft made fortunes.

L: Groovy—and a good, positive note to wrap up on.

Doug: Indeed.

Doug Casey on Castro and Cuba

Sept. 15, 2010

L: Doug, Fidel Castro is much in the news of late, with almost McNamara-like changes of heart, ranging from regretting the persecution of gay people under his rule, to admitting that socialism isn't working too well. The press reports him saying, "The Cuban model doesn't even work for us anymore."

I just heard today that the Cuban government plans to fire a half a million government employees, and the number may climb to a full million—those jobs were once sacred sinecures. I know you've been to Cuba and met Castro, so what do you make of all this?

Doug: I have to say, this gives me some hope. If only Obama could take a page from Fidel's new book. Perhaps Fidel is not a completely sociopathic criminal after all; perhaps he's just been deluded and a very slow learner; perhaps he's actually capable of admitting guilt and reforming. He seems to be trying to re-think things in a more moral way, as the grim reaper approaches him. Perennial optimist that I am, I like to give folks the benefit of the doubt.

L: Do you think that's what it is, a desire to set right what he can before he exits this stage? Or could he actually be more honest than we gave him credit for, and now he's facing the evidence that says he was wrong?

Doug: You can never really know what's actually going on in his mind. But it puts him a cut above hopeless sociopaths like Stalin, Hitler, and Mao who never evidenced an iota of regret that we know of. Or even lesser lights, like FDR and Nixon. If Dante's *Inferno* exists, all of them would be in low and nasty circles. Let's hope Fidel at least makes it to the *Purgatorio*.

L: So tell us about Cuba, why you went there, and what you thought of Castro when you met him.

Doug: I've visited Cuba four times over the years. The first time was not long after the Soviet Union collapsed. There was essentially nothing there.

Doug Casey, upper left, sips a drink while Pierre Lassonde enjoys a lengthy lecture, finger jabs included, by Fidel Castro. (Photo courtesy of Paul Zyla.)

The country had been living for years on handouts from the USSR, getting paid way above market for its sugar, buying oil way under market, and getting all sorts of miscellaneous freebies from the Soviets. But that game fell apart, taking the Cuban pseudo-economy down with it. There were about three or four blocks in Havana that have been renovated for the benefit of tourists wandering around, but the vast majority of the city looks like Berlin in 1945—and I kid you not. Hundreds of buildings with collapsed roofs, broken windows, no electricity or plumbing. Socialists have never understood the concepts of depreciation and maintenance.

L: The Soviets ran out of money before their government collapsed, so Cuba would have been on meager rations for some time when you were there…

Doug: And it couldn't be disguised. I went to a state dinner, and it was so bad, it was embarrassing. As I recall, the only thing they had to serve were some Spanish stuffed olives, which they'd bartered for some sugar, some bread, a few veggies, and a fish. Against all odds, somebody had gotten some gasoline and gone out in a boat and caught one. Things were really rough then.

L: Is that when you met Castro?

Doug: No, I think I met him on my third trip to Cuba. We were staying at a *casa particular*—a lot of times, when the government would host you, they'd put you up in a house that used to be owned by a rich Cuban who'd fled. It was a trip back in time. The furniture, the rugs, the curtains—all of it was stuff I'd last seen on 1950s TV reruns. It was all decades old.

L: Well, I guess the Cubans aren't going to make *Architectural Digest* anytime soon. But what about health care? Admirers say real strides have been made there.

Doug: I happened to have visited one of the vaunted Cuban biotech centers while I was there; it basically resembled the chem lab of a rural high school in the US. But first, we must be very careful to distinguish between "health care" and "medical care." The term health care is a fraudulent misnomer. Health is everywhere a strictly personal responsibility and determined largely by diet and exercise. It was laughable when that fat slob Michael Moore made the argument that the average Cuban was healthier than the average American because of their nationalized doctors and hospitals. He's right that the average Cuban is much healthier—but it's solely because he's got a simple, fresh, low-calorie diet, he necessarily gets a lot of exercise every day, and he's not taking a half dozen pills every day to assuage every real or imagined pain.

The fact is that medical care in Cuba is about 50 years behind the times. Their technology, and the education of the doctors, is antiquated and primitive. They don't even have Band-Aids and penicillin, forget about MRI and CAT-scan machines. Cuba is not a good place to get a severe trauma or acute disease—which is where American medical care shines. But the average Cuban is vastly healthier than the average American, for reasons that have almost nothing to do with medical tech.

L: And the education system? It's said every Cuban can read and write, which didn't used to be the case...

Doug: I think there's some truth to that. But, once again, *Boobus americanus* completely misunderstands what it means. First, learning to read and write isn't rocket science. Second, it's something an individual is responsible for, not a school system. People who think it's a fantastic accomplishment apparently believe the government is a solution to illiteracy. Of course, Castro wanted everyone educated in the basics, but only so they could read propaganda. There's certainly not much else to read there—no books in the libraries, no magazines, no newspapers besides *Granma,* the state rag—and you can forget about computers. I think it's tough to get a decent education with few pens and pencils to be had, and very little paper, a few books, and the teachers putting political education first. Cuban students are in a time warp. Claims about Cuban education are just nonsense. It's a huge failure. But so is American education.

L: Okay… But what was an anarcho-capitalist doing in Cuba at all, let alone as a guest of the communist government?

Doug: Well, Americans are theoretically allowed to go to Cuba, but they are not allowed to spend any of their own money there. That's why, if you enter the US from abroad and the officer who checks your passport has reason to believe you've been to Cuba, or if you reveal the fact that you've been to Cuba, you will definitely be interrogated. I understand that, at least during the Baby Bush years, the US had agents in places like Cancun, Toronto, and Santo Domingo, from where a lot of flights for Havana depart, looking for people with US passports at the check-in counter.

We'll have to do one of these conversations on dealing with Customs, Immigration, and TSA types sometime soon… Anyway, since it's hard to visit a place and not spend any of your own money at all, they figure you've probably broken the law, and you will probably be prosecuted. So, American businessmen usually go there as guests of their business associates, enabling them to make the claim that they never spent anything in Cuba. The Cuban government treats them well, because it gets a 50% equity stake in any deal they make—you're always in business with the government in Cuba.

L: What kind of deals?

Doug: I went there with Leisure Canada, a small Canadian company that had acquired some spectacular beachfront property in Cuba and was planning to build resort hotels. Another time, I was with a mining company that had a copper-gold deposit in the far west of the island. I went another time with a mining company that Pierre Lassonde had, with several projects around the country. And the other time was with another Canadian company that was trying to manufacture retail electronics in Cuba, taking advantage of the cheap labor. Those were my sponsors—and you needed to have a sponsor, of course.

It was always an adventure. One time we were flying to Santiago, in Santiago de Cuba province, where the revolution began, in an old Soviet An-1. I was talking to the pilot and told him I flew. He let me take the controls for 10 minutes—try doing that on a commercial flight in the US. Another time we were taking an Mi-8, the workhorse Soviet helicopter, someplace and the pilot couldn't get the damn thing to fire up. So the copilot came back and started messing around in the fuse box—if you can imagine a jet helicopter that has a fuse box—with a screwdriver. The whole thing filled with acrid smoke, and we exited posthaste. Believe it or not, those guys flew the thing away—but I guarantee we weren't on it.

It was on the trip with Pierre that I met Fidel. There were only about ten of us there, and he presented himself, unannounced. I believe he speaks quite acceptable English, but he prefers to speak Spanish, for nationalistic reasons, and so as not to be misquoted or misunderstood in English. He rambled on for hours, through his interpreter. At that time, he'd already given up smoking cigars—he was well known for smoking Cohiba Lanceros, the long, thin panatellas. They are absolutely one of my favorite cigars as well. Cuban cigars are the only way to fly.

L: If those are thin, how did the CIA hide a bomb in one when they tried to kill Castro?

Doug: I don't know—maybe they didn't give him a Lancero-type cigar. We gave him a cigar as a token, and he accepted it. Immediately, one of the three or four security guards took it out of Castro's pocket and put it in his own pocket. Fidel was wearing his signature green fatigues, but not combat boots. He was sporting a pair of Gucci-style calfskins that zipped up the side; quite fashionable and comfortable.

L: [Chuckles]

Doug: That really happened. My mistake that evening was to stand around listening to Castro go on and on about nothing, really, of any importance, when all the while, sitting off to the side by himself, was Carlos Lage. At the time, he was the bright young star of the next generation—everyone had their eye on him as the guy who was going to replace Fidel. Apparently, Lage spoke perfect English, and I could have sat down with him and had a good conversation for a couple hours, maybe planted some ideas that could have made a difference.

L: Well, Raul Castro got the job, so maybe, maybe not.

Doug: Yes, apparently, he's subsequently fallen from grace. But back to your initial question, I do think it's quite interesting that Castro has had some second thoughts about the Cuban revolution—though he also came out later with some second thoughts on his second thoughts.

When I met him, I got the impression that he's pretty sophisticated, although a complete egomaniac. Certainly not stupid. He's got to know that everything he's done with Cuba has been a disaster. But I'd guess that he just doesn't see a way out now, doesn't know how to finesse it. I wish I could have proposed my radical plan for privatization to Lage… I believe it could thread the horns of the dilemma Fidel finds himself in.

L: Do you think Cuba could actually embrace market reforms and rejoin the global economy? Or are the political realities such that Castro's generation pretty much has to die before progress can resume again?

Doug: I suspect they'll try to do it the way the Chinese did: economic freedom, but political repression. The guys who are running the place don't want their rice bowls broken, don't want their power scam to come to an end. But there are some things about Cuba that are hard to figure, some factors that are very hard to gauge. For example, the people who left in 1959 and the early '60s, they were mostly the rich and educated ones—which, in Cuba, meant mostly white people of European descent. They went mainly to south Florida, but also other places, where many have become extremely successful.

Now, are they, or their kids, going to be welcomed back? I suspect not. If they were to return—which many will try to—I suspect there'll be a bit of a culture clash. That's not a prediction, but it seems quite possible to me that the Cubans who stayed, who, on average, are of a different racial mix and have a different culture, aren't going to appreciate these rich carpetbaggers if they come back.

L: I've seen that in West Africa, where they call white people *obruni*, which, I'm told, means "swindler," but they also call their returning cousins *obruni*. There's a huge cultural difference, and perhaps a perceived racial one as well.

Doug: Sure. That sort of thing happens all around the world. It's often called "Uhuru jumping." A fat checkbook buys a lot of political favors. Underdeveloped countries are always run politically—which is basically why they're underdeveloped. Add money, and corruption enriches the political class.

L: Hm. Did you invest in any of those companies?

Doug: Yes, but I have to admit that none of these were winners. One of the reasons is what I said about the government always taking a 50% stake in any of these deals—and that's a completely carried interest. That, in effect, doubles your capital costs, and you still have to pay taxes and royalties. Another critical factor is that you've got to pay all the Cubans you hire a reasonable salary in dollars—but the money goes to the government, which pays them in Cuban pesos at the official exchange rate, even though the pesos are worthless. So the government captures most of their salaries too. You pay a guy $1,000 a month, and he winds up getting $20. It's just a scam, of course, but if a government does it, the sheep assume it's for the greater good. These things put even the best business plan on shaky ground in Cuba.

L: Why did you invest, then?

Doug: Well, Wally Berikov, the guy who ran Leisure Canada, is a good friend and a great guy to spend time with. He was also a close personal friend of Castro's and managed to get hold of some really beautiful property—just fantastic development properties, in downtown Havana, the Island of Youth, and elsewhere. It's still a mystery to me why Wally was never able to follow through... but they still have control of those properties, 20 years on. Maybe, when Castro dies, the thing will finally be a ten-bagger.

This was one that looked like a great speculation, but just never panned out. As you know, this is in the nature of dealing in small, volatile, risky, illiquid companies. If just one realizes its potential, it will make up for ten losers—and we hope to do a lot better than just one in ten.

L: A lot of deals never worked out in Cuba, not just Leisure Canada…

Doug: Yes. Whenever things go wrong there, the Cubans like to blame the US embargo—it's all the fault of the US. This is, of course, complete nonsense. *Only* the US has an embargo against Cuba, so they can get anything they want, including American goods, from anywhere else in the world. Cuba has perfectly fine relations with every other country in the world, besides the US. They can't buy things, but it's not because the US stops them. It's simply because they're bankrupt and can't pay for anything.

L: Can't say I'm surprised to hear that you're no fan of the embargo.

Doug: It's just one more stupid thing the US government has done. It handed Castro a credible excuse for failure as he stumbled from one economic disaster to another, and may well have significantly prolonged his rule. It did keep American tourists away, which is a shame, because a flood of American tourists would have made it abundantly obvious to the Cuban people that Americans don't have horns, and it may have inspired more of them to ask if their society was on the wrong path sooner.

Continuation of the embargo only damages American businesses. When Fidel dies, and Raul dies shortly after him, the place will definitely open up. Unfortunately for Americans, the Spaniards, Mexicans, and all the other nationalities that are big there will have locked up all the best deals and will have the best connections with the government.

It's a completely perverse policy that has done nothing but create a big PR black eye for America and punish American tourists and businesses, while giving Castro a great excuse that allowed him to continue failing for decades. Totally perverse, like almost everything the US government does.

L: Looking forward, then, if somebody came to you with a great Cuba deal now, before it's all tied up, would you be interested?

Doug: I don't see how Cuba can fail to boom…

L: The spring is pushed down about as far as it can go, so the place has nowhere to go but up?

Doug: That's right. And the place has thousands of miles of pristine beaches that have seen no commercial use for 50 years, which is to say, ever. I understand that about half of the real estate in Cuba is actually still privately owned—entirely apart from that which was taken from foreigners. Everybody has settled except for the Americans. Almost anything you could do there—as long as you have some confidence that it will come to fruition—could be a fantastic deal. But you'd want to get positioned now, make connections with entrepreneurial Cubans, etc., before the country opens up. The problem is the US government makes this hard for Americans, and even if you can get around that, you have to speak excellent Spanish and take a *lot* of time to meet the right people, learn how to do business in the place. There's always a way to skin the cat. But best to figure it out now, before the Cuban economy liberalizes and starts booming.

L: The only shortcut I can think of would be to hook up with one of these Mexican or Spanish businesspeople already doing business there—but then you'd have to be able to trust that person a lot.

Doug: Yes. And, especially if the deal were taking advantage of some gray area of the law, you'd have to *really* trust the Cubans you were making the deal with, because there's always a chance of them reneging later. But it's only 90 miles from Florida; at some point, it's going to be a fantastic place to be. And it's a fun place, even now, under the puritanical Castros. I can only imagine what it must have been like in the '50s, when Meyer Lansky was running it...

L: Location, location, location.

Doug: Just so. The only problem is that you just can't be everywhere at once. Maybe that doesn't bother most people, though, who even today tend to be as rooted in one place as a medieval serf.

L: Well then, food for thought. Thanks.

Doug: My pleasure. Talking Cuba has given me an urge to fire up a cigar and have a nice, aged, dark rum on the rocks.

Doug, cigar in pocket, under the watchful eye of Che Guevara. (Photo courtesy of Paul Zyla.)

Doug Casey on All Things Fun (ATF)

March 17, 2011

L: Doug, among the many things you find perverse in our world, I've heard you say that one of the most perverse is that the US government has created a bureau to regulate and suppress three of your favorite things in life.

Doug: Ah, yes. Alcohol, tobacco, and firearms—the three things you need for a decent hunting expedition. Or a Class One party. A Class Two party would also include sex, drugs, and rock-n-roll.

It really is strange that they have one agency to regulate these three particular things. Of course, none of them should be regulated at all. Regulating alcohol makes as much sense as... regulating water.

L: The government does that, too.

Doug: These people learn absolutely nothing from their mistakes—ever. To me, that's proof that the problem isn't intellectual; it's moral. Spiritual. And I don't mean on the part of the drinkers, smokers, and shooters. The bluenoses just *have* to tell others what they can and cannot do; they're uptight, nosy, unhappy, and small-minded. Not the type you'd want for a neighbor, but they are nonetheless quite successful at wheedling their way into political power. These types pushed the US into prohibiting the manufacture and sale of alcohol from 1919 to 1933, and it was an unmitigated disaster. It created a crime wave the likes of which had never been seen before, and not just because peaceful, otherwise law-abiding citizens became criminals with the stroke of a pen. It created a black market for liquor, and that spawned many related criminal activities.

L: When those activities become criminal, the people involved can't take their differences to the courts, so there's an increase in settling disputes with violence. And since the goods are traded in the black market, people can't complain too loudly if the quality is bad. Plus, prices go up, to account for the cost of evading the law, which attracts new people to enter a life of crime to cash in on the high margins. Bathtub gin was easy money, like meth today.

Doug: Right. Prohibition established the Mafia in the US, which became the main supplier of alcohol. The Mafia didn't really exist in the US before the Volstead Act initiated the Prohibition era. It was Prohibition that made crime profitable as a big business; Al Capone would never have been more than a small-time hood without it. Prohibition caused destruction and havoc, cost a lot of money, and affected the moral fabric of society—it was a total disaster.

L: I've read that women rarely drank spirits before Prohibition, and almost never in the company of men, before the speakeasies. Even though I rarely drink any alcohol at all, I'm not sure this fall from grace is entirely bad—but it sure does indicate a fundamental change in the fabric of society. All unintended consequences of busybodying.

Doug: They never learn. They've declared war, of all the stupid ideas, on various plant extracts that are unpopular with the neopuritans: cocaine, marijuana, heroin, etc. It's not a war on all drugs—really dangerous psychiatric drugs like Ritalin, Prozac, and scores of others are being actively promoted. The war is really just on recreational drugs—and not even all of them, just some of them. All these things were legal in the 19th century and were never serious problems, even when anyone could buy them at the corner drug store. Sure, some people abused them, just like some do today. But they were cheap in a free market, and no one had to resort to crime to support his habit. For what it's worth, alcohol is much more dangerous than marijuana. Cannabis has demonstrated medicinal uses, but don't try telling that to an anti-drug crusader.

L: What do you say to people who ask if drug addiction isn't a terrible thing that destroys families, etc.?

Doug: It's true—but mostly if kids haven't been brought up right to start with. A lot of fools want the government to do their job for them. But depression also destroys lives. Are you going to outlaw that? Overeating is a deadly vice, so busybodies are working to outlaw that now too, with laws against fat and salt. These neopuritans, who think they know best for everybody else, suffer from serious psychological aberrations. I'd say "So what?" except they insist on imposing their values, by law, on everyone else.

Tragedy is part of the human condition. You can't legislate it out of existence. And, as with Prohibition, the United States' disastrous War on Alcohol, most of the bad things we see in relation to drug use today don't come from the drug use itself, but from people being forced into criminal activity in order to engage in otherwise peaceful activity.

As I said, well before the insane War on Some Drugs, most of these drugs were known and commonly used as medicines, with no regulation at all, and the people with problems were few. Sigmund Freud prescribed cocaine to his patients and used it himself. I'm not advocating the use of recreational drugs, incidentally, and I generally eschew the company of users. I'm simply saying it's nobody's business if you indulge.

I could go on, but I won't. The point is that alcohol is no different and should be completely unregulated; the market would ensure cheaper, safer, better drinks, and everyone would be better off.

L: What's your favorite drink? I mean, we all know you like a good glass of wine, but is there a variety you like?

Doug: The technology of wine making has become so sophisticated, and widespread, that any wine above a certain level is quite acceptable today. It's a far cry from the days—not so long ago—when people crushed grapes barefoot or thought Mogen David was a special treat at dinner. Hell, things have changed from when, in college, we used to mix grain alcohol with Welch's grape juice and think we were living high on the hog. But seriously, above, say, $15 a bottle, the difference between most wines is largely promotion and marketing as far as I'm concerned. But to answer the question, everything being equal, I'll order a Malbec in a red—they're very hearty. And a Torrontés in a white.

L: And what about mixed drinks—martinis or manhattans?

Doug: I'm not a connoisseur, but when it comes to the hard stuff, I enjoy bourbon on the rocks. I used to be a fan of Old JTS Brown, mainly because it was the brand Fast Eddie drank in *The Hustler*—that movie was made in the days before paid product placements. But I haven't seen it for many years. The brand seems to have been killed—probably by some corporate "suit" who obviously didn't know either good bourbon or the value of free advertising.

Now the market is totally dominated by Jack Daniels and Jim Beam, which are perfectly acceptable products—but the alcoholic equivalents of McDonald's and Burger King. Of course now there are lots of very expensive small batch makers as well. But 90% of the cost of the product is taxes, which I resent. I hope someday Americans again have the guts to go back to rum running private stills—all the great NASCAR drivers of the '50s and early '60s got their start as bootleggers outrunning revenuers on back roads.

L: The parallels with tobacco are obvious. It's another victimless crime that Big Brother and all his busybody supporters have decided has got to go.

Doug: Yes, they're ratcheting up the anti-tobacco rhetoric in the same way these other substances were demonized before they were made illegal. I generally don't believe in conspiracy theories; it's hard enough to get four people all to agree on what movie to see, much less how to commit a giant malfeasance. But, clearly, people of bad will often think alike. And if they see some group of do-gooders has a new agenda, it's monkey see, monkey do. The anti-smoking hysteria is worldwide at this point.

L: I'm not a smoker either, and frankly, I hate the smell of cigarette smoke. But it's striking to me the way that habit is being rebranded in such a negative way. The little smokers' booths in European airports are bad enough, but making it illegal to smoke in bars is crazy. They are private property, where people *want* to go smoke and drink. It's even illegal in your own home, in some places. This is taking the anti-smoking witch hunt beyond apartheid to persecution.

Doug: It's actually insane. And a violation of property rights—the owner of the establishment should make the rules; the customers can abide by them or go elsewhere. People have become such whipped dogs in accepting government decrees. There's a cigar bar in Vancouver, right across from the Terminal City Club. They sell good Cuban cigars, and they have a tastefully appointed room that's air-conditioned, filtered, sealed, etc., set up so people could smoke cigars without affecting a non-smoker's most delicate sensitivity in any way. But the Vancouver government has outlawed any smoking in *any* commercial establishment. So, here we have a state-of-the-art cigar bar where you're not allowed to smoke.

It's just incredible. Stupid and destructive. It's a depressing sign of how degraded the average person has become that people are not out in the streets with pitchforks and torches, storming the busybodies' castles. And, of course, the police enforce any and all laws, like robots.

Back in the 1980s, when I flew the Concorde…

L: They let you fly one?

Doug: [Laughs] No, although I did fly a Cuban airliner once. It was a Russian Antonov-1, which is a gigantic prop plane. I went up to greet the pilot, who didn't speak very good English, and my Spanish wasn't very good at the time. He asked if I was a pilot, and I said yes, which was true, albeit for little Pipers and Cessnas, and he invited me to take over the plane. My friend Ben Johnson had the same thing happen to him in Russia on a Tupolev jet airliner… but that would not likely happen on a British Airways Concorde.

L: No, I wouldn't think so.

Doug: Anyway, not only could you smoke on the Concorde in those days, but they actually passed out a selection of Cuban cigars for you to smoke after your dinner.

L. Wow…

Doug: That's a genuine fact. And earlier, back when I was in high school, stewardesses would pass out free sample packs of cigarettes to all the passengers who wanted them, courtesy of the cigarette companies.

L: Things sure have changed…

Doug: Radically. It seems like all these chimpanzees get a new meme in their heads, and that becomes the new way it is. Fashion totally overrules principle.

L: It's like that thing about, first they came for the communists, and I didn't speak out because I wasn't a communist; then they came for the Jews, and I didn't speak out because I'm not Jewish, etc., then when they came for me, there was no one left to speak out.

Doug: Pastor Martin Niemöller, referring to the National Socialists, of whom, incidentally, he was an early supporter. Today, it'd be: "First they came for the smokers… "

L: What would you say to people who don't want to breathe other people's smoke? Isn't it a violation of their rights when a smoker fills the air with fumes they don't want to breathe?

Doug: It might be, but it might not. It's a matter of property rights. If someone comes into your house and blows smoke in your face, that certainly is a violation of your rights. But if you're in a restaurant or airplane and the owners are okay with smoking, no one is violating your rights. You have the right to leave or fly another airline, but you don't have a right to impose your personal air quality standards on others, in their places. In these types of situations, it's not the smoke that's the problem, it's unclear property rights.

L: Fair enough. So, what's your favorite cigar?

Doug: Well, I have to give the nod to the Cubans. I used to argue with my good friend Jose that the Dominicans were just as good—but he was right. Too bad Cuban cigars are illegal in the US. The best in the world is probably the Trinidad, and it's also the most expensive at close to $50 a copy, for some models. Next is the Cohiba, especially the Esplendido and Lancero. During the cigar boom of the late '90s—and cigar booms always coincide with tops in the stock market, it's uncanny—Castro idiotically put out a directive to triple production. Needless to say, quality collapsed; he almost single-handedly destroyed the industry. But the Cubans are now back up to snuff.

I think there's much more variation in quality and taste in cigars than in liquors. And marketing also is a major controller of price. Once, when I visited perhaps the best cigar store in Havana, I mentioned to the manager, who was a real aficionado, that I really liked Cohiba Lanceros but didn't like the $20 price. He suggested El

Rey del Mundo, Grandes de España. As far as I could tell, it was the same cigar—but at $4 a copy. The cheapest place I know to buy Cubans is at the Duty Free in Buenos Aires. The most expensive is anywhere in the UK—including the Duty Free at Heathrow, where they're over twice the price they are in Buenos Aires.

L: Well, I'll leave that experiment to those of our readers who share your taste in this regard. So, what about firearms?

Doug: In many ways, this is the most egregious, dangerous, and offensive stupidity of them all.

L: Why?

Doug: Times were that to be a freeman *meant* to be a person who could possess weapons. They were not just a symbol of freedom but the means for securing it and maintaining it. Only slaves were disarmed—or, for that matter, allowed themselves to be legally disarmed. But that's exactly the direction the US is going, and indeed most of the world.

I'm a firm believer that everyone ought to be able to carry any weapon they wish. It's a matter of your rights as a free and sovereign individual. And guns, the "great equalizers," put 90-pound girls on a level playing field with 250-pound men half again as tall.

L: That's not a level playing field; the guy's a much bigger target!

Doug: So much the better, if you're the girl and he's just broken into your bedroom. But my point was that the gun is just a tool. I don't just believe in the right to own a gun but the right to own and use any weapon—in self-defense. Self-defense is an essential human right. Without it, society is not possible. And without tools for self-defense that even the odds between the strong and the weak, society is reduced to the brutish level of "might makes right."

L: I think of guns as "life preservers," myself.

Doug: Just so—and you can't have a right to your life if you have no right to defend it. Disarming yourself is simply stupid in a world not inhabited by angels—unless you think it'd be fun to go up against a bad guy unarmed. The bad guy is almost certainly going to have a baseball bat or a knife, if not a gun—and I never want to bring a knife to a gunfight.

L: What would you say to our European readers or readers from other places with less tradition of firearms ownership than there is in the US? Many of them think that governments keep people safe, and that individuals should not have firearms (or any weapons at all), only the police should have them.

Doug: I think that's a ridiculous attitude that flies in the face of history and the abundantly evident darker side of human nature. I think such people are both deluded and degraded.

It's striking how much things have changed on this front as well. As late as the 1930s, the period of Indiana Jones, you could take a pistol with you anywhere in the world, even on airplanes—which they accurately portray the hero doing in the movies. In the '60s, when I was a kid, I put my rifle and my pistol in the overhead compartment on a couple of flights in the US, and nobody thought twice about it, including me. If you read Sherlock Holmes stories, which I've always enjoyed, you'll find that not only was Sherlock Holmes a notorious smoker of tobacco, but he was also known to indulge in other chemical substances that are illegal today. And he would often sit at his flat on Baker Street, shooting his revolver into the mantelpiece to practice his marksmanship.

L: I hope he was wearing ear protection. Maybe he loaded his own ammo and made some light rounds for practice? He must have gone through a lot of mantelpieces… and had to replace the masonry of his chimney often. But that was a different world—many people say that individuals don't need guns *today*, that they are an anachronism.

Doug: They are simply wrong. And fools. In places where it's assumed that almost everyone has guns in their homes, like West Virginia and Alaska, the crime rate is very low. In places where guns have been outlawed in recent years, like Australia, violent-crime rates have risen. And in Washington DC, once the murder capital of the US, the crime rate plummeted after the city's draconian anti-gun laws were reduced. Of course, that never gets mentioned in the popular press.

L: I just looked it up, and the stats I see say that violent crime dropped 46.9%, and property crime dropped 48.3% in 2007, the year the DC gun ban was struck down by the Supreme Court. (As Heinlein said, an armed society is a polite society.) But if your argument is moral—that humans have a right to self-defense—do the statistics matter?

Doug: You're quite correct, they really don't. It's improper to argue matters like this with statistics; it's purely a matter of ethics. It's an interesting observation that as a practical matter, society is better off if gun ownership is widespread, but that has nothing to do with the moral imperative: human beings have the right to defend themselves, their loved ones, and their property. It's unethical and stupid to deny that right by law. It may sound clichéd, but it's true that when guns are outlawed, only outlaws will have guns. A system that ensures that only the predators among us have the best weapons is one that's asking for mass-produced tragedy.

You can't rely on the police to be there when you need them. Even as societies are increasingly disarming themselves, relying more on the state for everything, the police are becoming more and more of a clique unto themselves.

In other words, the first obligation of police officers is to other cops—their co-workers. Their second obligation is to their employers—the government. And their third obligation—and it's a distant third—is to "serve and protect" society. "Serve and protect" is increasingly just a PR slogan. So, in today's world, you actually need a gun more, not less.

Besides, a free person should not rely on others to defend him or herself—that's a kind of dependence and no way to remain free.

It's a happy coincidence that the moral and the practical are the same. But I find that's almost always the case.

L: Rand would argue that the practical *is* practical because it is moral. So, what about the third leg of the "right to keep and bear arms" argument? As the character V put it so well in *V for Vendetta*, people should not be afraid of their governments, governments should be afraid of the people. A disarmed population is at the mercy of the worst thugs of all: those in uniform and their masters.

Doug: That's absolutely right. People have got to recognize that the state is not their friend. Big Brother is anything but brotherly, and the less those in power fear the people, the more bold and predatory they and their agents become. That's another reason to be armed, even if you feel safe where you live and work.

Not that I'm suggesting that anyone with a pistol and rifle would be able to stand up to an army, but it's better to have it and not need it than to need it and not have it.

L: Of course. An individual, no matter how great a marksman she or he might be, can't defend a home with a gun against artillery shells. However, there are more individuals in society than there are members of the army, and if the people are armed, the balance of power changes substantially. As we've seen in Afghanistan and Vietnam, peasants with light arms have been able to stand up to the most powerful armies in the world.

So, which of these three arguments is the most important to you? The moral argument (right to self-defense), the practical argument (gun ownership reduces crime), or the political argument (a disarmed populace ends up being treated like cattle)?

Doug: Oh, there's no question. It's absolutely the moral argument. If you're going to live with yourself, you have to do what's right. The only question is, what kind of guns should you own?

L: So, which ones?

Doug: Well, different people have different needs and tastes, of course, but answering this is a little more objective than it would be for alcohol or tobacco. There's a clearly discernible difference in the utility and quality of various firearms.

L: That reminds me of your story about the guy who put the same wine in three different bottles and invited some experts to a tasting… and they all imagined all sorts of differences that weren't there. But I think anyone can tell the difference between a .22 and a .44.

Doug: [Laughs] That's right. I have an S&W model 29—three, actually.

L: I like .44s too, but I've never had one of the famous Model 29s. A Dan Wesson .44 was my first gun.

Doug: I've got revolvers, like the .44, but I far prefer autoloaders. And there I like .45 autos. There have been improvements since John Browning invented the "1911 .45 Automatic Colt Pistol," but his same design is still in use, because it's one of the most accurate, rugged, and practical guns ever made. There's a reason that the 1911 almost always wins combat shooting contests whenever they're held.

Glocks are great too. They're extremely simple, very reliable, and they work perfectly right out of the box. You can get them in lots of different models, some very small and concealable. And because they're about half plastic, they're also very light. Great carry guns.

L: I like 1911s too, and so do my older sons. What about a battle rifle, something suitable for militia use?

Doug: The FN FAL is the Mercedes of battle rifles, in .308. But in rifles it's tough to beat the AK-47; the things are indestructible, they work no matter how dirty, and with the worst ammo. The SKS is almost as good, and half the price. Ruger ranch rifles in .223 are really mini M-14s, but rougher. The AR-15, especially a reworked one, is kind of a "must own" in the US. But, in .223, the best is actually made by Daewoo—they took the best elements of the AR, basically the lower receiver, and combined it with the best of the AK, the upper receiver. It's flawless.

But when it comes to a defensive weapon, nothing can touch a shotgun. A shotgun, along with a .45 pistol, is the absolute "must have." I'd go for a police model pump action, with a short barrel but a long ammo tube. Mossberg makes a very inexpensive but highly serviceable one.

L: I'm partial to the AR-10, myself, for a battle rifle. I like .308 much better than the .223 caliber the army has gone to. Sure, you can carry more ammo with the smaller round, which, I suppose, is an important advantage if you don't trust your troops to become good marksmen, but I like a round that carries a little more authority.

Doug: Well, I agree. But there's such a huge amount to be said on this subject that we haven't even scratched the surface. If someone wants an instant education, you can't go wrong getting a copy of _Boston's Gun Bible_[1] by our mutual friend Boston T. Party.

L: It occurs to me that maybe it's not a random perverseness that these three things, alcohol, tobacco and firearms, should be regulated by one agency. The BATF started out as a branch of the Department of the Treasury, not the Justice Department. And given the nature of these commodities—they are all Mad Max-type valuable goods—they have had great importance, at least historically, to tax collectors.

There's a demented kind of sense to lumping "ATF" together, from the state's perspective. Early on in America, you could pay taxes in tobacco—and marijuana too, by the way—and whiskey was used as money. After the revolution, there was a shortage of good money in America—people forget, but America does, in fact, have past experience using worthless IOUs for money. The Continental Congress had no gold, so they issued paper promissory notes. That's where the expression "not worth a continental" comes from. Whiskey, on the other hand, was so divisible, durable, convenient, consistent, and of value in itself, that its use as money—and the government's decision to tax it—sparked a second rebellion, which George Washington put down by force.

Doug: Yes, turning crops into whiskey was actually a good way of storing them, in those relatively primitive days—and that storage only increased the value of the whiskey. That sad episode, the Whiskey Rebellion, is one of the few things that besmirch Washington's otherwise rather good reputation. But I've read that he only did it because of Alexander Hamilton, who was secretary of the Treasury at that time. A momentary lapse of judgment.

L: Hamilton was a proponent of a single national government as well, which he was instrumental in foisting on the Americans of the day, instead of the confederation of thirteen independent states they had fought for. It's said that Washington could have made himself King George the First—he had it in the palm of his hand, but he chose not to, and that's worthy of respect. But anyway, my point is that when it comes to ATF, it always comes back to money and taxes.

Doug: And raw power, which draws the worst type of people, those who believe they should, and can, control others. What makes the anti-tobacco crusade all the more perverse in this context is that much of the early wealth and power that made America flourish came from tobacco farming. And, of course, there'd be no country if American farmers hadn't acquired large numbers of guns and trained themselves to hunt and protect their families. America, in

---

1. www.totallyincorrectbook.com/go/102

reality, was built on alcohol, tobacco, and firearms. It's ironic that the ATF, set up to regulate them, is notoriously among the most corrupt of agencies. Their misadventure at Waco back in 1993[2] is emblematic of their mindset.

L: True enough. But guns… People trade them, and they do hold value over time, and yet I'm not aware of them ever being used as a medium of exchange in any significant way. Perhaps that's because they are not divisible, convenient, or consistent. But ammunition is—I've seen ammo used as money on a small scale—and you can even make change with it.

Doug: Yes, and perhaps not coincidentally, I think that's the US government's next angle of attack on this issue. They'll keep pressure up, trying to take people's guns away, but the Second Amendment has, almost miraculously, slowed them down a bit lately. So, if they can't grab people's guns directly right now, I think they'll grab the ammo instead. They'll be indirect. They won't ban it, but they'll tax it and regulate it to the point where getting ammunition will be much, much harder and more expensive.

You know, perhaps it's convenient that they've rolled all these bureaucracies of thugs, including the drug enforcement thugs, into one Department of Homeland Security. It'll make it easier to round the bastards up after the next revolution. They send their minions out into the land so they can bedevil the little guy…

L: Maybe they can get spiffy black uniforms with armbands?

Doug: They're actually moving in that direction. I find it very disturbing that Homeland Security now has its own 400-acre campus in Washington. Fittingly, it's on the grounds of the old St. Elizabeth's hospital, the oldest mental institution in the United States. Once an agency gets its own building complex and fills it with bureaucrats and thugs, you can never get rid of it, not until the country collapses. To me, this is a really big nail in the coffin of what little is left of America.

L: Just the name itself gives me the heebie-jeebies: *Homeland Security*. Sounds like something the Nazis or Soviets would have come up with. A sign of the endgame approaching?

Doug: It's not just in the area of personal freedom but the economy[3], and the military situation as well. It all seems to be coming together at once.

L: We're not going to see you on the street with a placard saying "THE END IS NIGH!!" are we, Doug?

Doug: Not at all my style. But I've got to say that this is one of the things I like about living in Argentina in general, and Salta in particular: it's "ATF-friendly." You can smoke a cigar wherever you want, as long as the owner of the

2. www.totallyincorrectbook.com/go/103
3. www.totallyincorrectbook.com/go/104

place is okay with it. You can drink what you want, where you want to, including out in the street, if you wish, though there's almost no drunkenness that I can see. There's very little in the way of a police presence—it isn't needed, isn't wanted— and you can own a gun. It's unfortunate that you're supposed to register guns with the government, but it's no big deal to have a gun in Argentina. You must, however, be a resident. That's true everywhere, unfortunately.

One of the nice things about the place, besides the weather and low cost of living and so forth is that, especially when you're out in the provinces, it's like you're stepping back in time. Sociologically, it's more like what the US was like in maybe the '20s—or at the latest the '50s. It's just delightful and why I enjoy spending time there. I have all the benefits of today's technology, I have a vastly higher standard of living, and I have much more freedom than I do in the US. And a big measure of that freedom is the liberalism regarding alcohol, tobacco, and firearms.

Actually, although I'm a gun guy, I've never been a hunter. But I'm going bird hunting—ducks, partridges, doves, and pigeons—next month in Argentina with six friends from New Zealand who tell me some of the best bird hunting in the world is over in Santa Fe province.

L: Okay then. Investment implications?

Doug: Well, politically incorrect areas always offer opportunities. Tobacco stocks have high yields. And I don't think government will kill the industry since it cranks out so much in taxes. Gun manufacturers are also cheap. One of the more fun trades I made years ago was to short Ben & Jerry's Ice Cream, which was very overpriced because they were so fashionably lefty, and going long Ruger. My rationale was to be market neutral by being long and short simultaneously. It was a huge win on both sides of the trade.

Outside of the financial markets, I don't think you can possibly go wrong setting aside part of the basement to store a few crates of ammo—.223, 9mm, .45ACP, and .308. Prices there are probably going to skyrocket and availability decrease. The same is true of tobacco, which has always been an alternative currency. Buying a few cartons of cigarettes every time you're at the Duty Free or in a low-tax state and salting them away is a no-lose proposition.

L: And the suppression of All Things Fun is yet another reason to diversify your assets to friendlier climes.

Doug: Yes, and perhaps a barometer of sorts. Whether or not you smoke, drink, or like to shoot, if you can find a place where these increasingly politically incorrect activities are accepted, you may be on to a good place to diversify into.

L: Got it. Thanks Doug.

Doug: You're welcome. Till next time.

Doug Casey on the Morality of Money

Feb 8, 2011

L: Doug, every time we have a conversation, I ask you about the investment implications of your ideas, and we consider ways to turn the trends you see into profits. The assumption is that that's what people want to hear from you, since you're the guru of financial speculation. But this, your known status as a wealthy man, the fact that you have no children, and other things may lead some people to form an incorrect conclusion about you—that "all you care about is money." So let's talk about money. Is it all you care about?

Doug: I think anyone who has read our conversation giving advice to <u>people just starting out</u>[1] in life (or re-starting) knows that the answer is no. Or the conversation we had in which we discussed <u>Scrooge McDuck</u>[2], one of the great heroes of literature. However, I have to stop before we start and push back: If money were all I cared about, so what? Would that really make me a bad person?

L: I've <u>grokked</u>[3] Ayn Rand's "<u>money speech</u>[4]," so you know I won't say yes, but maybe you should expand on that for readers who haven't absorbed Rand's ideas...

Doug: I'm a huge fan of Rand; she was an original and a genius. But just because someone like her, or me, sees the high moral value of money, that doesn't mean that it's all-important to us. In fact, I find money less and less important as time goes by, the older I get. Perhaps that's a function of Maslow's hierarchy: If you're hungry, food is all you really care about; if you're freezing, then it's warmth, and so forth. If you have enough money, these basics aren't likely to be problems.

My most enjoyable times have had absolutely nothing to do with money. Like a couple times in the past when I hopped freight trains with a friend, once to Portland and once to Sacramento. Each trip took three days and nights, each

1. www.totallyincorrectbook.com/go/105
2. www.totallyincorrectbook.com/go/106
3. www.totallyincorrectbook.com/go/107
4. www.totallyincorrectbook.com/go/108

was full of adventure and weird experiences, and each cost about zero. It was liberating to be out of the money world for a few days. But it was an illusion. Somebody had to get the money to buy the food we ate at missions. Still, it's nice to live in a dream world for a while.

Sure, I'd like more money, if only for the same genetic reason a squirrel wants more nuts to store for the winter. The one common denominator of all living creatures is one word: Survive! And, as a medium of exchange and store of value, money represents survival… it's much more practical than nuts.

L: Some people might say that if money were your highest value, you might become a thief or murderer to get it.

Doug: Not likely. I have personal ethics, and there are things I won't do.

Besides, crime—real crime, taking from or harming others, not law-breaking, which is an entirely different thing—is for the lazy, short-sighted, and incompetent. In point of fact, I believe crime doesn't pay, notwithstanding the fact that Jon Corzine of MF Global is still at large. Criminals are self-destructive.

Anyway, what's the most someone could take, robbing their local bank? Perhaps $10,000? That's only enough to make a wager with Mitt Romney.

But that leads me to think about the subject. In the old days, when Jesse James or other thieves robbed a bank, all the citizens would turn out to engage them in a gun battle in the streets. Why? Because it was actually their money being stored in the bank, not the bankers' money. A robbed bank had immense personal consequences for everyone in town. Today, nobody gives a damn if a bank is robbed—they'll get their money back from a US government agency. The bank has become impersonal; most aren't locally owned. And your deposit has been packaged up into some unfathomable security nobody is responsible for.

The whole system has become corrupt. It degrades the very concept of money. This relates to why kids don't save coins in piggy banks anymore—it's because they're no longer coins with value, they're just tokens that are constantly depreciating, and essentially worthless. All of US society is about as sound as the dollar now.

Actually, it can be argued that robbing a bank isn't nearly as serious a crime today as robbing a candy store of $5. Why? Nobody in particular loses in the robbery of today's socialized banks. But the candy merchant has to absorb the $5 loss personally. Anyway, if you want to rob a bank today, you don't use a gun. You become part of management and loot the shareholders through outrageous salaries, stock options, and bonuses, among other things. I truly dislike the empty suits that fill most boardrooms today.

But most people are mostly honest—it's the 80/20 rule again. So, no; I think this argument is a straw man. The best way to make money is to create value. If I personally owned Apple as a private company, I'd be making more money—completely honestly—than many governments... and they are the biggest thieves in the world.

L: No argument.

Doug: Notice one more thing: making money honestly means creating something *other* people value, not necessarily what you value. The more money I want, the more I have to think about what other people want, and find better, faster, cheaper ways of delivering it to them. The reason someone is poor—and, yes, I know all the excuses for poverty—is that the poor do not produce more than they consume. Or if they do, they don't save the surplus.

L: The productive make things other people want: Adam Smith's invisible hand.

Doug: Exactly. Selfishness, in the form of the profit motive, guides people to serve the needs of others far more reliably, effectively, and efficiently than any amount of haranguing from priests, poets, or politicians. Those people tend to be profoundly anti-human, actually.

L: People say money makes the world go around, and they are right. Or, as I tell my students, there are two basic ways to motivate and coordinate human behavior on a large scale: coercion and persuasion. Government is the human institution based on coercion. The market is the one based on persuasion. Individuals can sometimes persuade others to do things for love, charity, or other reasons, but to coordinate voluntary cooperation society-wide, you need the price system of a profit-driven market economy.

Doug: And that's why it doesn't matter how smart or well-intended politicians may be. Political solutions are always detrimental to society over the long run, because they are based on coercion.

If governments lacked the power to compel obedience, they would cease to be governments. No matter how liberal, there's always a point at which it comes down to force—especially if anyone tries to opt out and live by their own rules. Even if people try that in the most peaceful and harmonious way with regard to their neighbors, the state cannot allow separatists to secede. The moment the state grants that right, every different religious, political, social, or even artistic group might move to form its own enclave, and the state disintegrates. That's wonderful—for everybody but the parasites who rely on the state (which is why secession movements always become violent).

I'm actually mystified at why most people not only just tolerate the state but seem to love it. They're enthusiastic about it. Sometimes that makes me pessimistic about the future...

L: Reminds me of the <u>conversation we had on Europe</u>[5] disintegrating. But let's stay on topic. So you're saying that money is a positive moral good in society because the pursuit of it motivates the creation of value, because it's the bridge between selfishness and social good and because it's the basis for voluntary cooperation, rather than coerced interaction. Anything else?

Doug: Yes, but first, let me say one more thing about the issue of selfishness—the virtue of selfishness—and the vice of altruism. Ayn Rand might never forgive me for saying this, but if you take the two concepts—ethical self-interest and concern for others—to their logical conclusions, they are actually the same. It's in your selfish best interest to provide the maximum amount of value to the maximum number of people—that's how Apple became the giant company it is. Conversely, it is *not* altruistic to help other people. I want all the people around me to be strong and successful. It makes life better and easier for me if they're all doing well. So it's selfish, not altruistic, when I help them.

To weaken others, to degrade them by making them dependent upon generosity, as we discussed in our conversation on charity, is not doing those people any good. If you really care about others, the best thing you can do for them is to push for totally freeing all markets. That makes it both necessary and rewarding for them to learn valuable skills and to become creators of value and not burdens on society. It's a win–win all around.

L: That'll bend some people's minds… So, what was the other thing?

Doug: Well, referring again to our conversation on charity, the accumulation of wealth is in and of itself an important social as well as a personal good.

L: Remind us.

Doug: The good to individuals of accumulating wealth is obvious, but the social good often goes unrecognized. Put simply, progress requires capital. Major new undertakings, from hydropower dams to spaceships, to new medical devices and treatments, require huge amounts of capital. If you're not willing to extract that capital from the population via the coercion of taxes, i.e., steal it, you need wealth to accumulate in private hands to pay for these things.

In other words, if the world is going to improve, we need huge pools of capital, intelligently invested. We need as many "obscenely" rich people as possible.

L: Right then… so, money is all good—nothing bad about it at all?

Doug: Unfortunately, many of the rich people in the world today didn't get their money by real production. They got it by using political connections and slopping at the trough of the state. That's bad. When I look at how some people

---

have gotten their money—Clinton, Pelosi, and all the politically connected bankers and brokers, just for a start—I can understand why the poor want to eat the rich.

But money itself isn't the problem. Money is just a store of value and a means of exchange. What is bad about that? <u>Gold, as we've discussed</u>[6] many times, happens to be the best form of money the market has ever produced: It's convenient, consistent, durable, divisible, has intrinsic value (it's the second-most reflective and conductive metal, the most nonreactive, the most ductile, and the most malleable of all metals), and can't be created out of thin air. Those are gold's attributes. People attribute all sorts of other silly things to gold, and poetic critics talk about the evils of the lust for gold. But it's not the gold itself that's evil—it's the psychological aberrations and weaknesses of unethical people that are the problem. The critics are fixating on what is merely a tool, rather than the ethical merits or failures of the people who use the tool and are responsible for the consequences of their actions.

L: Sort of like the people who repeat foolish slogans like "guns kill"—as though guns sprout little feet when no one is looking and run around shooting people all by themselves.

Doug: Exactly. They're the same personality type—busybodies who want to enforce their opinions on everyone else. They're dangerous and despicable. Yet they somehow posture as if they had the high moral ground.

L: Okay, so even if you cared only for money, that could be seen as a good thing. But you do care for more—like what?

Doug: Well, money is a tool—the means to achieve various goals. For me, those goals include fine art, wine, cars, homes, horses, cigars, and many other physical things. But it also gives me the ability to do things I enjoy or value—like spend time with friends, go to the gym, lie in the sun, read books, and do pretty much what I want when I want. Let's just call it as philosophers do: "the good life." It's why my partners and I built <u>La Estancia de Cafayate</u>[7]. We have regular events down there I welcome readers to attend.

But I don't take money too seriously. It's just something you *have*. It's much less important than what you *do*, and trivial in comparison to what you *are*. I could be happy being a hobo. As I said in the <u>conversation on fresh starts</u>[8], there have been times when I felt my life was just as good and I was just as happy without much money at all. That said, you can't be too rich or too thin.

---

6. www.totallyincorrectbook.com/go/110
7. www.totallyincorrectbook.com/go/111
8. www.totallyincorrectbook.com/go/112

L: Very good. Investment implications?

Doug: This may all seem rather philosophical, but it's actually extremely important to investors. What is the purpose of investing or speculating? To make money. How can anyone hope to do that well if they feel that there is something immoral or distasteful about making money?

Someone who pinches his or her nose and tries anyway because making money is a necessary evil will never do as well as those who throw themselves into the fray with gusto and delight in doing something valuable—and doing it well.

L: The law of attraction[9].

Doug: Yes, but I don't view the law of attraction as a metaphysical force—rather as a psychological reality. If you have a negative attitude about something, you're unlikely to attract it... even if you try to talk yourself into thinking the opposite.

L: Okay, but that's not a stock pick...

Doug: Sure. We're talking basics here. No stock picks today, just a Public Service Announcement: If you think money is evil, don't bother trying to accumulate wealth. On the other hand, if you want to become wealthy, you'd better think long and hard about your attitudes about money, work through the thoughts above and those you can find in the rest of our conversations via the links we provide. Cultivate a positive attitude about money, which is right up there with language as one of the most valuable tools man has ever invented. Think about it, and give yourself permission to become rich. It's a good thing.

L: Very well. Thanks for what I hope will prove to be a very thought-provoking conversation!

Doug: My pleasure. Talk to you next week.

---

9. www.totallyincorrectbook.com/go/113

Doug Casey on Your Health

Sept 2, 2009

L: Doug, we've talked a lot about what we might call financial health, which only makes sense, given what we do here at Casey Research. But I know you have a great interest in physical health, and you've just visited one of the best health spas in the world. What did you think—would you recommend it to our readers?

Doug: Yes, I just finished spending ten days at the Canyon Ranch spa in Tucson, Arizona. It's one of the oldest, and probably the premier US spa. You might recall that about three years ago, I spent some time at the Chiva Som spa in Hua Hin, Thailand, which is probably the best spa in Asia. These may be the two best spas in the world.

L: So, how did they compare?

Doug: I'd recommend the Canyon Ranch spa highly, if only because it's closer to where most of our readers are. The thing they do at both of these places is draw your attention to the fact that nobody—even those who try to engage in a healthy lifestyle—really does an adequate job.

Look, right now, I'm sitting in an airport lounge in San Francisco, getting ready to board a plane to the Far East in a few minutes. I just left the Canyon Ranch earlier today. And I'm finding that as nice as the food is here in the first-class lounge, I really don't want to eat any of it. The stuff we were eating at the Canyon Ranch was just so… wholesome. Organic. Perfectly balanced in terms of fat, protein, and carbohydrates. I'm truly feeling regret for having left.

I'm not overweight, but like almost everyone, I'm not at my ideal fighting weight either. In ten days there, I lost six pounds—and I could have done much better.

I had an even better experience at Chiva Som in Thailand.

These things are expensive, but for those who are able to afford them, going to one of these spas is probably one of the most important things they can do. You won't really, fully understand why, unless you actually do it. So I'm suggesting, in the strongest terms I can, that people actually go out of their way and *do it*. It's one of the smartest things you can do with your money, at almost any age.

L: Because if you don't have your health, you don't have anything?

Doug: Exactly.

L: Okay, but you didn't say how these two spas compared. Was the American one more high tech? Was the Asian one swarming with human attendants?

Doug: Actually, they are very similar. The medical technologies available at both places were equal and excellent. The costs are close, but Thailand is cheaper. But I've got to say—and this may simply be a function of the costs of providing services being so much lower in Thailand than in Arizona—that although the food in both places was excellent, the food in Thailand is a cut above excellent. And there were more people providing services…

From a consumer's point of view, I'd have to say that the oriental experience was probably better. There is the added effort involved in flying to Bangkok, and from there driving two hours to Hua Hin, but Thailand is something everyone should experience anyway. It's one of my two favorite countries on the planet.

But I suggest that you do both, so you get a full idea of what it's like and which environment suits you best. It's potentially life changing. You know, one thing about these proper spas is that they make an effort to actually get you to change your life, from your way of thinking about your health to your daily habits. It's not just an experience. It's not just about going there to "do the spa thing" for a few days so you can say you've done it. They make a real effort to get you to reform the way you live, following a philosophy set down by each spa's founders. I think it's a very important thing for people to give serious consideration to—and most have not.

L: Sounds intense—you actually had time to work while there?

Doug: Yes. It's amusingly coincidental that I happen to have been at a health spa when I wrote an article for the *Casey Report,* on the so-called national health care crisis. That is, of course, mostly hysteria. Overhauling the US medical system will do absolutely nothing to improve the health of the population. American medicine is extremely good for acute problems and diseases, but when it comes to health maintenance, it's next to useless.

You know, Michael Moore, who is physically obese, intellectually dishonest, and philosophically unsound (what a pathetic combination—he should run for Congress), made the argument in his ridiculous movie that the average Cuban is healthier than the average American. That's totally correct—but it has absolutely nothing to do with the medical care system. The average Cuban isn't healthier than the average American because his medical care system is better. Cuba has a horrible—actually, a primitive health care system. The technology stopped advancing there back in 1960, and the doctors stopped learning new things in that year… medicines… nothing has changed since 1960. But the average Cuban *is* in much better health than the average American.

There are two reasons for that: he has a much better diet, which is to say that he eats way fewer calories (and they are unrefined calories), and he gets a lot more exercise than the average American.

When things change in Cuba, so that they have a diet like that of the average American and the same kind of transportation as the average American, then the average Cuban will be in much *worse* shape.

People conflate the health of a population with a country's medical system, when these things really have almost nothing to do with each other. Health care is a matter of personal responsibility, and personal discipline; it's about proper diet, exercise, and lifestyle. Medical care is about extraordinary measures for acute conditions. Americans foolishly conflate the two things. It's an example of why using words accurately is so important.

What this actually shows is the degraded state of American society. Instead of taking some personal responsibility for their health and lifestyle choices, they try to rely on medicos to engage in heroic efforts to keep them alive with tubes up their noses after they've become flaccid and bloated from a lifetime of bad habits.

L: This reminds me of the way the Romans were said to have gorged themselves at banquets until they couldn't eat anymore, induce vomiting, and then gorge again… But that might actually be healthier than what so many Americans seem to want to do, which is to eat all they want and then have it removed surgically later.

Doug: Yes, it really is awful. It's all about disguising symptoms, instead of addressing the actual causes of the problems. I think that what they do at these spas could be a big part of the answer. Unfortunately, they are not cheap. They'll run you about $500 to $1,000 per day, all in, and that can add up quickly. Then again, five-star hotels in major cities cost almost that much today. Plus, at the spa, you're getting three excellent meals and all the exercise classes that you can take. It's money well spent—it's money invested in your health, which can reduce future health expenses.

If I could manage to take the time, I would definitely spend a month at one of these top spas next year.

And I've got to say, this is one of the reasons I'm so excited about what we're doing down at _La Estancia de Cafayate_[1].

L: Is that a shameless plug?

Doug: Yes, I'm not prone to feeling shame, but in this case, there's no call for it, anyway. The whole place is being built to promote a spa-type lifestyle. Everything from the quality of the gym and amenities, to the food that's going to be grown on site.

L: Okay. You mentioned a "proper spa." What does that mean to you?

Doug: Well, there are probably thousands of places in the US that call themselves spas these days or claim to offer a spa experience. They'll have a good gym, and you can get a massage. Fine. Great start. But my idea of a proper spa is a place where you can start the day with Qi Gong at 6:00 am…

L: Start your day with _what?_

Doug: Qi Gong. It's an ancient Chinese form of meditative exercise, with an emphasis on breathing and holding positions—some similarities with yoga. Then a yoga class at 7:00 for an hour, a water aerobics class at 8:00, and breakfast at 9:00. Chill out for an hour, pump some iron in the gym, and then have lunch. Do some work or reading in the afternoon, go for a swim, have a massage at 5:00, and then a nice dinner. And you might add some things according to your individual interest, like, say, adding a boxing class, or Tai Chi, which I enjoy whenever they are offered. Or a cooking class.

That's a day at a proper spa. Pumping iron in the gym and a massage are great, but only a start.

L: So, you're doing all of this every day, and you lost six pounds in ten days—

Doug: Yes, but the process would have accelerated if I'd stayed longer. It takes a while to get off the mark. I think that if I'd stayed there for a month, I would have dropped a solid 25 pounds and built a lot of muscle out of what remained. In your normal day-to-day life, there are just too many distractions.

L: Okay, okay, but I gotta ask: you're doing all this stuff and you lost weight while they were feeding you rabbit food—didn't you get hungry? Ever feel weak?

Doug: No—this is the most amazing thing! I honestly was never hungry while I was there. A proper spa diet is programmed to include enough bulk so that you are never hungry. Absolutely amazing.

L: I find that hard to believe…

---

1. www.totallyincorrectbook.com/go/114

Doug: I was never hungry the whole time. In fact, when I stepped away from the table, I sometimes felt like I'd had too much to eat. It was shocking. That's what a properly programmed diet can do for you.

You know, one impetus for my going to the spa this time is that I had a really bad horse accident. It was a new pony. I got on him and he started bucking—and he bucked, and bucked, and bucked—and then he got really serious about getting me off his back. He sent me flying, and I couldn't walk for a day. If I hadn't gone to this spa, I would have been sedentary for the last two weeks, nursing my wounds and feeling sorry for myself.

Getting down to the spa got me exercising, and all sorts of moving around that I would not otherwise have done, having just been severely injured.

L: So… If I'm interested in trying this out, how do you recommend I proceed?

Doug: Get started *now*. I'm just telling you this because I really believe it's important. You know what they say: when you're young, you trade health for money, and later in life, you trade money for health. I'm telling you that if you take advantage of proper spa services, you don't have to make that trade-off.

L: Very well. Thank you.

Doug: My pleasure—and I really mean it: do it.

Doug Casey on Civil War, Past and Potential

March 11, 2011

L: So Doug, we're on the cusp of a major turning point of US Federal Reserve policy. "QE or not QE?" That is the question. What do you think? Is The Bernanke going to pull the handle on the toilet he's thrown the dollar into or let it mellow for a while?

Doug: I think he'll be forced to pull the handle and create trillions more dollars. The government has over a trillion of debt it has to roll over in the months to come, plus it has to finance a trillion-dollar deficit—at a minimum. The Chinese and the Japanese want to get rid of the US paper they have—they're not going to buy more. The only logical buyer is the Fed, so the dollar's fate is sealed, as far as I'm concerned. Meanwhile, there's something else important on my mind I'd like to talk about: the US so-called Civil War.

L: [Blinks] Ah… Okay. Why now?

Doug: Several reasons. For one thing, we've just passed the sesquicentennial, or 150th anniversary of its start. For another, it's one of the most misunderstood events in American—and world—history, with consequences that still affect us today. And also, because we might be within a few years of seeing trouble on that level in the US again.

L: Are you saying the economic crisis will turn into a revolution?

Doug: No, not necessarily, but it could. I think Stephen Jay Gould was right with his concept of <u>punctuated equilibrium</u>[1] in terms of geological history. Basically, it holds that things progress very slowly for long periods of time, then evolve very quickly after some catastrophic event upsets the balance. You can make the case that human history is like that, too.

A good example is France of 1789. Nothing had really changed, politically, for centuries. Then a tipping point was reached, and the totally dysfunctional

1. www.totallyincorrectbook.com/go/115

and corrupt monarchy was overthrown. Unfortunately, it was replaced with something even worse—Robespierre and the Terror—and then Napoleon, who was really just a beta version of Hitler or Stalin.

Anyway, things can change rapidly and radically when they reach a certain point. It's like water; it heats and heats, then at 212° Fahrenheit, it changes into steam, which is totally different. I think a case can be made that we may be at a point like that now in the US. I think that 1861–1865 was like that for the US as well. Anyway, today's world is a different topic. Let's retro-rock for the moment.

L: Right then; where to start?

Doug: First, as always, with definitions. It's incorrect to call it a "civil war."

L: Can a war ever be civil, anyway?

Doug: No, but that's not the point. A civil war is a conflict between two factions for control over the government. The Spanish Civil War of the 1930s was a real civil war. The unpleasantness of 1861–65 in America wasn't. It was a war of secession—albeit a failed one. The Confederates never wanted to take over the government in Washington. To the contrary, they wanted no part of it.

L: Or as L. Neil Smith[2] puts it, it was the "Second American Revolution."

Doug: That's a good way to look at it as well. Just as the 13 colonies wanted to shake off their rulers in London in 1776, four-score and five years later the 11 states of the South wanted to shake off their rulers in DC. In 1865, however, the wrong side won.

L: I understand what you mean about the wrong side winning, but many of our readers don't share our context. Honest Abe freed the slaves. "A house divided cannot stand." America wouldn't exist today—QED.

Doug: To the victors go the spoils, but what's more important, the writing of the history books. A whole complex of myth has been created about the War Between the States, and it's politically incorrect to hold that there was any justice to the Southern cause. As with most everything everyone believes, a great deal of it is inaccurate—sometimes wildly inaccurate, or even the complete opposite of accurate.

First, Honest Abe (whom we debunked a little in our conversation on presidents) didn't care about the plight of the slaves. He did not free them right away, and when he did free them, his "Emancipation Proclamation" did so only in the South. He was losing an unpopular war—his move was a desperate attempt to incite insurrection in the South, and thereby debilitate his enemy.

---

2. www.totallyincorrectbook.com/go/116

So, although slavery was a bone of contention, it was only one cause for the war. Myth incorrectly portrays it as *the* cause. That makes the victors look righteous. More important, and basic, were the economic causes. The US had significant tariffs on imported machinery and goods, which benefited Northern manufacturers and penalized Southern planters. I urge anyone who's interested in the period to read <u>Lincoln Unmasked</u>[3] by Thomas DiLorenzo.

Second, a house divided *should* not stand. The argument was that America needed to remain one strong country to fight off powerful European nations that might turn hostile. That's bunk. America had already fought off the mighty British Empire twice, and Europe—as always—was embroiled in its own problems. If peaceful secession had been allowed, the two countries would have been each other's largest trading partners and allies. But even if the danger of foreign aggression had been real, it would not justify forcibly keeping people in a union they no longer wanted to be part of. It's like a husband forcing a wife he loathes—and who despises him—to stay married to him because their crops will fail if they don't work together on the farm. Other solutions could be found. But even if true, nothing justifies the use of force on someone who does not consent and does not aggress.

L: Well, the South did start the fight by firing on Ft. Sumter.

Doug: Yes—a stupid move. If they had just gone about their business and waited for the North to fire the first shots, people around the world would have seen it as they themselves described it: the "War of Northern Aggression." Hubris is the root cause of so many unnecessary failures throughout history. Hubris was behind the <u>first battle of Ft. Sumter</u>[4]. Anyway, even though nobody was killed in the battle, it inflamed the North, and the war was on. And it's very hard for a small agrarian society to beat a large industrial society.

But the point I was making was a matter of principle—the right of secession. I have zero inclination to defend the South in any other way. The Confederate government turned the South into a police state, just as the Federals did the North. But they had a right to secede. If any group of people decides to leave a larger group, that is not aggression, and there is no ethical way to stop them. Secession may have costs, and there may be contractual obligations to deal with, but secession itself is not violence.

L: I would call it a fundamental human right. No one should be forced to be part of a group they don't want to belong to. The same is true if it's a marriage, a church, a labor union, or a nation.

---

3. www.totallyincorrectbook.com/go/117
4. www.totallyincorrectbook.com/go/118

Doug: Right. So, if the South had been allowed to secede, there would have been two Americas, the USA and the CSA. If that had happened, enormous loss of life and property would have been avoided. Both North and South would have been far richer and freer—and the South would have avoided being a backwater for hillbillies for the next century. The war was a total disaster in every way.

And if Europeans or others had wanted to attack, the war so weakened America, it actually created the most appealing invitation possible to do so.

Getting back to the point about Honest Abe, if the South had split off, slavery wouldn't have lasted long anyway. It was an uneconomic, dying institution. Chattel slavery is an economic institution, not to be confused with the abduction and imprisonment of individuals for other criminal purposes. It only works for brute labor—in other words, in an agrarian economy. The industrial age put an end to slavery the world over—I think Brazil was the last to give it up, in 1888. It would have happened even sooner in the South. So the war was unnecessary and pointless from every angle.

L: Okay, but you spoke of lingering effects… This is all very interesting, but why does it matter now?

Doug: Well, principles always matter, and I do believe in the right to secede. Oddly, so does the US government, when it comes to other peoples in far-off lands, like Kosovo and Sudan. Consistency has never been Uncle Sam's strong suit. But to answer your question, there are two things that I think are important legacies that may become even more important in the years to come.

First is that since the slavery issue was settled by force instead of by consensus, it wasn't truly *settled*—one side's views were imposed on the other by force, and, predictably, the losers dug their heels in and did everything possible to resist the foreign solution. That resulted in the Jim Crow laws, the Ku Klux Klan, and general race hatred that bedeviled the former slaves for more than 100 years. It still divides the US along racial lines today.

People who think this was all solved by Martin Luther King and believe we now all live happily in one big multicultural family are sticking their heads in the sand. These forcibly united states are not one homogeneous culture. The melting pot has stopped working. The US is perhaps now more deeply divided than ever, along several different cultural lines, race being a part of the mix. Yes, blacks and whites are getting along better now than they did 50 years ago. But that's not a function of anti-discrimination laws and forced integration, it's a function of technology and communication. I'm of the opinion that the US would never have had the kind of serious race problems it has had, if Lincoln had simply let the South go its own way. Blacks in Canada or Brazil haven't had the kind of problems we've seen in the US. The War Between the States created hatred and distortions that lingered for generations.

L: Just to make sure we're clear here; you are not saying that abolishing slavery was a bad thing, nor that every day the laws enabling slavery were on the books was not a horrific violation of human rights. All you are doing is pointing out—as a matter of history and economics—that the way the matter was dealt with has consequences.

Doug: Right. Slavery is an institution of pre-industrial societies. It existed all over the world, across countries, cultures, and races, for thousands of years. It only really started disappearing with the beginning of the Industrial Revolution, in the mid-1700s. It's completely inconsistent with a free-market, capitalist society, partly because capitalism rests on strict property rights. And the primary and most basic form of property is your own body. One person can't own another.

But another legacy of the war is that it turned what had been a confederation of sovereign states, joined together out of mutual interest, into one super-state. That set the stage for the vast and destructive expansions of central government power we've seen since then, including the Federal Reserve Act, the Income Tax, Prohibition, involvement in the World Wars, FDR's New Deal, Lyndon Johnson's Great Society, the Forever War on Terror, and the current government's mind-boggling fiscal irresponsibility. One thing flows from the other.

At this point, the Super State is out of control. It took a long while for the whole contrivance to build up the head of steam it now has. I think it's over-heating and looks close to blowing. The War Between the States was a major turning point, and unfortunately the country turned in the wrong direction.

L: You make me feel like I really am sitting on a powder keg with the fuse lit…

Doug: Well… You are. A close friend, who's a generation older than I am, was just telling me that I never have anything nice to say. I can see that it seems that way, but I didn't fill the keg, and I didn't light the fuse. I'm just trying to warn people of what I see; every thinking person should take immediate steps to protect his property and person. If I'm wrong, you might spend more than necessary on "insurance"—but you buy insurance because the future is uncertain.

L: It is what it is, and if the world is in trouble, speaking the truth is going to sound negative. Here's something positive: as bad as it's gotten, the state has not locked you up. They use the so-called General Welfare clause of the US Constitution for everything else, why not use it as a justification for arresting you for undermining the economic recovery with your negative commentary? They think the economy's engine runs on confidence, not production (though we both know it's just a con job). So almost anybody can be a threat to national security. When they arrest you for being an "attitude terrorist," we'll know things have gone unmistakably and undeniably too far. You're more than a gadfly, you're our canary in the coal mine—watching for what happens to you could give us our last signal to head for the exits before they are slammed shut.

Doug: Glad to be of service. Actually, I may not be such a great coal-mine canary, because I have every intention of getting out, and staying out, of the US when it gets that bad. Going back to the Civil War, if you're smart, you'll follow the lead of Rhett Butler who—as I recall in *Gone with the Wind*—spent most of the war in Europe.

L: What would be your signal that it's time to head for an extended stay in Argentina, Panama, Switzerland, Thailand, or wherever people have set up their vacation homes/redoubts?

Doug: Hm. Good question. It already makes my skin crawl every time I arrive in the US and have to go through Customs and Immigration… The recent conviction of Bernard von NotHaus for "economic terrorism[5]" after he circulated warehouse receipts for gold and silver comes pretty close; he may be our canary. The use of black-armored riot police to crush an annual block party[6] at Western Illinois University comes close as well. There's something new every day. Since the death of Osama[7], the US has ramped up its terror fear factor several notches. *Boobus americanus* is being trained to "See something, say something." You've now got nincompoops like Alberto Gonzales saying domestic terrorists are everywhere[8], and Charles Schumer saying the TSA has to monitor trains like it does airplanes.

The writing on the wall is pretty clear.

L: And the pressure is building. But you still come back to the US for conferences—what would it take to make you stay away completely?

Doug: I'm not sure, but fighting in the streets would show that the pressure cooker is blowing its gaskets.

L: Something to think about. Okay, Sunshine, you say you always like to look on the bright side—any investment implications you can comment on constructively?

Doug: Well, you could invest in private prison corporations; they will probably do well as the state incarcerates an ever-larger fraction of the population.

5. www.totallyincorrectbook.com/go/119
6. www.totallyincorrectbook.com/go/120
7. www.totallyincorrectbook.com/go/121
8. www.totallyincorrectbook.com/go/122

You could look for companies that sell weapons and armor to law enforcement agencies. But those things are intolerably slimy in today's world—entirely apart from the fact that stocks are generally overpriced.

I'm sticking to basics: go short government bonds and long on vital commodities: energy, agriculture, and precious metals. And I'm keeping my eyes open for the appearance of new bubbles, which will arise from the trillions of new currency units The Bernanke will create. This is nothing new, but that doesn't make it any less important.

L: Everything the governments of the world have done in response to the economic crisis is only making the situation worse. The world is slipping into an inflationary spiral that's going to send commodities prices much higher.

Doug: Added to this volatile mix are uprisings in the Muslim world, fear of technology in the wake of the Japanese earthquakes, and all sorts of other black swans settling around us. Each one sends shock waves of panic through the global financial system, and gold, which I've always seen as a "fear barometer," responds.

L: A fear barometer. There's a great, positive note to end on, so let's stop there.

Doug: Until next week, then.

Doug Casey on Speculators' Fiction

Nov 11, 2009

Doug: You're in Chile, I'm in Argentina, and we're talking through our computers… for free. The next step might be the "communicators" of *Star Trek*. Actually, we're almost there with smartphones. Life increasingly resembles science fiction, and we often refer to sci-fi. So let's talk about it.

L: I'm an avid sci-fi fan too, but don't you think that a lot of our readers are busy professionals with little time on their hands for reading space fantasies?

Doug: If they are, they are neglecting their own education as speculators. That's because SF is not really "science fiction" but, as Robert Heinlein used to say, it's *speculative fiction*.

You know, there are all these think tanks that try to predict the future, but in my view, authors of speculative fiction have done a *much* better job predicting the future. It's much more entertaining to read their work than some dry theoretical paper, and the authors have to draw a broader picture of social implications and express the consequences of future developments in human terms, in order to write good stories. If you're subscribing to futurology magazines and reports, throw them all away and buy some good science-fiction books instead.

L: Can you give us some examples of such predictions, ones that matter? I remember that Heinlein invented the waterbed in *Stranger in a Strange Land*, but I'm not sure that changed the course of history.

Doug: That's true, he did, but he didn't file a patent on the idea and didn't profit from it. The most famous example is probably that of Arthur C. Clarke, who invented the idea of communication satellites—an idea that mattered a great deal, but sadly he, too, didn't patent it.

L: Wow, that's major. I didn't know that.

Doug: Totally true. I used to be in what we now call snail-mail communication with Clarke. At one point, a relative of mine was visiting Sri Lanka, where he lived. I mentioned it and he was gracious enough to spend a day with her. I also spoke with Robert Heinlein on the phone once.

L: Lucky you! The closest I got was a letter from Virginia Heinlein.

Doug: Well, I wish I'd really gotten to know them, since they're among the top SF writers of all time—though the genre really only came into its own in the 1950s. A third one, I'd say, was Isaac Asimov. But I feel very close to Clarke and Heinlein, especially Heinlein. His _Rocket Ship Galileo_[1] was the first SF book I ever read, when I was ten years old. Coincidentally, that happens to be the first SF book Heinlein published.

L: There are several SF authors I think of as being like fathers to my mind. It seems to me that a large part of the values I hold, and the way I think, not just about the universe, but man's and my own place in it, was deeply influenced by them. Especially Heinlein.

Doug: I would put Heinlein first as well. He was very prolific, and I haven't read all of his books, but he has written three that are among my all-time favorite works of fiction. Just fantastic books—no pun intended.

The Moon Is a Harsh Mistress[2] is a book about a future revolution—it's absolutely required reading. There are many interesting political themes in the book, as well as historical allegory, as a small and poor colony (the Moon) breaks away from a wealthy and much larger power (the Earth). There are also interesting technological points Heinlein was absolutely right about, as, from a military view, you always want the high ground, and the Moon _is_ the high ground over all of the Earth. It also has a thoughtful and unique take on the emergence of artificial intelligence.

L: It's also the only book in which Heinlein mentions Ayn Rand by name... at least as far as I can recall.

Doug: Indeed. Professor Bernardo de la Paz, who's sort of the intellectual leader of the revolution on the Moon, mentioned being able to find common ground with Randites, as they're called. The book is really a work of genius. It's inspiring. Required reading.

L: And number two?

Doug: _Stranger in a Strange Land_[3]. It's rather new-age for a writer with a military background, and a lot of military themes, but it's the same hard-thinking Heinlein, simply being more overtly philosophical. In the story, Michael Valentine Smith, the first human born on Mars (as a result of a mixed-gender

---

1. www.totallyincorrectbook.com/go/123
2. www.totallyincorrectbook.com/go/124
3. www.totallyincorrectbook.com/go/125

expedition that gets marooned on the red planet), comes back to Earth, with his mind full of Martian philosophy—and some seemingly supernatural powers that arise from that philosophy. The book was very popular in the 1960s, and it has stood the test of time.

L: It actually sparked something of a religion for a time. People were adopting Heinlein's Martian philosophy and starting "crèches" around the country.

Do you know if it's true that L. Ron Hubbard, another SF author, founded the church of Scientology as a result of Heinlein betting him he couldn't do it and make it stick?

Doug: There's no way to know the actual facts, of course, other than that Hubbard started researching Dianetics just after World War II. But they were friends, after all, and both SF writers. The model for the character of Michael Valentine Smith was supposed to have been Hubbard—there were supposed to be a lot of similarities between the two. The religion racket can be an easy way to make a million dollars, but I don't think that was on Hubbard's mind when he founded Scientology. A surprisingly large percentage of the human-potential movement was a direct result of his work. He was sincere in promoting it, notwithstanding a lot of negative PR surrounding the subject.

L: We'd need a time machine to find out. Okay, so what was your third favorite Heinlein book?

Doug: _Glory Road_[4], which is a fantasy. But I just really like the flavor of the book. I don't like all of his later books so much, but he was at his peak when he wrote this one, and it shows. There's another Heinlein book I've been told is superb, but which I haven't read. It's called _The Number of the Beast_[5]. Have you read it?

L: Yes, I have. I think I've read all his novels. That one was written when Heinlein started experimenting with the idea of multiple universes as a way to bring together characters from different story lines he'd written. Many Heinlein fans loved it, but I'm not sure anyone who chose that as a first Heinlein novel to read would find it to be more than a strange adventure. By the time Heinlein died in 1988, he'd written his most beloved characters into one happy family. I enjoyed it, but you're not alone in finding him past his prime in his later years.

Speaking of his prime, that's when Heinlein wrote his "juveniles" (great reads for adults as well) which are among his best. _Have Spacesuit, Will Travel_[6],

---

4. www.totallyincorrectbook.com/go/126
5. www.totallyincorrectbook.com/go/127
6. www.totallyincorrectbook.com/go/128

Podkayne of Mars[7], _Red Planet_[8], and _Star Beast_[9], among others, are books with great ideas, strong ethics, and fun stories.

Doug: Yes. Possibly in that class is _Farnham's Freehold_[10]. Moving on to the other top SF writers, my favorite book by Arthur C. Clarke, by far, is _Childhood's End_[11]. It's actually been quite predictive. He wrote that a long time ago—1953—and it seems to me that the way he described the social psychology of the world evolving was pretty much right on target. It's a great read, and cosmic in its significance—a book about the end of the world.

L: Or the beginning, depending on how you look at it.

Doug: If you wish. Asimov was great too. It's said that Clarke and Asimov decided between themselves that Clarke was the better SF writer, but that Asimov was the better science writer, and I think that's true—although Asimov's Foundation Trilogy is also something everyone should have on their lifetime reading list.

L: I read somewhere that Asimov's one regret about that story was the name he came up with for his super-science of the future. It actually explained and predicted aggregate human behavior. It was basically economics—Ludwig Von Mises' "praxeology[12]" writ large, but he called it "psycho-history."

Doug: Yes, and in some ways, you might say that what Strauss and Howe have done with their generation cycle theory[13] is the same. Great minds think alike.

L: Back to Clarke—you mentioned _Childhood's End_, but most folks who've heard of Clarke would think of him as the author of _2001: A Space Odyssey_[14]. What did you think of that book?

Doug: I thought it was excellent. The movie was great too, but as good as it was, the book was better. I recommend it, even to people who've seen the movie, as it was not quite the same.

L: Well, the book had an ending that made sense.

Doug: Yeah [laughs], that's right.

L: My friend James P. Hogan tells a story of getting to ask Clarke about the end of the movie after years of wondering what it meant. Actually, his complaining about that ending making no sense is what got Jim into writing SF and got

---

7. www.totallyincorrectbook.com/go/129
8. www.totallyincorrectbook.com/go/130
9. www.totallyincorrectbook.com/go/131
10. www.totallyincorrectbook.com/go/132
11. www.totallyincorrectbook.com/go/133
12. www.totallyincorrectbook.com/go/134
13. www.totallyincorrectbook.com/go/135
14. www.totallyincorrectbook.com/go/136

him invited to a science-fiction convention where he met Clarke. But when he asked Clarke what it meant, Clarke leaned over and whispered: "I have no idea!"

Doug: I was told by another SF writer, a past Eris Society attendee, that most of Clarke's ideas were actually mined from Olaf Stapleton's _Last and First Men_[15] and _Star Maker_[16]. I've got to say that in terms of pure scope, _Last and First Men_ and _Star Maker_ may be two of the most cosmic books ever written. _Last and First Men_ traces mankind over about two billion years into the future. The species devolves into rabbit-like creatures, then re-evolves into intelligent beings, and radically changes about two dozen times—and he wrote about this in the late '20s. Among other things, he predicted the atom bomb. It's not terribly well written from a literary point of view, I'm sad to say, but don't let that stand in your way if you haven't read it. It's just brilliant.

Back to Clarke, I also liked _Rendezvous with Rama_[17].

L: I did, too, but the sequels were not as amazing.

Doug: For some reason that's true of almost all sequels. But we can talk about that when we talk about movies someday.

L: Okay, what about Asimov? What else do you recommend, besides his _Foundation Trilogy_[18]?

[**Ed. Note:** The Foundation Trilogy is comprised of: _Foundation_[19], _Foundation and Empire_[20], and _Second Foundation_[21]. Late in his life, Asimov added more books to the series, and connected it to his _I Robot_[22] stories, but these three books are the story that influenced huge numbers of readers and writers for decades.]

Doug: He wrote a totally brilliant short story, _The Last Question_[23]. Literally cosmic.

Doug: Reaching back further, I'd recommend reading Jules Verne. It's all dated now, but remember that when he published his first two novels, the Civil War was still raging in the (now forcibly) United States. I just love all his stuff. The guy was a genius—he'd be on top of the heap if he were alive and writing today.

---

15. www.totallyincorrectbook.com/go/137
16. www.totallyincorrectbook.com/go/138
17. www.totallyincorrectbook.com/go/139
18. www.totallyincorrectbook.com/go/140
19. www.totallyincorrectbook.com/go/141
20. www.totallyincorrectbook.com/go/142
21. www.totallyincorrectbook.com/go/143
22. www.totallyincorrectbook.com/go/144
23. www.totallyincorrectbook.com/go/145

L: How about H.G. Wells? _The War of the Worlds_[24]? _The Time Machine_[25]?

Doug: I like both of those books. But Wells was an anomaly among SF writers.

L: He was a socialist.

Doug: He was a complete statist. And one of the great things about SF is that most writers in the genre are libertarian—some explicitly so.

L: I've wondered about that—why do you suppose that is? I know plenty of scientists and speculators who aren't libertarian at all. What is it about being the kind of thinker who can write good speculative fiction that makes such minds tend toward libertarian values?

Doug: I think that if you're drawn to science—or speculative fiction—you're drawn to the idea that people can maximize their personal opportunities, in every way possible. That naturally gives you a libertarian outlook.

L: Hmmm. That's a new theory to me—food for thought. What about newer writers—the ones still writing today? You've mentioned Neal Stephenson many times in our newsletters. The concept of the Casey Phyles (groups of people around the world who see things the way we do) comes from his book, _The Diamond Age_[26].

Doug: Yup—I'm a big fan of Neal Stephenson's. He's very sound and libertarian-oriented. I've also long been a big fan of David Brin, whose _Uplift_[27] series about humanity's lifting other species of animals to human intelligence will prove extremely predictive. His book _Earth_[28] accurately foresaw, among other things, what's now happening with everyone having web-linked video cameras, recording everything.

Two overtly libertarian SF writers today are L. Neil Smith, with his libertarian manifesto adventure novel called _The Probability Broach_[29] and J. Neil Schulman, in his now seemingly prophetic book about economic collapse in the US caused by too much government, called _Alongside Night_[30].

L: Yes, both Neils are strongly libertarian. L. Neil's books are particularly fun for folks who like guns. Other libertarian writers today include Jim Hogan, whom I mentioned before—his _The Mirror Maze_[31] is basically about libertarians winning a US presidential election. (Talk about fantasy!) F. Paul Wilson wrote the classic

---

24. www.totallyincorrectbook.com/go/146
25. www.totallyincorrectbook.com/go/147
26. www.totallyincorrectbook.com/go/148
27. www.totallyincorrectbook.com/go/149
28. www.totallyincorrectbook.com/go/150
29. www.totallyincorrectbook.com/go/151
30. www.totallyincorrectbook.com/go/152
31. www.totallyincorrectbook.com/go/153

economic-freedom-fighter-of-the-future story, _An Enemy of the State_[32]. Vernor Vinge is a fantastic writer who helped popularize the technology singularity concept we spoke of in our CWC on technology in his meta-novel, _Across Realtime_[33]. And Ken McLeod, the Scottish libertarian SF writer whose books like _The Stone Canal_[34] might be more carnal than cosmic, but they sure do stretch your mind.

What about non-libertarians?

Doug: A non-libertarian I like is Orson Scott Card, who wrote _Ender's Game_[35] and some follow-up books. I also like Greg Bear and Greg Benford— I'd read anything by those two guys. One of my favorite books of all time is called _Dragon's Egg_[36] by Robert Forward. It's a work of genius, about a civilization discovered on a neutron star. Very hard science, quite mind-expanding. Have you read it?

L: No… but… as you were talking just now, I ordered it from Amazon.

Doug: I'd recommend putting that high on the list to anyone. One more hard-science story is _Ringworld_[37], by Larry Niven—another mind-expanding "must read." More on the fantasy end of the spectrum, I have to say that I enjoyed C.S. Lewis's _Space Trilogy_[38].

[**Ed. Note:** The _Space Trilogy_ consists of: _Out of the Silent Planet_[39], _Perelandra_[40], and _That Hideous Strength_[41].]

Another brilliant must-read book I reviewed in _Strategic Investing_ years ago is A.E. van Vogt's _The Voyage of the Space Beagle_[42].

And I guess you'd have to classify Ayn Rand's _Atlas Shrugged_[43] as SF.

L: Not much on the science, but yes, there was some, and it proposed a future world undergoing great changes.

Doug: And like a lot of SF, it's becoming reality.

You know, maybe it shouldn't, but it astounds me that SF has not really broken into the realm of honored literature, at least not in the eyes of the powers that be. This is just more evidence of how intellectually constipated most literary types are.

---

32. www.totallyincorrectbook.com/go/154
33. www.totallyincorrectbook.com/go/155
34. www.totallyincorrectbook.com/go/156
35. www.totallyincorrectbook.com/go/157
36. www.totallyincorrectbook.com/go/158
37. www.totallyincorrectbook.com/go/159
38. www.totallyincorrectbook.com/go/160
39. www.totallyincorrectbook.com/go/161
40. www.totallyincorrectbook.com/go/162
41. www.totallyincorrectbook.com/go/163
42. www.totallyincorrectbook.com/go/164
43. www.totallyincorrectbook.com/go/165

L: As we discussed in our CWC on education.

Doug: Yes. I have little use for English professors. Their standard complaint is that SF isn't "great literature"—which is nothing more than a foolish and unsubstantiated opinion. The relevant fact of this matter is that a variation of Pareto's law applies: 80% of everything is crap. And of the 20% that's left, 80% is just mediocre. So, of course 80% of SF is crap—but so is 80% of everything else. The best speculative fiction, the top 4%, is world-class literature. And it has much greater ideational content—by an order of magnitude—than any other genre of literature. That more than makes up for the lack of poetry in some of the prose.

L: What matters more; a book that challenges your mind to think in new directions, or <u>onomatopoeia</u>[44]?

Doug: Exactly. No question. Anyone who wants to claim to be a well-read person has to read speculative fiction. In fact, my two favorite areas for reading have long been ancient literature and speculative fiction—bracketing the two ends of the spectrum of time, if you will.

L: Perhaps so, chronologically. But I suspect the ancients would have been looking around at a world that was new to them and full of mysteries and unexplained frontiers—just the sort of things SF authors tend to write about.

Doug: Yes, it's very interesting. Paradoxical, in some ways. The Greek and Nordic myths are actually a form of SF.

L: Okay, so, you've given us a long list of books to stretch our minds. Are there any investment implications to this, other than the general encouragement to embrace the kind of forward-thinking every speculator needs? Do you actually think about this stuff when you're considering new areas to speculate in, or writing for *The Casey Report*?

Doug: I would say this: you improve your skill in the markets by knowing more than your competitors about the world, in depth and in breadth and in all its aspects. Speculative fiction is one of the best ways to expand your knowledge level quickly and enjoyably. Since that gives you a leg up on your competitors, I don't think of this as mere recreational reading. Don't just think about things that are; think about things that could be. If someone does not explore this huge, undervalued form of education, they have a blind spot.

L: Makes sense to me. Thanks!

Doug: Remember: if you have a blind spot, you're much easier to blindside. Until next week.

---

44. www.totallyincorrectbook.com/go/166

Doug Casey on Tax Day

April 11, 2012

L: Doug, the Taxman[1] cometh, at least for most US citizens who file their annual tax papers on April 15. We get a lot of letters from readers who know about your international lifestyle and wonder about the tax advantages they assume it confers. Is this something you care to talk about?

Doug: Yes; something wicked this way comes, indeed. But first, I have to say that as much as I can understand the guy who flew his airplane into an IRS building, as we once discussed[2], I do not encourage anyone to break the law. That's not for ethical reasons—far from it—but strictly on practical grounds. The Taxman can and will come for you, no matter how great or small the amount of tax he expects to extract from you. The IRS can impound your assets, take your computers, freeze your accounts, and make life just about impossible for you, while you struggle to defend yourself against their claims and keep the rest of your life going. The number of IRS horror stories[3] is beyond counting. As the state goes deeper into insolvency, its enforcement of tax laws will necessarily become more draconian. So you absolutely don't want to become a target.

L: So… just bow down and lick the boots of our masters?

Doug: Of course not. People can and should do everything they can to pay as little in taxes as possible. This is an ethical imperative; we must starve the beast. It could even be seen as a patriotic duty—if one believes in such things—to deny revenue to the state in any way possible, short of endangering yourself.

Starving the beast may be the only way to force it back into its cage—we certainly can't count on politicians to make the right choices—they're minions of the state. They inevitably act to make it bigger and more powerful. It's

---

1. www.totallyincorrectbook.com/go/167
2. www.totallyincorrectbook.com/go/168
3. www.totallyincorrectbook.com/go/169

sad to see well-intentioned people supporting someone like Mitt Romney because they naïvely think he'll reduce the size of the state and its taxes. The man has absolutely no ethical center; he'll just try to change the government to suit his whims.

L: Can you expand on the ethical imperative aspect?

Doug: Yes. The first thing is to get a grip on who owns the moral high ground. The state, the media, teachers, pundits, corporations—the entire establishment, really—all emphasize the moral correctness of paying taxes. They call someone who doesn't do so a "tax cheat." As usual, they have things upside down.

Let's start with a definition of "theft," something I hold is immoral and destructive. Theft is to take someone's property against his will, i.e., by force or fraud. There isn't a clause in the definition that says, "unless the king or the state takes the property; then it's no longer theft." You have a right to defend yourself from theft, regardless of who the thief is or why he is stealing.

It's much as if a mugger grabs you on the street. You have no moral obligation to give him your money. On the contrary, you have a moral obligation to deny him that money. Does it matter if the thief says he's going to use it to feed himself? No. Does it matter if he says he's going to feed a starving person he knows? No. Does it matter if he's talked to other people in the neighborhood, and 51% of them think he should rob you to feed the starving guy? No. Does it matter if the thief sets himself up as the government? No. Now, of course, this gets us into a discussion of the nature of <u>government as an institution</u>[4], which we've talked about before.

But my point here is that you can't give the tax authorities the moral high ground. That's important because decent people want to do the right thing. This is why sociopaths try to convince people that the wrong thing is the right thing.

If an armed mugger or a gang of muggers wanted my wallet on the street, would I give it to them? Yes, most likely, because I can't stop them from taking it, and I don't want them to kill me. But do they have a right to it? No. And every taxpayer should keep that analogy at the top of his mind.

L: I also believe that the <u>initiation of the use of force (or fraud, which is a sort of indirect, disguised, form of force) is unethical</u>[5]. It doesn't matter what the reason for it might be or how many people might approve of the action. But some people claim that taxation is really voluntary—the price one pays for living in society… and if I'm not mistaken, the US government says the federal income tax is voluntary.

---

4. www.totallyincorrectbook.com/go/170
5. www.totallyincorrectbook.com/go/171

Doug: [Snorts] That is a widely promoted lie. It's propaganda to help statists claim the moral high ground, confuse the argument, and intimidate people who aren't critical thinkers. Just try not volunteering to pay it and see what happens. Taxation is force alloyed with fraud—a nasty combination. It's theft, pure and simple. Most people basically admit this when they call taxation a "necessary evil," somehow mentally evading confrontation with the fact that they are giving sanction to evil.

I question whether there can be such a thing as a "necessary evil." Can anything evil really be necessary? Can anything necessary really be evil?

Entirely apart from that, if people really wanted anything the state uses its taxes for, they would, should, and could pay for it in the marketplace. Services the state now provides would be offered by entrepreneurs making a profit.

I understand, and am somewhat sympathetic, to the argument that a "night-watchman" state—a minimal government that provides police, courts and military—is acceptable. But since the state always has a monopoly of force, it inevitably grows like a cancer, to the extent that the parasite overwhelms and kills the host. That's where we are today.

I think a spade should be called a spade, theft should be recognized for what it is, and evil should be opposed, regardless of the excuses and justifications given for it. Ends do not justify means—and evil means lead to evil ends, as we see in the bloated, corrupt, dangerous governments we have all over the world.

L: That runs counter to the conventional wisdom, Doug. Evil or not, most people think taxation is part of the natural order of things, like rain or day and night. Death and taxes are seen as the two inevitable things in life, and you are a silly idealist—if not a dangerous madman—if you believe otherwise.

Doug: That saying about death and taxes is both evil and stupid; it's a soul-destroying and mind-destroying perversion of reality. It's evil, because it makes people reflexively accept the worst things in the world as permanent and inevitable.

As for death, technology is actively advancing to vanquish it. Who knows how far medicine, biotech, and nanotech can delay the onset of death? And taxes are, at best, an artifact of a primitive feudal world; they're actually no longer necessary (if they ever were) in an advanced, free-market civilization.

People also once thought the world was flat, that bathing was unhealthy, and that there was such a thing as the divine right of kings. Many things "everyone knows" just aren't so, and this is one of those.

A government—for those "practical" people who think they need one—that stuck to the basic core functions of police and courts to defend people against force and fraud and a military to defend against invasion, would cost a tiny, tiny fraction of what today's government costs, and that could be funded in any number of ways that essentially boil down to charging for services.

As it is now, the average US taxpayer probably works half of the year just to pay direct and indirect taxes. That doesn't even count the cost of businesses destroyed by regulation and lives lost to slow approval of new medical treatments by regulators, or a million other ways governments burden, obstruct, and harass people.

L: I just looked, and Tax Freedom Day[6] this year is April 17.

Doug: That means that all the work the average guy does until April 17 goes to pay for the government that failed to protect him on September 11, 2001, failed to protect him from the crash of 2008, and continues failing him every day. We pay for an organization bent on doing not just the wrong things, but the exact opposite of the right things in economics, foreign policy, and everything else we've talked about in all our conversations.

It's rather perverse that Emancipation Day[7]—the day the first slaves in the US were freed in the District of Columbia in 1862—is April 16. But what is a slave? He's someone who is deprived by force of the fruits of his labor. Sound familiar? I disapprove of slavery, in any form—including its current form.

However, Tax Freedom Day[8] is an incomplete way of looking at things. What's the cost to business forced to install equipment to meet government regulations? That's not paid as a tax, but it's a serious burden. There's something called Cost of Government Day[9] that's a somewhat more inclusive estimate of the burden the state imposes on the average guy…

L: I just looked for that too and don't see that a date for 2012 has been announced yet; but Cost of Government Day for 2011 was August 12. According to that estimate, the average US taxpayer slaved away for about two-thirds of the year to pay for the state and got to keep only a third of the fruit of his labor for his own benefit and improvement.

Doug: That may be a more accurate way of looking at the burden of government the average guy has to bear, but it still doesn't even begin to address what economists call "opportunity cost[10]." Basically, I don't just look at what the state we have costs us in cash, but in terms of the innovation and growth we don't have because of government policies, laws, and regulations. This covers

---

6. www.totallyincorrectbook.com/go/172
7. www.totallyincorrectbook.com/go/173
8. www.totallyincorrectbook.com/go/174
9. www.totallyincorrectbook.com/go/175
10. www.totallyincorrectbook.com/go/176

everything from new medicines to all sorts of new technologies to different forms of social and business organizations, to the cleaner intellectual atmosphere I think we'd have without government propaganda machines cluttering it up.

I don't believe in utopia, but I do believe our world could be far freer, healthier, and happier than it is today—without any divine intervention, magic, or changes in the laws of physics. Just a different path, every bit as possible as the one we've taken to where we are today.

L: As in the alternative reality L. Neil Smith wrote about in his book _The Probability Broach_[11]?

Doug: At least as far as the humans in that story go, yes, it's a good illustration of how much more advanced the world might be, based on a different turn of events.

Back in this world, I think that without any major differences in technological development and without assuming that people can be angels, the average standard of living worldwide would be much higher if... Well, there are lots of turning points, some of which we've discussed. Just in the 20th century, things would be very different if America had stayed out of WWI, or had not ratified the 16th Amendment to the Constitution, or had not elected FDR.

L: Okay, but those things did happen, and we live in the world we have today—the one you call a prison planet. How should people try to do what's right in such a world without ending up in jail?

Doug: First, it's important to think about what's actually possible, because people will not even try to reach for what they are sure is impossible. The world needs idealists to challenge us all to aim higher... including idealists willing to go to jail for what they believe in, like Thoreau[12]. But even he said that while he encouraged all people to disobey unjust laws, he wouldn't ask those who support families to get themselves locked up and leave their families destitute.

So my take is as we started out saying: It is both ethically and practically imperative to starve the beast. The less cooperation of any sort we give the state—but especially the less money we give it—the less mischief it can get into. We're unlikely to get politicians to vote for getting the state off our backs, out of our pocketbooks, out of our bedrooms, and out of other people's countries as a matter of principle, but we could see the state get out of places it doesn't belong simply for lack of funds.

And if everybody treated minions of the state with the contempt they deserve, most of them would quit and be forced to find productive work. As

11. www.totallyincorrectbook.com/go/177
12. www.totallyincorrectbook.com/go/178

Gandhi showed us, <u>civil disobedience</u>[13] can not only be an ethical choice, but a very powerful force for change.

L: Any specific advice?

Doug: Get a good accountant, take every deduction you can, and look for ways to legally reduce your tax burden. For example, our readers should know that charitable contributions in the US get deducted *after* the alternative minimum tax wipes out other deductions. That means that a substantial fraction of every dollar you give a registered 501(c)(3) nonprofit does *not* go to the federal government.

Now, as you know, I don't believe in charity, at least not in the institutional sense, but wasting money on charities is far, far better than giving it to the government to use bombing innocents and creating enemies for generations to come. And if that charity happens to be something like the <u>Institute for Justice</u>[14], the <u>Fully Informed Jury Association</u>[15], or any of the other libertarian think tanks dedicated to reducing the size and scope of government, you get to help fight the beast and starve it at the same time.

L: I do my <u>economics and entrepreneurship camps</u>[16] in Eastern Europe under the auspices of the <u>International Society for Individual Liberty</u>[17]—of which I should disclose that I am a director. I have to admit that it pleases me greatly to see funds that would have gone into making bombs to drop on foreigners and hiring more goons in uniform to oppress people at home redirected to something I consider constructive.

But what about the international diversification question: can that help reduce your tax burden back home?

Doug: It's different for different countries, and each individual should consult a tax specialist with the details of his or her own case, or proposed case. However, there is an <u>exclusion for Americans</u>[18] who live abroad for a whole tax year—it was around $100,000 the last I looked. So there are very good tax reasons for Americans to live abroad. There are even better reasons for Canadians, Europeans, and almost everyone else to leave their native country—many can live 100% tax-free.

I guess it's just a sad testimony to the medieval-serf mentality that most people suffer from that few people take advantage of this. They're born someplace, and

---

13. www.totallyincorrectbook.com/go/179
14. www.totallyincorrectbook.com/go/180
15. www.totallyincorrectbook.com/go/181
16. www.totallyincorrectbook.com/go/182
17. www.totallyincorrectbook.com/go/183
18. www.totallyincorrectbook.com/go/184

they stay rooted there, like a plant. Oh well, everybody basically makes his own bed, reaps what he sows, and gets what he deserves…

However, as appealing as the "permanent tourist"[19] idea is, I recommend international living[20] first and foremost as a way to protect your assets. As we've discussed before, real estate in foreign countries cannot be repatriated or confiscated by the government that thinks of you as its milk cow. There is nothing illegal or nefarious about buying real estate abroad, and it could come in very handy if things get really chaotic back home, wherever that happens to be.

L: Okay… any investment implications to discuss?

Doug: Starving the state-beast is the right thing to do, ethically and practically, but I believe the state's days are numbered anyway. The thing to be aware of is that the beast won't go quietly, and in its death throes it can do a lot of harm. Still, like Nietzsche said, "That which is about to fall deserves to be pushed."

In the meantime, much higher taxes are on the way. More and more currency controls are coming. You may have heard that the US is contemplating a law denying issue or canceling the passport of anyone accused of owing more than $50,000 in taxes. I expect the transformation of what was once America into a police state to continue, and I expect other "developed" nations—especially Europe, Canada, and Australia—to follow suit. And this will happen whether or not the global economy exits the eye of the storm as I expect it to.

So you want to rig for stormy weather and invest for continuing crisis. Own gold for prudence, speculate on related stocks and other things that may benefit from government profligacy, and as we've just been saying, diversify your assets and personal living arrangements internationally.

The day is coming when your local government may stop seeing you as a milk cow and start seeing you as a beef cow, and you want to have options before that day.

L: The Casey mantra. Any chance you're wrong?

Doug: Anything's possible. But we just asked ourselves that question in our conversation on the illusion of recovery[21], and I just don't see a way out for the old economic order.

L: Hedging one's bets against social chaos may sound a bit extreme, but as an option, it sure is something that can help one sleep better at night.

---

19. www.totallyincorrectbook.com/go/185
20. www.totallyincorrectbook.com/go/186
21. www.totallyincorrectbook.com/go/187

Doug: I didn't formulate the rules for this crazy game; I'm just trying to play it competently.

L: Right then. Until next week.

Doug: Next time.

Doug Casey on Cars—
Past, Present, and Future

August 12, 2009

L: Doug, last week we talked about energy, including your thoughts on what's in store for the oil markets. That naturally leads me to ask about something that I know is near and dear to your heart: the automobile. Especially high-performance cars—which were the basis of your first capitalist venture.

Doug: It's appropriate that we talk about cars now, with the recent bankruptcy of General Motors. I've always been interested in cars. The first car I had was a 1964 Pontiac GTO, with the tri-power and all the extras. Throughout my life, I've always had high-performance cars. I had a couple 289 Cobras. I had a 427 Cobra.

And yes, the first business I got into was importing Ferraris to the United States. This was in 1967. In those days, there was a relatively small middle class in Europe. So you could either afford a new Ferrari (if you were rich), or a new Fiat (if you were not so rich), but there was no market for used Ferraris, because of the maintenance costs and social strictures that came with owning one. On the other hand, in the United States, there was even more of a middle class to society than there is today, and everybody wanted a used Ferrari. But there weren't many to be had in the US—so the prices were fairly high. Much higher than in Europe, where there was no market for them.

I was in college at the time, but I saw the opportunity and decided to act on it. I bought a 1962 250 GTE 2+2, in Milano.

L: Was that the four-seater?

Doug: Yes, although the backseats were pretty cramped. It was the car that Ford copied for their 1964 Mustang 2+2, and it was a lot of fun; it had a 3.0 liter V-12 with three 2-barrel Weber carbs. I drove it through a lot of Europe and went to a couple of driving schools, one at Montlhéry, the autodrome of Paris, the other at Monza in Italy. I then sold it, sight unseen, to a guy in Ohio. The price was so good, he couldn't resist it.

I went back to Milano to pick out a second Ferrari, a 330 GT 2+2. I had the bit in my teeth—I had plans to refine the business. Who knows, if I had done that, my entire life would have been different. But… stroke of fate. There was a truck passing a tractor on a blind curve in between the towns of Fribourg and Bern in Switzerland, and I had a catastrophic accident. It put me in the hospital for six weeks.

That put paid to my first business venture of importing used exotic cars to the United States, but I've stayed interested in cars.

L: What's your favorite car today?

Doug: Well, I've got to say that dollar for dollar, pound for pound, you can't beat a Corvette. Too bad it's a General Motors product—it's one of the very few that General Motors makes that's a decent car. More than decent; the Corvette is a fantastic car. It's a high-performance, light-weight, fine-handling economy car.

I have a Corvette I bought in 2004, and the car averages about 23 mpg in the city and about 26 or 27 mpg on the highway. In fact, I've noticed that while cruising in it over 100 miles per hour, even then, it averaged 26 mpg, according to the instant readout.

L: I always thought you were joking about Corvettes being economy cars, but it's true. My 2008 gets 30 mpg at 70 on a level highway—at that speed, it's barely ticking over at about 1,500 rpm. My average fuel economy, for the entire time I've had the car, including city driving and some racing, is 23.4 mpg.

I bought the car at your suggestion, because most of the time I drive, I'm driving by myself to an airport or to business meetings. It was silly to be driving my nine-passenger SUV like that—it gets literally half the mileage, and it's hard to park the beast in Vancouver to boot. For folks who drive a lot by themselves, or with just one passenger, the Corvette actually is an economy car.

Doug: Yes, they're fantastic cars. They don't need much maintenance. They use very little fuel. They don't rust. If anyone's looking for a high-performance car, I'd suggest the Corvette be the first on their list.

In New Zealand, where I live three months of the year, I've got a Toyota Supra Twin Turbo, which is almost as fast as the Corvette but isn't nearly as much fun. I've also got a Mazda RX-7, fantastic car, but I'm just too big to drive it comfortably. I let my normal-size friends who come to visit use it.

In Aspen, I've got a Porsche, the last of the air-cooled twin turbos with four-wheel drive, and it's a lot of fun to drive. But when I'm driving into town and I have to decide whether to take the Porsche or the Corvette, I usually take the Vette. The Porsche is actually faster, handles better, and in a road race, it'd probably win, but the Corvette is just easier to drive.

L: So, what's the ratio, dollar for dollar, as you say. The Porsche is a little faster, handles a little better, but it costs—what—three times more? Four?

Doug: In 1996, the year I bought my Porsche, it cost $105,000. That's about $144,000 in current dollars. In 2004, when I bought my Vette, I paid about $40,000 for it, which is about $46,000 today. So in real terms, the Porsche is more than three times more expensive—but it's not three times as much fun. The Porsche doesn't even give you a cup holder. And I promise you, when you change the oil or have anything done on the Porsche, it's going to cost you two or three times what it costs on the Vette as well.

The only car I'm looking at that I'd kinda like to get right now is a Ford GT. Perhaps that's because I have a soft spot in my heart for the Cobras from the '60s. I've driven one of the GTs—which they no longer make—and they're actually fantastic cars. The problem, however, is that the roads in the US are full of police, and they're full of other cars. These days, if the police pull you over for driving a car like the GT at the speeds that would be the whole point of owning the car, they'll take your license and they might even take the car.

I mean, in the '60s, when I was a bit wild and crazy, I was in a few road races with the police. And what would happen? They might throw you in jail for a night, give you a series of $50 tickets, and it was no big deal. I speak from personal experience.

But now it's serious business, and not just in the United States. In many countries in the world, if you're caught exceeding the speed limit by too much, you're in for some very serious consequences. That's one of the pluses about Argentina. Wide-open roads, few police, and they have a very Italian attitude towards speeding. Actually, I'm thinking of putting in a quarter-mile dirt track near Estancia de Cafayate as an additional amenity... dirt-tracking some cars with roll cages with a few friends is my idea of a good time.

L: You've got that right—fortunately, there's a track not far from where I live. With GM having gone bankrupt, what do you think will happen to the Corvette?

Doug: With GM having become a state-owned enterprise, I wonder if— just on general principles—they won't finally kill the Corvette. The administration might like to see it replaced with some dim-bulb Birkenstock car. So, not only should anyone looking for a performance vehicle put the Corvette first on their list, they should think about moving quickly if they want a new one.

Actually, when it comes to exotic cars, I think the market in them is going to collapse in the near future. That's especially so for Lamborghinis, Ferraris, Aston Martins, things of that nature.

That's for several reasons. First, there's every reason to believe that the price of oil is going to go way up, so people are going to be driving a lot less. Second, the social environment is going to be one in which you don't want to look like some rich guy who's still living in the '80s or '90s, driving an exotic car. Third, people are just not going to be able to afford these kinds of cars in the same numbers—and a lot of the people who have them are going to be selling them. Fourth, young people today are no longer car crazy; they'd actually rather play games on their computers.

There was a huge boom in exotic cars from the late '80s to the early '00s; people are treating them like instant collectibles, when they're really just depreciating consumer goods. By the time the public sees something as a "no lose" investment, the game is over; prices are going to collapse. Plus, the world really is going to switch over to hybrids and electric cars. So, if you want a Lamborghini and are willing to wait a few years, I think you're going to be able to pick up a real bargain.

In the mid-'80s, I recommended buying '60s muscle cars as a speculation. I personally bought a 1970 Herb Adams modified Trans Am but sold it way too soon because I didn't have a practical place to store it... really dumb of me. The peak came about four years ago when I saw a couple of Baby Boomers, guys my age, who bid a 1970 426 Hemi Dodge Charger up to $2 million. I couldn't believe it. Obviously they really wanted that car back in the day but couldn't afford it then.

But those days are over for a good many years to come. Probably a couple generations. Lots of cars like that will wind up in barns, and what was once $4,000, and then $2 million, could again go for whatever the equivalent of $4,000 is then...

L: So, how about those hybrids and all-electric vehicles—have you test-driven a Tesla Roadster?

Doug: No, but I'd like to try one. I have driven a Prius, which is not an unpleasant little car to drive, but it's just simple transportation. Hardly what I'd call a fun ride. The type of thing that makes a practical taxi for the city.

L: If I recall the numbers correctly, the Tesla Roadster accelerates at about the same rate as my Corvette—but it does it constantly from zero to 125 mph. And it does it without changing gears. So, in any situation in which you're not worried about your top speed, I could imagine that being a lot of fun.

Doug: Yes, I'm all for the new generation of electric cars that are going to be coming out. Some of them are going to have excellent technology and be great fun to drive. But it's still early days. I wouldn't buy one until the technology is thoroughly sorted and the market solidly established.

I think it's criminal, the way the government is trying to keep dinosaurs like General Motors and Chrysler alive. These things have been brain-dead—run by accountants—for decades, whereas there are new companies, like Tesla and others, being put together by a new generation of car guys that look to be able to build fantastic cars that are fun to drive. Unfortunately, the governments of the world make it hard to start a new venture, with all the regulations and so forth. So, instead of having hundreds of new electric car companies, which we would—and should—have, just as we had hundreds of gasoline-powered car companies a hundred years ago, we're going to have just a few. The state is the enemy of everything good and enjoyable in the world.

When I think of things as simple as cars, it really brings me back to a basic question I often ask people. It draws the line. And the question is: Do you hate the state or not?

You know my answer. The state is really the great predator. It's stalking you, and your standard of living, and your life. The state is not only keeping automotive technology twenty or thirty years behind the times, but it's keeping all technology from reaching levels most people think of as being only science fiction, like Star Trek.

L: I hope you're right, because forms of government change over time, and I believe the state as we know it was an industrial-era form that will not last long in the information age. Once it's out of the way, we may get to see some of your Star Trek technology.

Meanwhile, what about investment implications today? Obviously, you are not a GM fan, but they are coming out with an all-electric vehicle. So is Ford, and the Japanese too. Would you buy any of them, or the new innovators like Tesla?

Doug: I wouldn't touch the big companies, but getting into a start-up company in heavily regulated environment is really tough. With the government trying to keep the old dinosaurs alive and to keep their bloated, overpaid labor forces in their uneconomic jobs, they are not going to make it easy for the real green shoots—which would be the new entrepreneurs. Fact is, as I said before, that there should be hundreds of new auto companies, but there are only a half dozen or so serious ones around the world at this point.

Would I invest in them, if possible? That's very iffy. They are now going to be competing against what is becoming, effectively, a government monopoly.

L: Okay, well, how about farther up the food chain? What about suppliers, especially the battery manufacturers, and the energy metals miners?

Doug: Sure. I'd be much more prone to invest in a company that produces lithium, for example, because everyone's going to need it for car batteries. And that's true whether it's a government-run car company or an entrepreneurial company. That's because lithium batteries deliver the most power per weight of any battery technology on the market. So I'd be much more inclined to bet on something like a lithium explorer or producer than on a new car company.

Remember, Warren Buffett didn't become as successful as he is by buying every new start-up idea that came along (in which everything that can go wrong usually does). He can't look at small companies because of the size of the assets he manages, but if he could, he wouldn't even think of them unless they fit Graham-Dodd parameters. That means they've got to have a solid balance sheet, five years of growing earnings, etc., etc. Buying into a new car company is pure pie-in-the-sky speculation, not investing.

L: So, in your view, the best way to bet on the current automotive trend is to buy stocks related to the metals that will go into new generations of car batteries, and the energy commodities that will generate the electricity needed to charge those batteries.

Doug: Right. And if it's driving fun you're interested in, check out the new Corvettes. The Z06 packages give the new Vettes an agility more like that of a fast motorcycle than a car.

L: I sure love mine! Thanks for your time.

Doug: It's been fun. Till next week.

Doug Casey on Ethics

June 23, 2010

L: Doug, most religious people base their personal ethics on the moral mandates of their religions, and I know socialists who base their ethics on the utilitarian principle (or at least say they do). Both types seem shocked when someone like you or me—atheists, anarchists, and capitalists to boot!—refuse to do something that may seem profitable, on ethical grounds. So let's talk about ethics; what are they, what are yours, and how do you apply them?

Doug: Well, as always, let's start with a definition.

L: Sure. Webster's says:

1: The discipline dealing with what is good and bad and with moral duty and obligation.

2 a: A set of moral principles: a theory or system of moral values.

2 b: The principles of conduct governing an individual or a group.

2 c: A guiding philosophy.

2 d: A consciousness of moral importance.

3: (*Plural*) A set of moral issues or aspects.

Doug: These are all workable definitions, depending on the context we're discussing. Now, there are clearly some people who have no ethics at all, which is to say no principles. They act on the spur of the moment, just doing whatever seems like a good idea at the time. Then there are other people who have flawed principles that will consistently send them in the wrong direction. My own set of principles can be summed up in two statements:

1: Do all that you say you're going to do.

2: Don't aggress against other people or their property.

There are endless corollaries you can derive from this, but this is what it all boils down to.

L: The first one sets out the basis for contracts and fair conduct, the second one the basis for peaceful physical interaction. But the first is actually derived from the second, because breaking the first (committing fraud) is really just a deferred form of the second (initiation of force).

Doug: True enough, although I think it's helpful to make a distinction between force and fraud. I also think it's important to distinguish between ethics, an individual's own guiding principles, and morality, which is a set of community standards.

Morals, being politically derived artifacts, really only have a coincidental, or even accidental, connection to ethics. Morality is something that's dictated by a group or even imposed on a group by some kind of higher power. Ethics deals with the essence of right and wrong. Morality is just a construct of rules. It winds up being a bunch of precepts. Some have a basis in ethics. Others are just the consequence of people's fears, quirks, and aberrations.

The difference between ethics and morals is analogous to that between using a gyroscope or a radar to navigate. A gyroscope is an internal device that keeps you level and steady without reference to what's outside. Radar would use external cues, bounced off other people to tell you which way to go. Morality tells you what to do; ethics acts as a guide to help you determine, yourself, what you should do.

Similarly, ethics is a branch of philosophy, not religion. Ancient Greeks studied, wrote about, and placed a great deal of importance on ethics, the guiding principles of good action, completely apart from whatever their frisky gods were up to. For them, religion had basically nothing to do with ethics, except for providing edifying stories from time to time.

L: Okay, but what's the basis for your principles—or the one fundamental libertarian commandment of non-aggression that they resemble? Why is this any better than, for example, the Ten Commandments?

Doug: Which Ten Commandments? The part of Exodus 20 most people refer to when they say the "Ten Commandments" actually has more than 10 commands, and there's another version in Exodus 34, plus one in Deuteronomy 5. So the things are hardly written in stone, as it were. Some of the Bible's commandments are basic common sense, of course, especially if you use the "Thou shall not murder" translation instead of the "Thou shall not kill" version.

But the first three or four, depending on how you count them, are totally useless admonitions regarding a supernatural being, the existence of which is not supported by any evidence whatsoever. As ethical guidance goes, the list is rather confusing, with the parts governing the way people treat each other looking almost like afterthoughts, thrown in after all the instructions on how to worship.

The Ten Commandments impress me as an arbitrary agglomeration of moral precepts and commands. They lead to thinking you'll be all right if you do as you're told, instead of figuring things out for yourself. They get people into the mindset of following orders, even if the orders are goofy or irrelevant or arbitrary. The Ten Commandments got Western civilization off to a bad start.

L: In the New Testament, Jesus boiled it down to two principles, as you do: first, to love god, and second, to love your neighbor as yourself.

Doug: The second one, interpreted liberally, looks good at first. But it's not. Love isn't something you should hand out for free; it's something that should be earned and deserved. Otherwise, love is not virtuous—it's worthless and counterproductive. I believe in giving the other guy the benefit of the doubt and maintaining an attitude of good will towards others whenever possible. And I absolutely believe in cultivating a benevolent approach towards other people, creatures, and even inanimate objects. But to love any neighbor as one's self is idiotic and degrading; it leads to self-abasement and destroys self-respect.

The first one is nonsense to me. Which god? Allah? Zeus? Perhaps Yahweh, the one who calls himself "Jealous" in those commandments, periodically authorizes wholesale genocide, and says he will punish children for the sins of their fathers?

It appears most people in the US worship Jesus. Why not Baal or Quetzalcoatl? If you must debase yourself before some construct, it makes more sense to me to have a household god, as did the Romans, that represents and personifies the virtues that are important to you as an individual. My personal preference in gods are those that show nobility, as do many of the Greek gods, but especially the Norse gods. But I don't see what gods have to do with ethics. At least any more than Batman, Wonder Woman, or other super heroes do.

L: Okay, okay, but let's not get distracted. Religion is not today's subject. What's the basis of your two ethical principles? Why are they better than others?

Doug: They demonstrably work. They allow you to live with other people, in any society, and in any time, whether those people are enlightened philosophers or bloodthirsty pirates. Understanding those two laws is all one needs to interact peacefully and productively with others. Even more important, they're what you need to live with yourself—and you are the final judge of what you do; the values and morality of others are just opinions.

You could say the two laws are right because they obviously benefit others, but they actually benefit you the most—and it would be stupid to adopt principles that benefit you less. You could say, as an economist might, that they maximize efficiency and hence well-being among members of a society. They're quite practical, and it doesn't take a legal scholar to understand them. In fact, a six-year-old can understand them, rather intuitively.

L: Sounds like the utilitarian principle of the greatest good for the greatest number.

Doug: They happen to be pragmatic and utilitarian, although I must say I don't like pragmatists or utilitarians, because their principles are situational, fluid, and unsound. Someone who holds to those things could wind up committing all manner of depredations. But it's *because* my ethical principles are sound that they tend to produce the greatest good for the greatest numbers, not the other way around.

The problem I have with utilitarianism is that anyone can argue that anything, even the great atrocities committed by the Soviets, were right as rain, because they were intended for the greatest good. Pragmatism is anti-ethical because it holds something is right if it works; the Nazis fancied themselves to be pragmatists.

L: The guiding principle of pragmatists is expedience, which really offers no guidance at all. As for utilitarians, anything sacrificed on the bloody altar of the greater good, even an innocent child, is made sacred and holy by that excuse. Utilitarianism devolves into expediency, the perfect excuse for any atrocity. The 20th century sure showed how badly utilitarianism can be abused.

Doug: For sure. And all these cockamamie philosophies usually evidence themselves as some variety or another of economic collectivism and political statism.

My view is that free-market capitalism is the only ethical economic system. It maximizes everyone's advantage and does so without coercion. That's no accident; that's the proof of the soundness of the principles.

And it's no coincidence that the two ethical principles I outlined are also the only laws you need. You certainly don't need some council or Congress or Parliament cranking out new ones by the score every week. Or, as you pointed out, one being derived from the other, they could be boiled down to one single law. Just as physicists are trying to boil down the laws of the universe to one great law, here's my attempt for ethics: *Do as thou wilt… but be prepared to accept the consequences.*

L: We discussed that in our <u>conversation on judging justices</u>[1]. And that makes sense; on the most fundamental level, the law is a substitute for personal ethics when those fail or appear to be lacking. So they should have the same basis. There is little in our world that is more perverse than unethical laws that require people to do what's wrong or punish people for doing what's right.

Doug: Sure, but it happens all the time. These laws are cranked out by governments like there's no tomorrow—they are basically visible dramatizations of the psychological aberrations of lawmakers and the people they pander to. In brief, I have no automatic respect for either law nor morality—which I know sounds horrible. But that's only because they subvert people's judgment. They actually work to make a personal code of ethics unnecessary, by telling people all they have to do is obey the law and current morality. This tends to transform people into unthinking automatons who don't feel responsible for their own actions.

L: "I was just following orders!" Frightening indeed. But I want to stay on track here. Let's talk about how you apply your two ethical principles, and if such a simple system can really cover all situations.

Doug: Okay...

---

1. www.totallyincorrectbook.com/go/188

Doug Casey: The Ethical Investor

July 27, 2010

L: Doug, you said at the end of our last talk that I wouldn't like what you had to say about business ethics. Given your two principles:

1: Do all that you say you're going to do.

2: Don't aggress against other people or their property.

Why would that be? Sounds like good business to me.

Doug: Well, as far as completing your contractual obligations and not stealing from—or intentionally harming—people you do business with, that's pretty obvious and we've already covered it. No need to discuss that further.

Unfortunately, though, when most people think of "ethical investing," it has nothing at all to do with ethics. Most people have been deluded into thinking it has to do with not investing in tobacco companies, gun manufacturers, miners, timber companies, oil companies, many drug companies, many agricultural and food companies... in fact, whatever is on the ever-growing hit list of the politically correct. Pretty soon the silly bastards will be saying you shouldn't invest at all but give your money to NGOs.

L: Hey, you might be on to something there; if everyone gives their money to everyone else, everyone will get lots of money for nothing—free cash for everyone, what a great idea!

But let's come back to that in a moment. It's true that murdering your competitors is a rather short-sighted business strategy. It's also true that failing to deliver what your customers expect is an even shorter path to insolvency and dissolution of your business. And so forth. But a *lot* of businesses do things that are not ethical—or at least fall into legal gray areas that allow executives to claim they didn't do anything wrong. If that's such a bad idea, why do so many businesses do it?

Doug: I can't speak for other businesspeople, but you know that after hydrogen, stupidity is the most common thing in the universe.

I can say that in our own business, *reputation* is critical. We offer investment advice through our various publications—why would anyone take advice from someone they don't trust? Of course we comply with all the laws and regulations imposed on our industry—even though I disapprove of any regulation—but we go beyond that. As you know, we not only do not sell at the same time we tell people to buy, we disclose when we already own shares of companies we recommend, and we let subscribers sell first when it's time to head for the exits. This may sound self-serving, and perhaps it is, but it remains true that people know that Casey Research can't be bought; companies cannot pay us to write them up.

We certainly have one of the best track records of investment results in the business. It's sometimes hard to know what to make of our competitors' claims. Some of our colleagues in the business are absolutely first class in every department, including ethics and competence. But others…

Reputation is a strange commodity from a philosophical viewpoint. On the one hand, a good reputation is of high value. On the other hand, it's only an opinion held in the minds of others, and like all opinions, it can be based on incorrect information or interpretation. I think we have a superb reputation, but as far as I'm concerned, reputation is strictly secondary to our actually acting ethically.

I don't, however, worry about it. I almost never do or don't do something because of what other people would think. The mob is fickle, thoughtless, and easily swayed; the best proof of that is the type of people elected to public office. Look how the mob turned on Jesus when nothing had changed but perception.

I prefer to rely on reality. Damon Runyon was correct when he said, gainsaying Ecclesiastes, that the bread may not go to the wise, nor the battle to the strong, nor the race to the swift—but that's the way to bet.

L: So you adhere to ethical business practices because you adhere to ethical action in general, but for people without quite the same strength in their ethical backbones, reputation can be a powerful market force for the good.

Still, there are companies that put out cheap, shoddy products, relying on the fact that few people will complain or take the trouble to return the items. The market is large enough that they can make money for years before they run out of customers who don't know how poor their quality is. Why doesn't reputation seem to work in such cases? Is this a case of so-called market failure?

Doug: Well, there's a place for shoddy goods. People calculate costs and benefits subjectively. Maybe junk is all the buyer can afford. Maybe the buyer plans on just using it once and then discarding it. Maybe it's just part of the buyer's learning process. For instance, I hate cheap suits, but I've bought them when I didn't know any better. Cops prefer them, however, since getting in a fight, which they often do, is a sure way to ruin a good suit; and if they owned a good one, their fellows would assume they were on the take.

My view is that I'd rather have one good suit than three crappy ones. One good lawyer than a dozen shysters—one good doctor, friend, whatever, than a dozen mediocre ones. Quality is what counts. But it's a question of both having judgment in figuring out what "quality" is and having the means to procure it.

Of course, there are companies that take advantage of novices, the unwary, the fools, and the greedy, by misrepresenting their wares. But that's to be expected. Pareto's Law dictates that if 80% of businessmen are honest, then 20% might be iffy, and 20% of that 20% are scoundrels. Generally, the scamsters prey on the fools, the greedy, the novices, and the unwary. It's a naturally balanced ecosystem. And if you try to protect idiots from themselves, even if you succeed, you just wind up filling the world with idiots.

That's what government does[1]. The problem, as is so often the case, is when the state sticks its nose into the situation, as when government regulators assure people that minimal standards are met. This gives companies an excuse for doing as little as they can get away with—and legal protection from claims in court—because they can show that they met the government's minimum requirements. That's why the FDA should be renamed the Federal Death Authority, because they kill more people every year (through vastly raising costs, distorting tests, and slowing approvals, among other things) than the Defense Department does in a typical decade. The SEC should be called the Swindlers Encouragement Confabulation, since they don't just increase costs immensely but make John Q. Public think someone is actually protecting them.

Regulation creates an environment in which reputation is less important because consumers think the government is protecting them. They think they don't have to worry about it, so they don't. If this weren't the case—if people knew they had to rely on their own judgment, experience, and expertise, as well as that of sources they trust—reputation would become much more important in all markets around the world. Having a reputation for striving for the highest standards of business ethics, as well as in quality of products or services, would become a powerful competitive advantage and regulating force. So government regulation doesn't protect the consumer, it really just makes things easier for the swindler.

---

1. www.totallyincorrectbook.com/go/189

L: Pretty grim. But I'm an optimist. As we progress into the 21st century, people and capital alike are becoming more mobile. That means that more and more people can essentially shop for governments, based on their reputations, tax rates, corruption, etc. You're doing it by moving to Argentina. Others are headed for Thailand, Panama, Switzerland, Costa Rica, etc. Eventually, it may dawn on even the densest politicians that they are going to have to compete for customers. Tax slaves evolve into voluntary fee payers…

Doug: In my dreams. At the moment it seems things are going the other way: all over the world, people seem to be clamoring for the magic cornucopia of government to kiss things and make them better. They'll get what they deserve… good and hard.

L: We'll see. But okay, back to so-called ethical investing. The term refers to things like the fad for not buying shares in companies that did business in South Africa during the apartheid years. Or not investing today in companies that would ever, ever hurt cute furry creatures in the Amazon rain forest. Right?

Doug: Exactly, and I have to say that this type of ethical investing is bunk. To me, it's nothing but another form of political correctness. It's complete nonsense. It's the type of thinking that's resulted in Warren Buffett and Bill Gates encouraging other billionaires to give away half their money to charity while they are still alive. These people are *idiot savants*—excellent at their businesses, but fools outside of their narrow spheres.

L: And we all know what you think about charities.

Doug: That's the polite version. Conventional charitable giving is an entirely stupid, counterproductive, and perverse idea. If the goal is to improve the lot of their fellow human beings, conventional philanthropists are achieving just exactly the opposite by giving their money to charities, which only serve to dissipate that wealth so it can no longer be put to productive use.

Green investing is just as stupid—mired in the same moral morass. Investing with *any* criteria in mind other than maximizing return is, by definition, rewarding inferiority—or mediocrity, at best. Putting wealth to any use other than maximizing its growth is to squander it, to the detriment of the person who accumulated the wealth and all those he or she might employ. And charity often damages its recipients even more, by making them feel entitled, just because they're poor, unlucky, incompetent, or whatever.

The best thing to do with your money—from an ethical, economic, and social point of view—is to deploy it in such a way as to make more money, that is to say, that it makes more wealth. When you increase the amount of wealth in the world, *everybody* benefits.

People who invest in these so-called ethical funds do so because it makes them feel good, perhaps assuaging their guilt if they've bought into the whole "money is the root of all evil" nonsense. Or, more accurately, hatred of the "love of money," which is actually even more pernicious. Maybe they actually believe it will save the planet…

L: I guess they didn't agree with <u>George Carlin when he said the Earth doesn't need their help</u>[2].

Doug: George Carlin was a genius; I love all his stuff on YouTube. But "green" investing is a stupidity, in the specific sense of that word I favor: an unwitting tendency towards self-destruction. It's absolute idiocy. It shows that these people know nothing about ethics or economics, or investing. Or the environment, for that matter. I'll go further. These people don't love the environment, so much as they just have a covert—and sometimes even overt—hatred for other people.

L: Okay, but it's their money. If so-called ethical investing is as stupid as you say it is—you could think of it as a self-imposed stupidity tax—doesn't that make it self-correcting? Anyone foolish enough to do this will deprive himself or herself (and his or her heirs) of the means for funding other really stupid ideas?

Doug: Maybe so; Darwinian principles should result in their being culled from the gene pool. They're certainly at its shallow end. But they have probably already passed on their genes by the time they're thinking of dissipating capital. The <u>memes</u>[3] they promote, on the other hand, are even more virulent, propelled by squandered wealth. I'm not sure what you can do about that, other than have conversations like this and try to spread positive ideas around to nullify the destructive ones. It seems as if the good guys are losing the battle at the moment…

L: Hm. According to <u>T.H. White</u>[4], the night before King Arthur's final battle with his son Mordred, when Arthur was in despair about the failure of his Round Table to improve society and prevent war, Merlyn told him that no one can really be saved from anything. The only thing one can really do to improve the world is to add to the pool of ideas. That way, ideas conflict—with each other and reality—and over time the better ideas survive, raising the whole aggregate of the human condition.

[Ed. Note: L is referring to T.H. White's version of the Arthurian saga, specifically *The Book of Merlyn*[5], part of the tale of *The Once and Future King*[6].]

---

2. www.totallyincorrectbook.com/go/190
3. www.totallyincorrectbook.com/go/191
4. www.totallyincorrectbook.com/go/192
5. www.totallyincorrectbook.com/go/193
6. www.totallyincorrectbook.com/go/194

Doug: I'll second that emotion. Looked at over the long term, there's cause for optimism, I suppose. Mankind has risen from the primeval ooze and a world of 100% theft, to a reasonable level of technology and perhaps just 50% theft—if you look at the government's percentage of the GDP as a proxy for theft. The real problem seems to be the psychological aberrations seemingly ingrained in the human psyche. A pity, really. But the majority of human characteristics are good.

L: So… this might be a bit of a tangent from business ethics, but what the heck—it's interesting. What do you do when you're at the end of your rope? You're not going to give the money to charity, and you won't be around much longer to keep producing more wealth… What do you do with it?

Doug: Well, you're certainly at liberty to disperse it to the four winds, with high living. But if you don't consume it all, you're going to have to put it under the management of *someone*. So, you'd better choose that someone as wisely as you can.

Obviously, that's almost *never* a foundation of any kind—especially not one of the big, popular foundations. They are bastions of politically correct stupidity, and the type of people who serve on their boards should never be given a lot of money to play with. They shouldn't even be given a little money to play with. Those types are generally just political hacks, highly conventional, mostly concerned with their position in the social pecking order. Wealth shouldn't be played with; it should be kept whole and focused on creating more wealth. At least if you care about other people and the future.

L: What about foundations with missions written out explicitly to honor the donor's intent, and created with sunset clauses that require the foundation to go out of existence after working on and spending (investing) the money into whatever the donors believes in?

Doug: It doesn't matter. First of all, who's to say the donor won't be as hare-brained as Buffett and Gates? Anyway, entropy conquers everything. All systems have their flaws, and they all wind down. Once you're gone, the board will find legal loopholes to take advantage of; they will wrench the wealth away from fulfilling your intent. I suspect Ford, Rockefeller, and Carnegie—not that I consider them models—would roll over in their graves if they could see what was done with their wealth. Foundations are just not a good idea—most often, they are disastrous ideas. Their only redeeming feature is that they deny revenue to the state because of their tax-free status.

L: Okay. No surprise there. What about children? You don't have any, but most people do, and that's a natural thought for them.

Doug: Well, even if I did have kids, there's no guarantee I'd end up with one I trusted to run with the family business—or even with any I liked. I know several brilliant, successful people with children I wouldn't trust to run a lemonade stand. It's a total genetic and environmental crap-shoot what you end up with. Even if you're an ideal parent who makes your kid the focus of your life.

And if giving money to a foundation that might drift from your instructions for the wealth is a bad idea, leaving your wealth to children who did nothing to create it, know nothing about how to increase it, and don't deserve to squander it, is just as bad an idea. Of course leaving it to your kids is ideal if they're worthy of it. My suggestion is that you at least make a proper education available to them to increase the odds they turn out right. But you never know. Look at Marcus Aurelius—his son was Commodus. And the tutor of Nero was Seneca. There are lots of examples.

Speaking of which, I like the Roman approach much better; choose your heir from among those you know. Pick whoever you judge to be the most sound, ethical, and competent. You may not even like him. But if he's the one who'll do the best job of keeping the ball rolling and growing, he's the one you want.

L: Or her.

Doug: Or her. Or maybe, for lack of a better alternative, instead of giving it to anyone, invest it in a profitable company. You could buy the shares in a company that you really believe is creating wealth and has the best chances for continuing to do so, and bequeath the shares to the company in your will—a sort of free buyback.

The essence of the question is whether you're interested in improving the general state of the human race—really eliminating poverty, improving nutrition, education, medical care, and what have you—or just indulging your idiosyncrasies and playing big-shot on the charity circuit. If it's the former, then you must invest money and make it grow; there's no other alternative that's even close.

L: You don't generally invest in big companies, so I guess you'd pick some entrepreneurial small company with management you really believe in. That's a bit like the Roman idea, again.

Doug: That's true. If you choose wisely, the small company will grow faster. As companies grow, they all eventually become victims of entropy and bureaucracy, and end up like General Motors: run into the ground by brain-dead suits. But that process can take decades and in the meantime can create a lot of wealth. If you put it in a foundation, however, it's a guaranteed automatic write-off. And, worse, maybe it will show a negative return, since most foundations are actually destructive, giving money to promote destructive memes and support human weasels and cockroaches.

L: So, it's all building sand castles in the surf.

Doug: [Chuckles] Yes, it is. The good news is that in 1,000 years, what you do with your money won't amount to a hill of beans anyway. But that's the danger of taking a long-term view, I suppose.

L: But you know, if you build your sand castle well enough, even if it's doomed, it can give you time to build the next one. You make that one even bigger and better, and it can give you time to build the next one, and so on. Progress is possible in the face of the ever-corrosive effects of entropy.

Doug: You may be right, in which case the <u>second law of thermodynamics</u>[7] can be beaten, if only for a while. And we've got to fill those idle hours somehow.

L: [Laughs] Okay then. Food for thought. Until next time.

Doug: Until next time.

---

7. www.totallyincorrectbook.com/go/195

Doug Casey on Presidents:
The Good, the Bad, and the Ugly

Oct 21, 2010

L: Doug, I've heard you say you find Presidents' Day objectionable. I know that's not just you being a gadfly, but a comment driven by your study of history and your thinking on psychology, sociology, and economics. It seems worth following up on.

Doug: Yes, that's true. For one thing, as we discussed in our conversation on anarchy[1], political power tends to attract the worst of people, the four percent of any society that's sociopathic. So declaring holidays to honor these people is a tragic mistake in and of itself. It, like so many things in our world, is completely perverse, as people celebrate and reward mass murderers, industrial-scale thugs, and con-men who fleece entire societies.

Who is idolized in the history books? Is it people like Edison, the Wright Brothers, Leonardo, Newton, Ford, or Pasteur? Not really; they just get a passing nod. The ones who get statues built to them and are engraved on the collective memory are conquerors and mass murderers—Alexander, Caesar, Genghis Khan, Napoleon, and a whole bunch of US presidents.

L: Do you ever get to thinking that perhaps people get the government they deserve?

Doug: I do indeed. People who vote for free lunches—knowing full well that someone needs to pay for them, and they are fine with that as long as the someone is someone besides themselves—deserve to become tax slaves for those who view them as milk cows. If economically ignorant, greedy, and short-sighted people vote for bad government, they should start by looking in the mirror when they wonder what went wrong. But few people are that introspective. Further, most people apparently lack a real center, an ego in the good sense. That's why they create these false gods to worship; by becoming part of a group, they think they gain worth. Pity the poor fools...

---

1. www.totallyincorrectbook.com/go/196

There's no doubt in my mind that the US has devolved to that level. Something like 43 million people get their food from the government. About half of workers pay no income taxes (although I wish no one did, of course), and about half of those are significant net recipients of government funds... and many millions are employed directly by the state. It's why I no longer refer to "America" when discussing the US—America was a wonderful idea, which unfortunately no longer exists.

A bad leader can bring out the worst in people, making them think the government is a cornucopia; and then the people demand more of the same from future leaders. It's a downward spiral—never, for some reason, an upward spiral. It's why, after Augustus, Rome never returned to being a republic, even though they pretended—just like the US does today. My conclusion is that people basically get the kind of government they deserve. Which is a sad testimony to the degraded state of the average person today.

L: Okay, but as far as presidents go, and as much as I wish everyone valued freedom more than (imagined) guaranteed comfort, the fact seems to be that most people need leaders to prod them along into at least somewhat effective action. I don't know why—perhaps it stems from childhood needs for heroes who show us that the world can be tamed and life secured. Whether it be a company CEO or a club president, people often seem to work more effectively in groups with hierarchical structures and strong leadership at the top.

Doug: Well, first, it may seem that way simply because that's the way it is now. But I don't have a problem with hierarchies *per se*; it depends on the kind of hierarchy.

I'm not opposed to leaders or leadership. Leaders are an organic part of society; all mammals that live in groups appear to have them. They're essential for group effort. Natural leaders arise because of their competence, intelligence, wisdom, and virtues. I am only opposed to coercive leadership—the kind where you must follow orders or be punished. I prefer a society where peer pressure, moral opprobrium, and social approbation get people to do things—not laws and penalties. A formalized political structure doesn't draw natural or benign leaders so much as thugs who are interested in controlling other people.

L: And once an establishment gets in place, they try to cement themselves there with laws...

Doug: Exactly; they don't want their rice bowls broken. But more than that, the way most people raise kids in an authoritarian family structure with the father at the top, educate their children, with teachers who must be obeyed and powerful figures like school principals at the top, and send them off to work for hierarchically organized companies with, as you say, presidents and CEOs at the top, it's no surprise that most people think the world must be organized into hierarchies with some ultimate authority at the top.

But as you know first-hand, there are ways of parenting that don't revolve around a family structure that's a mini-dictatorship. As we discussed in our conversation on education, there are ways to teach young people that don't involve submerging their impressionable egos in rigid, bureaucratic, authoritarian "school systems." And there are ways of organizing companies and other very effective organizations that have very little hierarchy.

L: Casey Research, for one. You never tell me what to do, just ask me for results. And I taught my kids reading, writing, and arithmetic without relying on punishment. These things are not just theories to me but ways I live my life.

Doug: And of course, I believe there are ways of organizing effective societies that don't revolve around a central authority structure or leader. Personal responsibility is what it's really all about. Free societies centered on cooperation—through markets, rather than coercively through the state—would be much healthier, richer, and more just and moral societies to live in.

So, of course I object to anything that tends to prop up authoritarian ways of organizing society. Celebrating presidents—even the less stupid, evil, and destructive ones—is counterproductive to the direction I'd like to see society evolve, and incidentally, the direction I think it *is* evolving. President's Day is one holiday that deserves to be abolished absolutely.

L: Understood. Hm. I'm sure you've got a long list of evil, stupid, and destructive US presidents—probably most of them, in one way or another—but what about the good ones? Or the less bad ones—who's your favorite president and why?

Doug: Well, start with the caveat that they were all flawed. Plato's ridiculous notion of the Philosopher King is an illusion—that type of person wouldn't dream of being a president, because he'd realize that you shouldn't control other people. That said, I like guys like Chester A. Arthur, John Tyler, Calvin Coolidge, and Grover Cleveland.

But we should define what constitutes a good president. In my view, it would be one whose actions resulted in peace, prosperity, and liberty for the country. Peace means no foreign wars; war is the health of the state. War is the meat that feeds the beast. Prosperity means extremely low taxes and regulation, and a peaceful environment where enterprise can flourish. And liberty means being able to do what you wish, as long as you don't violate other persons or property.

Perhaps my favorite really ought to be William Harrison, because he only ruled 32 days before he died from a cold in 1841. He had no time to do any damage.

L: I'd bet most Americans don't even remember that there was a president by that name—the true mark of a great president.

Doug: What about you, Lobo, who's your favorite president?

L: I can't quite bring myself to believe that any man could win the ultimate pandering contest and be an individual of real integrity, so none are heroes in my eyes. That said, I do find myself persuaded by the <u>argument Larry Reed used to make</u>[2] back when he ran the Mackinac Center for Public Policy, that <u>Grover Cleveland</u>[3] might have been the best of the lot. He was a sound-money advocate, generally pro-market, and had both the personal ethics and the backbone to face down Congress and the powerful interests behind the annexation of Hawaii.

The conquest of Hawaii, in my opinion, was one of the most shameful episodes in US history, because of the massive level of fraud and deceit involved, which was quite different from the relatively simpler xenophobic extermination of other natives. Grover Cleveland basically said that Hawaii would never be annexed while he was president, and that's exactly what happened.

Doug: I remember that story.

L: I also have to give credit to George Washington, in spite of the major turn down the wrong road he took for the whole country when he suppressed the <u>Whiskey Rebellion</u>[4] by force, because he could have set himself up as king after the first American Revolution—and he didn't.

Doug: He had the army, was very popular, and he could have done it—I agree, he could have made himself king or been reelected until his death. But I can't forgive him for crushing the Whiskey Rebellion; that set the precedent for federal taxation and power that eventually led to the Civil War and the bloated monster in Washington that has now burst almost all of its chains.

L: So, who was the worst president?

Doug: That's a really tough question to answer, because there are so many deserving candidates for that title. A short list would have to include McKinley, Teddy Roosevelt, Wilson, Hoover, FDR, Truman, Johnson, Baby Bush, and Obama. But I'd have to say Lincoln was by far the worst. He plunged the country into a totally unnecessary and immensely devastating war, and violated every

---

2. www.totallyincorrectbook.com/go/197
3. www.totallyincorrectbook.com/go/198
4. www.totallyincorrectbook.com/go/199

important part of the Constitution. But he was such a great rhetorician that he made Americans feel good about all the horrors he brought about, setting a doubly bad precedent.

L: I think I know what you'll say, but for our readers who are used to hearing Lincoln described as some sort of saint, and probably America's greatest president, can you expand on that? He preserved the union and freed the slaves...

Doug: The union was *not* preserved. A union of free and sovereign states was cemented into a single super-state, in which each individual state became nothing more than an administrative region. Who's to say that a bigger US was a better one anyway?

Anyway, it wasn't a civil war, which is technically a contest for the control of a single government; it was a war of secession, like that of 1776. I'm no fan of the Confederacy, but the wrong side won, overthrowing the federal organization that restrained national power, maximizing political and economic freedom.

L: Not for the slaves.

Doug: No, not for the slaves. But slavery was an uneconomic institution that was on its way out anyway—the Industrial Revolution was about to put an end to it in the US, just as it did most everywhere else around the world. Brazil was the last major country to be done with it, in the 1880s, and its abolition was peaceable everywhere but in the Land of Lincoln. And Lincoln was *not* an abolitionist—he didn't give a fig for the plight of the slaves. His "emancipation proclamation" freed the slaves only in the South. Its real purpose was to incite the slaves to rebellion in the South and weaken his enemies, and to enlist the support of the abolitionist movement in support of his disastrously expensive and unpopular war.

L: Lincoln, the great emancipator, was also the first president to institute the draft, impose a federal income tax, and to smash opposition press (literally sending soldiers to break their printing presses into kindling).

Doug: That's all true, although George Bush Jr. arguably had the potential to be an even worse president. At least Lincoln was intelligent and articulate. Baby Bush was stupid, evil, pig-headed, thoughtless, *and* hugely destructive.

L: So, was Bush Jr. worse than, say, Obama?

Doug: I'm not sure—Obama could be worse. He's smart and persuasive, like Lincoln, which makes him very dangerous, because his ideas are totally destructive. He's not just doing all the wrong things, but exactly the opposite of the right things—and not just economically, but in every field. Obama could well be the president who pushes the US over the edge.

One major problem is that people conflate a president's style and personality with his quality as a leader. An example of that is Teddy Roosevelt. He was athletic, personally brave, a great outdoorsman, a prolific writer, something of an intellectual—the kind of guy who would make for an altogether amusing dinner guest. But he was also a militarist, an imperialist, and a complete economic fascist. Teddy the Trust-Buster popularized the idea that business is evil from his "bully pulpit." He gets an A+ for charisma and style, but an F- if you value peace, prosperity, and liberty.

There's a lot of similarity with his relative, FDR, who was a total and complete disaster on absolutely every front. Of course one can argue FDR was just a man of his time—his contemporaries were Hitler, Stalin, Tojo, Mussolini, Chiang Kai-shek, Mao, Peron, and Franco, among others. All of them, and other world leaders at the time, were cut from basically the same socialist/fascist cloth. FDR just cloaked most of his depravations in traditional American rhetoric—"reforming" capitalism in order to "save" it and similar nonsense.

Reagan was a fairly good president in terms of his rhetoric—but like Roosevelt, one can argue he was also a man of his time, because all over the world, in the UK with Thatcher, China with Deng, Argentina with Menem, everywhere really, there was a lot of free-marketization and reduction in taxes. But Reagan also started putting deficits and increases in the military into hyper-drive. And those are trends that will prove nearly as disastrous as some of those started by Roosevelt. Reagan is a bit like Jefferson—he talked the talk, but didn't walk the walk.

What about you—who would you pick for the worst US president of all time?

L: Well, I have to say I have an abiding dislike for Bill Clinton, who, among other crimes, used tax money stolen from me to bomb friends of mine in Serbia—civilians. But I think that after Lincoln, whom you've already discussed, FDR was probably the worst. The New Deal was almost a Third American Revolution, a sweeping wave of socialism that changed America forever, undermining the individualism and independence of the American people as well as setting the country on a path to economic self-destruction, the endgame of which I believe we are now entering into.

Doug: I'd have to agree with you there, FDR was perhaps the second worst. Wilson was perhaps the third worst, for getting the US into a totally pointless world war that he promised to keep the US out of, and thereby both greatly increasing the scope of the destruction and also setting the world on the path to WWII. It was also on his watch that the Federal Reserve was set up and the income tax initiated. Of course the slippery slope had already started getting steeper when a dead president was put on our money for the first time, in 1909, with the Lincoln penny.

And, going back to Jefferson, he set up a terrible precedent for socialized education in Virginia with the University of Virginia and made the unconstitutional Louisiana Purchase. Great writer and thinker, but he turned into Mr. Hyde once in office—there's much more that was bad about him that made him a mediocre president, at best.

L: On the other hand, he did oppose the slave trade. And I have to admit, I admire him for all of his inventions.

Doug: That was a pretty courageous thing to do at that time—but it would have been even more courageous to free his slaves while he lived and then protect them.

L: Can't argue that. What about today, see any candidates out there who don't seem stupid, evil, or destructive to you?

Doug: No. I'd like to say Rand Paul, but although he's riding on his father's coat-tails, he appears to be just another weakly principled Republican, who seems to think "supporting our troops," promoting "traditional values," and thumping the Bible will somehow restore peace, prosperity, and liberty to the US. I hope that's an unfair assessment of the guy, but I think not, because the longer people spend in Washington, the more corrupt and conventional they tend to become. As a lone voice, his father was a breath of fresh, more principled air, but he didn't change anything at all that I can see; the US has continued headlong for the economic and social cliff he saw as clearly as I did.

L: A pity.

Doug: Maybe, or maybe not. If he'd made more of a difference, it might have encouraged other good people to enter politics, instead of doing something useful with their lives—might have helped prolong the false belief that anything good can come from politics. At this point, I don't think we're going to see any meaningful constructive change until the US government itself implodes. Which is very likely to happen this decade. The problem is what comes next... We're in for truly interesting times.

Doug Casey: Waiting for WWIII

Mar 11, 2011

Editor's Note: At the time this edition was due, Doug was very busy at the annual conference of the Prospectors and Developers Association of Canada. For readers' enjoyment, we dug up an article from the July 2001 edition of the *International Speculator* that almost predicted 9/11, even mentioning Osama bin Laden by name. In light of recent world events, it was a truly precognitive piece of writing, and worth including in this collection.

What are the greatest problems facing us today? Domestically, I'd say the continual and accelerating loss of freedom, compounded by the prospect of what I suspect could be the biggest financial/economic crisis of modern times. What might that crisis be like? That's unpredictable, although the odds are it will be unlike any others that are still fresh in people's memories, simply because people tend to be most prepared for the things that have most recently scared them. The big problems usually come from an unexpected quarter, and/or at an unexpected time. Like the monetary crisis of 1998 that materialized in Thailand.

That said, the question remains of where to look. My guess (although it sounds so unprofessional to use a word like "guess," a government briefing would substitute a phrase like "our research shows" or "expert opinion indicates") is that it will come from outside American borders, in the form of war. War is perhaps the worst thing that can happen, not only for the destruction it will cause in itself, but because it will immensely exacerbate America's domestic problems. As Bourne famously said, "War is the health of the State."

But neither a declared war nor a war in the conventional sense is likely in the cards. US troops have been in combat in a dozen countries since our last "official" war ended in 1945; the US troops stationed in over 100 countries are an accident waiting to happen. Besides the Balkans and Iraq, Colombia is probably highest on the dance card, but almost anyplace could erupt unpredictably. Who, after all, could have predicted that the US would invade Somalia in 1991, a country few people other than stamp collectors even knew existed? No place is safe from being attacked in The National Interest of the world's self-appointed policeman.

Anything is possible within this context, but I discount the possibility of another Vietnam, again because of the "recent collective memory" phenomenon. Vietnam is possibly the major reason why the Iraq attack ended so quickly; quick withdrawal obviated any danger that ground troops might get stuck in a major tar baby. But when you're sticking your nose absolutely everywhere it doesn't belong, there are lots of ways to get it bloodied. My guess is that something resembling a Crusade is developing against those who live in the Koran Belt. It won't be overtly religious like the crusades of the Middle Ages, but it will have major cultural undertones. And there's every prospect it will be highly unconventional in nature.

Attack and Defense

This is why all the talk about a strategic missile defense system (ABM) for the US is so totally ridiculous.

Why would an enemy of the US spend a fortune building ICBMs, a clunky, inaccurate, 1950s-era technology, when a plethora of ABC (atomic, biological, chemical) weapons can be sent by FedEx? They'll arrive exactly where you want them, and precisely on time. You may think I'm joking, but the most effective delivery system is one that's cheap, reliable, unexpected, redundant, untraceable, and hard to detect until it's too late. If you have an especially large device to deliver, it can be shipped as cargo in a conventional boat or plane. Indeed, as good as a car bomb is for taking out a building, an equally innocuous boat or plane can take out an entire city.

When the attack comes on the US, that's the form it will take. Ballistic missiles may have some terror/propaganda value for countries like North Korea or Iraq, for use against regional enemies. But these people aren't stupid; they know that if they launched a strike on the US with a missile, there'd be no question about its source. And no question about the response. No government or group would dream of attacking the US in that manner, since it would literally amount to signing their own national death warrant. It's simply not going to happen that way. If they want to take out some US cities, it won't be with a missile.

Why, then, does the US government want to spend scores of billions on a missile defense system that's worth less than a Maginot Line? In fact, they should nickname the ABM (in the manner that's long been the case for US weapons) the "Maginot." Are they really that stupid? Or is the money flowing to defense contractors really that important? Or is it a PR stunt to convince *Boobus americanus* that he's safe? Or all of the above? I don't know. But to me, it's absolute proof that the generals and their masters are just as intent on fighting the last war as has been the case every time in the past.

This isn't unexpected. The US has (depending on who's doing the accounting, and how many are built) spent $2 billion on each B-2 "Sitting Duck" bomber, and will spend $250 million on each F-22 "White Elephant" fighter, aircraft superbly suited to fight a non-existent hi-tech enemy.

Even if building these hi-tech showboats was a good idea, I question whether these devices aren't overpriced by an order of magnitude. You'll recall that the P-51, the best fighter of WWII, went from the drawing board to production in seven months and was cranked out at $50,000 a copy. OK, say that's $500,000 in today's money, and the F-22 is vastly more complex and capable. But the real prices of raw materials have plummeted, and the advances in technology have done the same for both design and manufacturing costs. If nothing else, it's a testimony to the inefficiency and corruption inherent in the procurement system.

Entirely apart from that, any (serious) potential enemy will make sure they're taken out on the ground with saboteurs, special operations units, or ABC weapons. When you're dealing in aircraft that cost a few million, and you've got thousands of them widely dispersed, these things are manageable. But when you've got the very limited numbers you can buy at hundreds of millions a copy, it's a different story. The US will hardly dare deploy these weapons because the loss of only one in combat would be a catastrophe.

But these are strictly tangential points. Weapons like these are as useless as the ABM against what's coming in the next war.

The Only Defense

It's a truism that the best defense is a good offense. But it's only true once you're in an active war and are trying to win it. Regrettably, the US is confusing a good offense with running around the world giving offense, and it will only result in starting a war.

The only defense against the kind of attack that will open the next conflict is, frankly, to give the attacker no reason to attack. Does Argentina, or Canada, or Italy, or Thailand or, really, any country in the world besides the US, have reason to fear a massive ABC attack? The answer is no. Sure, the Indians and the Pakistanis, the Chinese and the Taiwanese, the North and South Koreans could attack each other. But the source of the threat is discrete. Only the US is running around the world, whacking a hundred different hornets' nests.

A major power could get away with this in the past. The most the natives could do in retaliation was assassinate the odd dignitary or ambush the odd patrol. But the world has changed. Now, if you antagonize a group badly enough, they're entirely capable of bringing the war to your home ground. The World Trade Center bombing, which should have, by all rights, been a success, and the USS Cole bombing, which was a stunning success, are only the most trivial examples of what's in store.

Almost anyone can build a nuclear device today. Various designs are published, and the methods of enriching uranium are not complex. It's not rocket science any longer. Moreover, why bother when a million dollars passed to a Russian general (or maybe just a sergeant, since he actually handles the things) can buy you state-of-the-art equipment? That's even more true of biological and chemical weaponry.

The question isn't whether it will be used. That's a certainty. Anything that can be imagined can probably be done; and anything that can be done probably will be done. It's simply a question of when. And by whom. The most likely attackers are members of the Muslim community.

The Next Enemy

Although there's no innate reason for a conflict between the US and the Islamic world, the odds are high there will be. *Boobus Americanus* has been programmed for a generation to see Muslims as The Enemy. Most recent wars and terrorist activities center around places like Iran, Iraq, Somalia, Lebanon, Bosnia, Sudan, and Afghanistan, and people and organizations with names like Gaddafi, Hamas, Black September, and Osama bin Laden. The US government consistently supports Israel, which the Muslims view as an outlaw, terrorist state. Show me a single movie since "Lawrence of Arabia" in which Muslims are portrayed sympathetically. There would be lots of support for a crusade against these folks.

Not surprisingly, the Muslims see their lands and culture as having been under constant attack since the Crusades of the Middle Ages. The romantic image of knights in armor battling to free the Holy Land from the infidel is reversed in their eyes. They see hordes of unwashed European barbarians having invaded their homeland on a pretext, intent on rape, pillage, murder, and wholesale looting. And, being as objective as possible about it, one has to credit their view.

And that was just the start of the Crusades, which continue to this day, in the eyes of Muslims. Over the last two centuries, European armies have run roughshod over every Muslim country, now replaced by American armies. The "ragheads" and "kaffirs" in question don't like it any more than Americans would if the Iraqis were bombing New York every day and had a "no fly" zone set up over the Deep South to protect a black separatist movement in the area. We see Saddam Hussein as the devil incarnate (as do many Iraqis). But, his personal foibles aside, he's viewed as a hero by most Muslims for having fought against enormous odds from the Crusaders and remained standing.

I think it's worth a look at the Muslims and what they believe. You may be asking yourself what relevance that has to us. In a perfect world, where people minded their own business, the answer would be, very little. But that's not the world we live in.

Islam

Islam may be the world's largest religion, at least if you consider the number of real, as opposed to just nominal, believers. It's certainly the world's fastest–growing, dominating the lives of about a billion people who live in what a wag might call the Koran Belt, extending from North Africa through all of the Mideast and Central Asia, right through western China and down to Indonesia. It's a part of the world with lots of poor people and little capital. Many repressive governments and little freedom. To what degree, if any, is that the fault of Islam?

We are told the Prophet (Peace Be Upon Him, a phrase the faithful usually append to a mention of his name, often abbreviated to p.b.u.h.) was a merchant until, at age 40, he was visited by the angel Gabriel. Gabriel related the wishes of Allah (The Compassionate, The Merciful—perhaps the most common of the many benefactions used by the faithful) to him, which Muhammad transcribed as the Koran.

Islam attracts people for the same reason all religions do: It offers a neat package explaining the meaning of life, while promising eternal bliss after death. But it has some characteristics and makes some promises rendering it especially attractive to the poor and downtrodden. And that means its potential market is about 75% of the world's people.

The Essence of Islam

Islam has a number of sects and variations, but only a tiny fraction as many as Christianity. It won't serve a useful purpose to go into them now, except to observe that the reason for the relatively small number of variations is that it's necessarily a much more cohesive faith than Christianity, being based on one rather short book, promulgated by one man whose status is clear; the religion leaves relatively little open to interpretation. The basic pillars of Islam tend to unify believers, whatever other differences they may have; internecine warfare between Muslims over religion has been the exception. It's unclear to me what actually constitutes an observant, or perhaps a "saved," Christian; opinions differ widely among the religion's many sects. There's no question, however, about who is an observant Muslim: One must only adhere to its Five Pillars.

> 1) **The Shahadah, or Profession of Faith.** This is the essence of Islam. One must say aloud, sincerely and purposefully, "There is no God but Allah, and Mohammed is his prophet."

> 2) **Prayer.** One must pray, in a ritualized manner, five times a day, in congregation if possible.

> 3) **Zakat**, or tithing. One must give a certain percentage of one's assets to the poor each year.

> 4) **Fasting.** One cannot eat, drink, or smoke from dawn to dusk during Ramadan, the ninth month of the lunar calendar.

> 5) **Hajj**, or pilgrimage. One must journey to Mecca at least once, if it's possible to do so.

There you have it. And it certainly seems like a small price to pay to gain paradise, where one engages in pleasures of the flesh for eternity, surrounded by doe-eyed houris. Infidels and apostates, meanwhile, may expect to burn in sulfur for eternity.

Islam offers benefits in the here and now, as well. It cultivates a brotherhood of believers cutting across racial, ethnic and linguistic barriers not just in theory but in practice. It allows the believer to communicate directly with

Allah, dispensing with an intermediary priesthood. It's a very fraternal and democratic religion.

The word Islam means "submission." Since Allah is all-powerful and all-knowing, as well as merciful and compassionate, it means that whatever happens is the will of Allah, and the faithful do well to accept it. This leads on the one hand to a mellow, destressifying view of life, which is a good thing. On the other hand, it can lead to an overly fatalistic view of life, wherein hard work and striving can be pointless. This may be one reason for the relative backwardness of the Muslim world.

If you want to convince others of something, the most important thing to remember is: "Keep it simple!" And Islam does that extremely well. The key to salvation is observance of the Five Pillars, and they're quite specific and well defined. There's no room, or need, for complex theological wrangling to confuse the issue. In addition, Islam cultivates a great deal of certainty, and that certainty is mightily abetted by its simplicity. If you want someone to believe, certainty—total, unwavering confidence in the correctness of your position—is 100 times more effective than any amount of intellectualism. Simplicity and certainty are the two indispensable elements of a successful mass religion. With this solid foundation laid by Allah, through the Prophet, enthusiastic early adherents were able to take the show on the road.

The Reason for Islam's Early Success

The question often arises how Islamic civilization, which conquered much of the known world in the 150 years after the Hegira (Muhammad's flight from Mecca to Medina in 622 A.D), preserved much of ancient civilization and made innovations in mathematics, architecture, science and literature, could have regressed to its present sorry state. Was it because Allah smiled on Muslims in their early years but, for some reason, has frowned upon them in more recent centuries? Or could there be some other force at work?

My theory is that Islam's flowering had relatively little to do with religion, per se, and a lot to do with a military organization, which was enabled by religious fervor. Great conquests usually begin with a unifying ideology, most often some form of nationalism or religion, and the simpler and more certain the better. That's exactly what Islam gave the Arabs. I suspect any number of ideologies could have done as well, but it's tough to argue with success. The conquests led to wealth, and wealth to civilization and progress.

War, Wealth, and Hypocrisy

It's worthwhile examining the relationship between war and wealth. After all, most wars seem to have economic roots. At least until very recent times, conquest was the key to wealth and success.

Losing a war was a step to poverty (simply because the enemy stole everything you owned) and probably slavery. Largely because of the unity and fervor generated by their religion, the Arabs were extraordinarily militarily successful. I would hold, therefore, that the wealth Islam displayed early on, during its Golden Age, wasn't so much a direct product of Allah's Will, smiling on the piety of his believers, as the result of conquest. Conquest is what you call simple theft when it's perpetrated by a large, well-organized group. So the Arabs became wealthy just like every other successful pre-industrial empire. In pre-industrial, pre-technological times, conquest was a formula for success. Nobody had qualms about it. The thought of war-crime tribunals, had they even existed, would have been laughable in times when the standard recompense for soldiers of a conquering army was three days of unrestricted looting, raping, and general mayhem in a fallen city.

Historically, when you conquered an enemy and confiscate (another nice word for "steal") his possessions, you became wealthier. This was, however, much, much more true in pre-industrial times, when wealth was static (land, gold, livestock, etc.). As the Soviets found, it's less true in industrial economies, because they are based on continuing massive production, and because the means of production depreciate and obsolesce. In today's hi-tech economy, simple theft is much, much less productive than used to be the case. In the old days, if you were able to steal some land or gold successfully, you were ahead of the game; land and gold defined wealth.

Today, if you steal a computer, you have nothing but a depreciating asset. You can't effectively steal know-how, because it's a process, not a concrete object. The higher the technological level of a society, the less sense theft makes. The whole story of civilization is one of the replacement of theft by production as a means to live. It's why, for instance, I never believed the Soviets would attack Western Europe; the very fact of conquering it would have destroyed the wealth they wanted. In a hi-tech world, theft is actually counterproductive, much as stealing the answers to a test really gains one nothing. That's not the way it was in the ancient world, however.

But if the act of conquest allowed the Muslims, tent dwellers riding out of the desert, to become wealthy, then hypocrisy allowed them to stay wealthy at least for a while. A good Muslim, even more than a good Christian, makes his religion not just the centerpiece of his life, he makes it his life. If the Koran is the exact and indisputable word of Allah, then it's almost a blasphemy to read anything else, or learn about anything else, or do anything that doesn't relate directly to what Allah expressly tells you to do, unmistakably, in black and white. Unfortunately, this presents a conflict with about a thousand other things a human may need or want. So compromises are inevitably made, rationalized, and justified. Hypocrisy is necessary, even admirable, if you believe and say things that make no sense to do.

Don't get me wrong. Islam does not endorse either theft or hypocrisy, and these faults are in no way unique to it. The Roman Empire, whatever its numerous other virtues, gained most of its wealth by stealing it from the peoples it conquered and taxed. When it stopped expanding (with the reign of Hadrian), it almost necessarily went into decline. The same was true of the Spanish, Portuguese, British, and French Empires, among others. I attribute their glories not to their righteousness but to their temporary military prowess. The same is true of Islam. It's just that the unifying aspects of the religion aided mightily in their conquests. Muslims are no more hypocritical than followers of any other faith. And theft (unless it's called conquest) is much rarer in Muslim than Christian societies.

Just as stock investors often confuse a bull market with genius, religionists often confuse happy accidents of history with the fruits of righteousness.

Fundamentalism

What really concerns people in the West, however, aren't the economic but the political ramifications of Islam. While many other religions, from Voodoo to Hinduism to Mormonism, may be viewed as quaint, nonsensical, or bizarre but at least well intentioned, Islam is seen as threatening. That's because of Islam's political ramifications, including what was once the 6th Pillar, known as Jihad, or Holy War, to defend or spread Islam. That, understandably, scares Christians (and others). But no more, I suspect, than hearing a congregation sing "Onward Christian soldiers, marching as to war" on a Sunday scares Muslims (and others), while the US Air Force is plastering various Muslim countries.

Some say that Islam is fine in itself and, as with Christianity, the problem is fundamentalism. Fundamentalism is basically living your life exactly according to the dictates of The Book, as least as you understand it. And this gets us back to the problem of hypocrisy. If Allah, via the Prophet, says it is wrong to charge interest on a loan, under any circumstances, how can you rationalize that with modern banking practices and economic theory, in which interest is the time value of money? If Jesus, who many Christians believe is God, says that it's easier for a camel to go through the eye of a needle than for a rich man to get into heaven, how can you rationalize being rich?

Well, Muslim banks have at least 18 ways of getting a return on loans without calling it interest (fees, return gifts, commissions, tokens of appreciation, percentage of profit, etc.). As for how Christians solve the wealth conundrum, I'm sure we've all heard the answers in Sunday school. Query: Is this why Jews are famously richer than either Christians or Muslims?

Actually, despite all the problems fundamentalists of all religions cause (and have), you've got to respect them, if only because they're not hypocrites. They don't just talk the talk; they walk the walk. The real question is whether the talk itself should be relegated to the scrap heap of history. There may be cause for optimism. After all, Marxism was nothing but a secular religion, and today nobody but acknowledged morons, and some college professors, ever admit to having been believers.

The Future of Islam

Having far too briefly and inadequately looked at why Islam arose, and what it is, let's explore where it's going. Should Islam be considered a threat to Civilization As We Know It? That question requires two, equally valid, answers.

One answer is a definite yes, Islam is a huge threat. That's because there's every reason to believe any number of groups in the Islamic world will attempt to defend themselves from the medieval Crusaders disguised as modern Americans. They'll fight back not with planes, missile cruisers, and tanks, but with weapons they can afford, which are, ironically, not just vastly cheaper but vastly more effective. We won't call their warriors "soldiers" but "terrorists" while forgetting that "I'm a Freedom Fighter, you're a Rebel, he's a Terrorist."

Some, especially those in National Security circles, discreetly ask what should be done about the Muslim threat. My answer is: Absolutely nothing. I don't see the Muslims as any more of a threat than the Christians, the Jews, the Hindus, or any other religious group. The ones I know are every bit as nice and decent as anyone else. Once, however, you start looking for an answer to the "Muslim question," you're looking for trouble of the worst kind, as did the Germans when they sought an answer to the "Judenfrage." Unfortunately, that's the direction America is moving. I don't doubt that, before this decade is out, those of us with Muslim friends may be watched as potential terrorists for that reason.

A second answer is a categorical no. Islam is not a threat at all. Paradoxically, one of Islam's greatest strengths is also one of its greatest weaknesses: namely, the fact it's more than just another religion; it's a complete world view. It doesn't just prescribe how one deals with the supernatural, or even just morality, but dictates one's approach to finance, science, art, politics, and life in general. This has a certain utility in uniting primitive people for the purpose of military conquest, using simple technology. If you can get a horde to think alike in most ways, even convincing them they're going to go to Paradise if they die on a Jihad against the enemy, you've got a formidable low-tech military force. In warfare, as Napoleon said, the psychological is to the physical as two is to one. But group-think doesn't much help in any other area of civilization.

To the degree Muslims take their religion seriously, they will necessarily fall behind in every other area of human endeavor. That's because their religion takes absolute precedence over everything else and regulates everything they do. The consequences of that are poor, at least if you value things like capitalism, freedom, science, and technology. And their consequence, prosperity. With no disrespect intended, slavish belief in a book that came to an illiterate Arab merchant in his dreams in the 7th century is less likely to lead to success in a wealthy high-tech world than one where people lived in tents and counted their wealth in terms of camels.

For that reason, I've got to say the economic future of countries with Islamic traditions is not going to be what it could, or should, be. And that's a pity. But, as most people will acknowledge, there are more important things in life than money. Everyone has to make his choice. As for me, it means that, everything else being equal, stocks traded in these countries have to be cheap indeed before I'd consider buying them.

Doug Casey on Juries and Justice

Nov 3, 2010

L: Doug, in our conversation last week, we touched on the topic of jury duty, and I could tell that you had a lot of thoughts on the subject. It's an important topic, since the jury system is, theoretically at least, meant to be the ultimate bastion of justice. But you spoke of how, although most people evade summons for jury duty if at all possible, for you it's academic, because you'd never be allowed to sit on a jury anyway. Where does that leave things—do you think the jury system is a good idea?

Doug: My view has always been that what really holds a society together is not the body of law enacted by a legislature or handed down by a king, but peer pressure, social opprobrium, and moral approbation. When somebody breaks a society's rules, a trial of some type ensues, to determine who's right, what harm has been done, who should be compensated, and so forth. Juries are one way people have developed for helping to determine these things. But I would argue that the state is not a necessary part of any of this.

L: You would argue that the state shouldn't be part of anything[1] at all…

Doug: Yes, but it might be easier for many readers if we start with the minimal "night watchman" sort of state described by Ayn Rand. In her view, the proper role of government is simply to defend you from force (and fraud). That implies an army to defend you from force external to your society, a police force to defend you from force within your society, and a court system to allow adjudication of disputes without resorting to force.

I could live in a society like that—it would be a vast improvement over what we have now—and the jury system would be part of it. But, as you say, I'd go on to argue that juries and courts should be privatized.

L: Justice is a service for which there is a market. We'll probably have to come back to that, to explain how it might work—and why it would be better

---

1. www.totallyincorrectbook.com/go/200

than what we have now—but whether private or state run, you are agreeing that juries are a good idea?

Doug: Yes, especially when they're composed of independent thinkers, who aren't easily swayed by rhetoric or pressured by groupthink. They are a good balance against the tremendous power of judges. And judges, these days, are either elected officials, which means they have to campaign like any other politician and are subject to the same perverse incentives any other politician is, or they are appointed, which is even worse. Appointees are usually just collecting political favors and, while allegedly more independent, are in many ways even less accountable.

So, in theory, a jury is a good counterbalance to the power of the judge. You need some way to weigh the facts and decide who's in the right. If all of that were on one elected or appointed man or woman's shoulders, there could be a lot of problems. But the way juries work in the US today is far from optimal.

L: How so?

Doug: Well, the way juries are run today is really a form of involuntary servitude. You get your notice for jury duty, and you either have to serve, whether you want to or not, or come up with excuses the state will deign to accept. Most productive people feel that they have more urgent priorities in their lives than helping to decide court cases, and a court case can go on for months. So the type of people that end up serving on juries these days are generally people with nothing better to do, or people for whom the trivial fee they pay is good money. Neither is necessarily the best kind of person to be deciding weighty matters, perhaps even life and death. In addition, many trials center on highly technical concepts, and forms of evidence, that these people are simply unqualified to interpret.

Worse, there's the jury selection process we mentioned last time, called _voir dire_[2]. The notion is to give both sides' attorneys opportunities to remove a few individuals from the jury who might be biased against their case, thus ensuring a more unbiased jury. But in practice, it's an interrogation process by which the lawyers try to ensure they get a jury that will believe whatever they tell them. That usually means that anyone exhibiting the least bit of independent thinking, or who is prone to value justice over law enforcement, gets removed and will never serve on a jury.

L: My friend Vin Suprynowicz[3] at the _Las Vegas Review Journal_ says _voir dire_ is French for "jury tampering."

2. www.totallyincorrectbook.com/go/201
3. www.totallyincorrectbook.com/go/202

Doug: He's right. And the result is that the quality of juries today is several standard deviations below what it should be. Any intelligent person has opinions, and in this day of the Internet, almost any person's opinions are easy to find out. No matter which way your opinions line up, one side or the other in any case isn't going to like them, and you won't make it past *voir dire*. On the other hand, the qualities in a juror both sides will like to see are malleability and an easily influenced mind. The typical juror has no opinions other than on the weather, sports, and *American Idol*. People who think in concepts are weeded out as troublemakers. The typical juror is somebody who might be a candidate for appearance on Jay Leno's *Jay Walking*[4].

L: You could say it's the process by which the system ensures that no qualified person serves on a jury, which could be dangerous to the state.

Doug: It also makes a shambles of the concept of a "jury of your peers." The type of people they could rope into jury duty wouldn't be my peers—they wouldn't even be the peers of the average person. If I were facing a trial, I'd much rather be tried by twelve people randomly selected out of a phone book than by the type of people who get selected for jury duty.

L: So, what you're saying is that juries are a good idea, in theory, but in practice, the jury system is so distorted, it's actually a liability against justice?

Doug: Right. If we're to have juries, they ought to be truly juries of our peers—people who can understand you and the facts pertaining to your case. But we're far, far from an ideal system. It's worse than arbitrary; given that most of those employed by the justice system work for the state, and that it's the state vs. an individual in so many cases, there's a huge inherent bias on top of the whole problem with today's stacked juries.

L: So, what would an ideal system look like to you?

Doug: In my ideal system, courts, judges, and even jurors would compete with each other to offer their services. They'd promote their proven records of intelligence, fairness, speed, and low cost.

L: I know what you mean, but the idea of private courts, judges and juries is so alien to most people, the idea won't compute at all. To explain, justify, and illustrate how such a system might actually work would make a book out of this conversation. So let me suggest a book that already does a good job of doing just this, as well as explore other important ideas: Robert A. Heinlein's *The Moon Is a Harsh Mistress*, which we discussed in our conversation on speculators' fiction.

---

4. www.totallyincorrectbook.com/go/203

In this book, the Moon is used by Earth authorities as a penal colony. The prisoners have no laws—are not *allowed* to have laws—so the entire society is regulated by custom, or culture. There's a part of the book that describes effective justice being done in a lawless society—the hero, in fact, gets asked to judge a case by a gang of youths who are offended by a man from Earth who kissed one of their girls without asking permission first. Both sides have to pay the hero to accept the case.

Doug: L. Neil Smith's North American Confederacy books also describe privatized legal systems. And for a full explanation, in a straightforward nonfiction context, I recommend Tannehill's <u>*The Market for Liberty*</u>[5]. It's one of the two or three most important books I've ever read, and it can be downloaded as an <u>audio book for free</u>[6].

L: What do you say to people who argue that private justice services would be biased—they are for *hire*, after all—and that you need the state to insure impartial justice?

Doug: I'd say that they must have had no exposure to the current legal system, which is anything but impartial and has very little to do with justice. If you separate justice and state, for one thing, it eliminates the ability of the state to prosecute phony, made-up crimes, especially crimes with no victims. If the state can't be party to a case, then there needs to be an actual victim to press charges. That right there would eliminate all the stupid, counterproductive, wasted resources and trashed lives that result from the US's various wars against victimless crimes. No one could be prosecuted for having unorthodox sexual preferences, using unpopular drugs, drinking on Sunday, or smoking in a private establishment. Or for evading taxes.

L: That'd be pretty far-reaching... If whatever governance system such a society had could not prosecute for tax evasion, that system would have to rely on collecting fees for services it renders. That'd limit those services to ones people are actually willing to pay for. Instead, in the US, the justice system has become a machine for enforcing laws. It's not about defending people from force or fraud, but about imposing the will of the rulers upon the people. I hadn't thought of it in just this way before, but separation of justice and state would end the ability of any government to ride roughshod over the people it allegedly serves.

Doug: And it would focus legal action on actual matters of <u>tort</u>[7] and breach of contract, where it belongs. Further, ignorance of the law is impossible, when

---

5. www.totallyincorrectbook.com/go/204
6. www.totallyincorrectbook.com/go/205
7. www.totallyincorrectbook.com/go/206

the laws are all derivations of the <u>two great laws</u>[8]: Do all that you say you're going to do, and don't aggress against other people or their property.

L: Some people might think you're talking about a sandwich, or a cake when you mention a tort...

Doug: Those are the kind of people who end up on juries today. The point is that justice has to do with righting actual wrongs that have been done to people, not enforcing laws. Today justice means enforcing the will of the politicians, which amounts to being the brute squad for the king, as in old times.

At any rate, with privatized justice, someone would accuse another, both sides would choose an arbitrator (professional or otherwise), and those two arbitrators would agree on a third to make sure there were no tied votes. They would look at all the facts—not just the arbitrary subset of facts allowed by legal precedent and state machinations—and they would decide. That decision would not be about punishing anyone, but about making the harmed party whole again. Compensation.

L: The key concept here is restitution. A justice system should not be a penal system but a system to set wrongs aright, at least as much as is possible. You steal a hundred dollars, you have to pay back a hundred dollars, plus something for the time and effort involved in recovery. Some harms can't be undone, like murder. In *The Moon Is a Harsh Mistress*, a man who killed another would be responsible for the deceased's widow, children, bills, etc. for life. If he didn't honor those responsibilities, no one would hire him, sell to him, serve him food, or clean his boots. It would become a virtual death sentence, not by execution by the state, but by ostracism—the near impossibility of living in our modern world without any transactions of any kind with other people.

Doug: That reminds me, I oppose the death penalty.

L: I know you agree with me that violence in self-defense is justified, so I know you are not opposed to murderers dying at the hands of their intended victims, who defend themselves at the moment of the attempted crime. You mean that the power to kill citizens in custody should never be given to the state?

Doug: Why people assume the state should have godlike powers amazes me. On an ethical basis, once you've disarmed a criminal and tossed him in jail, he's no longer an active threat to anyone, and so lethal force can't be called self-defense. On a more practical level, once you give the power to kill to the state, that power will be abused, and that's very dangerous.

---

8. www.totallyincorrectbook.com/go/207

Entirely apart from that, executing someone makes it impossible for him to ever compensate the victim, or the victim's estate—at least to the greatest extent possible. Locking people in cages as punishment only costs the victim more money in the form of taxes. It also tends to harden the convict, and the whole enterprise degrades the moral tone of society. And, most important, imprisonment makes it impossible for a criminal to do anything productive to pay off damages owed victims.

L: I'd expect that having to actually pay for your crimes would be more instructive than simply "doing time." And, if the driving concept is restitution, the harm you do by locking someone up cannot exceed the harm they have done to your person or property. The moment they balance, the offender goes free, or you end up owing him, or her, restitution for your unjust infringement of rights.

Doug: Once again, the key concepts are justice and restitution, not punishment. Punishment, if you actually think about it, rarely serves any useful purpose; it just gives vent to the basest and most reactive emotions of the victim. It may set a "good example" to deter future miscreants; but it definitely sets a bad example for society as a whole, by institutionalizing and justifying cruelty.

L: Okay, but what if you kill someone who has no relatives? If the state can't prosecute you, and the only one harmed is dead, do you go free?

Doug: Almost everyone has some connections. The victim's employers might sue you for the disruption you caused them... but the main line of defense would probably be insurance companies. It could be anyone with an interest in the victim's life.

L: Lends a whole new meaning to the idea of life insurance. And I suppose that if someone were such a destitute hermit that he or she had no connections to any others, such that no one would step forward to press charges against, we'd be talking about the sort of homeless wretch who gets no protection in our current society anyway. A breakdown of the system in such an extreme case can't be said to be a fatal flaw when it'd be an extremely rare fluke. And it's one the current system is just as vulnerable to, if not more so, given the mistreatment many in the underclass suffer at the hands of thugs in uniforms today.

Doug: That's right. And this is not a set of ideals limited to science fiction novels. Private arbitration exists today and is very common. Many contracts you sign these days include consent to arbitration clauses, because people know that any disputes that arise will be resolved faster and cheaper if handled outside the state's legal system. The state legal system today is a disaster. It takes forever to get your case heard. It will bankrupt you with legal and court costs while you're there. And once you're in, you will despair of ever getting out.

The idea you describe from Heinlein's book is neither new nor that fantastic; it's been done. In several ancient societies, especially the Nordic ones, if you had a judgment against you and failed to abide by the terms of the judgment, you became an outlaw. You were literally outside the law. Since you would not accept the judgment of the society, that society would not protect you in your turn—that made you fair game for anyone who decided to make furniture out of your bones.

L: Okay, so it's not just science fiction—but it's certainly not how things are today. Today we have a penal law-enforcement system instead of a justice system. What do you do if you do get dragooned into involuntary jury service?

Doug: If that happened, I might have a chance to use the power of the jury to overturn unjust laws. Some years ago, I was a director of the <u>Fully Informed Jury Association</u>[9] (FIJA). That organization's *raison d'être* is to inform everyone in society that a jury's proper and historical function is not to enforce laws but to stand as the final arbiter of law, and thus to protect people from tyranny.

In other words, every jury on every case could act in the way the Supreme Court acts today, judging the law as well as the facts of a case. This is the way America's founders saw juries—their purpose was not to see if any laws were broken but to see that justice was done.

L: While you've been speaking, I've pulled up the FIJA web site, and found some quotes to back you up:

Thomas Jefferson: "I consider trial by jury as the only anchor yet imagined by man, by which a government can be held to the principles of its constitution."

John Adams: "It is not only the juror's right, but his duty to find the verdict according to his own best understanding, judgment and conscience, though in direct opposition to the instruction of the court."

Alexander Hamilton: "Jurors should acquit, even against the judge's instruction… if exercising their judgment with discretion and honesty they have a clear conviction the charge of the court is wrong."

I'm not a big fan of Hamilton, but I'd have to agree with him on that last quote. And this is exactly the opposite of what a judge will tell a jury today, when giving instructions before deliberation.

---

9. www.totallyincorrectbook.com/go/208

Doug:Yes, judges' instructions today are entirely improper and a subversion of what juries are supposed to be. But the fact of the matter is that judges are just government employees. They're the king's men, on his payroll.

L:What would you say to people who say that jury nullification—juries refusing to convict lawbreakers—is what allowed white good old boys to literally get away with murder in the old South?

Doug: Lynching was certainly a terrible thing, but in a society so biased and hostile against a minority, the law was not much protection either—and, in fact, many unjust laws were put in place to perpetuate inequality and injustice. But also, as a matter of fundamental principle, it's worse to convict and punish people unjustly than to let a few guilty ones escape.

Jury nullification is a tool, and like any tool, it can be abused. But though this is a tool that lends itself to occasional failures to see justice done, robotic enforcement of laws by juries is a practice that guarantees and mass-produces injustice. Remember that the states' laws are not made by infallible gods but by fallible politicians. It was once legal to own another human being, and jury nullification by abolitionists—who refused to convict those who helped escaped slaves—was a powerful force for justice and social change.

L: Hm. So, if you did get summoned to jury duty, would you ever consider playing the role of Joe Six Pack, to try to get on a jury and see if you could help justice triumph over law enforcement? I see that FIJA actually has a pamphlet on <u>surviving _voir dire_</u>[10].

Doug:Well, I don't think you or I could ever get past the _voir dire_ process and onto a jury, but if by some miracle someone of goodwill and interested in justice were to do so, I'd say yes. By all means, get on a jury if you can. Striking a blow for justice is worth some inconvenience and effort.

L: Is there hope for the future in fully informed juries, then, Doug?

Doug: No, the situation is truly hopeless. It's so far gone, I think the best we can hope for is a controlled demolition. But in the meantime, good people who get on juries can help prevent the legal system from creating more injustice, at least from time to time. Even if you're the only one willing to vote your conscience and refuse to convict on some ridiculous traffic case, or prostitution case, or drug case, you can still hang the jury and prevent conviction, at least at that time. I think it'd be wonderful if people did that—by all means, if you believe in justice, go ahead and see if you can get yourself onto a jury.

---

10. www.totallyincorrectbook.com/go/209

L: To get past *voir dire*, you might have to lie or at least refuse to give fully honest answers to questions.

Doug: I would say it's entirely ethical to keep some of your thoughts to yourself in the interests of seeing justice done. Just act uncertain and confused—like all the others certainly are. You'll be indistinguishable, you should be fine, and might do some good.

L: I've thought about that; it'd be fun to help our legal system achieve some justice, in spite of itself. But to show up at a court, *as ordered*, and to cooperate with a system that presumes to command me to give it my time—it just runs so counter to my nature, I'm not sure I could do it.

Doug: I understand, but if I could get onto a jury and foil an unjust prosecution, I'd love to do it. And I'd encourage each of the 100,000 people reading this to do the same—and more, to spread the word to everyone of goodwill they know. As long as the jury system holds, there's a chance for people of conscience to overturn unjust laws, at least on a case-by-case basis. This could actually have a far, far larger effect on society than voting.

L: That's a key point; if we can't get the skittering creatures under the rocks in Washington to do the right things, we can do the right things ourselves in the courts, which is where the hard edge of the law actually hits people. Especially for those who are unable or unwilling to vote with their feet, this is a way to fight back, without violence, and without participating in coercion.

Doug: That's exactly right. And they can take comfort in the fact that as little as 100 years ago, this would not be a subversive act, but was exactly what was expected of a juror. The whole system has been turned upside down, and become the opposite of what it was meant to be.

L: It's perverse.

Doug: Good word.

L: Are there any investment implications to this? Or is this conversation just a public service announcement?

Doug: Well, I see people being convicted under ridiculous applications of the securities laws, tax laws, and more. In fact, almost all the administrative laws of the myriad of three- and four-letter agencies—ATF, FTC, EPA, SEC, FDA, etc., etc., are totally bogus and nonsensical "crimes." And even if you aren't convicted, it costs you hundreds of thousands or even millions of dollars in legal fees, plus time, plus lost business and reputation. All that just to defend yourself from this blindly rapacious system. And as the state grabs more and more power with each passing crisis, the risk of this sort of unhappy attention from the state increases, even for the people with the most innocent and honest of intentions and deeds. This is almost bound to get worse before it can get better, and that has very negative implications for anyone with any wealth the state might decide to question.

That has very serious implications for people in business, for investors, and for the stock market. This is one reason I'm so bearish on the prospects of the current world order; not only are there decades-long distortions in the economy that have to be liquidated, but the whole legal system is rotten to the core. It needs to be scrapped—someone needs to push the reset button and restore justice as its guiding principle—and that, too, is a distortion that can't be corrected easily or painlessly.

This is just one more thing to think about as we watch the global crisis deepen, one more trend to be aware of as we make our plans and shift the allocation of our assets.

L: Understood. Another sobering conversation, but it needed to be said. Thanks.

Doug: You're welcome.

Doug Casey on Education

Oct 21, 2009

L: Doug, in our recent conversation on global warming, you made some critical remarks about modern education. I know that wasn't mere drive-by disparagement—can you tell us why you're so hard on teachers today?

Doug: Sure. Since the school season started recently, it's probably a good time to talk about schools and education.

L: School season? Is there a bag limit on how many schools you can take down?

Doug: Well, I think that most of the money that's spent on so-called education is, if not wasted, definitely misallocated.

There was a book written a few years ago called something like *All I Really Need to Know I Learned in Kindergarten.* I have to admit I never read the book, but the title resonated with me—I think there's a lot of truth behind the notion. To me, it implies that a person should have absorbed basic ethical values and an understanding how to relate to other people, animals, and objects, by the time he's six years old. Those are the most important things anyone can learn, and should be the first things one learns. But it doesn't seem any institution, and fairly few parents, think to teach them.

But the first thing to do is to ask: What *is* education?

L: Okay, I'll bite. What is it?

Doug: Education is the process of learning how to perceive and analyze reality correctly. That would include subjects like ethics, science, history, and important literature.

L: What about logic? You'd have to include logic.

Doug: Yes, definitely. All things of that nature. The ancients developed the idea of liberal arts, which had a different meaning to them than our current usage. The root of "liberal" is "liber," meaning *free*. So the liberal arts were subjects that a free man—as opposed to a slave or a menial—was assumed to be acquainted with. They were divided into the arts and the sciences. The idea was, these things gave you the tools of thought and the building blocks of culture. They were distinct from the mechanical arts—which were means of earning a living. You'd learn the mechanical arts as an apprentice.

Put it this way. The quality of a person can be determined by how he relates to three critical verbs: Be, Do, and Have. The classical liberal arts show you how to "be"—they help form your essence, your character, your will. The mechanical arts show you how to "do"; they are important, but really are just acquired skills. As a consequence of what you are and what you can do, you "have"—acquire goods and money and reputation.

But it seems pretty clear that most people have the sequence totally backward. They want the "have" part, the material goods, but they don't understand it flows as a consequence of being something and having the ability to do something. Having things is trivial. It's why trailer-park trash will win a million-dollar lottery and wind up back on the dole a year later.

I fear that most of what kids get today, whether in grade school, high school, college, or post-grad, is not education. It's *training*.

Entirely apart from that, it seems to me that most institutions degrade as time passes. They naturally and inevitably become constipated, concrete-bound, and corrupt. That certainly appears to have happened to education in the US, and probably most other countries.

I'm sure you've seen that eighth-grade test from 1895 that's been floating around the Internet for some years. Snopes.com had a go at debunking it[1], but they didn't claim the test isn't real, and it does cover a lot of basic stuff few people today know anything about. What every educated person should know may change from age to age, but the basics of *thinking* and its application to language, science, etc. are enduring. And there are certain minimums of knowledge, tools for living, that everyone should have. The US education system is not delivering these basics.

Training is different. Training is rote learning with a view towards productive behavior in the future. It's what you'd learn on the job, as an apprentice laborer. This would cover most high school and college courses, which are not designed to produce educated young people but useful employees, ready to enter the labor force. But they don't even do that well.

I'll go further. Most schools today are state schools, or if they are not state schools, they teach state-approved curricula. There's an implicit orientation to

---

1. www.totallyincorrectbook.com/go/210

train the kids to be good little cogs in the wheel, as in obedient subjects, and as opposed to independent thinkers and citizens. That's probably the most important reason not to send your kids to a state school.

Homeschooling is a great alternative, though so many homeschoolers are religious fanatics, they've given the whole idea an unfortunate and undeserved aura of nuttiness. And in my view, filling your kids' heads with all sorts of religious superstition is no better than filling their heads with statist superstition. What they need is a classical education in the liberal arts—starting in grade school.

L: Do you really think homeschooling has such a bad reputation? Aren't homeschooled kids burning up the track at the spelling bees, geography bees, etc.?

Doug: Perhaps it depends on which circles you travel in. You homeschool, and you're not religious, so maybe you see things differently. But my sense is that media portrayal tends to emphasize the religious homeschoolers, and perhaps rightly so, since they constitute (I believe) the majority of homeschoolers.

But I'll give you a good reason to favor homeschooling, regardless of who most homeschoolers are. I had a good enough time in school, and I generally enjoyed the social interaction with the other kids. But it was a misallocation of my time; there's little of value you can learn from other kids. It's simply a bad idea to put your kids in an environment where they spend most of the day associating with young yahoos, many or most of whom have a lot of bad habits. The average school is full of unrefined young chimpanzees. Sure, kids need to learn how to work together and socialize, but school is not the only, and certainly not the best, place to do that.

Another reason is that every class, like a group traveling together, tends to move at the pace of the slowest kids in the group. An environment tailored for the lowest common denominator bores the smart kids to tears—or trouble. I was perpetually bored and distracted by the "one size fits all" program of my schools.

It's the same in college, which was an even more serious misallocation of four years of my time—and a bunch of my parents' money. And it's much worse today, in either current or constant dollars.

Like most of my friends, I'd end up cutting a lot of classes, because I'd stayed up too late the night before. When I did go to class, I'd fall asleep half the time. And even fully awake, my mind would wander and I wouldn't take good notes, so then I wouldn't bother reading the notes. Of course you learn stuff, but I think it's mostly through osmosis. Entirely apart from the fact that the profs varied greatly in quality.

Most people go to college today because they actually think someone is going to *give* them an education, when in fact, an education is something you have to give yourself.

You absolutely do not need a college to do that. The old saw about "Those who can, do, and those who can't, teach" is all too true. Professors can't educate anyone, though a few of the good ones can help motivated students educate themselves. But the college business is now structured like a manufacturing business; Aristotle and Seneca wouldn't know what to make of it.

L: My Webster's dictionary says the word educate has two roots: *e-*, "out," and *ducere*, "lead, draw, or bring." In other words, to draw out, or bring out what's in the student's ability to grasp and remember—not to cram whatever the teacher thinks is important into the student's head.

Doug: That's what "education" today fails to do—and why it's such a waste of money. There is no point at all in going to a college today, unless you're looking to learn a trade. Or, perhaps, because the people you meet in college might be of some future benefit to you. In other words, it's pointless unless it's Harvard, Princeton, Yale, or the like. Because of the classes? No. It's because the kids that go to such schools are the most intelligent and ambitious "up and comers"—so the connections you make and the patina you get at these places can open a lot of doors.

But if you look closely, the very best and brightest—people like Bill Gates or Steve Jobs—drop out, or don't even go.

I would suggest that a parent thinking of allocating $40,000 to $50,000 per year for four years of college education instead grubstake their kid with that same money. You could even make it a fraction of that, to be put into actually doing something, like starting a business or trying out different investment strategies, and get a lot more experience and knowledge for your kid as a result.

You certainly don't need a college to gain knowledge. For example, there's an outfit called <u>The Teaching Company</u>[2] that hires the very best professors in the world in all sorts of subjects to deliver superb audio courses. I listen to these things all the time in the car. I watch the ones that have important visual components on my computer, and I can go back and repeat anything I don't understand clearly—when my mind is receptive to it. It's *much* more effective than going to college would be, and it's vastly cheaper. Superior in every possible respect.

Another thing I'd do if I had a college-age kid is plan out a travel schedule. He'd have to spend at least a month in a dozen countries and report on what he does there. Travel may be the single best type of education, at least if done with a method and an objective.

---

2. www.totallyincorrectbook.com/go/211

There are many ways to get an education besides going to college—and going to a second-rate, third-rate, or community college is a complete waste of time and money. It serves no useful purpose whatsoever.

L: I've long thought similarly about what we call a "liberal arts education" today. Paying lots of money to read literature with friends seems patently silly, and to have someone tell you what some long-dead artist really meant seems arrogant to boot. But there are also things like physics, chemistry, and medicine. When I was a physics major at RPI, I was glad to have all sorts of laboratories and machine shops at my disposal—stuff I could never have built in my backyard…

Doug: I totally agree with you on that. Aside from the patina and connections I've been talking about, there are two valid reasons for going to a university. One is to study a hard science. You can still learn these on your own, but you're right; it helps a lot to have the labs and so forth. That's worth paying for.

The second reason is if you need a piece of paper that shows you've jumped through hoops other people recognize. In other words, if you're going into a trade, like doctoring, lawyering, or engineering, for which you need a certificate in order to be able to hang a shingle without getting arrested, that's okay because it's necessary.

Well, maybe not for lawyering—we have entirely too many lawyers in the world today. They've turned from expert helpers to parasites at considerable risk of overwhelming the host body.

Another degree I would strongly advise anyone against getting is an MBA, which has, regrettably, become a very fashionable degree. In our shop, if anyone applies for a job, an MBA is an active strike against them. They'd have to come up with a really good explanation for why they spent all that money and two years of extra time to get something that serves no useful purpose.

It's amazing, when you stop and think about it. The professors who teach MBA courses are not successful business people out making millions in the economy—they're academics! Successful business people with proven track records wouldn't work for their wages. These academics have no hands-on experience and are teaching theories, most of which are based on completely phony and fallacious economics.

Don't get conned into this gross misallocation of time and money. An MBA is worse than useless. Only a fool would rather have one than the $100,000, the lost income, and the two years of lost time and experience it costs.

L: I guess that explains how I got this job, with no relevant papers.

Doug: Of course—you're not a dog or a horse, for cryin' out loud. We don't need pedigree papers to identify talent we can see.

L: Another example in which training is desirable, and not a corruption of education, would be the military schools. Generals like rote, conditioned behaviors.

Doug: They do indeed. And soldiers need to learn practical skills, deeply ingrained, that can keep them alive under very difficult circumstances. Military academies are like advanced trade schools.

I very nearly went to West Point. The only reason I didn't is because I went to a four-year military boarding high school. In those days, military boarding schools were rather gruesome. I decided that I'd had quite enough of shining shoes, marching in squares, and saying "Yes, Sir!" to people I had no respect for.

L: Is that why you're an anarchist, Doug—was your response to that training to go as far in the opposite direction as you could go?

Doug: Well, let's not say that I have a problem with authority. I just have a problem with people telling me what to do.

L: Okay, well, I get the criticism of higher education, and I see the broad strokes of your proposed alternative educational strategy, but what about younger children? You seem to be saying that the very idea of the classroom is a bad one, public or private.

Doug: As a matter of fact, when I got out of college in 1968, I needed a job—and I got one: teaching sixth grade in Hobart, Indiana—the heart of Blues Brothers country. I only did it for one semester, but one thing really impressed me deeply: most of my co-workers were complete morons. They were people Jay Leno would feature on his *Jay Walking* videos if he'd ever met them. They had so little knowledge of the world and anything that matters, I was embarrassed to be called a teacher.

There are exceptional teachers, of course, but by and large, they are not the best and the brightest, they're losers. I wouldn't want to expose my progeny, if I had any, to a random collection of people who want to be government employees imprisoning kids for six hours a day.

L: Does that apply to private schools as well?

Doug: As I said, I went to a private military high school. Were my teachers any better than others? I suspect they were—but can't prove it. I'm sure there are some places, like Exeter Academy in New Hampshire, that pay more and probably attract a better grade of teacher. But if anything is worth doing, it's worth doing well, and in education, that means doing it yourself. Which means read, read, read.

L: So, your general view is that homeschooling is the way to go for younger children?

Doug: Exactly. Though I'm sure you'll sympathize with me when I say that I think toddlers ought to grow up for a couple years with wolves, so they can toughen up a bit and learn some survival skills. Kids are way overprotected these days. They are so isolated and insulated from reality, it's totally counterproductive. Sadly, it's hard to find a good wolf today.

So it's homeschool, then college only for technical trades and for the largely cosmetic advantages of an Ivy League pedigree. For most people, just reading books and then going out into the real world and doing stuff is way smarter, cheaper, and more productive. The difference between a properly educated kid and one subjected to conventional training is the difference between the Arnold Schwarzenegger character and the Danny DeVito character in the movie *Twins*.

And for God's sake, don't send your kids to business school. Better they should try some real businesses instead. Whether they succeed or fail, they'll learn much more.

L: That would put hundreds of thousands of people in the education business out of work. According to you, they are ill equipped for productive work—doesn't sound like a politically viable reform plan, Doug.

Doug: The ones who are any good would rise to the occasion and do something better with their time. And those who are not… well, we need people to clean toilets and sweep streets. At least they'd be away from our kids.

And all this dead weight is expensive. I understand that the per-pupil cost of public schooling in the US is running $10,000 to $12,000 per year. And college is $40,000 to $50,000 per year. There's no reason, no excuse, for it to cost so much.

Teachers who are any good could do as they did in ancient Greece and Rome, and solicit students. They could teach in their houses or in rented facilities, and compete with each other. They'd have every incentive to strive for the lowest-cost and highest-quality service—and they'd make more money, because most of the money spent on so-called education these days goes to administration and overhead. Not towards getting superstar teachers.

L: I can imagine a future in which the best teachers are celebrities, rich superstars. People would compete for spots in their classes. What would someone with a real passion for astrophysics pay to be able to study with Stephen Hawking?

Doug: That's exactly what I mean. And instead of having reason to conform as teachers do now, being members of unions, they'd have reason to excel. Unions have a well-established interest in making sure no one stands above the average, so they foment a culture that guarantees mediocrity. The whole educational system in the US needs to be flushed.

Unfortunately, just the opposite is happening. The Obama people want to give everyone a college education, probably including really useful mandatory courses in Gender Studies, Global Warming, and Marxist Economic Theory. Why stop there? Everyone ought to have a post-grad education as well.

L: Like Luna, in Woody Allen's *Sleeper*, who has a Ph.D. in oral sex?

Doug: Yes. It's insane. It's another sign that the whole system in the US, not just education, is upside down and overdue for collapse.

L: There's no reforming such an entrenched system, supported by such powerful unions and a population that believes it can and should be fixed. On the other hand, the education system in the US is such a dismal failure, people are opting out their kids in droves. So, with reality-reality vs. political reality, it could actually collapse. Maybe there is hope for a future in which there's real education, simply because the old system implodes and disappears.

Doug: It could happen. The US Department of Education should be abolished. The National Education Association building in Washington DC should be boarded up or dynamited. No, better yet, cleaned out and sold on the market, so some entrepreneur can put it to some useful business purpose.

L: It could be turned into a brothel. It would be more honest.

Doug: It would—you'd actually get value for your money.

L: Investment implications?

Doug: I expect I'll expand on this theme with an examination of publicly traded online universities. They represent an interesting trend.

L: Okay, well, thanks for another interesting talk.

Doug: My pleasure.

Doug Casey on Obamacare and Bioethicists—the TSA of the Intellectual World

Mar 28, 2012

L: So, what's on your mind this week, Doug? The coup in Mali? The black comedy provided by the US election circus? The latest market-moving pronouncements of The Beard?

Doug: No, I've never been to Mali, and I prefer to comment based on first-hand experience, not just parsing what some journalist writing from New York puts in his article on the place.

L: I thought you had been… You should have gone with me.

Doug: Next time. And the election is too pathetic to comment on at this time—a pox on both their houses. Maybe after the GOP selects its candidate for Clown in Chief. And there's nothing new in Bernanke's blathering. Though I do have to say that link you sent around, regarding this complete moron who is <u>Argentina's central banker saying that printing money does not lead to inflation</u>[1] just goes to show how hopeless the political situation in Argentina is. But I shouldn't be too hard on Argentina; every country in the world is headed in the wrong direction.

L: Isn't that a bit redundant, saying the central banker is a moron?

Doug: My apologies; you're quite right. As a class, central bankers are morons in $1,000 suits who've gone to prestigious universities and then play big shot at outrageously expensive international conferences. The head of Argentina's central bank is only slightly better than Zimbabwe's Gideon Gono and only a bit worse than Bernanke, in terms of foolishness.

L: Since speculators like to take advantage of predictable trends, and nothing is more predictable than government stupidity, is this an Argentinean buying opportunity in the making?

Doug: Yes; I think the cost of living in this place is about to get much lower. But we've already talked about why I like Argentina so much. What I want to

---

1. www.totallyincorrectbook.com/go/212

talk about today is the dangerous absurdity of so-called "bioethics." For years, every time I've read anything by a self-appointed bioethics pundit, it has made my skin crawl. Stupidity is bad enough, but aggressive, self-righteous, corrupt, and manifestly destructive stupidity just makes me want to scream.

L: Ah. You saw that pompous pile of buffalo chips[2] in support of Obamacare?

Doug: Yes, and with The Supremes about to take up the constitutionality of that particularly counterproductive piece of legislation, it's worth calling attention to this particularly despicable cadre of self-proclaimed experts on ethical matters. But, as always, we should start with a definition.

L: Here's what Wikipedia says[3]:

> Bioethics is the study of controversial ethics brought about by advances in biology and medicine. Bioethicists are concerned with the ethical questions that arise in the relationships among life sciences, biotechnology, medicine, politics, law, and philosophy. It also includes the study of the more commonplace questions of values ("the ethics of the ordinary") which arise in primary care and other branches of medicine.

Doug: It's all high-sounding hogwash. Bioethics is a phony science, recently concocted by busybodies working for pharmaceutical companies, governments, and medical institutions looking for excuses to justify what they have already decided to do. That's dangerous enough, but these are not just fools sowing confusion, they are mostly of a particular mindset—that is to say, they are a bunch of collectivists and statists—who pretend to be objective. Worse, they espouse policies with wide-reaching implications, almost universally wrong-headed and disastrous, which are a reeking part of the rotting fabric of what was once American society.

I don't know where they dig up these people—how can anyone be so corrupt, blind, and stupid at the same time, and still manage to tie his shoes in the morning? These people are like the TSA of the intellectual world. They are worse than useless; they are counterproductive, making people more confused on ethical matters, thereby making the world more dangerous. They hide under rocks and in sub-cellars in stable and happy times. But given an opening, they come out, and you have an infestation that's extremely hard to expunge. The kind of people who join the TSA are one species, but bioethicists are even worse.

---

2. www.totallyincorrectbook.com/go/213
3. www.totallyincorrectbook.com/go/214

L: I really wish you'd stop beating around the bush and let us know what you really think.

Doug: I guess I'll never be a diplomat—partly because it's against my nature, and partly because I'd then have to associate with other diplomats. We're dealing with fundamental issues of good and evil here; I urge everyone to read my article on the ascendancy of sociopaths in US governance[4]. Essentially, the powers of darkness have gotten the upper hand almost everywhere, and we're looking at a dystopian future, where *1984* might be used as an instructional manual.

But what really gets me about these bioethicists is that they are not technical experts contributing to debates among scientists—they're just a bunch of busybodies who want to tell everyone else what to do, based on their own opinions of morality and notions of political correctness. This is especially dangerous because people make decisions and act based on their ideas of what is right and wrong—on ethical grounds. By setting themselves up as the great determiners of what is ethically correct, these supposed experts become a sort of new secular priesthood to guide us all. They're worse than run-of-the-mill busybodies, however; they want to play the role of Gríma Wormtongue[5] in counseling rulers. They are generally sociopaths who want us to accept their statist, collectivist ethics, and thereby exert control over the direction of society, taking it down paths they deem best.

L: But even if this is all true, are these people really that dangerous? I mean, does the average guy switch the TV from Monday Night Football to watch a bioethicist deliver techno-drivel on C-SPAN?

Doug: Fortunately, few people listen to bioethicists. But unfortunately, those who do tend to be among those battling for control of public policy. These so-called ethical experts insinuate themselves into the bureaucratic machinery of the state, into the flow of intellectual and academic debate, into the course material taught at universities, and they exert influence.

It's especially dangerous because when people read about a consensus of Ph.D.s agreeing that X or Y is ethical, they may be seduced into letting these others do their thinking for them, instead of holding on to the vital responsibility of thinking through matters for themselves.

From the beginning of the Dark Ages up until the early 1500s, the Church of Rome was the arbiter of morality in the West. That was highly problematical, because it substituted the judgment of a priest for that of each individual. It's one reason that the medieval era was so backward. Individual responsibility to

---

4. www.totallyincorrectbook.com/go/215
5. www.totallyincorrectbook.com/go/216

understand ethics and act accordingly is a cornerstone of Western civilization, going all the way back to the Greeks. It's what the play _Antigone_[6] is all about. This is one reason that Islamic countries are basket cases—they're at the same stage of philosophical evolution as the West was in the medieval era.

Anyway, the decline of religion in the West over the last century—a trend I applaud for many reasons but won't go into now—has left something of a moral vacuum. It's been partially filled by secular religions like Marxism, but Marxism has been debunked everywhere but on college campuses... so the bioethicists are the latest fad trying to fill the space.

Individual responsibility, rather than diffuse responsibility among classes of people, is a major reason for the individual accomplishments and innovations that led the West to global eminence. Bioethicists are trying to set themselves up as a new priesthood, attempting to reverse an essential element of Western thought. These people are termites eating at the foundations of Western civilization and are contributing to the West's fall from eminence.

Bioethicists are irksome because they're a visible cutting edge of the knife destroying our sense of individual responsibility and freedom, they're trying to weave us into a socialist/fascist fabric, and yet they are given unearned respect and material prosperity.

L: For example?

Doug: I was reading an article by an alleged bioethical expert, spewing about medical advances, and the man, one Dan Callahan, Ph.D., actually said that <u>one of the problems with medicine is technology</u>[7].

L: What?! Medicine _is_ technology.

Doug: Yes, you're exactly right. Needless to say, he conflates healthcare with medical care, which are two totally different things. But beyond that, this luminary actually says that technology "is one of the barriers to an equitable and sustainable healthcare system." Why? It "drives up costs with little return on investment."

L: Tell that to the people who are alive today because of technological breakthroughs.

Doug: You have to see clearly what he's saying. He didn't say technology was a barrier to _effective_ medical treatment, he said it's a barrier to an "equitable and sustainable healthcare system." He doesn't give a fig if you or I live or die, it's the system—the collective—that matters most to him and all his socialist ilk. This is classic. These frauds are not experts in ethics at all, but socialists

6. www.totallyincorrectbook.com/go/217
7. www.totallyincorrectbook.com/go/218

using big words that sound scientific and objective to con people into buying their collectivist values.

The collectivist mindset is a pathology. Socialists have been discredited by the collapse of the USSR and the economic boom in China—which is now socialist in name only. So, they've migrated from economics to "ecology," where they have become "watermelons"—green on the outside, red on the inside. And they've redoubled their efforts to capture the legal and academic arenas. Bioethics offers a chance to do that, plus corrupt science, plus gain the high moral ground. It's a wonderful scam. And if these people are good at anything— actually it's the only thing they're good at—it's perpetrating a scam.

L: I have a friend who lives in a country with socialized medical care. His family ate some poisonous mushrooms several years ago. He ate few and lived. His wife and son ate many. His son went to a children's hospital, where they routinely pump the stomachs of children who swallow things, and the son lived. His wife went to an adult hospital, where the doctors didn't bother pumping her stomach, saying it had been too long already. She died. It also turned out later that there was a new medicine the doctors did not try—did not even mention—because it was very expensive and not covered. This is what you get when you place greater value on an "equitable and sustainable healthcare system" than on the individual's right to pursue the best health care possible.

Doug: That would be your friend Virgis in Lithuania?

L: Yes.

Doug: I remember—I'm sorry for your friend… but you're exactly right. These lickspittle pseudointellectuals are on their way to becoming a leading cause of death in the US and elsewhere. They are metastasizing into a giant force for government control of science and suppression of "unsustainable" research not aligned with the goals of those in power. Instead of allowing innovators to create new treatments wherever new ideas take them, we could end up with pseudoscience following a course of research set by the dominant political agenda of the day.

It should not be up to lunatic busybodies like this Callahan to tell people how much they can spend trying to keep themselves alive; it should be up to individuals. If some people can afford expensive new treatments, bully for them. If some people can't, they are no worse off than they were before the new treatment was invented. Nobody gets out of here alive.

But of course, to a socialist this is a big problem, because in that view everyone should have equal and unlimited access to all treatments. In this perverted view of things, it doesn't matter if an expensive treatment is better, it doesn't matter that rich people who pay for new treatments open the path for less expensive and better treatments in the future—it matters only that the system cannot afford to provide something for everyone now. This only shows that the man is not an expert in medical technology, nor economics, and especially not ethics.

L: An example of subservience to political agendas being this article in support of the so-called <u>Affordable Care Act</u>[8] (ACA) we started with?

Doug: Yes. The op-ed's authors argue that since medical companies can avoid state regulation by basing operations in other states, the "interstate commerce clause" of the Constitution gives the federal government the authority to regulate medicine. Of course what's going to happen is that medical entrepreneurs will not just locate to a different state but to a different country, where they can develop products freely and cheaply. And more and more Americans will go elsewhere for medical care. Even more will renounce their citizenships and go elsewhere to avoid everything from being forced to buy medical insurance to being forced to support the Welfare-Warfare State in general.

L: People are already <u>voting with their feet</u>[9]. The clauses allowing regulation of interstate commerce are one of the most serious flaws in the Constitution; it's opened up a gigantic can of worms.

Doug: I know that. You know that. So does any intellectually honest person who follows the evolution of the Constitution. There's a huge body of legal precedent and subsequent legislation that uses the interstate commerce clause to justify all sorts of federal intervention into the economy, and has done so for decades. I'd argue that the distortion of the interstate commerce clause into a *carte-blanche* excuse for everything the federal government wants to do but is not given the power to do in the Constitution was, in fact, the end of the rule of law in what was once America. Of course, the whole Constitution is really a dead letter. It's been selectively interpreted out of existence and is now simply disregarded whenever it suits our ruling cadres.

But we digress. These bioethical poseurs actually argue that the interstate commerce clause gives the federal government the right to *force* individuals to buy medical insurance they don't want—the "individual mandate" part of Obamacare:

> Striking down the individual mandate would introduce a new and deeply problematic chapter in the history of the Commerce Clause. For the first time since the New Deal, Congress would no longer

---

8. www.totallyincorrectbook.com/go/219
9. www.totallyincorrectbook.com/go/220

hold a vital power of national concern, namely, the authority to regulate all economic subject matter substantially affecting commerce.

Before the government became involved in medical care—first because of Roosevelt and then especially under Johnson—medical insurance wasn't even necessary. But this guy enthusiastically wants more state intervention, not less.

L: It's hard to imagine anyone using the interstate commerce clause in this way with a straight face. The Bill of Rights is all about protecting individual human rights. That's what once made America great; it was set up with a focus on the well-being of the people, not the state. To use one part of the Constitution to ride roughshod over the rest is an Orwellian nightmare.

Doug: A nightmare we've been living for decades—and a nightmare that will lead to its lamentable but inescapable conclusion—in the not-too-distant future, I believe[10]. At any rate, the Congress has no business regulating interstate commerce—or any economic activity. That's what's taking what's left of America down the path of Mugabe and into depression. There should be separation of economy and state for basically the same reasons we have separation of church and state.

L: Sure, but you think there should be a separation between all human activity and state, since you don't think the state should exist.

Doug: But that's a conversation we've already had[11]. Maybe the advent of these bioethicists is a sign that the ascendancy of state power has reached a peak and things have gotten so bad that they have to get better going forward.

L: Nah—things can get worse. They can always get worse.

Doug: Well… you're right. But I'm a perpetual optimist. The fact is that the trend is accelerating—not reversing or even slowing—toward total state control of everything in the US. Back to bioethics: Far be it from me to defend a Republican argument, but there's something to what they say about "death panels." If you socialize medicine, who will determine what treatments are allowed? What treatments are within *budget*? There will have to be panels of supposed experts—like these bioethicists—who will literally have the power of life and death in their hands. As you pointed out with your friend's experience in Lithuania, people may be denied treatment simply because it's not routine or because it's not in the system's best interests because it's too expensive.

There are two ways you can allocate scarce resources: economically or politically.

---

10. www.totallyincorrectbook.com/go/221
11. www.totallyincorrectbook.com/go/222

L: "Economically" meaning based on what individuals can afford or find support to pay for. "Politically" meaning based on what the day's rulers deem fit. The former may seem unfair to some, but the latter is a disaster for almost everyone but those in power—and even them, eventually, when they run the system down.

But okay, I think we've made our case. Investment implications?

Doug: Just another sign of the times—the decay of Western civilization, the continuing decline and transformation of America into the United State. This supports everything we've been saying in *The Casey Report* and other conversations we've had: rig for stormy weather, because we're going through the wringer.

L: All right, then. Thanks, and 'til next week.

Doug Casey on the US's Most Consistently Wrong-Headed Journalist

Jan 11, 2012

[Skype rings. It's Doug calling. Sounds like he's got a fistful of papers he's waving around in agitation.]

L: Hola, Doug—what's on your mind?

Doug: Well, you know I try not to read much in the popular press. It's mentally unsanitary. But occasionally, a few things catch my notice. For example, I've got an article I tore out of the September 3 *Wall Street Journal*—it's been in a stack of papers for a couple of months, and I just uncovered it. I couldn't decide, when I first tore it out, whether it was simply beneath contempt or actually worth commenting on. It's an absolutely shocking indictment of the depth to which the moral and intellectual character of what was once America has descended. The title is "How to Turn in Your Neighbor to the IRS[1]." The author's theme is that the IRS is offering big rewards to people who turn in tax cheats—but there are catches. As though the depravity of denouncing your neighbors to a ruthless, brutal, and predatory government bureaucracy were a good thing, as long as one is careful in going about it.

The person who wrote the article, one Laura Saunders—probably the kind of creature who's angling for a cabinet post in the Department of the Treasury at some point—starts off by writing: "Maybe it's your brother-in-law, who has a new Mercedes and likes to quip that only fools pay all their taxes." The article then goes on to list other sorts of people whom the envious losers and assorted sociopaths of the world may want to use the IRS to punish for being what they are.

[Sounds of paper being crumpled violently]

L: That reminds me of Ray Bradbury's *Fahrenheit 451*, a novel in which houses are fireproof and books are banned because they made people think—which makes them unhappy with the way things are. So there are Fire

---

1. www.totallyincorrectbook.com/go/223

Department drop boxes you could use to denounce your neighbors who might be hiding books in the rafters, and the Fire Department would show up and burn them, with prejudice.

Doug: Yes, that's right. Even in prisons, among the dregs of society, the snitch—the squealer—is viewed as the lowest form of life, next to a child molester. But here we have someone alerting the public how to rat out their neighbors and relatives in a feature article in the *Wall Street Journal*. To me, this is an indication that the *Wall Street Journal*, supposedly a bastion of capitalism, is no bastion of anything. There are clearly no standards, either in its editorial department or among its reporters. It's appalling and disgusting—but, that said, still far superior to the *New York Times*, *The Washington Post*, and *USA Today*.

[More crumpling of papers, possibly followed by the sound of a toppling wastebasket, knocked over by said crumpled papers]

L: Better take it easy crumpling papers by the microphone, or people might think you're trying to sound like Rush Limbaugh.

Doug: Anything but that. There's another sign of the decay of the US. Limbaugh has done great harm to the cause of free-market thinking. He was actually quite funny back when he was making fun of Clinton. One might have thought, hating the Clintons as he did, that he was a friend of liberty. But the enemy of your enemy isn't necessarily your friend. As it turned out, he was just a Republican lickspittle. It's especially rich that he advocated the execution of drug users and then went and got himself busted for Oxycontin abuse. I despise hypocrites. I have many vices of my own, most of which I rather enjoy, but I'd hate to be called a hypocrite.

L: I could never stand listening to the man. Much as I value self-esteem, his ego pushed me right out of the room whenever he was on the radio.

Doug: But the brain-dead "dittoheads" who idolize him couldn't care less. Anyway, another journal out of New York that I read is the *New York Review of Books*. It's a sort of in-house publication for left-wing intellectuals and the literati. It's a house organ for concerned, socially active, overeducated—or rather, indoctrinated—liberals. I've nonetheless subscribed to it for over 20 years. The reason is that I like to know what's going on in these people's bent minds. It's a kind of early warning system to see what they talk about among themselves. But that's hardly enough to justify $60 per annum, or whatever I pay. Forgetting their politics and economics, they frequently have excellent articles and obviously, reviews of books on the sciences, ancient literature, and various odd areas of intellectual arcana I'm interested in.

L: And it'll confuse the Thought Police when they go through your garbage.

Doug: That's always a good thing. At any rate, a case in point is a review of a new book by Thomas L. Friedman, who is the intellectual Wrong-Way Corrigan of our day. He's a professional busybody who's ethically and economically on the wrong side of everything. Now, I have to say that I haven't read the book, called *That Used to Be Us: How America Fell Behind in the World It Invented and How We Can Come Back*. That's partly because I don't want a single penny of my money going into his pocket and partly because this is one of the reasons I subscribe to *NYRB*. However, I've read enough by him in the past to understand his thinking. The book review itself, which is written by a highly sympathetic foreign-policy wonk—these people all review each other's books, it's quite incestuous—is worth commenting on.

My friend Bill Bonner of *The Daily Reckoning* and I tend to agree on most everything. We have a laugh riot whenever we talk about a Friedman editorial, although it's a black kind of comedy.

As a professional busybody, Friedman has *the* answer for how to improve everything—how we can all make our lives better, if we'd only do as he says... which almost always involves giving the government more power to enforce his prescriptions.

L: So, what are these prescriptions that will save us all?

Doug: The reviewer summarizes the book, saying Friedman describes four challenges America faces. First is the expansion of globalism.

L: Ah yes, that evil force that is raising the standard of living of some of the poorest people across the planet, because now they can compete for jobs with laborers in richer countries.

Doug: Yes, that's the one. Because everyone knows that Americans deserve to get paid more for the exact same work that others will do for less. It says so in the Constitution. Or the Bible. Somewhere. That's the natural order of things, so naturally, we can't even consider eliminating minimum wage laws, mandatory insurance and retirement plans, and fat benefits packages extracted and accreted by labor unions[2] over the years. That'd make it possible for Americans to compete for jobs on a level playing field. That obviously just wouldn't do, having some overfed gender-studies graduate competing with an Indian engineering major. We must have government tame the evil force of globalization with more regulations, fees and fines, or what-have-you.

L: It'd be funny if it weren't tragic, how quickly people come to regard historically recent social arrangements, like so-called Social Security, as though they were carved in stone at the time of Moses.

---

2. www.totallyincorrectbook.com/go/224

Doug: Indeed. The next challenge is education, which in the Information Age must be upgraded to enable Americans to compete with all the smart, hardworking people globalization is empowering. This, of course, according to Friedman, will require much more government spending and involvement in education—the very thing that has led to such dismal educational levels in the US now. State-provided "free" education (ignore the man behind the curtain and the taxes you must pay, whether you have children in school or not) is the primary reason for the appalling level of ignorance in the US today.

Although schools in the US have become little more than babysitting centers, indoctrination institutes, or juvenile prisons, it's obvious to any right-thinking person they can be made better simply by throwing more money at them.

L: Of course. By the way, when I'm out and about with my children—who are homeschooled—and they see a school bus, they like to shout: "Prisoner Transport!"

Another thought: I was just talking to my son's sports coach, and he was telling me that schoolteachers are increasingly not allowed to fail anyone. Might hurt their feelings. Yet the children are increasingly unprepared to work hard or endure any discomfort, because everyone passes regardless of effort. Everyone is wonderful regardless of results. All the system needs is more money—and maybe sedatives, which will surely teach the kids not to do drugs—and all will be well.

Doug: This is typical of the statist mind-set: People like Friedman never saw a bureaucracy they didn't like, and if the bureaucracy fails in any way, it's not the fault of the bureaucrats or stupid regulations and laws. It's because they need more money and power to do the job right.

L: A pity Reagan didn't have the spine to kill the Department of Education as he said he would.

Doug: That and about 100 other counterproductive, expensive, wasteful, and unethical agencies that ought to be completely abolished and salt sown in the ground where their buildings once stood.

L: Just to show that it *doesn't* take a village, did you see that MIT—a private school—is now giving education away[3]?

Doug: I did see that. And of course, you know I'm a big fan of The Teaching Company's products[4]—a much better way to learn than paying tens of thousands of dollars to have administrators babysit you while you read textbooks. Education isn't something that you receive by paying money; it's something you do.

3. www.totallyincorrectbook.com/go/225
4. www.totallyincorrectbook.com/go/226

Anyway, the third challenge is debt. Now, I'd have to agree that debt levels are in urgent need of addressing. But, true to form, Friedman looks at it completely backwards. He says: "Our habit of not raising enough money through taxation to pay for what the federal government spends, and then borrowing to bridge the gap... "This is typical of Friedman. He never even considers the possibility of not spending so much money to start with. It's not even a logical possibility in his mind.

L: Isn't it peculiar that in the US—which is thought of around the world as a capitalist society—the idea of actually cutting government spending in any significant and meaningful way is a total non-starter? It's not even an option on the table in Washington, D.C. But in Europe—long a bastion of more openly socialist public policy—the EU is actually demanding austerity measures of its more profligate members, including actual cuts in government spending. Since the member countries can't just print more money now, they are—at least half-heartedly—trying to comply.

Doug: Yes. That is the bright side of all these governments going bankrupt; they will be forced to dump many of their cherished projects and programs. That won't be because they believe in free markets, but simply because it won't be possible to keep the Ponzi schemes going.

L: And the fourth challenge?

Doug: You're going to love this: It's the threat of fossil fuels to the planet's biosphere. Somehow, the US will save itself and make itself more competitive country in the global economy by embracing more economically suicidal policies based on misinformed—if not actually malign—pressure from environmental extremists.

I have to be careful here, because I'm not a climatologist nor an expert in any of the many technical fields one would really have to master in order to come to a truly, fully well-informed opinion about anthropogenic global warming.

L: Sure, but I'd guess Friedman isn't either, and that doesn't stop him from pronouncing his sage advice on the topic.

Doug: Of course not. On the other hand, I am somebody who makes it his business to read a lot of scientific publications and I try to understand the basic theory, as well as keep abreast of current scientific developments. As we've discussed, I've actually done a lot of digging into the subject, trying to sort through the hysteria and highly politicized coverage.

I've got to say that it makes me very uncomfortable that US Republicans generally come down against the notion of anthropogenic global warming, because they tend to be scientifically ignorant and wrong-headed. I almost wish they were on the other side on this one, because I feel very uncomfortable being on the same side with them—it's rather like making an argument for states' rights and then finding yourself in the company of KKK members making the same argument.

L: Ouch.

Doug: But it is what it is, and at least we can say that the Democrats are almost equally scientifically ignorant, with their fetish for being anti-technology. It's rather odd, really. The Republicans are reflexively anti-science—especially evolution theory. And the Democrats tend to be reflexively anti-technology—things like fracking and nuclear power.

At any rate, global warming is Friedman's fourth big challenge, and the reviewer says that Friedman asserts that all four "require a collective response."

L: Can't rely on the private sector when you believe it takes a village.

Doug: Or a mob. Never mind that a collective has never discovered or invented anything. It was individual geniuses who brought cheap light and heat to give us comfort and productivity in what was once the cold, dark night. Friedman seems to sincerely think that Congress is wise. He really believes that if our wise leaders would only say, "Make it so," then the peons could go out and collectively create the millennium.

I hate to be in effect reviewing a book without reading it, but I have a lot of confidence in the *NYRB* to accurately represent a writer's philosophy when they agree with it. That said, I see this more as an opportunity to review Friedman who, although an excellent writer, is even more shallow than he is earnest—and he's very earnest. He'll probably sell some books, since shallow isn't a problem when marketing to *Boobus americanus*, and the public is anxious for easy solutions. They also love certainty, which is something he radiates. Unfortunately, Friedman not only comes up with bogus challenges but foolish solutions to the problems he fabricates.

L: I'm looking on Amazon.com, and the book is currently ranked 415th on its best-sellers list. Nowhere near the top, but still getting some sales.

Doug: Friedman desperately wants the ruling classes to take him seriously. And they do—because they're cut from the same cloth. Politicians love ideas that can serve to increase their relevance and power. Friedman is a point man for those who believe that there actually should be a public-private partnership between the state and businesses. For example, he goes on about the need for government support for basic research.

L: Well, Al Gore <u>invented the Internet</u>[5]. Don't you remember?

Doug: Ah, yes. I forgot about that. And I'm sure at this point that Al would like to forget about it as well… although he'll likely be best known as an inventor of global warming. But back to Friedman. He's one of the most popular journalists in the US, and the vision he's promulgating is for more taxes, more regulation, and more government generally, to "help" the US recover.

L: From its addiction to too much government?

Doug: Right. And then the reviewer goes on to say that, "as Paul Krugman reminds us"—

L: The guy who thinks <u>fear of space aliens</u>[6] would be good for the economy.

Doug: Yes, him. You can tell where the author and reviewer are coming from. Krugman is almost certainly the most embarrassing choice they've ever made for the Nobel Economics prize; he's not even an economist. He's only a political apologist and an intellectual clone of Friedman. But, to give credit where it's due, I will say that Friedman says in the book that he regrets his support for the war in Iraq.

L: Well, at least he didn't wait 30 years like McNamara did.

Doug: Yes. I think I've mentioned that one of the things I most regret not having done in my life is related to Robert "the Strange" McNamara.

On the other hand, I don't want to give Friedman too much credit, because after what seems like a duplicitous neglect to mention the role of public education in producing ignorant and ill-trained workers, he just calls for more government spending to provide training. And at the same time, he advocates more corporate welfare, to help with "research" and "job creation."

Without the wise direction of the state, individuals wouldn't have the sense to educate themselves. Without state money—which was originally taken from them—corporations couldn't afford to do R&D.

L: Clear as day. He doesn't see that when government pays companies to create jobs, they get jobs that don't need doing—otherwise the market would have met the demand. And the money they extract from the economy to do these things is taken from more productive uses, weakening the economy.

Doug: Friedman is clearly a fascist, believing that the government should splurge even more on welfare—not only to those at the bottom but to the big companies at the top.

L: Note to readers who don't know Doug well: He's not just calling names—a cornerstone of Mussolini's fascist vision for Italy was a public-private partnership.

---

5. www.totallyincorrectbook.com/go/227

6. www.totallyincorrectbook.com/go/228

Doug: Hitler's too, for that matter. So, it's no surprise that two of the worst presidents from a libertarian view are Friedman's favorites: FDR and LBJ. Why? Because they "exploited crises"—the Great Depression and the assassination of JFK—to ram through "bold and daring" government programs. Anyway, fascism isn't essentially about jackboots, mass rallies, and starting wars—although it always winds up with those things. It's about meshing the state with large corporations. Unlike socialism, it's about allowing corporations to be privately owned, so thoughtless people easily conflate it with capitalism. Then favored classes can become wealthy, through fat salaries, bonuses, and share options. But corporations are state controlled—through regulation, taxation, and directed spending.

L: Friedman is like an anti-Doug. I wonder if you were to shake hands with him... Would you both cease to exist, like matter and antimatter colliding?

Doug: It'd be an interesting experiment... I've shaken hands with Castro and Clinton and I'm still here. But perhaps it was partly fear of a matter-antimatter flash that kept me from shaking Cheney's hand.

That's probably just about enough on this subject, but there is one more thing I'd like to comment on. The reviewer goes on to say: "At a time when Tea Party enthusiasts, determined to oppose, discredit, and ultimately defeat the first black president of our country... " as though Obama's race were even an issue for most Tea Party members, and more so than his blatant socialist philosophy.

L: If the reviewer is making it about race, then he's actually the one acting as a racist, because such decisions should be made on merit, not skin color.

Doug: Exactly. And people like this are archetypes among the chattering class who control the mainstream media in the US. They never hesitate to support and praise people like Thomas Friedman, no matter how ill-informed and destructive his ideas are, because like them, Friedman wants to see more government control of our lives. These people all slop at the trough of the state. At the same time, they do their best not to even acknowledge the existence of people like Ron Paul, who's trying to do the opposite.

More nails in the coffin of the place that was once America.

L: Okay then, thanks for another interesting—if not exactly cheerful—conversation.

Doug: My pleasure, as always.

Doug Casey on Political Correctness

Sept 16, 2009

L: So, Mr. Wilson (R–SC) went to Washington and called the president a liar, an action I can't help but approve of. Regrettably, he didn't have the spine to stick with the truth and later apologized to the president. Knowing that you don't have any more use for politicians than I do, Doug, I suspect you have some thoughts on this subject.

Doug: Yes. First of all, I have to say that it does speak well of Wilson that he would do something like that. But a little research shows that his comment had little to do with principle and more to do with the battle over medical insurance for illegal aliens and his desire that they not be given any. A few years ago, he voted to insure them—just the opposite. The point is that he might have yelled out, "You lie!" just to get some free publicity, to garner his 15 minutes of fame. Like almost everyone else in Congress, he's a hypocrite who stands for absolutely nothing. Certainly not the truth. Interestingly, he was censured by Congress for simply pointing out a fact.

But reprimands are rare. The last two I recall were Traficant in '02, after a federal bribery conviction, and Gingrich in '97 for ethical breaches to do with a multimillion-dollar book deal. Wilson is being reprimanded for what amounts to a speech crime or, really, just impoliteness.

One nice thing about the spat was that it allowed a glimpse behind the facade of gentility Congress tries to project. One problem with Congress—one of very many—is that it's entirely too politically correct. They have rules about how they are supposed to treat each other with respect, not call each other names, etc. But I'm of the opinion, assuming we have to have a Congress at all, that the country was much better served during the 19th century, when these creatures would physically fight each other on the floor and invite each other outside for duels. Self-removal of hotheads and blowhards from the political process was a public service.

I don't like the idea of Congress trying to make itself appear august and worthy of respect when its members are basically all thugs, at least psychologically and philosophically. It's false advertising.

L: This reminds me of the way the Constitution prohibits titles of nobility. The founders were vehemently opposed to the establishment of a new American aristocracy and even more so of a new American monarchy. And yet, we have a set of government administrators who wear black robes—thank goodness the powdered wigs are no longer fashionable—and ask us to call them "Your Honor."

Doug: Right. I've been in court a few times and had to address the judge, and I've never addressed him as "Your Honor." I've addressed him as "Judge."

L: That's simply a statement of fact.

Doug: Exactly right. But to take what you're saying a bit further, I don't like the way media interviewers address the politicians by their titles in an honorific way. I saw an interview with Newt Gingrich the other day, and he was still addressed as "Mr. Speaker." Even if he were still the speaker, he shouldn't be addressed that way—he should be called "Newt" or "Mr. Gingrich," if one wanted to be polite. It's entirely too close to the European custom of addressing certain persons as "Your Highness," or "Your Eminence," or "Your Holiness," or "Your Lordship."

L: How about, "Hey, scumbag?"

Doug: If you wish. Gingrich is a particularly unprincipled creature. None of them should be called "Senator," nor "Representative," just "Mr.," at best. I don't want to be thought of as a Jacobin who thinks everyone should be addressed as "Citizen," nor as a Soviet, who thinks everyone should be called "Comrade." But I think addressing people by their first name, once you've been introduced, or by their last name, or "Mr." if you want to show respect, is the proper way to do it. Why should a government employee be treated with any more deference than a shop clerk?

L: Okay—back to Mr. Wilson. I don't suppose there was any chance of him doing anything honorable, like throwing a shoe at Obama? Wilson wasn't really objecting to lying in general, but to a particular lie that upset his own political agenda.

Doug: Unfortunately. I certainly think there have been so many blatant lies, and gross and willful misinterpretations of reality by Obama, that there's nothing wrong with calling him a liar. Just because he's the president doesn't mean he shouldn't be called a liar. In fact, this should be done much more often...

L: [Interrupts, laughing.]

Doug: I'm serious. Politics is nothing but a body of lies. It's given entirely too much respect, and that is unhealthy for a society. That fellow who threw his shoes at Bush, Muntazer al-Zaidi, he's a hero. He took his life in his hands to do the correct and honorable thing. I have immense respect for him.

This is why the Soviet Union and Nazi Germany lasted so long: people were too afraid to speak up and yell "Liar!" at Hitler and Stalin. And you can see that Wilson was afraid of what might happen to his career if he didn't apologize, so he rolled over on his back and wet himself. We're headed in the wrong direction.

L: The Thought Police are coming.

Doug: You can hear their sirens; soon you'll hear them banging on your door. You know, when the phrase "politically correct" came out in the 1980s, I thought it was a spoof of some kind, a line from a Saturday Night Live skit. The Soviets had "political officers" to make sure everyone thought—or at least spoke—in approved manners, not America. But political correctness has woven itself into American society over the last generation. We're not allowed to say anything politically incorrect.

L: You're not kidding. Children used to be taught not to let anyone's mean-spiritedness bother them. "Sticks and stones may break my bones, but names will never hurt me." But now, if you work for a large corporation—or even an evangelically correct smaller one—you can be tried and sentenced on pain of losing your job to "sensitivity training" for nothing more than boorish words. And there is at least one place in America where a joke or even polite words spoken with heat can get you arrested: an airport.

Doug: For sure. These 50,000 TSA people take themselves more and more seriously. I mean, you can't even look at them askance, or they'll interrogate you. And you better speak respectfully when you give your answers, or missing your plane will be the least of your worries.

You know, people often wonder where the Nazis found the bedbugs willing to join the Gestapo and the SS, and where the Soviets found the worms who worked for the KGB. Well, they were exactly the same sort who join the TSA. They are largely nothing/nobody people who were doing nothing with their lives—middle-aged people who were recruited out of their nothing/nowhere jobs, to go to work for a government agency, literally going through people's dirty laundry and asking them impertinent questions.

L: Don't forget the spiffy uniforms. They're important psychologically.

Doug: We mustn't forget the spiffy uniforms. That fetish is part of the psychological profile of these creatures. They love uniforms; they make them feel a part of something bigger than themselves, giving them a sense of self-importance and meaning to their meaningless lives. It's all part of this atmosphere of political correctness.

You know, the only people who can say overtly politically incorrect things today are comedians. This is one reason I really enjoy the comedy of George Carlin, in particular. He was a genius. People like Sarah Silverman, Lisa Lampanelli, Dave Chappelle, and Chris Rock have really grown on me for the same reason. These people are capable of saying absolutely anything, and they can get away with it, unlike the non-professional comedian. Their role is roughly analogous to that of the court jester in the Middle Ages, the only ones who could insult the king. It's a pity the average guy now has to "outsource" his sense of humor.

L: Maybe they get away with it because they are "just telling jokes," so they "don't really mean what they are saying." Intentions matter more than deeds to so many people today, so the fact that they are trying to amuse gets them off the hook. But really, why should it matter?

Doug: That may be right—and where does it lead us? Will you need to get a license to say funny things? It's part of the increasingly corrosive atmosphere in America that you have to watch not only what you say, but whom you say it to and who might overhear what you are saying. We really are entering the era of Thought Crime and Double-Think.

L: Doubleplusbad! Or should that be, "Doubleplusungood?"

Doug: You'll have to re-read *1984* to find out.

L: Heh. "Freedom is the freedom to say that two plus two make four. If that is granted, all else follows."

Doug: Can't have that…

L: I find it mind-boggling that it's American liberals, who traditionally held the First Amendment to the US Constitution to be a sacred thing—who are so ready to decry homophobia and book burning—that it's these same self-described *liberals* who have become the main voice of censorship in America today.

Doug: It used to be that you could count on liberals to at least give lip service to free speech, but you knew they hated economic freedom. And in the past you could count on the conservatives to at least give lip service to economic freedom, but you knew they hated free speech. But the fact of the matter is that, as shown by their actions, neither group really likes any kind of freedom at all.

"Liberal" and "Conservative" no longer define philosophical positions—they only designate a variety of psychological aberration. The Republicans used to be the Warfare Party and the Democrats the Welfare Party. They've been merged for some time into the Demopublican Party, and there's not enough difference between its two wings to be worth the powder it would take to blow them both to hell.

L: So, do you see this as a sort of "Crisis & Leviathan" scenario? All these politicians pander to various interest groups, adding to the layers of attempted thought control… Or do you see a deliberate design behind the erosion of free thought in America?

Doug: Well, I'm not inclined to believe in conspiracies. As anyone who's tried to get three friends to agree on a movie or a dinner knows, it's hard to get even such a small number of people on the same page on something as simple as that—much less hatching plans to take over the world.

But the fact that politicians can successfully pander to things like that tells me how very degraded the average American has become. The way to get a following these days appears to be to appeal to people's most base psychological aberrations. This tells me that it's not the political class that's the problem, but the average American himself.

These horrible people who rise up in the political system, as incredible as it may seem, could actually be among the best, and not the worst, America has to offer. I find this a most disturbing thought. One that is reinforced by watching reality TV or the *Jerry Springer Show*.

L: Very disturbing. And depressing. America might actually be getting the government it deserves.

Doug: Well, justice is defined as getting what you deserve. And justice is a cardinal virtue to me. We've evolved a long way from a sturdy yeoman republic, in which everyone was responsible for himself, took care of his own business, and *minded* his own business. Now, everything is everyone's business—which is to say, the government's business. I don't see any way to turn this unfortunate trend around at this point. It's taken on a life of its own, and we'll just have to see where it goes. Although I'll lay odds it's going to go badly, and the downtrend is going to accelerate.

L: It will have to go to *reductio ad absurdum*. People don't have the philosophical foundations necessary to even see the problem, let alone embrace the painful cure.

Doug: There's little cause for optimism. That's one reason I don't believe the United States will still exist in its present form in 100 years—probably not even 50, though I hate making predictions like that. That's because what we're going into now—certainly from an economic point of view, but also from a psychological point of view—is really much more serious, and potentially much more devastating, than what happened in the '30s and '40s. What this country will look like when it comes out the other side is an open question.

L: So, looking at this as speculators, what are the implications of mass willful ignorance and entrenched stupidity? As we've discussed already in our conversations on currency controls and living abroad, the most obvious answer is to get your ass and your assets out of harm's way. But is there a way to bet on the rise of the American Thought Police?

Doug: I'll tell you a true story. About 15 years ago, I was at a luncheon group that meets every Friday in Aspen. Bill Bennett, the former "Drug Czar," was the speaker. After he gave his perfectly horrible speech, the guy who was moderating knew my mind, so he called on me to ask some embarrassing questions.

L: I remember seeing Bennett tell a TV reporter that he didn't need drug laws to stop him from abusing drugs, but that "people" did.

Doug: That's him all right. So, of course my question turned into a denunciation, and his lackeys there were booing and hissing at me. Anyway, one thing he said that was very interesting was: "Buy stocks in prison companies—we're going to be building a lot more of them."

L: He actually came out and said that?

Doug: He did. That's a fact. And it was actually good investment advice. Though it also showed me the guy's basic character, which I see as a deformed, criminal personality.

L: Suppose you were convinced that shares in a company in the business of making devices for eavesdropping on people in their homes were about to go to the moon—would you actually invest in such a company? You wouldn't feel any moral qualms about it?

Doug: That's a good question. I certainly wouldn't buy stock in an IPO of such a company, because then I'd be actively capitalizing it. I don't want to be selling the rope they'll use to hang me with—as Lenin, presciently, said the capitalists would do. But if I bought the stock on the open market, my payment would go to a private individual, and I'd be making my money off some other guy that came along later. Although, I admit, that's just a rationalization…

A good speculator should look at the financial aspects of a deal and not let psychological squeamishness get in the way. That said, I have to admit that there are some deals I just wouldn't touch. But, hell, you can make a moral argument that you shouldn't buy T-Bills, because they will be repaid with stolen money—taxes.

L: Understood. Much to think about this time.

Doug: Indeed. But don't get depressed. Remember what my friend Robert Friedland, the founder of Ivanhoe Mines, always says: "The situation is hopeless, but it's not serious."

Doug Casey on the Military

Dec 2, 2009

L: I'm sitting with Doug Casey in his apartment in Buenos Aires, Argentina. Above me, on the wall behind the sofa, is a mural depicting the brutality of war. Every time you write about the military, Doug, we lose a large swath of subscribers. But I know it's something you've given a great deal of thought to, and you've never been shy about broaching taboo subjects, so we might as well cull the herd now. Let's talk about the boys in green...

Doug: Sure. Like most young males who grew up on a diet of John Wayne movies, I used to think that the military was great and romantic. As you know, my attitude has changed very much over the years. I'm actually very glad I went to a four-year military boarding high school, back when they were pretty tough places. That's because I'd wanted to go to West Point, and going to a military school helped cure me of having any desire for four more years of spit-shining shoes, marching in formation like an automaton, and saying "Yes, Sir!" to all kinds of unsavory people.

L: It's a little-known fact that I once thought of doing Air Force ROTC. I wanted to fly F-18s and had pretty good qualifications for doing it. But I knew I'd have to hock my soul for the chance and just couldn't make myself do it.

Doug: Well, at any point in life, a left turn instead of a right can result in an entirely different life.

L: That's right. You could be a used-car salesman right now if you hadn't crashed that Ferrari.

Doug: That's true. And there was another point in my life when I was in Europe and was thinking that it might be fun to join the French Foreign Legion; I'd read *Beau Geste*. It was an idiotic idea that can only be entertained by someone who is 22 and at loose ends. Anyone could go to the recruiting depot in Marseille and sign up for all the military adventure they could want—I guess they still can. Although Americans have always been discouraged; they prefer people from desperate countries—people who won't complain so much about a life, as Gibbon put it, characterized by violence and slavery.

But there is very little romance, and a lot of marching, discomfort, and minimum wage-type labor. I don't think the Legion is much different from other militaries, except that conditions are tougher and the recruits are rougher. But they say the food is better. French influence.

L: And you get French citizenship if you do join.

Doug: Yes, you serve five years in the Foreign Legion and you gain French citizenship. That's quite correct. I've met a number of legionaries over the years, and it seems that that organization draws individuals who tend to be either the roughest criminal types or rogue intellectuals. It's a bit like the US Army's Special Forces... you don't get your average Joe.

After WWII, they were all ex-Wehrmacht guys, then there was an influx of Eastern Europeans. It's quite an interesting organization. But would it have been worth five years of my life? Not likely. I probably would have deserted or shot my officer long before then.

L: So, you don't hate the military, per se.

Doug: No. But over the years of writing the newsletter, I found that my remarks repeatedly culled the herd, as you said, of people with overly conventional, collectivist, or statist views of it. This type of "My country, right or wrong!" "Support our troops!" (no matter how many villages they level), and "If you value your freedom, thank a soldier!" thinking is a sacred cow. It's just one of many examples of what Will Rogers used to say: it's not what people don't know that's the problem, but what they think they know that—

Doug and L: —just ain't so.

Doug: Right. So, to begin with, you've got three kinds of armies: slave, mercenary, and militia.

For many years, from WWII forward, the US had a slave army. If you were of the right (or wrong) age and didn't have the political connections to get out of it, you were conscripted—forced into involuntary servitude—typically for two years.

L: Wasn't it our saint, Abraham Lincoln, abolisher of slavery, who instituted the first conscription in the United States?

Doug: Yes, he was. Jeff Hummel pointed this out in his book, _Emancipating Slaves, Enslaving Free Men_[1].

---

1. www.totallyincorrectbook.com/go/229

L: So, the US Civil War started with volunteers and ended with conscripts, at least on the Union side, and WWII was largely fought with conscripts, but what about WWI? I remember reading about big 15-year-olds lying about their age so they could sign up and go kick the Kaiser's butt.

Doug: There was a "Conscription Act of 1917," enacted not long after the US declared war. So, popular myths notwithstanding, it's questionable how many young men really wanted to go off and kill or die in horrible conditions. But it's interesting how war hysteria can build up in a society for absolutely no good reason at all. That was absolutely true of the War Between the States, the Spanish-American War, and WWI. There's never been a good reason for Americans to go to war against anyone; the US has never been invaded, at least not since the War of 1812. And war has always been the biggest impetus for debasing the currency, raising taxes, taking on debt, vastly increasing the size of the state, and decreasing personal freedom.

L: "War is the health of the state." But back to the types of armies. The US had volunteer armies—militias—until Lincoln instituted the first conscription in the Civil War, then again during WWI and WWII. But Vietnam changed American attitudes, and the draft ended in 1973.

Doug: Yes. Although a case can be made that it wasn't necessary for America to enter WWII, it was different from WWI and other military adventures, like the Spanish-American war or Korea, because it wasn't a "sport" war. I don't believe conscription was necessary, since many people felt a need to defend the country after the attack on Pearl Harbor sucked America into the war. Anyway, if the common citizen doesn't see a need to defend a country, perhaps it shouldn't be defended. Peer pressure and social opprobrium are what really hold societies together, not execution squads chasing those who don't believe in a war.

The best example of what happens when you have a slave army, however, is Vietnam. Young men were forced into it, they hated being there, and it's no surprise that it became a complete disaster. There were widespread drug problems, problems with soldiers fragging officers and NCOs—the effort was just falling apart at the seams.

L: For those who don't know: fragging meaning killing. The classic example of military slaves getting back at their masters that comes to mind is that of Vietnam soldiers on gunboats setting off up-river, only to loose thousands of rounds into the jungle as soon as they were out of sight. That way, they didn't have to confront enemies who would actually shoot back, and they could return and report a successful pacification of imaginary swaths of jungle.

Doug: Right. Running out of ammo was a good excuse for having to run back to base. A lot of soldiers didn't have anything against the VC or the NVA, other than the fact they were designated the enemy. Don't forget what Muhammad Ali said: "I ain't got no beef with any VC. No VC ever called me nigger." In today's world, slave armies are completely ineffective anyway. Cannon fodder armies are, at a minimum, technologically obsolete.

Mercenary armies make more sense. You have people serving who actually want to be there, for whatever reasons of their own. The American army now is a mercenary army, in which the soldiers are actually pretty well paid, not just while they are in, during which time they get meaningful bonuses and promotions, but also because of the huge benefits they get when they get out. Those benefits include preferred hiring within the US government, which creates another whole problem.

Historically, I think the military has drawn two types of people: those who were interested in the adventure and experience, and those who were on the bottom rungs of society and wanted to elevate themselves.

Today, the US Army is apotheosized: it's PC to say soldiers are our "best" and "brightest" young heroes, but they are largely refugees from the barrios, ghettos, and trailer parks. Nothing wrong with that, it's just an accident of birth. But people from the same social strata and with similar motivations, all being trained to be blindly loyal and learning to kill on command—people forget that's what armies do—can become problematical in a civil society.

L: Wait a minute. Is that still true post-9/11? A lot of people felt called to "serve and defend."

Doug: Well, there's been a lot of jingoism since then. Maybe there are a lot of people who want you to believe that that's why they have joined, because they think that's what they're supposed to believe. I doubt they really think about it. I don't believe that the average sailor or soldier has ever really enlisted for such seemingly high purposes. Generally, the degree to which they perform their jobs well and act courageously is basically because of peer pressure. They don't want to fail in the eyes of the people around them, as opposed to fighting for any high ideals.

Anyway, 9/11 was no excuse to join the military and fight a war. The attacks were a large-scale criminal action that should have been pursued on that basis. Attacking Iraq because of suspected weapons of mass destruction, which is a misleading term, and Al Qaida links was ridiculous—Iraq was a secular state and no friend of Muslim extremists, and there were no atomic weapons—it was clearly grandstanding by the US government, which had to appear to "do something."

Attacking the Taliban in Afghanistan had absolutely nothing to do with 9/11. The 15 Saudi guys who were hanging out in Afghanistan at that time could have been hanging out anywhere, including the US 9/11 was a police matter, not a military matter.

L: Okay, but that's logic. I can imagine an ordinary twenty-year-old buying the "defend the homeland" spin on TV and being encouraged by the "Support our troops" mentality to enlist to "protect America."

Doug: I suppose a few might, but I'd question their thinking. I mean, what if it had been 20 Italians who had hijacked the planes and crashed them into those buildings. Would they have joined to go fight Mafiosi in Italy? How well would that have worked?

L: Good point. I rather doubt it. Okay, so let's finish up the army types. If a mercenary army is better than a slave army because those involved actually want to be there…

Doug: A militia is the best of all, because it's one that really does come together to defend a society—the places where the people live and work. They are highly motivated by hearth and home. Militias are strictly defensive, which is good, because their very nature precludes the possibility of an aggressive over-seas war. In a way, a militia is a kind of guerilla army, which is almost impossible to defeat, short of genocide.

L: You have to sterilize the area.

Doug: Exactly. And now, our mercenary armies are in Iraq and Afghanistan, fighting guerilla armies. If you're fighting guerilla armies, you've got to ask yourself why you're there, attacking *their* hearth and home. I mean, how would the average American react if a large army of young Muslims were on American soil, kicking doors in, shooting resisters, and so forth? There would be no end to the number of Americans willing to take up arms and fight back, with or without training, with or without leadership—which is exactly what American forces face over there.

L: You know I strongly favor the idea of volunteers fighting in self-defense. I like the way the nature of a militia, which is drawn up in times of need, means there would be no standing army that could be sent overseas on some politician's meddlesome errand. But because militias are composed of ordinary people with non-military jobs who volunteer to defend hearth and home, there would be no professional soldiers among them, and no one standing guard in case of surprise attack. Some people would argue that for these reasons, relying on militias is archaic and leaves a people vulnerable to attack.

Doug: Well, I think it makes sense to have a cadre of professional sol-diers, a skeleton that can be fleshed out should the need occur. They can themselves respond quickly, and be the trainers of the new forces drawn up for legitimate defense.

In today's world, the entire nature of warfare is changing—again. Before WWI, the military consensus was that cavalry was a useful tool and that marching into battle in straight lines was a good idea. Trenches and machine guns changed that, although it took the generals millions of casualties to figure it out.

Before WWII, battleships were the cat's pajamas, but they turned out to be sitting ducks for planes launched from carriers. Today, they're spending $2 billion a piece for B2 bombers designed to fight a Cold War that no longer exists. And, of course, aircraft carriers are now just gigantic sitting ducks, especially hanging out in places like the Persian Gulf.

L: Okay, but wait, before we get into discussing hardware and modern warfare, let's finish up with the three types and your preferred type of army. I understand your skeleton crew answer to the concern about a lack of professional soldiers, but what about surprise attacks? If there's a sudden offensive, do you have to lose half your ground before your skeleton crew can train raw recruits to begin fighting back?

Doug: I think it was Yamamoto who said that the Japanese could never conquer America, because behind every rock, there'd be an American with a rifle. I've always believed that if America were a free society and the Chinese invaded and overcame our first line of defense, the surfers, the Chinese general would have someone dragged up and say, "Take me to your leader!" And the guy would take him home to his wife. After a few months, half the Chinese army would desert to open McDonald's franchises, and the other half would be treated as common criminals; they'd disappear at night.

L: A free society would be an armed society.

Doug: Absolutely. In today's world of very powerful individual weapons, I don't think that invasion of a place like America makes any sense. Some people say that enemies might launch nuclear weapons at the cities, but that makes neither military nor economic sense. In the first place, you don't attack a society that doesn't threaten you. And if conquest and loot were your goal, you wouldn't vaporize everything of value. That's why it would have served no purpose for the Russians to overrun Western Europe in the '60s, '70s and '80s, which many people were worried about.

It's not like in the Roman days, when you could conquer a country and cart off all the gold, women, and cattle to fund yet more conquest. That's not the way wealth works today; if you tried to do what the Romans did today, you would destroy the basis of wealth itself. There's nothing to milk afterwards, and the conquered land becomes nothing but a cost to you—just as Afghanistan and Iraq are to the US today. Conquest simply makes no sense in today's world.

L: Hmmm. So. In spite of what people have said about your "anti-military" remarks, you're not actually anti-military. You're anti-slave-army. Not so keen on mercenary armies. And you're pro-militia.

Doug: That's a good summary. And it's relevant to the future, because I think the whole concept of a national military is going to change radically in the near future. Why do I say that? First, because the nation-state as we know it, which has only been around since about 1600 or so, is on its way out.

There's an evolution here. The idea used to be that you were loyal to your tribe, which at least had some survival value. Then, as kings took over the world, you were loyal to your king, for some reason—it looks like it was pretty much blackmail, a double-negative sort of survival value. And then the nation-state took over, and you were loyal to your government. That looks like a losing proposition to me, with negative survival value. It doesn't make any sense.

In the future, facilitated by things like the Internet, people are going to be loyal to whatever groups they choose, bound together by the things the individuals think are important, not by simple accident of location of birth. These emerging voluntary societies are what speculative fiction writer Neal Stephenson called "phyles."

L: A concept many of our readers have taken to. There are now Casey Phyles in many major cities around the world.

Doug: When your first loyalty is to people you have chosen to give it to, whether they live in Cambodia or Chile, because of the things you yourself think are important and that you share in common, you're much more likely to stand by them than you are for types in America whose goal in life seems to be leaching off producers. I'm sure there are many phyles of different types coming together all over the world whose members feel more loyalty to each other than to whatever neighbors random chance has put next to them. Why should the fact some nation-state considers two people subjects automatically command mutual loyalty?

L: And the military implication is that it's very unlikely that distributed societies like this would mount physical, military invasions on one another. It'd be very difficult to do, and what would be the point?

Doug: Right. I think the world is evolving differently. And let me re-emphasize that military technology is changing too. All these aircraft carriers, B2s, M1 tanks, and so forth are basically junk. They serve no useful purpose in the kind of battle that's likely to happen in the future. If someone wants to attack the

US, they're not going to use an ICBM; those are extremely expensive, clunky, and you can see where they come from, guaranteeing retaliation. It's total idiocy that even a maniac wouldn't bother with. Not when you can deliver a backpack nuke by FedEx, cheap and on time. Or you could use any commercial aircraft, container ship, or truck.

But the real handwriting on the wall is the sort of thing we saw in Mumbai last year in November. There it was a matter of two dozen people with ordinary guns turning the whole city totally on its head for days. That was an extremely cheap and easy thing to do—and warfare has always been a matter of economics.

L: It's not a question of what's possible, but what you can pay for.

Doug: Yes. And that Mumbai attack was just one variation on a very large theme. An even more effective one, cheap and easy for a handful of individuals to pull off, would be to destroy a city's or country's critical infrastructure: electric power plants or transmission lines, water treatment facilities, gas pipelines…

L: That would do much more harm.

Doug: *Much* more harm.

L: They are soft targets that are too numerous to protect adequately.

Doug: But that won't stop governments from doing as they always do, fighting the last war. It's like with all these zombies at the TSA pretending to prevent another 9/11—which no one is going to try again because it can never be a surprise again. It's completely insane to make all travelers suffer at the hands of these nitwits for no useful purpose whatsoever.

L: But wait a minute, what you're saying is that all three types of armies, even the militia, are going to be useless. An army can't defend a population against pinpointed terror attacks. So, the army of the future may be *no* army. The nature of conflict is evolving to where you'll have to hire highly specialized field agents to seek out and neutralize particular threats.

Doug: Quite possibly. If for some reason you wanted to go on the offensive against a particular group of people somewhere in the world, you might hire a group of specialists to go after the soft targets and paralyze the place. It's almost undetectable, low cost, and effective. Even a militia wouldn't be able to stop them.

L: On the other hand, *only* a militia would stand any chance of stopping such attacks, because everyone would be part of the defense force, and all people would have the need for eternal vigilance on their minds at some level—instead of assuming the professionals will protect them—and they'd have some training and weapons. It'd be part of the culture, as in a place like Alaska, where everyone has guns and knows how to use them.

Doug: Sure—a militia isn't a perfect answer, but it's the best one we've got. It's interesting that that soldier who went berserk in Fort Hood a couple weeks ago was able to kill so many people. It was on a military base, of all places, where people are supposed to be trained to fight...

L: That was my first thought: why didn't anyone shoot back?

Doug: Apparently, you're not supposed to go around armed on a military base—just goes to show you what disarming people makes possible. It's completely insane.

L: So... how does this apply to a current conflict like Afghanistan? A militia wouldn't work, because a militia wouldn't go there, but the other two types of armies can and have been sent there, and they haven't done so well.

Doug: The only way to win is not to play. You simply can't win against a guerilla. And the worst thing about this is that the main conflict in the coming years is likely to be the West's unadmitted war against Islam. Since there are over a billion Muslims in the world, and since as a general rule, Muslims take their religion much more seriously than most other people around the world, and since it says in the Koran, which is supposed to be the direct word of Allah, that they must spread their religion around the world, the conflict is not going to go away. Especially since there is also a small but quite virulent minority of Christians in the US that have similar views, and a rather disproportionate number of them are in the military.

It's become a redux of the Crusades, at this point. Actually, the Crusades never really ended; they've just waxed and waned since the Middle Ages. Using the distributed warfare tactics we've just discussed, the Muslims are going to win on a cost-benefit basis. The new crusaders will attack their countries with expensive junk, and the Muslims will counter with unstoppable, low-cost violence. Even though they are largely primitive societies, they are going to win both on the attack and on the defense, creating huge chaos in the process.

You can't conquer a primitive society. There's nothing to destroy or hold hostage. The only way to win is to commit genocide.

Everything Western governments, and the United States especially, are doing politically and militarily is counterproductive.

L: You could defeat Germany, for example, in the past world wars, and Germany would surrender. But in these places, if you kill ten percent of the people, the other 90 will still fight you, and if you kill 90 percent of the people, the other ten will still fight you.

Doug: That's a real problem when you're fighting what amounts to a religious or tribal or race war. And just destroying materiel serves no useful purpose. If you live in a desert, a threat to blow up nearby sand dunes doesn't deter you much.

It's very interesting to me that during the Vietnam War, a large part of US society completely disrespected and hated the US military in all its forms. Soldiers would come home and people would throw garbage at them and spit on them. They became ashamed to be US soldiers. Today, things are completely different. Soldiering is an honored profession these days—and people act as though that's the way it's always been and always should be.

But it isn't. Soldiers are trained to follow orders, to do as they're told, and never to question authority; it's not an occupation for free, independent thinkers. And as I said: the current institution of the military, the way it's constituted, organized, run—everything—is an anachronism. It's a dead duck.

L: So... You're not anti-military—not in the way people were back in the late '60s and early '70s, when they spat on soldiers. You're anti-*stupidity*, in things military. You would favor morally constituted and effective military tools and structures.

Doug: Yes. And I feel very bad for these poor teenagers who are joining the military. Once they're in, they learn a few good habits, like shining their shoes and shooting straight, but once they go to a war zone, the chances are excellent that they'll pick up some *really* bad habits... like shooting first and asking questions later. It's not just the things that might happen to them, like having their brains scrambled when a high explosive goes off nearby, but the things they'll end up doing, perhaps unthinkingly, that will weigh on them for the rest of their lives.

L: Shooting a child you mistook for an enemy soldier...

Doug: It could be an honest mistake, but you still have to live with it. The US's current military setting, with bases in 100 foreign countries, is very bad, from top to bottom. And most of the bad habits those kids learn will stick with them when they come home, because most will go to work for government agencies, especially the armed ones. Police, like soldiers, tend to be loyal first and above all to each other. Their secondary loyalty is to their employers, and only as a distant third are they loyal to the people they supposedly serve and protect. This is a very, very bad trend; these soldiers are picking up bad habits and then coming home to work in government jobs where they have power over others.

L: Okay. Well... Lots to think about. Thanks.

Doug: You're welcome—till next week.

Doug Casey on His Favorite Sport

Nov 25, 2009

L: Doug, we've talked about cars, gold, and real estate. Another well-known passion of yours is horses, and your love of the game of polo. In fact, I see that you're wearing a tie that has polo horses on it. But I know you've had more than a few accidents—why do you do it?

Doug: Well, I started playing polo in about 1994. Regrettably, I started at about the age when many players are hanging up their spurs and getting out of the game, because polo is one of the most dangerous sports in the world—but it's also one of the most exciting.

It's as close as you can come to unarmed combat in the form of sport. We call it horse hockey, because it's really like playing hockey except you're on a horse instead of on skates.

L: Forgive my ignorance… You said it's like hockey on skates. Hockey is well-known as a brutal game. The fans love to see the players fight. They literally pull off their gloves and start fighting on the ice. Are you saying stuff like that happens in polo? I've seen a polo game. You need binoculars to watch it, so it's hard to tell what's happening out there, but I didn't see anything like fighting.

Doug: No, fighting with other players on the field is not looked upon with favor. But, except for the lack of encouragement of fights, it's very much like hockey. People do get hit with those sticks—they knock people's teeth out and break their arms. You can get hit by one of those balls—which move up to 120 miles per hour—and it's like getting hit with a line drive from a good baseball player. I personally had my foot broken, right through my boot, when I got hit by a ball. There's all kinds of things that can go wrong in polo. I mean, if somebody turns in front of you when you're riding 40 miles an hour, two horses and riders, and maybe more, all go down in a parcel. That can be ugly if you've got a thousand-pound beast rolling over you.

L: And... this is fun?

Doug: Yes! It's a dangerous sport, but it's also extremely exciting. And usually nothing untoward happens. I've played for years in a row with no injuries, as do most people. When I started playing polo, I thought I knew how to ride because I knew I could stay on a horse when it went faster than a walk. But I quickly found out that there was much more to it. One nice thing about polo is that I would have been too bored learning to ride by taking lessons. I like to be entertained and excited while learning, and polo did that for me. But unfortunately, in my case, learning to ride and learning to play at the same time meant that I picked up bad riding habits and bad playing habits. I had to go back and get rid of those bad habits, and that slowed me down a lot. But I was only in it for the fun, nothing else.

I've played polo in several countries now and have kept a string in the US for the last 15 years...

L: String?

Doug: String, string of horses...

L: You need more than one horse to play a game of polo.

Doug: Yes. You typically play six chukkers in a game.

L: Sorry—six what?

Doug: A chukker is a period of seven minutes. You typically have six chukkers in a game, divided by a break of three minutes between each chukker.

L: And the horses can't run that fast for so long?

Doug: Yes; you are basically going more or less full speed for seven minutes. So you change your horse every chukker, although you can double-chukker a good horse if you allow recovery time.

So, I've had a string of horses in the US (in Aspen or Palm Beach) for years. I have a string of about sixteen horses in New Zealand, where I've played since the year 2000. And now I've got the same number in Argentina. So I've played in all three countries, although mostly in Argentina and New Zealand now. And that's very expensive, I'm sorry to say.

Anybody can play it; we've got cowboys in the US and gauchos in South America who play it, and they don't have a lot of money. But, unless you are going to shoe your own horses, stable and groom them, and do all the work yourself, you've got to hire people to do it. You've got to buy new shoes for every horse every month, which is like buying a pair for yourself every month, multiplied by maybe eight horses at a minimum (you need at least one extra, because one is always getting sick or injured and can't play).

It's like running a small business that only loses money, with no upside potential whatsoever. On the plus side, polo drew me to Palm Beach, where I bought a nice property before the real estate boom. The appreciation in my property actually covered the couple hundred thousand dollars a year I was losing on polo. Of course that was while the late great property bubble was still inflating. (My guess is that won't reoccur for a generation—but that's another story.)

I left Palm Beach because I disliked the social climate—and the weather—so I went to New Zealand, where there was basically a bunch of tough farm boys that liked to play horse hockey when they weren't playing rugby. I enjoyed that, and the social structure was very different from Palm Beach. An additional bonus was that polo was so cheap in New Zealand, I couldn't resist. That was partially because at the time the kiwi dollar was at forty cents US. Since then, the kiwi dollar has peaked at close to double that level, and there's been a real estate boom as well. So even with the expenses of playing in New Zealand, I've more than paid for it with another gain in real estate.

Now polo has drawn me to Argentina, where I'm spending most of my time. So, although polo is the most expensive sport you can play, except for auto racing, air racing, or yacht racing—things of that nature—believe it or not, it's more or less paid for itself in my case.

Except for inevitable accidents… You can't replace your body, and that's a significant cost.

The other thing about polo is that it's the only sport in the world you can play with the professionals as an amateur. I mean, how are you going to get on the court with Michael Jordan or Shaq O'Neal? There's no way you are going to get to play basketball with those guys. Nor will you get to play football or baseball with the top pros. But in polo, you can hire the pros to go out there and play with you. And it's a lot of fun playing with the best people in the world.

L: What does it take to become a pro?

Doug: What Wayne Gretzky said about hockey is equally true about polo: "You don't skate toward where the ball is, you skate toward where the ball is going to be." You've got to assess who's currently got the ball. And once you know who's got the ball currently, you can figure out what he is capable of doing and what he is likely to do with the ball. And if you are good, you play it from there.

L: You're saying that playing polo is not just riding around and hitting the ball, it's a psychological game. You're assessing the other players and predicting their behavior…

Doug: Absolutely. If you are looking at an amateur player, you've got to assess the odds that he's going to maintain control of the ball and put the ball where it ideally goes. You've got to decide whether to ride ahead of him to cut off the ball or wait for him to miss the ball and then pick it up behind him. But if you're dealing with a top player, it's a different story entirely. So you've got to play the man as well as play the standard strategies of polo.

L: Perhaps like reading faces in a boardroom?

Doug: I would say it's more like an ultra-high-speed poker game. We can talk about poker sometime in the future too. From a business point of view, I think one interesting thing about polo is that all the sponsors that play polo (you've got the sponsors and the pros—the two groups of people that play polo) are individual rich guys. They have enough money to pay for themselves and their grooms and their horses and hire pros—and pay for their horses and their grooms too.

L: Pros never have money on their own?

Doug: They're professional athletes. The sponsors in polo tend to be rich guys, business owners… It's generally a rich guy's sport, frankly. And going to the parties with these guys and seeing what they are thinking about and talking about is always interesting. I know that in the past, when I started getting questions about gold at polo parties, it was almost inevitably an indicator that it was time to sell, because guys that didn't know anything about it were interested. Actually, polo helped me financially as a contrary indicator.

L: So what are they saying now in the locker room and at the parties?

Doug: Well, I stopped playing polo in Aspen a year ago. And I'm glad I've been out of Palm Beach for much longer. I don't really know what other guys are saying today, because I'm so busy, I just wasn't able to play this summer. I'm not *dans le vent* at the moment, as the French would say.

L: Well, summer is arriving in Argentina, so, whether you play or watch, please tell us what your polo pals say at the parties, so we can do the opposite.

Doug: I will. My Spanish is improving all the time.

L: Thanks, Doug.

Doug: My pleasure.

Doug Casey on Voting

Oct 28, 2010

L: Doug, last week we spoke about presidents. We have an election coming up in the US, one many people believe is very important—an election that could have significant consequences on our investments. But given the views you've already expressed on the Tea Party movement[1] and anarchy[2], I'm sure you have different ideas. What do you make of the impending circus, and what should a rational man do?

Doug: Well, a rational man, which is to say, an ethical man, would almost certainly not vote in this election, or in any other—at least above a local level, where you personally know most of both your neighbors and the candidates.

L: Why? Might not an ethical person want to vote the bums out?

Doug: No. I've thought about this a fair amount, and I believe the conventional wisdom on voting is totally wrong. So let me give you five reasons why no one should vote.

The first reason is that voting in government elections is an unethical act, in and of itself. That's because the state is pure, institutionalized coercion; as Mao, certainly an expert on the subject, said: "The power of the state comes out of the barrel of a gun." If you believe that coercion is an improper way for people to relate to one another, then you shouldn't engage in a process that formalizes and guarantees the use of coercion.

L: It's probably worth defining coercion in this context. I know you agree with me that force is ethical in self-defense. A murderer I shoot might feel coerced into accepting a certain amount of hot lead that he did not consent to, but he intended the same, or worse, for me, so the scales are balanced. What you are talking about is forcing *innocent,* non-consenting others to do things against

---

1. www.totallyincorrectbook.com/go/230
2. www.totallyincorrectbook.com/go/231

their will, like paying taxes that go to pay for military adventures they believe are wrong, etc.

Doug: Right. The modern state not only routinely coerces people into doing all sorts of things they don't want to do—often very clearly against their own interests—but it necessarily does so, by its nature. People who want to know more about that should read our conversation on anarchy. This distinction is very important in a society with a government that is no longer limited by a constitution that restrains it from violating individual rights. And when you vote, you participate in this unethical system. Voters are dupes; they're classic examples of what Lenin called "useful idiots."

L: It's probably also worth clarifying that you're not talking about all voting here. When you are a member of a golfing club and vote on how to use the fees, you and everyone else have consented to the process, so it's not unethical. It's participating in the management of the coercive machinery of the state you object to, not voting in and of itself.

Doug: Exactly. Unlike a golfing club, or something of that nature, the state won't let you opt out. In some countries it's a misdemeanor if you fail to vote, and they don't even have a space on the ballot to write in "None of the Above."

L: Even if you're not harming anyone and just want to be left alone.

Doug: Which relates to the second reason not to vote: privacy. It compromises your privacy to vote. It gets your name added to a list government busybodies can make use of, like court clerks putting together lists of conscripts for jury duty. In many states, you have to identify yourself with a particular party, which could be disadvantageous. This is perhaps not as important a reason as it used to be, because of the great proliferation of lists people are on anyway. Still, the less any governments know about you, the better off you are. This is, of course, why I've refused to complete a census form for the last 40 years.

L: We've talked about the census[3]. Good for you.

Doug: A prudent individual wants to be a non-person as far as the state is concerned, as far as possible.

L: And your third reason for not voting?

Doug: That would be because it's a degrading experience. The reason I say that is because registering to vote, and voting itself, usually involves taking productive time out of your day to go stand around in lines in government offices. You have to fill out forms and deal with petty bureaucrats. I know I can find

3. www.totallyincorrectbook.com/go/232

much more enjoyable and productive things to do with my time, and I'm sure anyone reading this can as well.

L: And the pettier the bureaucrat, the more unpleasant the interaction tends to be.

Doug: I have increasing evidence of that every time I fly. The TSA goons are really coming into their own now, as our own home-grown Gestapo wannabes.

L: It's a sad thing... Reason number four?

Doug: As P.J. O'Rourke says in his new book[4], and as I've always said, voting just encourages them.

I'm convinced that most people don't vote for candidates they believe in, but against candidates they fear. They vote for the other guy; but the "other guy" sees that as vote for him, not just against his opponent. The more votes the "other guy" gets, the more he thinks he's got a mandate to rule.

Some people try to justify this, saying it minimizes harm to vote for the lesser of two evils. That's nonsense, because it still leaves you voting for evil. That's entirely apart from the fact that there's no real difference between the left wing of the Republicrats, and the right wing of the Demopublicans. Why even choose between the Evil Party and the Stupid Party? Tweedledee or Tweedledum?

Incidentally, I got as far as this point in 1980, when I was on the *Phil Donahue Show*. I had the whole hour on national TV all to myself, and I felt in top form. It was November, actually the day before the national election, when Jimmy Carter was the incumbent, running against Ronald Reagan. After I made some economic observations, Donahue accused me of intending to vote for Reagan. I said that I was not, and as sharp as Donahue was, he said, "Well, you're not voting for Carter, so you must be voting Libertarian... "

I said no, and had to explain why not. I believed then just as I do now. And it was at about this point when the audience, which had been getting restive—especially after I'd already debunked the idea of going to college—started getting really upset with me. I never made it to point five.

Perhaps I shouldn't have been surprised. That same audience, when I pointed out that their taxes were high and were being wasted, contained an individual who asked, "Why do we have to pay for things with our taxes? Why doesn't the government pay for it?" I swear that's what he said; it's on tape. If you could go back and watch the show, you'd see that the audience clapped after that brilliant question. Which was when I first realized that while the situation is actually

4. www.totallyincorrectbook.com/go/233

hopeless, it's also quite comic... And things have only gotten worse since then, with decades more "public education" and mass media indoctrination behind us.

L: That guy probably works in the Obama administration now, where they seem to think exactly as he did; the government will just pay for everything everyone wants with money it doesn't have.

Doug: He'd now be of an age where he's collecting Social Security and Medicare, plus food stamps, and likely gaming the system for a bunch of other freebies. Maybe he's so confused and discontent with his miserable life that he goes to both Tea Party and Green Party rallies, while voting Democrat. I do believe we're getting close to the endgame. The system is on the verge of falling apart. And the closer we get to the edge, the more catastrophic the collapse it appears we're going to have.

Which leads me to point number five: Your vote doesn't count. If I'd gotten to say that to the Donahue audience, they probably would have stoned me. People really like to believe that their individual votes count. Politicians like to say that every vote counts, because it gets everyone into busybody mode and makes voters complicit in their crimes. But statistically, any person's vote makes no more difference than a single grain of sand on a beach.

That's completely apart from the fact, as voters in Chicago in 1960 and Florida in 2000 can tell you, when it actually does get close, things can be, and often are, rigged. As Stalin once said, it's not who votes that counts. It's who counts the votes.

Anyway, officials manifestly do what they want, not what you want them to do, once they are in office. They neither know nor care what you want.

L: The idea of political representation is a myth and a logical absurdity. One person can only represent his own opinions—if he's even thought them out. If someone dedicated his life to studying another person, he might be able to represent that individual reasonably accurately. But given that no two people are completely—or even mostly—alike, it's impossible to represent the interests of any group of people.

Doug: The whole constellation of concepts is ridiculous. This leads us to the subject of democracy. People say that if you live in a democracy, you should vote. But that begs the question of whether democracy itself is any good. And I would say that, no, it's not. Especially in a democracy unconstrained by a constitution. That, sadly, is the case in the US, where the Constitution is nearly 100% a dead letter. Democracy is nothing more than mob rule dressed up in a suit and tie. It's no way for a civilized society to be run.

L: Okay, but in our firmly United State of America today, we don't live in your ideal society. It is what it is, and if you don't vote the bums out, they remain in office. What do you say to the people who say that if you don't vote, if you don't raise a hand, then you have no right to complain about the results of the political process?

Doug: But I do raise a hand, constantly. I'd just rather not waste my time or degrade myself on unethical and futile efforts like voting. That argument is more than fallacious, it's spurious. Actually, it's only the non-voter who has a right to complain. The voter endorsed the whole charade; he voted for his ruler, and now he has to do as he's told.

L: Okay then, if the ethical man shouldn't vote in the national elections coming up, what should he do?

Doug: I think it's like they said during the war with Vietnam: suppose they had a war, and nobody came? I also like to say: suppose they levied a tax, and nobody paid? And at this time of year: suppose they gave an election, and nobody voted?

The only way to truly de-legitimize unethical rulers, and the whole corrupt process, is by not voting. When tin-plated dictators around the world have their rigged elections and people stay home in droves, even today's "we love governments of all sorts" international community won't recognize the results of the election.

L: De-legitimizing evil… and without coercion, or even force. That's a beautiful thing, Doug. I'd love to see the whole crooked, festering, parasitical mass in Washington—and similar places—get a total vote of no-confidence.

Doug: Now, I realize that my not voting won't make that happen. My not voting doesn't matter anymore than some naïve person's voting does. But at least I'll know that what I did was ethical.

L: You won't have blood on your hands.

Doug: That's exactly the point.

L: A friendly amendment: you do staunchly support voting with your feet.

Doug: Ah, that's true. Unfortunately, the idea of the state has spread over the face of the earth like an ugly skin disease. All of the governments of the world are, at this point, growing in extent and power—and rights violations—like virulent cancers. But still, that is one way I am dealing with the problem; I'm voting with my feet. When the going gets tough, the tough get going. It's idiotic to sit around like a peasant and wait to see what they do to you.

To me, it makes much more sense to live as a perpetual tourist, staying no more than six months of the year in any one place. Tourists are courted and valued, whereas residents and citizens are viewed as milk cows. And before this crisis is over, they may wind up looking more like beef cows. Entirely apart from that, it keeps you from getting into the habit of thinking like a medieval serf. And I like being warm in the winter and cool in the summer.

L: As people say: "What if everyone did that?" Well, you'd see people migrating towards the least predatory states where they could enjoy the most freedom and create the most wealth for themselves and their posterity. That sort of voting with your feet could force governments to compete for citizens, which would lead to more places where people can live as they want. It could become a worldwide revolution fought and won without guns.

Doug: That sounds pretty idealistic, but I do believe this whole sick notion of the nation-state will come to an end within the next couple generations. It makes me empathize with Lenin when he said, "The worse it gets, the better it gets." Between jet travel, the Internet, and the bankruptcy of governments around the world, the nation-state is a dead duck. As we've discussed before, people will organize into voluntary communities we call phyles.

L: That's the name given to such communities by science fiction author Neal Stephenson in his book *The Diamond Age*, which we discussed in our conversation on speculators' fiction. Well, we've talked quite a bit—what about investment implications?

Doug: First, don't expect *anything* that results from this US election to do any real, lasting good. And if, by some miracle, it did, the short-term implications would be very hard economic times.

Most important is to have a healthy psychological attitude. For that, you need to stop thinking politically, stop wasting time on elections, entitlements, and such nonsense. You've got to use all of your time and brain power to think economically. That's to say, thinking about how to allocate your various intellectual, personal, and capital assets, to survive the storm—and even thrive, if you play your cards right.

L: I like that: think economically, not politically. Thanks, Doug!

Doug: My pleasure.

Doug Casey: Learn to Make Terror Your Friend

Mar 24, 2010

L: Twelve years ago, and almost exactly three years before the 9/11 attacks, Doug Casey had one of his famous Guru Moments, writing in the September 1998 edition of the *International Speculator*:

> Terrorism is becoming a major force in the world, as evidenced by Clinton actually referring to the use of nuclear, biological, and chemical devices in the US I've thought their use against US targets was an inevitability for years. But with the US government launching its own terror strikes against Third World targets, the inevitable is starting to look imminent. Let's put it this way: Living in Washington, New York or other population centers is not terribly prudent.

And again, the *International Speculator* that arrived in mailboxes mid-July 2001—rather good timing—had a feature article entitled "Waiting for World War III," which discussed, at great length, terrorism and Islam and even mentioned Osama bin Laden.

And more recently…

L: Tatich, we've touched on terrorism a number of times in our conversations, particularly when we discussed the military and in our <u>conversation on the implications of the attack on the IRS</u>[1] building a few weeks ago. Let's stop beating around the bush and talk about terrorism.

[**Editor's Note**: "Tatich" means "Big Chief" in the Mayan language.]

Doug: Okay, but, as with most areas where there's a lot of sloppy thinking, we should first start with a definition. If words are used too loosely, or inaccurately, then it's really impossible to know what is actually under

---

1. www.totallyincorrectbook.com/go/234

discussion. "Terrorism" is a concept that everybody talks about, but almost nobody bothers to define.

According to *Webster's New World Dictionary*, terrorism is "the use of force or threats to intimidate, especially as a political policy." This implies that all governments engage in terrorism daily against their own citizens—which is actually true, as anyone who's been audited by the IRS can tell you. A somewhat narrower definition of terrorism is: "an act of wholesale violence, for political ends, that deliberately targets civilians."

As we discussed in our conversation on the IRS attack and unintended consequences, the government's definition of terrorism is "the unlawful use of force or violence against persons or property, meant to intimidate or coerce a government or the civilian population as a means for achieving political or social goals."

L: What a great, self-serving definition.

Doug: It really is funny. And more than a little Orwellian in the way the meaning is twisted. By the government's definition, it's perfectly all right to do these things—as long as it's legal.

L: Hence the dodge of sending prisoners accused of no crime in any court of law to Guantanamo, to get around the illegality of indefinite detention. The message is that terrorism, even torture—waterboarding—is just peachy, as long as it's the authorities doing it. Did you hear Karl Rove defending torture of the Guantanamo prisoners? He said he was proud of it, and that the intelligence gathered was invaluable. Apparently rights, and even right itself, is of no concern.

Doug: Last year, I debated Rove in New Orleans—you'd never know what a moral cripple he is from the pleasant and personable exterior. We should discuss the banality of evil at some point.

L: I heard <u>that debate</u>[2] and was proud of you for telling him to his face that he ought to be ashamed for Guantanamo and other crimes committed by the administration he was part of. But back to terrorism. Given your definition of "an act of wholesale violence, for political ends, that deliberately targets civilians," why is this important to us in particular—other than as something to be avoided?

Doug: Because terrorism is the future of warfare. Far from going away, it's going to become the most common form of military conflict.

L: You don't think America can win the War on Terror?

Doug: [Sighs deeply] No. Not only is that impossible, the very idea is meaningless. Terrorism is not an enemy—it's a tactic. You can't have a war on

---

2. www.totallyincorrectbook.com/go/235

terror any more than you can have a war on artillery barrages, cavalry charges—or a war on war, for that matter. The first step in winning a conflict is to identify the actual enemy. And the fools in DC can't even do that.

But before we look at the future, it's worth noting that terrorism has long been a favored tool of those in power, going all the way back to ancient times.

L: Sure. As with your IRS example; that's why they periodically crucify ordinary Joes—it keeps the rest in fear and hence quiescent. People don't pay taxes out of pure love for the homeland—it's plain terrorism that keeps them in line.

Doug: Of course. It's just not on the scale of Genghis Khan or Tamerlane, who used to stack skulls into pyramids. Or the Romans, who literally did crucify people to show what happens to those who go up against the state.

L: Agreed, but on a moral plane, it's the equivalent; it's not about what's right, it's about enforcing submission.

Doug: Sure, you could say that "the state" is actually terrorism on a grand scale. It's bizarre how most people view the state as necessary or even benign. It may offend some of our readers, who have been programmed into believing the military can do no wrong, and that the US always has God on its side, but logically, the bombings of Hamburg, Dresden, and Tokyo are prime examples of state-sponsored terrorism.

World War II, in effect, legitimized the concept of mass murder of civilians. As late as World War I, the concept of incinerating whole cities would have been totally beyond the pale; WWII turned the moral clock back to the Middle Ages, when the wholesale slaughter of civilians was considered acceptable. I suspect the "Long 19th Century," from about 1776–1914, will be looked back on as a golden age, a peak of civilization, when the individual was ascendant, the state was under control, free-market capitalism was lauded, and progress seemed natural and inevitable. Technology has improved since then, but it's a mistake to conflate technological progress with moral progress.

L: I can't think of a clearer example than the bombing of Hiroshima and Nagasaki. It's said that using atomic bombs on Japan saved American lives—but the lives saved were those of combatant soldiers, and the lives taken were of noncombatants, including many thousands of women and children. The US government vaporized Japanese babies with the sole object of forcing submission. I'm not saying the Japanese were saints. I'm just pointing out that this was not a traditional military victory, in the sense of the US armed forces beating those of Japan; it was simply use of massive force on a civilian population for US goals—terrorism.

Doug: Yes. Although Germany and Japan—both of which were ruled by psychopathic criminals—originated the use of terror during WWII, it was the

US that perfected it and brought it to an industrial scale. That was most unfortunate, in that it deprived the US of the high moral ground. And, as Napoleon observed: in warfare the moral is to the physical as three is to one. That loss of moral high ground has really hurt the US in its war against Islamic radicals—which is really what the so-called War on Terror is all about. After Bush started the renditions (basically kidnapping and "rendering" the victim to some amenable jurisdiction), institutionalized torture, and set up the Guantanamo prison, the US became just another degraded country in the eyes of the world.

But the whole post-WWII era has been a moral as well as a strategic and tactical disaster for the US. Remember that the threat of societal annihilation against the Soviets was called the "balance of terror?"

L: Mutually Assured Destruction. I remember. When I was in college, the acronym seemed appropriate: it was MAD to assure everyone's destruction! But I have to admit that it seems to have worked. It kept the Soviets contained until they fell apart from their internal contradictions and stupid economics. (Stupid in your technical sense of the word: an unwitting tendency towards self-destruction.)

Doug: I remember that as well; people recognized the seemingly insane nature of the MAD policy at the time. _Dr. Strangelove_[3] showed its comedic aspect. Be that as it may, MAD does seem to have worked. But it may have been wiser for the US to have just let the Soviets expand and not gotten into Korea, Vietnam, and numerous smaller wars. The US would have become much wealthier without those huge expenses, and the Soviets would have bankrupted themselves much more quickly. One Afghanistan almost did them in; two, three, many Afghanistans would have done so, much, much sooner.

At any rate, the nature of warfare has changed forever, just as it did after WWI, and again after WWII. It's now once again mutating. Terrorism, as a method of warfare, is definitely the wave of the future. That's partly because "total war" enlists the country's civilians, through propaganda and mass media; they've almost become combatants without rifles. Whipping up "patriotic" fervor and intimidating people with charges of "treason" and being an "enemy combatant" tends to make the whole country, at least psychologically, an armed camp. So striking out against civilians today actually makes some military sense—much more than in the past.

Terrorism is also extremely cost effective—and _anyone_ can use it, with or without training or experience. It's a bit like Forrest Gump described

---

shrimp. You can fry it, boil it, stew it, fricassee it, sauté it, bake it, steam it, or just have it raw.

It's been called "open-source warfare," a phrase that seems right on target to me. One terrorist sees what another does and learns from it. People can invent infinite variations and programs of attack. A failed act of terror, like that of the "shoe bomber"—which couldn't have brought down the plane even if he succeeded—or this recent Nigerian case, is almost as good as a successful one. The government response is, predictably, more destructive than the act itself. Further, terror is massively parallel. There is no "leader" to kill; there are hundreds of heads to the hydra.

Deadly devices, sometimes even with somewhat larger-scale destructive capability, like that backpack full of nails and explosives found during the Atlanta Olympics, can be made with cheap, off-the-shelf supplies. And with every attack and attempt, the ideas of how to mount such attacks spread, just like open-source software.

L: The guy flying his plane into the IRS building sure seems to have been copying the 9/11 terrorists.

Doug: Maybe. And maybe he was just using the most effective means at his personal command. Terrorism is like jazz; it's all about improvisation and variation. That's why conventional forces are dead in the water against it; they're all "by the book," with top-down command and control. And as we discussed in our conversation on the military, standing armies are dead ducks, just like aircraft carriers. They have no chance against small groups of individuals carrying out deadly attacks against "soft targets," like small towns, pipelines, and so forth. As much as it may seem like a throwback, something like a militia is really the only form of organized force I can see having any chance of success in this environment. But it's better not to give the enemy a reason to fight at all... That's why the only correct foreign policy is one of "Trade with all; alliances with none."

L: You've given speeches before on "Making Terror Your Friend." Perhaps this is an opportune time to point out that you don't have any interest in blowing up people in their homes to achieve political ends, or any other ends. The point is that since it's a trend very firmly in motion, there are investment implications. Like it or not, terrorism is here to stay, and it's stupid to ignore it.

Doug: Quite so. In spite of the impression our conversation on alcohol, tobacco, and firearms may have made, I'm an extremely peaceable type. I don't want to be anywhere near any place where people are hunting and killing one another. It's just unpleasant, and the chances are excellent your number will come up. I'm speaking from what you might call an academic point of view.

That said, only an idiot fails to recognize that in an advanced technological economy an individual can have an immense, disproportionate effect if he wants to do damage. It's not like in pre-industrial days, when a single person was limited to perhaps setting a fire or maybe stabbing someone. Today, an individual terrorist can alter the direction of society. And there are hundreds of millions of candidates for that role.

In my view, the trend towards terrorism as the next evolution of warfare is about as certain as they come. It's not just the US; all the big nation-states are on the ragged edge of bankruptcy. Their huge bureaucracies, oppressive tax systems, complicated regulatory regimes, subsidies, bailouts, fiat currencies, and welfare programs are—every one of them—near collapse. They were confidence schemes. It's not just standing armies, but the nation-state itself is a dead man walking at this point.

L: Because the lumbering dinosaur can't compete with the fleet little mammal?

Doug: That's a good analogy. These giant dinosaur-states are thrashing around in their death-throes, but they are still extremely dangerous—at least while they can still pay the salaries of their minions in the police and the military. And that very fact is stirring up a lot of little creatures that are going to want to see them die sooner.

L: I can see that; the more villages around the world they bomb, the more enemies they make. Those new enemies provoke even more thrashing about, which creates even more enemies, leading leviathan to even more violent and oppressive responses. It's a vicious cycle taking the current world order down the spiral towards oblivion.

Doug: Yes, I'm completely convinced that all of the world's major nation-states are going to become much more oppressive as they try to keep things together. But it won't work. They are perpetually behind the curve, always fighting the last war.

Today, they talk about al-Qaeda being "our enemy." But, first off, al-Qaeda isn't a country. You can't invade it nor capture its capital. It's such a decentralized and amorphous entity, there's simply no military way to defeat it.

L. It's not even a military organization. There's no top general to assassinate. It's a disorganized movement of Islamic people pissed off at the West—it's an idea more than anything else.

Doug: That's right, and now that the US has whacked the hornets' nest, I believe there are scores, maybe even hundreds, of al-Qaeda look-alikes all around the world. They don't take orders from some al-Qaeda chief—they watch each other and take ideas from those who pull off successful attacks.

Actually, it's a sign of how backward the thinking is on this subject that the US apparently still sees al-Qaeda as a hierarchical organization. At most, it has franchisees and licensees. The best analogy is perhaps the drug business, where there are dozens of large organizations, unrelated to each other, often mutually antagonistic, but sharing the same general objective and similar methodologies.

They need not think alike, nor even like one another. But they have a common enemy, learn from each other, and improve their methods with each iteration. So, even if the US were to somehow, miraculously, wipe out every living member of Al Qaida today, new volunteers would pick up the banner, and the fight would continue. It would make absolutely no difference to the way the world is evolving.

L: And at an accelerating pace.

Doug: Yes. The War on Terror is being fought mainly in Muslim countries. The fact that most US allies in the Islamic world are oppressive regimes doesn't help at all. Iraq, Afghanistan, Egypt, Saudi Arabia, and Pakistan, among others, are all run by quislings, puppets, or stooges of the US. The average citizen of those places despises his corrupt government and recognizes that the US is propping it up—which gives them good reason to hate the US. The demographics in these places are a time bomb—half the population is under 30, and they're mostly un-employed. Many would form terrorist groups out of boredom, except they have much better reasons. The US doesn't have any real friends in those suppressive governments anyway; those people will change sides in a New York second. And it's getting worse.

What do the people in those countries perceive? Christian soldiers kick-ing in doors and shooting people—echoes of fighting that's gone on for over a thousand years. The West may think they are fighting a War on Terror, but Muslims are going to see it increasingly as a War on Islam. And when they react accordingly, it will become so.

L: If they come to see the War on Terror as a War on Islam, a religious war against a more powerful oppressor, they will fight tooth and nail, to the last man, woman, and child. If that's the shape of WWIII, it'll be a bloodbath to eclipse all others, combined.

Doug: I'm sorry to say that I agree, and that's the way things are headed. And what method of fighting will they use? Terrorism. And what will be the West's response? To escalate the fight, using the wrong strategies and tactics— still looking to decapitate a beast with no head—and using the wrong tools: all that expensive junk meant to fight a defunct USSR. You can't beat a *popular* guerrilla movement without widespread killing. Genocide, essentially.

If things continue down this path, Islam will win. Decentralized guerrilla terrorism is simply much more efficient and effective than national armed services could ever be. A $1,000 RPG can take out a $5 million M-1 tank or a $50 million helicopter. A $2 million cruise missile is expended to kill a few fighters, plus a bunch of innocents. Meanwhile there's a new crop of several million potential fighters being born every year.

L: That, I understand, is what brought the Soviets down in Afghanistan; the economics of the war were totally disastrous for them, losing entire choppers full of people and materiel to one fighter on a camel with a shoulder-fired missile.

Doug: It is an economic war. Osama bin Laden has even said so; the US will bankrupt itself. It won't just be Afghanistan and Iraq; it could spread to Pakistan, Somalia, and a dozen other places. It's going to be Che Guevara's dream—two, three, many Vietnams.

L: And there's no way to stop it?

Doug: Do you think the West will suddenly pull an about-face in foreign policy?

L: No.

Doug: And remember, there's no really effective way to defend against this. Remember that a couple dozen guys paralyzed the whole city of Mumbai, creating total havoc and inflicting a major blow on their enemy, with nothing more than small arms.

But that took some organization, which you don't even really need to create havoc and strike a blow. One lone wolf (no offense) can create widespread hysteria, as Ted Kaczynski, the Unabomber, demonstrated. And the chances of an individual acting on his or her own being caught are extremely low, precisely because they are acting on their own. There's no one to rat on them.

L: Just look at the chaos caused by those two guys driving around Washington DC a couple years ago, one in the trunk with a rifle. That took neither great planning nor strategy; it was just a bit of reasonably effective camouflage and mobility—and it was dirt cheap. Even with people being shot in broad daylight, it took the machinery of the state weeks to catch the guys. Just two guys. What happens when there are hordes of individuals acting similarly? There's no way to stop it.

Doug: That's my point. That fool Bush said the US was attacked because "they hate our freedom." I can't imagine a more ridiculous assessment. Especially when bin Laden clearly spelled out why the 9/11 attack occurred—three reasons. One, foreign troops in Muslim countries. Two, the US propping up puppet regimes in Muslim countries. Three, the US supporting Israel, which they view as a usurper of Palestinian land. In point of fact, these are reasonable objections on his part.

What should be done about this insane War on Terror before it gets totally out of control and we get everything from the kind of attacks we've discussed above, all the way up to nuclear explosions going off in US cities? All the while the US is bankrupting itself? I suggest the manly and honorable thing to do is sincerely apologize for past aggressions. That, combined with disinvolvement of the US government and military from the Mideast, could defuse the situation. Otherwise, this thing will almost certainly escalate and get out of hand.

When it comes to the next generation of warfare, terrorism, the only way to win is not to play.

L: Okay, so, I'm feeling pretty terrified. How is it we make this trend our friend?

Doug: Well, one obvious consequence of this trend is higher energy prices. However the War on Terror, or Islam, plays out, there's a good chance the Middle East will go completely up in flames before long. And even if the sands of Arabia do not end up getting turned to glass, the tensions alone make higher energy prices a foregone conclusion. I just don't see any way around that at this point.

Iran seems like the obvious flashpoint. If the US strikes Iran, oil will go to $200 a barrel. In the long run, that oil could be replaced, especially at the higher prices that make oil sands, shale oils, heavy oils, and such more economical—but in the short run, the supply is extremely inelastic. You can't just throw a switch and get more oil from some other source. Combine that with the financial chaos that would ensue, and even decreased usage wouldn't make up for the crunch. Higher oil prices seem like a lock-sync at this point.

L: The *caveat emptor* there would be to caution our readers not to try to time this. Playing the energy field for short-term gains is extremely tricky. You buy and hold for a major transition in the world to unfold.

Doug: Yes. The key would be to buy the companies that have the goods, are well managed, and are businesses you would actually like to own a part of, to capitalize on the megatrend. That's the way to do it.

L: Would it make sense to focus on companies with North American assets?

Doug: Not necessarily—buying at the right price is much more important. You can't come at these things with a cookie cutter. It's like knowing 100 years ago that the auto industry was going to boom and grow—if you bet on any but one or two of the hundreds of car companies that sprang up, you'd have lost money. Same thing with the air travel and television businesses; most of the companies went bankrupt and most people in early lost money. The same thing will happen with energy. You've got to be extremely selective, or you'll be right about the trend but still end up with nothing but pretty stock certificates to use as insulation in your walls.

L: Can't argue with that. So, what else—how else do we make this trend our friend?

Doug: Plan to profit from the coming diaspora.

As I've said many times in these conversations, diversifying your assets—and your personal presence—across different political jurisdictions is one of the most important things you can do in our world today. That's simply prudent at this point.

But as the wealthy countries of the world continue spiraling down, they will become increasingly Orwellian, and that will send out droves of people with resources in search of friendlier climes. The next real—or imagined—terror incident in the US could take things in a really ugly direction in very short order.

L: So… if you can predict where rich Americans, Brits, Europeans, and others will flee to and buy real estate before they get there, you can profit? Sounds like another plug for Argentina coming…

Doug: No question, that's my favorite pick, but I have bets on New Zealand and Uruguay as well. But, as per our conversation on All Things Fun, you could do worse than to look for any place you like that's ATF-friendly. Perhaps a small country, even if corrupt, with a government too disorganized to cause you any serious inconvenience.

L: Okay. What else? If the police state is coming, would you invest in companies that make shiny black boots? Prison companies? Surveillance cameras?

Doug: That's tricky, harder to spot clear winners. Private prison companies, for example, might have seemed like a good bet, especially given the ever-expanding War on Some Drugs. But they've pretty well filled the country with new prisons; I suspect, and hope, that party is over. The prison population actually declined last year, for the first time in decades.

L: What about defense companies?

Doug: Well, I think it's a misnomer to call them defense companies, just as it was an Orwellian twist to rename the War Department, the Defense Department after WWII. But apart from that, I suppose they'll keep getting fat contracts until the US government imposes the way the Romans did at the end of the 4th century.

L: Okay then. Thanks for another very informative, if not exactly cheerful, conversation.

Doug: Sure thing—talk to you next week, here in Argentina.

Doug Casey on *Avatar* & Pop Culture

Feb 3, 2010

Doug: Lobo. I saw it. Let's talk.

L: Ah, you mean the latest, greatest, highest-grossing blockbuster movie of all time—and not incidentally, environmental extremists' wet dream—*Avatar*.

Doug: Yes. I want to start by saying that I did actually enjoy the movie, though it's certainly no cosmic breakthrough on any intellectual front. It's a little bit of Romeo and Juliet, a bit more of Pocahontas and John Smith. Elements of Bambi meeting the soldiers and battle equipment from *Aliens*. The *South Park* guys nailed it, as they usually do, with their spoof, "*Dances with Smurfs*[1]." But the visual effects were stunning.

L: *Dances with Wolves* came to my mind right away as well, featuring a soldier with a heart of gold going over to the natives. It also reminded me of a cartoon movie released back in the early 1990s called *FernGully*, about a magical rainforest inhabited by wonderful creatures that some evil company wanted to chop down.

Doug: Yes, it appears that whenever a resource company sees a beautiful rainforest, they simply can't resist destroying it, as if wanton destruction were their Prime Directive. And mining companies in movies must have recruiting posters that read: "Join us! Visit exotic, distant lands. Meet strange, interesting people. And kill them."

But it's understandable. If you invade a place, devastate it, and take whatever you want without even asking if you can pay for it, it wouldn't make for much of a drama if the natives were just nasty brutes that needed killing. Where would the moral conflict be? That's where a mining company comes in. Every movie-going moron knows that only a mining company could be evil enough to attack Smurfs living in a rainforest.

---

1. www.totallyincorrectbook.com/go/237

That said, I *did* enjoy it. I watched it in 3D, in an IMAX theater here in Auckland. But the question is what people take away from it. Is it mainly the entertainment provided by the fantastic graphics showing an alien world full of amazing plants and animals? Or is it the… not so subtle ideological values that permeated the movie?

L: Subtle as a sledge hammer.

Doug: One of the things I noticed—and this is true of many things—is that even though the movie is full of typical left-wing Hollywood values, there were still things in it that were good from a libertarian viewpoint. There had to be, if only so people wouldn't be completely bummed out. But I got to wondering if this might be part of why so few people have internally consistent values. Most people never sit down and sort out the grains of salt from the grains of pepper in their intellectual diets. They are so thoroughly mixed up together in films like this, it can actually be hard to do.

L: I understand just what you mean, but some people haven't as yet seen the movie, or may not do so, so let's get a synopsis.

Doug: The movie is a science-fiction scenario in which humans have gone to a planet in another star system far from Earth to mine a super-valuable mineral called "unobtainium." Gotta love that name. Unobtainium has long been an engineer's catch phrase for pixie dust—but it's still funny.

The planet, called Pandora, is populated by giant, blue-skinned aliens who live in harmony with the rainforest that covers the place. These guys are the heroes, resisting the humans who, among other things, want to chop down a giant tree, which is a tribal totem. A human soldier's mind remote-operates an artificial body like that of one of the natives, called an avatar, and he is tasked with infiltrating the native society and getting them to leave their sacred tree. He ends up switching sides, of course, as the soldier does in *Dances with Wolves*.

L: And of course the Bad Guys work for a *mining* company, which has hired a private army to boot the natives out of the way. This scenario is so contrived—not to mention copied from a half-dozen predecessor stories—that the richest deposit of unobtainium within 200 kilometers is right under the beautiful natives' sacred tree. *Kilometers!* As though a civilization that can look for minerals across light years of space couldn't look for them more than 200 kilometers away…

Doug: [Laughs] You'd think that if $400 million couldn't buy you an original screenplay, it could at least get you one with some common sense…

L: The Bad Guys are such cold-hearted, money-grubbing stereotypes, they were like cartoon caricatures. On the other hand, you've got heartless bad guys and underdog good guys fighting for their homes and freedom from oppression—that's a good, positive theme. It's mixed in, like you say—it often seems to me that they have to stick some sort of libertarian message in, or they just don't get the audience as emotionally involved in the cause as they want.

Doug: That's why it's hard to sort out. If you're on the human side, you have to accept the genocide of the natives. If you're on the other side, you still have to totally suspend disbelief and be anti-technology, since it might hurt the planet. The alien natives are so pure and good and noble that you can only be living in an alternate reality. Apart from the fact that it's all geochemical fantasy: there are 92 naturally occurring elements in this universe, and unobtainium isn't among them. Clearly, at least to me, the director was trying to make this a morality myth. Too bad the morality is so confused.

I'd like to see a movie in which the hero is an unalloyed good guy.

L: Well, there was the 1949 film adaptation of Ayn Rand's *The Fountainhead*[2], starring Gary Cooper. That one's not very realistic either, but Rand didn't write the character of Howard Roark to be realistic; she created him to be a pure archetype. He's a moral example—unalloyed good.

Doug: Well, yes, that would qualify—but that movie was made in a different era. Perhaps one movie every 50 years with an unalloyed good guy is all the public can handle… we're about due for one. I can't wait.

L: One of the things I find most insidious about this movie is this business of the alien natives being portrayed as an environmental extremist's ideal of pure goodness.

Doug: Yes, they are primitives, with bows and arrows being their most advanced technology—all human technology is depicted as being destructive in the film. The primitive society is just the way extremists would like to see all people living on our world today—those that don't want to see humans wiped off the earth. This completely ignores the diseases, chronic risk of starvation, savage wars, and other terrors that were the daily fare of primitive humans. In this fantasy, these noble savages live in harmony with nature. But, frankly, who wants to live in harmony with germs, viruses, fungi, and carnivores that are actively trying to kill you?

Enviro-extremists fantasize that Mother Earth is alive—they call her Gaia—and that we nasty humans are killing her. Somehow volcanoes that spew mountains of toxic chemicals into the air don't count. Nor do asteroids and space debris that periodically crash into the planet, destroying most living things.

But in the movie, Pandora *really is* alive. The natives can communicate with animals via natural fiber optics that are part of their hair, and with the trees

---

2. www.totallyincorrectbook.com/go/238

that network the whole planet and store the memories of their ancestors. If that were true on earth today, then cutting down the forest really would be the crime environmental extremists make it out to be. But it's not. And the movie reinforces values driven by the environmental left, based on a pure fantasy that does not apply to the real world.

L: That's what I'm saying. The movie is a realization of a vision of indigenous peoples that's not true. It's never been true. Primitives on earth have almost universally been war-like. It was not only white people who practiced slavery. There's a reason why Hobbes describes primitive life as "solitary, poor, nasty, brutish and short."

My concern is that people will transpose the values from the movie to reality. They'll see international mining companies as being like the one in the movie, even though real mining companies go to great lengths to avoid conflict with local populations and in most cases actively try to help them. Many viewers will see the poor natives in Bolivia or Bangladesh as being like the ones in the movie, even though they are as often as not trashing the local environment in scores of ways, including mining using unsafe chemicals. The movie is a fantasy, but the stereotypes have direct analogs in our world today—and they are wrong.

Doug: Yes. The Na'vi—the blue people of Pandora—are portrayed as living in a real garden of Eden. As you say, reality on our planet is different. For one thing, many real primitive tribes were devastating to their local environments. For example, at least before the evil white man imported horses, it was very hard for North American Indians to take down big prey like buffalo unless they stampeded the whole herd over a cliff. They weren't environmentally friendly on principle; that's just currently fashionable enviro-imagination. They weren't trying to maintain the balance of nature; they simply lacked the technology to do more damage.

But it's a false dilemma. What's missing here is an understanding of property rights.

If the Sky People, as the humans are called in the movie, came and found something of value on Pandora, it would have been incumbent upon them to respect the property rights of those already there and find a way to trade for what they wanted. This apparently never occurred to the humans in the movie, who simply show up and take what they want by force. That's called "stealing," and it has natural consequences...

L: The movie even makes that point, if perhaps unwittingly. If you steal something, people resist. The Na'vi resist, so the evil mining company pays a fortune to hire an army, create avatars, etc., and eventually suffers a great economic loss as a result of having disrespected the locals' property rights. How could that be more profitable than finding places to mine where there were no Na'vi? Or mining underground and then restoring the minimal surface disruption to its original state? Or coming to some kind of a mutually beneficial agreement?

Doug: Right. The movie makers created a straw-man enemy, just to be able to knock him down. They don't even bother to explain how it was legal for a private company to murder natives in this future. Usually only governments or their minions, like <u>Blackwater</u>[3], can do that with impunity…

That reminds me of another thing that bothered me about the movie. In it, the soldiers and their more powerful technology are depicted as the Bad Guys, attacking the nice blue people. But if the blue people had had superior alien technology and had been ruthlessly wiping out the humans, those same soldiers would have been the Good Guys. In <u>*Aliens*</u>[4], the excellent movie I referenced earlier, Sigourney Weaver uses a robot to fight the bad alien.

And then there's the female helicopter pilot who switches sides at the end of the movie. It's just a matter of how you look at it, whether she's a hero or a traitor. Did everyone she killed deserve to die? If you're caught in the wrong war, do you have the right to shoot your officer? Joseph Heller, in <u>*Catch-22*</u>[5] said that the enemy is anybody who's going to get you killed. There are moral ambiguities in the movie that are never clearly dealt with. It's almost like they rolled dice to assign character values, just to get your emotions worked up. I prefer to have the motivations of characters explored. There's a difference between a real catharsis and just having your emotions played with…

That is a real problem with professional soldiers, of course; they do whatever they're told, including attacking and killing whoever they're told, because that's their job. There's very little moral reasoning among such people.

L: That's an interesting point, and perhaps a redeeming feature of the film. As you pointed out in our conversation on the military, when you have people trained to act without thinking, it's dangerous. This movie did show that, especially when, towards the end, the guys in charge tell all the humans in their base that the natives have amassed an army, and they now need to exterminate them, or the humans themselves will be exterminated.

That's typical of politicians in the real world; they push people into conflicts where they must kill or be killed. Look at Vietnam—the commanders and

---

3. www.totallyincorrectbook.com/go/239
4. www.totallyincorrectbook.com/go/240
5. www.totallyincorrectbook.com/go/241

soldiers on the ground did some bad things, but the people who are really to blame were those bastards in Washington, or Hanoi, or wherever, who put them in such a situation to begin with.

Doug: I agree. There were definitely some sergeants that deserved fragging. And some captains, colonels, and generals. And some presidents. But the higher up the command chain you are, the more likely it is you'll escape punishment for the crimes you commit in office—even though you deserve it far more. It's quite perverse.

L: Any other redeeming aspects of the movie? Usually with these anti-human environmentalist movies, it's not enough for the corporations to be simply making money in some disapproved way. In order to really get the audience riled up, the companies have to start killing people or committing other serious crimes. In this case, we have a moral underdog fighting genocide and winning— that's a positive message, isn't it?

Doug: Sure. In human history, whenever a more advanced civilization has encountered a less advanced one, it's been bad for the less advanced one. Every time. For one thing, the larger, conquering empire usually brings diseases the smaller, isolated tribe hasn't encountered. And, of course, throughout history, might has made right. There's value in pointing this out.

But this is not a function of capitalism as it's portrayed in the movie. To the contrary, capitalism is a matter of trade and voluntarism. The way I see it, the essence of capitalism is good and pure and noble. The problem is that humans suffer from flaws—which movies like this are correct to point out. For all I know, humans wound up on Earth as a prison planet for crimes they committed elsewhere in the universe. Maybe C.S. Lewis was right in how he portrayed the Silent Planet in his *Space Trilogy*. The possibilities certainly appeal to my solipsistic tendencies, as well as my love of SF.

But with these stupid movies, it's always a case of mistaken identity; they can't identify the real malefactor in the tragedy, which can turn the whole exercise into a black comedy if the viewer is a cynic.

In any event, as we discussed in our conversation on the military, conquest is not profitable in the modern world, as it was in the ancient. War destroys the value in a conquered society—it's just not profitable to cart off the women and the gold like they used to do.

L: Nukes don't conquer, they simply obliterate.

Doug: Another interesting thing is that the movie was banned in China, except for the 3D version in the few theaters that can handle it. Apparently the powers-that-be fear that the Han extracting resources from Tibet and other poor areas in western China might start sympathizing with the locals and stop working in the mines and so on.

I suppose any state naturally dislikes any movies that depict anything other than support for the state and its programs. All Soviet movies were basically propaganda. But when they try to censor things like this, it inevitably backfires on them. People resent it and go looking for it. People may in fact be idiots, but they don't like to be treated that way.

L: I always wondered if *V for Vendetta*[6] was allowed to show in China.

Doug: I sincerely doubt it. "V" is one of my favorite movies of all time—and it's seriously subversive. Everybody should watch it every year.

I wonder if there's a way this movie, *Avatar*, could have been made so that it was just as exciting and visually impressive, but so that it was morally uplifting instead of morally confusing.

L: What about investment implications—see anything in this mix?

Doug: Well, as a straw in the wind, this movie's $2 billion take at the box office can be seen as an argument for expecting metals supplies to continue being restricted for some time to come. As you know from your work, traveling around the world looking for good metals projects for *International Speculator* subscribers to invest in, governments everywhere are raising the cost of mining through ever more onerous regulations and ever higher direct taxation.

L: That's when they aren't shutting off vast tracts of mineral-rich lands to exploration completely.

Doug: Right. This movie is a clear sign of strong public sentiment in favor of policies that restrict mining, even as the Earth's population keeps growing and is going to need more and more metals. A hundred years ago, when you found a deposit, you could put it into production in a matter of weeks. Now, it takes nine years on average—if you can get the permits at all.

So, with demand on track to continue rising for decades to come, existing supplies in depletion, and new supplies being restricted, the trend is for higher metals prices for the foreseeable future.

L: Short-term corrections aside.

Doug: Yes.

---

6. www.totallyincorrectbook.com/go/242

Doug Casey on WikiLeaks

Dec 21, 2010

L: So, Doug, North Korea shelled South Korea—do you think that's the sound of an approaching black swan we hear?

Doug: It could be, but I doubt North Korea wants a real war, and South Korea absolutely wants to avoid one. Of course, North Korea's government is a hereditary monarchy, run by the thoroughly degraded Kim family—which is a bit confusing, in that everybody in Korea is either a Kim, a Park, or a Lee. Who knows what's going on in the abnormal psychology of Kim Jong-Il or whoever is really running the place? It's perverse.

The key is that North Korea is already a wasteland, so a war would do them relatively less harm; in a way they have nothing to lose. South Korea is a G20 economy, however, so even if they win a shooting match in short order, they still lose, in terms of the damage they would suffer in the process.

From a *realpolitik* point of view, it makes sense for the North to occasionally kill a few South Koreans, make threatening noises, and keep the "us vs. them" rhetoric hot. It provides an excuse for their extraordinarily low standard of living and a reason for having a police state. They use nationalism and patriotism very effectively to prop up their pathetic regime. In that regard, they are like most governments, just more extreme. But I consider the chances of an actual war to be slim.

It was interesting to see gold shoot up the day the Koreas traded artillery shells. Coincidentally, it was just after the EU's announcement that all is well and everyone can go back to spending as usual. I don't think it's likely that the Koreas will go for all-out war and push the teetering global economy over the edge. It's possible, because we're dealing with certifiable lunatics, but it's more likely the EU itself will provide a black-swan event. The bankruptcy of the euro, and then the EU, was always inevitable. It may now be imminent as well.

Regarding North Korea, though, what's really interesting is the information leaked through <u>WikiLeaks</u>[1] that China—basically their only ally—may be pulling back its support. The Chinese can see that maintaining a lunatic regime in North Korea no longer serves any useful purpose. They don't need a loose cannon on their border. I expect it will collapse in the near term. The Chinese, likely with the collusion of some North Korean generals, will oust the Kims and set up something that's less of a liability.

L: I saw that news. It's quite striking that after the wikileak, some Chinese officials have apparently come out and said that <u>they do, in fact, favor reunification</u>[2] of the Koreas.

Doug: The whole idea of WikiLeaks is terrific. They've become one of the most important watchdog organizations on the planet, helping to expose a lot of government action for what it really is.

This latest leak of a quarter of a million classified US embassy cables is quite a coup, not just for revealing China's changing attitudes about North Korea, but for exposing discussions the US had with other countries about bombing Iran, <u>espionage conducted by US diplomats in Paraguay</u>[3], Chinese government attacks on Google, and more mundane things like the <u>lavish lifestyles of Kazakhstan's political elite</u>[4].

Shining a light on the sociopaths who hide in the dark places under the rocks of government is always a good thing. That's what they just did in their exposé of what is going on with the counterproductive US wars in Iraq and Afghanistan. It's great to have a whistleblower organization like them. Julian Assange, who runs it, is a hero, and deserves the Nobel Peace Prize—although it's a shame that prize has become so meaningless and degraded.

L: The more skeptical people become of the Right and Honorable So-And-So, the better.

Doug: Exactly. And on a more fundamental philosophical level, this is in keeping with my sense of justice. Crooks should not get away with their crimes just because they hold lofty titles, wear spiffy uniforms, and call their crimes great deeds necessitated by "national security," "economic stimulus," or whatever other nonsensical lies they come up with.

I'm fond of saying, "Do what thou wilt, shall be the whole of the law—but be prepared to accept the consequences." Well, exposing secrets is an important

---

1. www.totallyincorrectbook.com/go/243
2. www.totallyincorrectbook.com/go/244
3. www.totallyincorrectbook.com/go/245
4. www.totallyincorrectbook.com/go/246

part of enabling the natural consequences for dastardly deeds to follow.

The whole idea of "national security" has gotten completely out of control. It has about zero to do with protecting what little is left of America; it's all about protecting, and building, the US government and the people who participate in it and profit from it. People fail to understand that the USG doesn't represent them or care about them—or at least not any more than a farmer cares about his milk cows. It's an entity unto itself at this point. It has its own interests, which have only an accidental or coincidental overlap with those of America. Government is by its very nature duplicitous and predatory; it always puts itself first. By cynically paying lip service to traditional values and whipping up a nationalistic, patriotic fervor, they can get *Boobus americanus* to go along with almost anything they propose. Just like *Boobus north koreansis*.

L: Hm. Sarah Palin apparently does not agree[5] with you about WikiLeaks. She's reported saying that WikiLeaks personnel should be treated like terrorists.

Doug: And people thought I was being too hard on the Tea Party[6] movement. This is exactly the sort of knee-jerk conservative reaction that shows that such people really don't care about freedom at all. I suspect Palin is cut from the same cloth as Baby Bush—ignorant, unintelligent, thoughtless, reactionary, and pig-headed. She belongs on reality TV, not in a position where she could damage the lives of billions of people.

L: The report says she wants to know why governments didn't hack the WikiLeaks website. Well, apparently somebody did last Sunday when these diplomatic cables were leaked—and who is a more likely culprit than the US government? On the bright side, the attack failed. A handful of nonviolent individuals took on the world's greatest superpower, as a matter of principle, and won. That just goes to show yet again how technological advances tend to flatten the power pyramid of society.

Doug: Yes; we talked about that in our conversation on technology. Every advance in technology puts the little guy on a more even footing with those at the top of the intra-human food chain. This is why the Colt revolver became known as "the great equalizer." For the first time, the little guy was not only the equal of the big guy but, because he presented a smaller target, was his superior.

The Internet is the best thing that's happened for freedom since the invention of the printing press. Technology is the biggest force for individual liberty and politics the main enemy of it. But people idiotically idolize politicians and generals much more than scientists and inventors. Despite that, with the

---

5. www.totallyincorrectbook.com/go/247
6. www.totallyincorrectbook.com/go/248

development of very powerful, homemade laser weapons, and 3D printers that will soon allow anyone to make almost anything at trivial cost in their garage, the cat will soon be out of the bag. We should discuss those in the future. These things are very opportune at the very time that the bloated states of the world are going into collapse, much like the Roman Empire in the 5th century.

L: In an interesting counterpoint, Reuters reports that Hillary Clinton defended WikiLeaks as she arrived in Kazakhstan—at the same time the embarrassing assessment of Kazakh leadership was leaked. Sometimes liberals do defend liberal ideas, like freedom of the press.

Doug: Sometimes. But not if it's politically incorrect press. You can rely on them only to make government larger and more expensive at every turn—you can rely upon that like a Swiss train. Hillary, like any Secretary of State, is a skilled and enthusiastic liar. Her stock in trade is deception. Everything she says is intended to forward her drive to become president. I wonder if she'd be worse than Palin? But that's like asking if Nero would be worse than Caligula.

L: No argument. And you know I agree with you on the watchdog principle, but what if they go after private-sector entities? CNN reports that <u>WikiLeaks' next target</u>[7] is a major US bank.

Doug: It's a mistake to think of banks in the US as being private-sector entities. US banks got into bed with the state decades ago, and got even more closely entwined via the latest set of regulations and bailouts. At this point they're really parastatal entities. Plus, I'd guess that whatever whistle-blowing WikiLeaks is planning, it probably has to do with the bailouts or other government interactions with the banks anyway—exactly the type of thing that needs to be exposed.

L: Fine, but their mission is not to fight the state, but simply to publish "important" news and information. What if someone uses their secure drop-box technology to reveal salacious material on private individuals... say, a complete list of all of Doug Casey's mistresses?

Doug: Unfortunately, that list would be rather small at the moment. Not that WikiLeaks would deem that sort of thing important enough to bother with. But, look, it doesn't matter; there are tabloids that cover that ground already, and they get the respect they deserve. If you aren't prepared to accept the consequences of something, don't do it. The only sure way to avoid having your mistresses exposed, if you really don't want that to happen, is not to have mistresses.

L: So... do you believe in a human right to privacy?

---

7. www.totallyincorrectbook.com/go/249

Doug: In the sense of having a right to remain silent, yes. No one should ever be forced to reveal anything they don't want to reveal. But in the sense of having a right to use force to stop people from saying, publishing, or broadcasting information about you, no. The information in their heads is theirs, and they have a right to do whatever they want with it. If it happens to be about you and you don't like it, tough. Develop better security measures. Or better, "If you can't do the time, don't do the crime."

L: What about libel?

Doug: If information put out by others about you is wrong, defend yourself with the truth. If you have a solid reputation accumulated over years of interactions with many people, your side of the story should get a good hearing. If you've been a jerk to many people or not always honest, you'll have a tougher time—which is as it should be.

The potential harm that lies might do does not justify giving power to the state to control what other people say—that's a far greater harm. A complete free market in information will necessarily make people much more discriminating and less gullible. They'll become much less likely to believe things without solid evidence.

L: Sounds a bit like an intellectual Wild West.

Doug: Yes, but that's a good thing. We have laws against libel and slander now, and people violate them constantly. It's not just ineffective, it's counterproductive, because the existence of libel laws makes people more likely to believe what they hear. In a society without laws against libel, people would be much more skeptical, and the potential harm from lies would be diminished.

L: I can see that… and why you favor the WikiLeaks technology. You remain an optimist; things have to get worse before they can get better, but the longest term trend of them all is "the ascent of man."

Doug: Yes. The trend is towards rapidly accelerating advances in technology. So, certainly in this case, the trend is your friend. Don't fear technology—it's what brought us out of the caves and primeval slime—it's everybody's best friend.

L: After the dog?

Doug: Poodles in particular. I suspect this isn't the time for a sidebar on standard poodles. But I will mention it's one of the many subjects on which I'm in total agreement with my friend Richard Russell.

L: Poodles. I'm not going to go there now. Investment implications?

Doug: Unfortunately, WikiLeaks is not itself an investment opportunity, being a non-profit organization.

L: If it were for profit, would you invest?

Doug: I'd have to look at the actual business model and projections, but there's reason to be skeptical. By its nature, WikiLeaks is always going to be outside the mainstream of the economy, with rabid governments trying to shut it down, maybe even imprison its people, as they get more desperate. This thing has "scapegoat" written all over it. I hear Interpol has suddenly decided to bring Assange in on charges of sexual assault—transparency and accepting the consequences of his actions should apply to him like anyone else, but I'm very suspicious of the timing of these accusations. WikiLeaks is an encrypted, moving target, but a target nonetheless.

L: Do you contribute to WikiLeaks? You like the service, but don't believe in charity.

Doug: I wouldn't consider it charity; I value their service. If I sent them money, it would be because I want to show support and reward their efforts. Sending them money and giving them other support amounts to a fair exchange, in my view. Not because of charity, which very often just assuages the guilt of the donor, while subtly encouraging bad habits in the recipient.

But this is also a technology story. WikiLeaks itself is not an investment opportunity, but there are new technologies that are fantastic opportunities.

L: Roger that.

Doug Casey on "Occupy Wall Street"

Nov 9, 2011

L: Doug, we're here in Cafayate, Argentina, far, far from Wall Street, which is being "occupied" by protesters with a very clear message. Doug, as a prime cut of meat on the "eat the rich"[1] menu, would you like to respond?

Doug: I assume you're being sarcastic about the clear message, but one can never tell in today's world. Otherwise, I would have thought Paul Krugman was joking when he said that a pretend alien invasion would be good for the economy[2]. We increasingly live in an Alice in Wonderland world.

L: Truth is often stranger than fiction. We'd have been laughed at if we'd predicted that people in Spain would shine lights on solar cells at night[3], because the subsidies make it profitable to do so.

Doug: Indeed. But back to Wall Street. I have very mixed feelings about the occupation movement, because these people are 100% correct to be angry about these banks—from Goldman Sachs on down—that received scores of billions of dollars of taxpayers' money after doing the opposite of what banks are supposed to do (losing money instead of keeping it safe), and then paying themselves lavish bonuses.

L: It's actually the largest bank heist in history.

Doug: You could say that. Was it Al Capone who said that one accountant with a pen can steal more than 100 thugs with guns? A central banker like Bernanke can facilitate the looting of an entire country, though. You might also say it's the Chinese whose money they stole, because the Chinese will never be able to redeem their long-term Treasuries for anything like the value they put into them. You could also say it's the next generation's money, because they're

---

1. www.totallyincorrectbook.com/go/250
2. www.totallyincorrectbook.com/go/251
3. www.totallyincorrectbook.com/go/252

going to have to pay for it all. No wonder so many young people are outraged—they have a right to be.

L: But... ?

Doug: But on the other hand, a lot of these Occupy Wall Street (OWS) people seem to be of the same sort who would have been loosely wrapped hippies back in the '60s. I was also sympathetic with the hippies in many regards, by the way, because I agreed with their anti-war and anti-drug-law stances. It's hard to see these people as allies, however, when one of their most popular slogans equates me to a beef cow. They seem to have a strong collectivist/socialist animus. They seem to hate the 1%[4] just because they have money. They don't have the sense to make distinctions as to how different people might have gotten that money.

I am, clearly, one of the 1%. So are you. In fact, almost everyone who has worked hard, saved money, and invested it wisely is at least in the top 10%. What the OWS people are angry about—or should be angry about—are the people who made their money through government contacts or connections. They didn't produce anything; they're really just sophisticated thieves. I have only contempt for those who feed at the public trough.

But here we are in one of the nicest places in the world, where I'm living high off the hog, smoking an expensive Cuban cigar—that's probably a waterboarding offense in the US these days—so I guess that puts me on the menu.

However, I haven't yet been to one of these protests to speak with any of these people, so maybe I shouldn't presume too much about what they think. It's likely their level of discourse would be no more cogent than what you read in the *New York Times*, perhaps even less cogent than *USA Today*. I don't like to be around angry people—although, to be honest, I'm angry myself because I hate to see what's left of America, and Western civilization itself, on the skids...

L: I haven't talked to any of the OWS people either, but, not wanting to rely solely on hearsay, I sent someone to the epicenter in Manhattan. We asked people there: "What does Occupy Wall Street mean to you?" I published the results in the current edition of the *International Speculator*. Here are some of the more comprehensible quotations:

The 99% are getting more distribution. Corruption in government. Peaceful overthrow.

---

4. www.totallyincorrectbook.com/go/253

There are people who have a lot of money and then people with nothing. I'm a student, and I don't want my future to be the way it is now. Make the country equal again.

If something is not right, do something about it! Inspire unity. Everyone knows something is wrong.

Mad at bailouts. Very little difference between political parties. [Everyone] knows Democrat = Republican! Lockheed Martin makes money from taxpayer-funded wars. Gold standard! Bitcoins! Disenfranchise the 1% plutocracy. Root out corruption.

I don't have my clear answer for this.

One of the interesting things about this is that there's a clear streak of very strong anti-government sentiment from people who usually can't get enough government. Granted, they don't necessary call for less government, but they do seem to want to throw the bums out. All of them. Except maybe Ron Paul.

Doug: That is interesting, and I think it's also interesting to compare the movement to the Tea Party[5]. Both groups feel powerless, disenfranchised, and betrayed. Both groups are under severe economic pressure—which, I promise, is going to get much worse.

L: I hadn't thought of that, but in spite of the ideological differences, I can see a similarity in that both are angry with the status quo but not clear on what they propose to improve on it.

Doug: Exactly. It's a very inchoate kind of anger. Most of the people involved, in both groups, seem to have zero understanding of real economics and don't understand the way the world works. They just correctly perceive that they're getting screwed. But I see little or no cultural or sociological overlap between the groups.

L: Well, I haven't been to a Tea Party event, nor have I sent an investigator to one, so I'm not in a position to compare them, but it is interesting to me how diverse the OWS people are. There were people there in favor of Ron Paul, as well as for typical New-England Democrats. One fellow even mentioned the gold standard. On the other hand, one photo I didn't publish—because the guy's face is clearly identifiable—is of a young man sitting on a cinder block, smoking marijuana... so the neo-hippie component does seem to be part of the mix.

---

5. www.totallyincorrectbook.com/go/254

Doug: In the photos I've seen, a good number of these protesters have taken to wearing Guy Fawkes masks, which I find encouraging. "Remember, remember, the fifth of November, gunpowder, treason and plot. I know of no reason it should ever be forgot." My avatar on Facebook, Skype, and other such venues is always a Guy Fawkes mask. I'd love to see everyone use one. That's how things ended in the movie _V for Vendetta_[6].

L: But that's just the thing: To you and me, a Guy Fawkes mask is a symbol for anarchy as a better organizing system for society than government—any government. But for many, the mask is just a symbol for resistance to tyranny. To some, it may not represent much at all, besides appropriate attire to wear during a riot.

Doug: Yes, and regrettably, in real life Guy Fawkes was apparently a Catholic fanatic who just wanted to replace a Protestant-dominated government with a Catholic-dominated government. That's hardly a solution. It overlooks the real problem, which is government itself, sticking its nose into every aspect of human existence.

L: So, here we have a movement, composed of very different people from different walks of life, that has gone viral, spreading all across the US, even to smaller towns. It has spread overseas as well and has turned violent in some cases, with mass arrests in Oakland being a recent example. This could get pretty ugly. This is how revolutions start—we've seen this sort of pattern in the Arab Spring, as well as in the fall of Eastern European dictators, and more. But starting a revolution with no clearer goal than "eat the rich" is... a dangerous thing to do.

Doug: It may sound rather extreme—

L: Not that that has ever stopped you...

Doug: —but I don't think it's out of the question that there could be a second American revolution ahead.

L: A third—the War Between the States being a failed attempt at a second one.

Doug: Right. Formal or informal, there could easily be a secession movement as things come further and further unraveled. And yes, it could turn into a shooting war. These things happen. A lot of Americans are getting to the point where they feel they have little to lose. And things are just starting to get bad; the Greater Depression[7] is still very young.

You know, the Obama administration is making noises about a rising threat in Iran. They might just be tempted to attack them, either as a great distraction from troubles at home or in the hope it might unite America—which, incidentally, I think would be a bad thing at this point. It would be like uniting

---

6. www.totallyincorrectbook.com/go/255
7. www.totallyincorrectbook.com/go/256

lemmings as they plunge over a cliff together. Being united amounts to group-think; it caters to the lowest common denominator. Uniting around a political leader is a symptom of moral bankruptcy. What made America great was individuals thinking and acting as individuals.

L: On the plus side, there was also an anti-war streak in the people we surveyed occupying Wall Street.

Doug: That's true in the Tea Party too, although to a lesser degree. But on the minus side, we have large numbers of people in uniform in the US—lots of police and soldiers—who have been trained to obey orders without hesitation. Just like everywhere else in the world, men in uniform are extremely dangerous. They're loyal above all to their peers in uniform, secondarily to the government that pays them, and last to the people they're supposed to "protect and serve." If Americans in uniform are ordered to beat and imprison American citizens petitioning their government for redress of grievances, they will obey. It could get very, very ugly.

L: If there's an insurrection with no goal other than to overthrow those in charge now, it seems like an invitation to "the man on the white horse" to come in and lead everyone boldly into a new slavery. This bubbling cauldron of anger is like a lit stick of dynamite. Who knows who's going to pick it up and where they're going to throw it?

Doug: It has to end badly. Every revolution I'm aware of, including the American revolution, leads to a period of things getting worse before they get better—if they get better. The French revolution is a classic case, in which it was good they got rid of Louis XVI, but then they got Robespierre, and then they got Napoleon, who was even worse. This is the standard pattern; revolutions unleash the most violent and fanatical people to rise to the top. So, if the trend continues, I don't expect it to have a happy ending.

L: And do you expect it to continue?

Doug: Unfortunately, yes. The economy is going to continue getting worse. People are going to become much more unhappy, and they are going to feel like they have much less to lose. Trends in motion tend to stay in motion until they reach a genuine crisis.

L: Whether OWS is the beginning of the violent end to this saga or whether things calm down, is there no way out for the US?

Doug: No. Partially because this country is really no longer America. The country has already changed in character from being a unique beacon of individual liberty to just another of the 200 degraded nation-states in the world. It's hopeless to wish for an easy out, not just for what's left of America, but for the West and the current economic order in general. Even though I'm an unabashed optimist about the long-term future, I just don't see how things can avoid getting much, much worse over the next decade or so. This is barely a beginning—we're just at the leading edge of the storm, as we exit the eye of the global crisis hurricane.

L: Mr. Cheerful again, Doug.

Doug: You know I call 'em like I see 'em. I don't make the rules, except in my personal life.

L: Right. Investment implications?

Doug: Nothing new. We've been saying for some time to rig for stormy weather; buy gold, buy silver. They are not at giveaway levels, but they're going a lot higher. Gold stocks are actually quite cheap now, relative to gold. I'm more enthusiastic about the potential for gold stocks to go into a huge bubble than I ever have been.

I also like quality energy plays on the dips and productive agricultural land a lot. Great new technological innovations, especially those that save people money, should also do well in the deepening crisis.

L: Okay, Doug. Thanks for another thought-provoking conversation.

Doug: My pleasure, as always.

Doug Casey on Poker

Dec 30, 2009

L: Doug, you often make a point of distinguishing speculation from gambling, as in our recent conversation on <u>winning speculations</u>[1]. But I know you also you like to gamble. Poker, specifically. Is that a vice or a virtue?

Doug: Well, I've always enjoyed poker, ever since I was a kid, actually. Part of the poker experience is sitting around with some friends in an informal environment. But unlike, say, bridge, it lends itself more to smoking, drinking, and pleasant conversations on unrefined topics. Bridge draws a much more straight-laced, even uptight, crowd; alcohol, tobacco, and colorful language are discouraged around a bridge table—which is limited to four people in any event. Bridge didn't grow up in gambling halls and cathouses where the denizens were often armed.

Wild Bill Hickok wouldn't have fit in well at your typical bridge tournament, although, it must be said, that might have extended his life. Poker is, after all, more of a gambler's game than bridge. The luck of the draw is important in both games, of course, and there's a mathematical element in both, albeit a stronger one in bridge. A good memory is also much more important in bridge.

But much more than bridge, poker is a game of psychology—it's one of the most important aspects of the game. It's why there are world-class poker players who almost always win, over the long run, and other players who almost always lose—even though over the long run everybody gets the same cards. With pure gambling games, like roulette and baccarat, everybody loses in the long run.

L: Hm. I never really thought of it that way, but of course, everyone does get the same distribution of probabilities over time... So, what does "psychology" mean in this context? Do you play by looking at people's faces and guessing whether they are bluffing?

---

1. www.totallyincorrectbook.com/go/257

Doug: "Reading" the other players sounds romantic.... and there are people who are good at it. The idea is to look for "tells"—quirks in your opponent's personalities, such as squinting when they have high cards, or breaking out in a sweat when they have nothing. But I find it overrated. It's not that people don't have these quirks, but that it's harder than people think to read them in the brief time you have to do it, with people you don't know at all.

The first book on poker I ever read when I was a kid was a book by a guy named Herbert W. Yardley, called _The Education of a Poker Player_.[2] Yardley had actually been a spook, employed by the US government in the 1930s, sent on errands of mischief all around the world—and playing poker all around the world. The most interesting part of the book is in the beginning, where he tells anecdotes about the guy who taught him how to play poker.

Incidentally, the guy's name was Monte, and there's an old adage that you should never play poker with a guy named Monte, nor a guy named Doc. It's always a mistake. [Chuckles] Monte spoke of a game played with some farmer called The Swede with an obvious tell, after which he ended up with the deed to the farm. Horrible, sad story, actually. I don't believe I can read other people's tells reliably. It's an art. It's easier to make sure you don't have a tell others can read.

The standard text on the game today, incidentally, is probably David Sklansky's _Sklansky on Poker_[3]. Some of his other books are worthy as well. You won't go wrong starting there.

L: So how do you play?

Doug: Well, it's not about what you have in your hand so much as what people think you have. Bluffing _is_ very important in poker. But more than occasional bluffing is not a good, long-term strategy. Neither in poker nor in life. Eventually, somebody is going to call your bluff with the real goods. Or make you think they've got the goods to call your bluff—it's a question of double-reverse psychology sometimes. As an occasional strategy, of course, bluffing can and does work because, as I say, it's not about what you have but what other people think you have.

It's like that old joke about two campers sitting by the campfire. A bear comes out of the woods and charges towards them, and one camper starts putting his shoes on. The other camper screams, "You can't outrun a bear!" And the first camper yells back, "I don't need to outrun the bear, I just need to outrun you!"

---

2. www.totallyincorrectbook.com/go/258
3. www.totallyincorrectbook.com/go/259

L: [laughs]

Doug: Poker's a bit like that. There are many, many forms of poker, of course, but historically, it started out with two main forms. There's five-card draw, in which you're dealt five cards, you can bet, and you can discard anywhere from none, up to all five cards, and then bet again. And then there's five-card stud, in which you're dealt one card face up, one card face down, and then new cards are dealt to each player individually and you can bet on each. Then it evolved into seven-card stud and many other variations.

Championship poker, as played today, is Texas Hold 'em, which is basically seven-card stud. You're dealt two cards, face down, and five cards are dealt in the middle, face up, which everyone shares to make up a five-card hand.

This is played all around the world. Casinos are going up everywhere, encouraged by many governments because they find they can tax casinos more than other businesses. That makes the game even more interesting to me, because you can sit down at a table anywhere in the world with whoever is playing cards, and match your wits against theirs.

L: Okay, I can see that. But back up to the actual playing of the game. If it's not about what anyone has in their hands but about what people think others have in their hands, does that make it important to learn to communicate false signals? Do people develop false tells so they can set others up and then swoop in for the kill?

Doug: I wish I were good enough to do that! But if you watch really good poker players—and you can see them on television all the time—they typically keep a good "poker face." Many wear dark glasses to disguise what their eyes are doing—which isn't very sociable. The game has actually become a very popular spectator sport around the world. Although it's not a sport. It's an activity, a hobby. Then again, they call golf and bowling sports, too. Personally, I don't consider something a sport unless you have to break a sweat playing…

L: They have those special tables with cameras built into the edges, so people watching on TV can see when the players lift up their two face-down cards to see what they have.

Doug: Yes. Anyway, if you watch, you'll notice that the best players—most of them—keep a poker face. They try not to reveal anything, true or false. But there's nothing to stop someone very, very clever from trying to give out false signals and use other forms of reverse psychology.

You know, one of the things the computer revolution has done is make online poker possible—and you can't even see your opponents' faces. The biggest online site is called PokerStars.net. At any given time you log on to that site, there are between 150,000 and 250,000 people from all over the world, playing poker. The stakes you put up to play are anything from one cent to thousands of dollars. They even have numerous free tournaments with cash prizes. Theoretically, a player could leverage himself from zero to the world championship, which usually pays over $5 million for first place. Tournaments are run all the time with $50,000 and $100,000 prize pools. The really big ones have million-dollar or more pools. So we're talking serious money—and there's no possibility of playing tells.

L: So... Is it even any fun then? No cloud of cigar smoke, no politically incorrect conversation, and no trying to read the other guys' minds? Are you even matching wits at that point, or is it all about weighing probabilities?

Doug: Oh, you're definitely matching wits. What does it mean, for example, if the other guy starts out with a big bet? Is he bluffing, or has he really got the goods? You can't know, at the start. So the correct response is based on the quality of the cards in your own hand. If you have an unsuited 2-7, you should drop. If you have a pair of aces, you may want to raise with your whole stack. But it also depends on how many people are betting after you, how much is in the pot at that moment, how close you are to being "in the money" if it's a tournament, and how much money you have versus the other players, among other things.

And there are advantages to playing online poker versus playing in person. For one thing, it's faster. In any given hour, there are more hands dealt—you get timed out if you wait too long to play your cards. And you can play several games at once. There are some very competent players who play many games at the same time. There's a guy named Hevad Khan—I don't know how he does it—who plays up to 20 online games simultaneously.

L: I guess that if you knew you had a tell of your own, you'd prefer to play online poker.

Doug: For sure. As you watch these guys play online, you see only an avatar for them. But you can watch their style of play and still try to figure out what's going on in their minds, who's bold, who's conservative. You always look for any indications you might find for what the others are thinking, and the main one is to watch their bets. You see what he bets and you ask yourself, what could he possibly have? And then after the flop, what could he have now?

L: Flop?

D: When they turn the next three of the five cards in the middle over, all at once. You see that, and what you think he might have, and try to figure what his hand is—"put them on a hand," we say—and the odds that it's better than yours.

There's an excellent poker movie with Matt Damon, _Rounders_[4], that offers a great look at the world of no–limit Hold 'em. There's a great scene in it where Damon's character watches a bunch of amateurs playing a friendly game and tells them all accurately what cards they're holding, based on the way they're betting. It's not unrealistic that a good pro could do that. And any player should get in the habit of trying to put every other bettor on a hand. I'll also recommend _The Cincinnati Kid_[5] with Steve McQueen, as the other classic poker movie. They're both worth watching, whether you play poker or not.

In any event, I find all the elements of poker quite entertaining. But unless you're a natural, it probably takes as much time as any other activity to become truly expert at it. Which is to say, about 10,000 hours of actually doing it and studying it. This is a point made (although not about poker) in the book _Outliers: The Story of Success_[6], which I also recommend. It amounts to the equivalent of several years of full-time work. Probably more than a game is worth.

L: So, is it just a pastime, then?

Doug: I find that everything you do in life can be improved by anything that gives you an insight into how people think and helps you get better at estimating odds. This is true of studying, sustaining healthy relationships, investing—speculating, of course—just about everything. The Law of Large Numbers is at work everywhere.

And watching your own psychology is equally—or actually more—important. Poker is an excellent school for doing that, if you're introspective enough to assess where you make your mistakes. The nice thing about poker is that the stakes are generally much lower than in investing.

L: Or even in relationships.

Doug: Sure. Like anything, too much of it can become a bad habit, but I think poker teaches useful skills anyone would benefit from improving. Watching how your friends and associates play the game can give you great insight to how they're likely to act away from the table. Does the guy lose hope after a couple of bad bets? Does he go "on tilt" in a desperate but foolish effort to get out even? Is he too timid, or too bold, or heedless of the odds? It's actually much more valuable playing with associates than strangers for exactly these reasons. The game can cut away the social veneer of normal life and give you an insight into who you're actually dealing with—good or bad.

---

4. www.totallyincorrectbook.com/go/260
5. www.totallyincorrectbook.com/go/261
6. www.totallyincorrectbook.com/go/262

It's first and foremost a game of psychology. I don't know of anything else as good. My old man once told me, when I asked him a long, complicated, somewhat cosmic question: "It's all a matter of psychology." That was his complete answer, which is probably why I remembered it.

L: So, you're making a case that poker is a virtue, not a vice. Has there ever been a time when you were making an investment or speculative decision, and consciously drew on the lessons you've learned playing poker in making your choice?

Doug: Yes, but it's probably more help subconsciously, and subtly. The broader your experience, the more you have to draw upon in any situation. And there is an element of gambling in playing the markets. You calculate the odds and do what you can to improve them, but there's still always the luck of the draw.

It's a lot like what Damon Runyon said: "The race is not always to the swift, nor the battle to the strong, but that's the way to bet."

L: Okay then, 'til next time.

Doug: Next time.

Doug Casey on Nobel Prizes

Oct 14, 2009

L: Doug, our savior Obama won the Nobel Peace Prize for boldly intending to wage peace. Really. Any day now. I know you must have some thoughts on this... Did you lose your lunch when you saw the news?

Doug: I was having a rather gruesome nightmare before waking and seeing the news—then I wished I could go back to sleep. No such luck; it was real. My first thought was that it was a spoof from *The Onion* that somebody had swallowed. Or maybe a comic doing a riff on Orson Welles' *War of the Worlds* broadcast. Those politically correct morons in Oslo really did give the man the peace prize for nothing more than stating intentions that are contradicted by his actions.

L: Such as?

Doug: The unconstitutional detention of individuals convicted of no crimes in Guantanamo Bay continues. The war in Afghanistan—a country that never attacked the US—continues, and may even escalate if General McChrystal gets the troops he asked Obama for. The war in Iraq—another country that never attacked the US, and we all know now that the WMD scare was a lie—is keeping the reaper busy. Obama is given much credit for scaling back plans for future missile defense spending, but reports have it that the military itself had already requested a reduction in that program, citing higher priorities.

Besides, the nomination deadline was February 1st, just days after Obama took office, so you know his nomination can't have had anything to do with actual accomplishments. And the fact of the matter is that Obama has not done a single thing to actually implement a more dovish military policy. In fact, it's not unlikely all the chaos in Central Asia will morph into a civil war in Pakistan. That's especially likely if either the Israelis or the Americans—I'm not sure who's the puppet and who's the puppet-master—attack the Iranians.

The US doesn't appear to have a "defense" policy, only an "attack" policy. They really should rename the Department of Defense. Calling it the Department of War, as we did the DoD's predecessor, pre-1947, was much more honest, if not pretty.

L: Well, he talks about peace a lot. I guess we shouldn't be surprised, in a world dominated by moral relativism, that intentions and feelings matter more to most people than deeds and facts.

Doug: Yes, and there's precedent. Don't forget that Al Gore won the peace prize in 2007. I confess that as low an opinion as I already had of the Norwegian Nobel Committee after they gave peace prizes to the likes of Yasser Arafat, Shimon Perez, and Yitzhak Rabin in 1994 (all of whom might as easily have been tried for war crimes), I was shocked and disgusted to see Gore get one.

All evidence to the contrary notwithstanding, part of my brain still likes to think that Nobel Peace Prize recipients *should* be almost preternaturally endowed with virtue. I would much prefer to have seen that Iraqi journalist who threw his shoes at Bush get the prize; at a minimum, he is a man of courage and conviction.

L: Well, after all, Gore is the genius who invented the Internet—I'm sure he must have thought about proposing to study the possibility of intending to do something peaceful, if elected president...

Doug: No, no; he got a peace prize for terrorizing children around the world about global warming.

L: Ah, yes. I'm sure they determined that all the Gore family enterprises have a significantly smaller carbon footprint than average.

Doug: I'm sure looking at the facts was the farthest thing from any committee member's mind. The Nobel Peace Prize committee is a bit different from the others, being appointed by the Norwegian legislature instead of the usual Swedish science academies. They seem to love political hacks above all others, even though an exceptionally popular and politically correct commoner like Mother Teresa can occasionally get the nod.

I actually met Al in 1980, when he invited Herman Kahn to debate me before (I think) the Senate Caucus on Technology and the Future. The whole story of that encounter, in four-part harmony, is in my book, *Crisis Investing for the Rest of the '90s*. But I met him again not long before he won the peace prize, at a lunch with some friends at the Aspen Institute (a prestigious but highly constipated establishmentarian outfit in Colorado). Normally, I don't bother celebrities in public. What's the point? They're usually just ordinary people who are famous for being well known. But since we'd met previously, I wanted to get an updated read on the man, so I walked over and said "Hi."

Not knowing that I was of the "Pave the Planet" persuasion, Gore was friendly and pleasant. Could I see into his soul, the way Bush thought he could do with Putin? No. My only impression was that he should lose a little weight. But that hardly made him unique…

Anyway, when I met him 29 years ago, he reached out to me. I had just given a gloom-and-doom speech (I was wrong, while Herman, who correctly foresaw the subsequent Long Boom, as he called it, was right). But Al wanted to talk to me, since my views reinforced his own. He's always been, I think, psychologically receptive to some great disaster teaching us all a stern lesson. The economy didn't do the job back then, but maybe climate change will now.

But Al and his thoroughly bogus thoughts on carbon, anthropogenic global warming, and the like are yesterday's news. Obama's prize is iron-clad evidence of just how corrupt and utterly meaningless the Nobel Peace Prize has become. The odds are overwhelming they gave it to Obama because he happens to be black and they happen to be stupid and corrupt. But in the Alice in Wonderland world we live in, there's a long-shot chance they have a quirky sense of humor and gave it to him to draw perverse attention to how warlike he actually is, and embarrass him into acting less like Bush…

L: Seems to me that the Nobel Prizes in general have become nothing more than a popularity contest these days. In our world of politicized science and other human endeavors, a Nobel Prize could actually be a contrary indicator to the kind of creative, original thinking needed to make a real breakthrough of any kind.

Doug: Yes, and the Nobel Peace Prize itself needs debunking. If Obama can win it for good intentions, they should give a special posthumous prize to Princess Di, because she wanted to give the world a hug and buy everybody a puppy.

L: Let them eat cake and have it too. (For free—as long as you ignore the man behind the tax curtain…)

Doug: Right. As I see it, like the prizes for literature and economics, the peace prize is awarded according to the totally arbitrary and, to my view, often irrational and self-indulgent opinions of the judges. As I said before, most of the recipients are political hacks. If you look over the list, you see a bunch of names unknown to almost any modern readers—and rightly so. A few are people I'd like to learn more about, but most wouldn't be worth the time it would take to skip over their names.

Let's just look at a few of the better-known winners—or more egregious choices—to see what the track record tells us. Things started off fairly well in 1901, when the first Nobel Peace Prize was split between Frédéric Passy, founder of the first French peace society, and Jean Henri Dunant, founder of the International Red Cross. But then, in 1906, Teddy Roosevelt won for drawing up the peace treaty between Russia and Japan.

L: The guy who led the "Rough Riders" in the Spanish-American War won a Nobel Peace Prize?

Doug: Yes, it's odd. Teddy had, to all accounts, great personal charm, style, and numerous accomplishments, but he was a horrible president—very statist and economically collectivist, and certainly one of the most warlike.

It gets worse: in 1919 Woodrow Wilson won one. That's an all-time low that will be hard to beat... But never say never—Mussolini, Hitler, and Stalin were all nominated. Wilson got it for founding the League of Nations. The fact that Wilson was single-handedly responsible for World War I going on as long as it did and ending with the disastrous Treaty of Versailles was apparently of no concern. I'm convinced that if it hadn't been for America's pointless entry into that war, the French, British, Russians, Germans, and Austrians would likely have signed a reasonable and much earlier treaty. Subsequent history would have developed quite differently—perhaps with no World War II and no Soviet Union.

L: I find it interesting that they gave out no prizes during the thick of WWII. I know there were actual advocates of peace back then, like T.H. White, author of *The Once and Future King*, but that would have been unpatriotic (politically incorrect), wouldn't it?

Doug: Yes, the prize money went mostly back into the main prize fund. But speaking of WWII, in 1953, George Marshall won a peace prize for his Marshall Plan, which is unjustly credited with Europe's recovery from World War II. What should be credited are the investments made by American corporations and individuals into productive enterprises in Europe. The Marshall Plan was just a gift from American taxpayers to socialist European governments. Worse, it served as a model for subsequent decades' worth of almost completely counter-productive foreign aid—perhaps the equivalent of a trillion of today's dollars.

L: And there have been more warmongers and political posers since then.

Doug: Sadly so. There was Kissinger, who should have been indicted for war crimes, who split the prize with Le Duc Tho in 1973. But Tho was principled enough to decline the prize.

Anwar Sadat and Menachem Begin split it in 1978 for peace in the Middle East. Both accumulated a lot of blood on their hands throughout their lives. I think a better choice in this regard would have been the US taxpayers who, since then, have given Egyptians and Israelis hundreds of billions in bribes not to kill each other.

One of the crowning ironies of the history of the Nobel Peace Prize, in my opinion, was when Gorbachev won in 1991 for bringing the Cold War to an end. What really ended the Cold War was the economic collapse and dissolution of the USSR, which Gorby—a hardline communist who subsequently went into the ecology business—tried his best to prevent.

A medal, a million dollars, and an E for Effort. It's really funny; he migrated from communism to ecology, from one scam into another, and gets a big payday instead of being pilloried.

L: What about the good guys? Do you give the committee a break for any of the deserving recipients?

Doug: Well, to me, the most deserving ever was the brilliant Muhammed Yunus, who founded Grameen Bank. Capitalist enterprises like Grameen (along with technology and good ethics) are what will bring peace and prosperity to the world, not blathering politicians, who are the majority of the recipients.

And, in spite of my generally negative view of charity, as a matter of principle as well as of practical consequences, I've got to approve of the prizes for Amnesty International (1977) and Doctors Without Borders (1999).

L: That's it?

Doug: Hmmm. Other deserving winners, but with reservations, I might add are Albert Schweitzer (1952), Martin Luther King (1964), Andre Sakharov (1975), Mother Teresa (1979), Lech Walesa (1983), Elie Wiesel (1986), the Dalai Lama (1989), Aung San Suu Kyi (1991), and Mandela and De Klerk (1993).

By the way, my old friend Leon Louw of the <u>Free Market Foundation</u>[1] of South Africa has been nominated several times, and I think he deserves it.

L: Could a hard-core free-marketeer like that actually win?

Doug: If Obama can win, anybody can win. It's a function of being the right cliché at the right time, which I admit Leon is not likely to be anytime soon. But who knows, when the dust settles after the coming economic collapse (it's not over by a long shot), things might be different. Maybe Obama deserves it for keeping McCain, who likely would have been an even bigger disaster than Bush, out of office. Even the wildest conjectures are well within the realm of possibility. The whole thing is so… goofy.

L: Okay, so… The Nobel Committees are not actively evil, just so politically correct as to have rendered themselves meaningless.

---

1. www.totallyincorrectbook.com/go/263

Doug: That's the way I see it.

L: Okay then. Thanks for your time.

Doug: Sure thing—till next week.

Doug Casey on the Coming War with Iran

Feb 1, 2012

L: Doug-sama, I've heard you say you think the US is setting Iran up to be the next fall guy in the <u>wag-the-dog</u>[1] show—do you think it could really come to open warfare?

Doug: Yes, I do. It could just be saber rattling during an election year, but Western powers have been provoking Iran for years now—two decades, really. I just saw another report proclaiming that <u>Iran is likely to attack the US</u>[2], which is about as absurd as the allegations Bush made about Iraq bombing the US, when he fomented that invasion. It's starting to look rather serious at this point, so I do think the odds favor actual fighting in the not-too-distant future.

L: Could they really be so stupid?

Doug: You know the answer to that one. We're dealing with criminal personalities on both sides, and criminals are basically very stupid—meaning they have an unwitting tendency to self-destruction. One thing to remember is that most of those in power in the West still believe the old economic fallacy that war is good for the economy.

L: The old <u>broken-window fallacy</u>[3]. Paraphrasing Arlo Guthrie, it's hard to believe anyone could get away with making a mistake that dumb for that long. Our friends at the Institute for Humane Studies put together a great, brief <u>video debunking the fallacy</u>[4].

Doug: People like those in power still suffer the delusion that it was World War II that ended the Great Depression for the US. Actually, it was only after the end of the war that the depression ended, in 1946. In his book

1. www.totallyincorrectbook.com/go/264
2. www.totallyincorrectbook.com/go/265
3. www.totallyincorrectbook.com/go/266
4. www.totallyincorrectbook.com/go/267

World Economic Development: 1979 and Beyond[5], Herman Kahn documented long-term growth throughout the 20th century. Between 1914 and 1946—a very tough time, with WWI, the Great Depression, and WWII—the world economy still grew at something like 1.8%. I believe real growth would have been several times as great, were it not for the state and its wars. But people still believe that spending money on things that explode and kill and destroy is somehow good for the economy.

L: I suppose they think it's okay if it creates jobs here and destroys lives and livelihoods "over there." But aside from the fact that it's not safe to assume today's enemies are not capable of bringing the battle onto US soil, it still ignores the fact that you're spending money on stuff that gets destroyed—like broken windows—and that impoverishes us all. Worse, the cost is not just economic.

Doug: That's right. This coming war with Iran has the potential to turn into something resembling WWIII, with enormous consequences.

Now, it's hard to speak with any certainty on such matters, because most of what we have to go on are press reports. Governments keep most really critical facts on their doings to themselves, and what you read in the press is as likely as not just a warmed-over government press release—in other words, propaganda. Meaningless, if not actively deceptive. It is correctly said that in war, truth is the first casualty.

L: But we do have the Internet these days, with indie reporters offering coverage ignored by the talking heads in the mainstream media.

Doug: True; it doesn't keep the chattering classes honest, but it does provide some diversity of spin, from which we can try to infer what's really going on. And from all the various sources—mainstream and alternative, Western and from within the Muslim world—I have to say that it appears to me that the Iranians are *not* actually developing nuclear weapons.

L: Then why do they act in such aggressive and bombastic ways?

Doug: Western powers are pushing them around, telling them what they can and cannot do, and treating them like children or mental incompetents with no right of self-determination. How else would you expect them to react? They may have a collectivist theocratic regime, but also a proud and ancient culture.

Now, as you know, I don't think there should be any countries at all—not in the sense of the modern nation-state[6], and I'm certainly no fan of the Tehran regime, but Iran *is* a sovereign state. The Iranians resent people from other countries telling them what they can and cannot do with their uranium

---

5. www.totallyincorrectbook.com/go/268
6. www.totallyincorrectbook.com/go/269

enrichment program, just as people in the US would if Iranians told them what to do with... well, anything.

L: Do you have specific data to substantiate your view that Iran is not focused on creating nuclear weapons?

Doug: I was just reading about an <u>official report</u>[7] that says that Iran is still not able to enrich uranium to the level needed to make nuclear weapons.

Uranium occurs basically in two isotopes with half-lives long enough to make it possible to find reasonable amounts of them in the Earth's crust: U235 and U238. Most of it is U238—99.3%—but it's the U235 that's fissile, meaning, it's the one you want for making nuclear reactors and weapons. So you have to enrich your uranium—to about 4% U235 to make reactor fuel and 90% or better to make weapons.

L: That's why the Russians are able to sell "downblended" uranium from decommissioned nuclear weapons for use as reactor fuel. So, you're saying the reports indicate that Iran is not capable of enriching uranium beyond the level needed for reactors?

Doug: Yes. But again, I have to stress that reliable information is very hard to come by. Remember when the US accused Iraq of having a program to develop so-called weapons of mass destruction? Apart from the fact that, except for nuclear weapons, that term is a complete misnomer, they had no such thing. It was either lousy intelligence or outright fabrication—and I suspect the latter. So how can we trust what they tell us today? Only a fool would be so naïve.

In any event, why shouldn't Iran have nuclear weapons? I wish none of these countries had them, but they do. No one stopped China, no one stopped North Korea, Pakistan, Israel, India, France, nor any of the others in the disreputable club that have them.

L: Wasn't it too late to intervene by the time those countries announced their nuclear capabilities?

Doug: I don't think so. Israel was friendly, so Western powers looked the other way. North Korea was too rabid, so they were left alone. The other countries are too big. The cat's out of the bag at this point; any country can develop nuclear weapons if it really wants to. But it's easier and cheaper to bribe a general—or maybe just a supply sergeant—in India, Pakistan, or Russia to get what you want.

Moreover, with the US on the rampage, prosecuting its counterproductive and unwinnable War on Terror, a lot of governments, especially ones unpopular in the West, have got to be thinking about acquiring nuclear capabilities. If

---

7. www.totallyincorrectbook.com/go/270

Saddam had actually had nukes, the US would have left him alone, just as they've left the Kims to rot in the workers' paradise they've made out of <u>North Korea</u>[8]. It makes sense for a country stricken from the US's official "nice" list and moved over to the "naughty" category to have some nukes. Everyone needs and wants a slingshot to keep the bully of the block at bay.

If you oppose nuclear proliferation, your first target should be US foreign policy, which is the biggest impetus behind the scramble to arms.

L: What about the argument that Iran would use nuclear weapons on Israel, if it had them?

Doug: That's ridiculous. It's true that just one or two nukes would turn most of Israel to glass, but it's a matter of mutually assured destruction (MAD), just as the *détente* between the US and USSR was. Israel is reported to have about 200 nuclear weapons, and the Iranians know it. Even if they launched a successful first strike against Israel, they would get wiped off the face of the earth in response. The regime in Iran is repressive and borderline lunatic, but they aren't *that* stupid. No way are they going to attack Israel with nukes. They not only cannot, but should not, be singled out for exclusion from the nuclear club.

L: But they're part of the axis of evil, don't you know?

Doug: Speaking of evil, it's evil to initiate the use of force or fraud. If Iran enriches uranium or even builds tools for war, that's not evil *per se*. But using force to stop them from doing something that is not in itself wrong *is* wrong, and that would make Iran's attackers the axis of evil.

In my mind, the US is the biggest threat to peace in the world today. I can easily imagine those in power in the US starting a war over any silly pretext, real or imagined. It could easily happen by accident at this point. Things go wrong. Maybe some young hotheads in Iran's Revolutionary Guard decide to take a boat out and attack a US frigate—launch a few RPGs at it before they're blown out of the water. Then the US feels it needs to mete out some punishment and launches a strike against the base the boat came from—which would be attacking the Iranian mainland—and the thing spins completely out of control. Could happen at the drop of a hat. Maybe the commander of a US ship has a streak of General Jack D. Ripper from Kubrick's *Dr. Strangelove* in him. Maybe the Russians or the Chinese—who are aiding the Iranians—mount a false-flag incident, because they want to see the US get involved in another tar baby.

L: So... another case of not just doing the wrong thing but the exact

---

8. www.totallyincorrectbook.com/go/271

opposite of the right thing, with economic, political, and ultimately physical world consequences.

Doug: That's right. Just look at what they're doing now, trying to isolate Iran from the world with an embargo. That could be seen as an act of war.

L: Well, wait a minute. A blockade is regarded as an act of war, but if Western countries decide to harm their own economies by not trading with Iran, that's unfriendly, but not force or fraud.

Doug: Well, it would be forcing citizens in those Western countries to pay higher prices for things, denying them the choice of buying oil from Iran if they wanted to. But I agree; that's more a matter of criminal tyranny and stupidity than an act of war. Still it sure is prodding Iran, throwing rocks at the hornets' nest.

The US did the same with Japan before WWII. The Japanese basically have no domestic oil production and were getting their oil from the US and the Dutch East Indies. The US cut off both supplies, backing them into a corner, leaving them little choice but an aggressive response.

At any rate, I think all of this could backfire on the US. Since the Iranians apparently can't clear deposits through New York, where international dollar trades clear, they've made a very commonsense move to cut the US out of the middle and sell their oil directly to India, without using dollars. I think other countries will follow—and then what? Iran isn't going to want bushels and bushels of rupiah or yen or whatever. I think the odds favor them turning to gold. It's said that's one of the means of payment the Indians will be using.

Gold is the logical choice and the next step in the demise of the US dollar as the world's reserve currency. There's a lot of demand for the dollar to buy and sell oil. If countries stop using it, demand for the dollar would fall, at the very time the US is greatly increasing the supply of dollars. The day is coming when trillions of dollars outside the US will only be spendable *inside* the US. At that point, it's game over for the dollar.

L: Would you care to put odds on open war between the US and Iran?

Doug: I'd say it's probable within the next two to four years—say, between 50% and 75%—that an actual shooting war will break out.

L: Thanks for your thoughts. I think.

Doug: You're welcome.

Doug Casey on His Favorite Place in the World

Feb 10, 2010

L: Doug, we've gotten a lot of follow-up questions to our conversation on currency controls[1]. People want to know more about Argentina and why you like it so much. So, let's talk about Argentina.

Doug: Sure. This is a good time, too, because I'm having a sort of house-warming party at the world-class resort we're building in Salta province, northwest Argentina. With the stipulation up front that I obviously have a financial interest in that project, I still think that, for a number of reasons we'll get into, Argentina is one of the best places in the world to weather the economic crisis. Yesterday is not too soon to start working on getting your assets and yourself out of harm's way.

L: Okay, so let's start with basics: why Argentina?

Doug: Well, I've been to 175 countries, most of them several times. I've lived in 12, defined as having spent enough time in the country to have rented a place to live or bought real estate and set up housekeeping. The thing is, technology has now progressed to the point at which any sufficiently motivated person can pretty much live wherever he or she wants. But most people still have a medieval serf mentality in this area and tend to live in or near the place where they were born and grew up. And they tend to think that the country they were born in is the best country in the world… I guess because they were born there.

L: All evidence to the contrary notwithstanding. And the more poverty-stricken and backward the place, the more fiercely patriotic its inhabitants tend to be. I suspect this is a modern expression of tribalism.

Doug: I've noticed that too—you travel now as much as I used to, so I'm not surprised we see most things the same way. But, as you know, I've never had a tribal inclination myself. And having been to so many places, seen their

---

1. www.totallyincorrectbook.com/go/272

pluses and minuses, it's all the more clear to me how ridiculous it is to see the world that way.

Although, it must be said, the tribal way of organizing a society actually makes more sense than the nation-state does—at least in a tribe you basically know everybody, typically have a blood or family relation with them, and almost certainly share values. The nation-state is just a piece of geography controlled by a central government. This is another subject for another time, but I believe the nation-state is on its way out.

Anyway, I asked myself, "Where is the best place to live, in order to enjoy life to the max, be freest, and enjoy the highest standard of living with the least amount of aggravation?" I looked at all the countries around the world, their pluses and minuses, and came to the conclusion that Argentina offers the best risk/reward and cost/benefit ratios of any country on the planet at this time.

L: Can you tell us more about how you came to that conclusion?

Doug: By a process of elimination. A couple generations ago, if you'd asked me where the best place to live was, I'd have put my finger on the United States. Back when it was still America, it offered a lot of freedom, a lot of opportunity, and had a lot of domestic capital. But things have been changing, and are changing very rapidly in the US now. It's no longer what it used to be. So the US, regrettably, no longer makes the cut—at least not if you have some capital.

And Europe is worse. It's hide-bound, constipated, heavily taxed and regulated, highly socialistic, and is suffering from what may turn into a demographic collapse.

L: My ex was from Germany. She told me families were basically paid by the government to have children.

Doug: It's not working; few people are having kids. But there's massive immigration, primarily from Muslim countries.

L: Those people are often very hard working and entrepreneurial—but they are not assimilating.

Doug: They are not assimilating, and Europe is becoming less European. Worse, the cultural clash could turn into something more serious, given the increasing tension between the West and Islam. The Crusades never really ended—they just seem to have time-outs between rounds.

L: Europe could turn into the battlefield the Cold Warriors feared it might, but in a totally different war.

Doug: Yes. It's a conflict that goes back to the 8th century, and I don't think it will be resolved anytime soon. So, I'd rule out living in Europe.

L: Africa?

Doug: Completely hopeless for anything other than a hit-and-run speculation. Too much racism, too many other serious and deeply entrenched problems.

L: And the Orient?

Doug: I'm a big fan of the Orient—I really like it. But while you can have a great life in the Orient, frankly, if you're of European extraction, you'll never become part of society there. It's just not going to happen.

L: Why is that so important? When I moved to Utah, people told me the same thing; the Mormons wouldn't invite me to their picnics if I didn't convert. But I didn't want to go to their picnics. I just wanted to be left alone. I loved it.

Doug: I understand, and value my privacy as well. But I enjoy going out to dinner with good friends at great restaurants. I like playing polo, and that's not something you can do alone. I like a friendly poker game once in a while. There are many benefits to society, and I enjoy them. But as pleasant and convenient as the Orient is, it's also pretty crowded; I like wide-open spaces.

L: You just don't want the cost of participating in society to exceed the benefits.

Doug: As a practical matter, that's right. There are moral issues as well, but that's another conversation.

L: Okay. So, eliminating the US, Europe, Africa, and Asia leaves Latin America and Down Under.

Doug: As it happens, I'm in New Zealand right now. Rick Rule and I bought a big ranch on the ocean ten years ago, and I also bought a smaller ranch on the Clevedon River. I first came here, as you know from our conversation on the subject, for the polo. It was kind of a joke. People used to ask why I came to New Zealand, and I would say it was for the kangaroos. "But," people would say, "there are no kangaroos in New Zealand." "Yeah," I'd reply, "I was misinformed." But it was really for the polo.

New Zealand is a delightful place. I think I'll keep my ranch here, because I like it. But the fact is that, for all of its advantages, New Zealand is an island, and it's pretty much at the end of the road. It's not very sophisticated, quite frankly, and it's become quite expensive.

When I first moved here and was recommending the place highly in the *International Speculator*, it was almost as cheap as Argentina is today. It was so cheap buying a meal in a restaurant, you'd almost feel guilty. But since then, the currency has doubled in value and domestic prices have risen more rapidly than in the US, so the general cost level is about the same as in the US. It's not a bargain anymore.

That's even more true for Australia, which is bigger but isn't as pleasant, to my way of thinking. Entirely apart from the fact that everything that moves there, on the land or in the sea, tends to be deadly.

L: And that leaves Latin America.

Doug: Exactly. Within that, what do we have? Central America, to be brutally brief, is "okay." But those countries simply have no class. When it comes to South America, I'm very partial to Argentina, Chile, and Uruguay. Of these, I prefer Argentina. Why? Because it has a down-at- the-heels but very classy elegance. That kind of reflects the fact that, a hundred years ago, it was the major competitor to America for the best place to go if you were a European looking to immigrate to the New World. It attracted many of Europe's best and brightest—and their capital.

Argentina blew it, of course, transforming itself from a country with one of the highest standards of living in the world to an economic basket case, over the course of the 20th century. The government of Argentina is monumentally stupid, with controls and regulations on everything, a big bureaucracy, and so forth. But that's compensated for by the place being very, very inexpensive. Whether you're looking at real estate or day-to-day expenses, it's much cheaper than either Chile or Uruguay. Also, I've found that on a practical level, the government leaves you alone more than most.

Uruguay, of course, is just across the Plate River from Argentina. It's got some advantages, but it's rather like a backward, yet more expensive, province of Argentina.

L: Why's that?

Doug: It's a smaller country than Argentina, one-tenth of the size, both in population and land area. It's long been known as a kind of "Switzerland of South America." It's a banking haven. Until recently, there was no income tax in Uruguay. Idiotically, they just slapped one on domestic income, but foreign income is still tax-free there. That draws a lot of rich foreigners, who have a disproportionate effect on prices. They bring a lot of capital, and the country's currency has risen about 30% against the Argentine peso in the last year. So, it's nice, but it's a quiet backwater—except for Punta del Este during January and February, when it's one of the most hopping places on earth.

Uruguay is considerably more expensive than Argentina at this point. A lot of Uruguayans, if they're in a position to, tend to want to live in Buenos Aires instead of Montevideo.

Montevideo is a place that still has horse-drawn wagons and gauchos standing around on street corners, drinking mate.

L: And the Graf Spee in the harbor.

Doug: I can't help but think of that when I'm there. The place is in a time warp, although a lot less than it used to be. When I first went to Argentina, in 1980, I felt I was taking a trip back to the 1950s. Then, when I went across the river to Uruguay, I felt I was taking a trip back to the 1930s. They still had the old black Bakelite telephones. That's all changed, but these countries are still caught in a bit of a time warp.

L: And Chile?

Doug: Chile is the unsophisticated mining province that made good… It's modern, everything works, and the capital city of Santiago is clean and nice, if plagued by air pollution. But it's a lot more expensive than Argentina or Uruguay, and doesn't have the same charm. Pinochet, for all his faults, put the place on the road to success. It's estimated the average Chilean has more net worth than the average American now.

L: So it's Argentina.

Doug: Yes. For one thing, I like its wide-open spaces. It's like the western US. Argentina is the size of the eastern US, but it has only 40 million people, and about 40% of those are centered around Buenos Aires. BA is one of the great cities of the world: sophisticated, marvelous, you can get everything and anything you want there, just one of my favorites. But once you get out of BA, you really are in the countryside. In most places, you can drive for hours through incredible scenery and not see another car. I like that.

Sometimes people who haven't been there are surprised when I praise Argentina, because they've heard how bad the government is. But it's not evil, or dangerous, like many. It's just corrupt, incompetent, and inefficient—which is actually much better than the alternatives, when we're talking about governments.

That said, there are disadvantages, too. Through one of the most impressive acts of government stupidity I've ever seen, Argentina, a country world-renowned for its beef, might actually end up having to import beef this year. It's insane. Like Saudi Arabia importing oil. But, that's what governments do.

Still, you can get the best beefsteak in the world for, oh, I would say a sixth of what you'd expect to pay for something equivalent in the US.

L: I've been to *El Rey del Bife* in Salta City and verified this for myself. One of the best steak dinners I've had, with salad and wine, and it was just over five bucks.

Doug: It's unbelievable. And I think I've found a place that's even better than *El Rey del Bife*, so we'll have to go there next time we're in town together.

L: I'll look forward to that. Did you start buying land all the way back in 1980, when you first visited?

Doug: No, I bought a ranch in Patagonia about a dozen years ago. One of my best Argentine friends said, "You'll make some money on that. It's okay for gringos, but if you really want something special, you'll go up to Salta province." I did, and he was quite correct. Patagonia is pretty, but it's not a center of culture.

L: I've been there. I think I saw more penguins than people.

Doug: It's basically a large expanse of wind-blown desert, except for a narrow band along the border with Chile, which is very pretty. Salta, indeed the whole northwest area of Argentina, is much more interesting. Salta, by the way, was recently named in *Frommer's Top Ten Destinations: 2010*. I especially like Cafayate, a town about the size of Aspen, Colorado, and strikingly similar in a number of ways. It's got a beautiful central square, with lots of sidewalk cafes, a couple dozen nice restaurants. It's very *gemütlich*, very enjoyable.

L: And it's not overrun by leftist environmental extremists.

Doug: Definitely one of its great qualities. But as nice as it is, it didn't have everything I wanted in a place to live. I thought, "Well, I'll just have to bring the things I want here." So, some friends and I bought 1,500 acres on the edge of town, and we're building a world-class resort.

We're very fortunate in that Cafayate is in a wonderful grape-growing region—that's one of the reasons it has so many nice things. All around the world, places that are good for vineyards are generally very nice places to live, as anyone who's been to Tuscany or Napa Valley knows. This is very much like that. It's a bit like Taos, New Mexico, meets Napa-Sonoma, California.

But there wasn't a polo field, so we've put a couple in, in our resort, which is called *La Estancia de Cafayate*[2]. We've also put in 40 miles of hiking, biking and jogging trails, an 18-hole, world-class golf course, tennis courts, a lap pool, a Gold's-type gymnasium, and a spa. The clubhouse will have everything from a cigar bar, to a billiards room, to a library, to a bocce ball court, to a quiet place where you can play go or chess. I don't think we've missed a single element, providing what a civilized person could want. We've got about 200 acres of grapes, so all the homeowners will get their own allotment of wine. Grapes are very aesthetic, which is the big thing, but we want to keep running costs as close to zero as possible—and they're a big help.

L: Okay, so be honest with me here. We had a conversation about spas, and you went to great lengths to distinguish between little wannabe spas, where you can get a massage and they put cucumber slices on your eyes, and a real spa, which is a total living experience that includes diet, education, sports and

---

2. www.totallyincorrectbook.com/go/273

physical training, as well as the saunas and massages, etc. Are you really going to be able to provide that kind of world-class spa experience?

Doug: Well, softly, softly, catchee monkey. So far, about 130 people have bought lots, and about 30 houses are under construction. More will be built over time, and that will get us to the level at which we can sustain a spa such as I described. It's a software issue. We'll have the physical facilities soon, but it will take a while to build the clientele that would justify having the people there who would provide the services. My intention is to start next year, hiring a couple Thais, or Filipinos, who are multi-talented. They'll know how to teach Tai Chi, Qi-Gong, do proper Thai cooking, and give proper massages.

As far as the spa cuisine is concerned, we're well on our way, because almost everything we'll eat grows in the valley. A wide variety of fruits and vegetables are being planted on our own land right now. The chickens and the beef and the milk are all local and organic.

With a little bit of luck, we'll eventually be as good as the Canyon Ranch or the like. You know, it takes a little time to develop the software. But I think it's very important to have the facilities for a full life. *Mens sana in corpore sano*, as the Romans said.

L: How much is ready to use?

Doug: We've built the golf course and golf clubhouse. The construction of the social clubhouse, gym, tennis courts, etc. should start next month. It should all be pretty well done within a year. By then, there should be 40 or 50 houses built or under construction, and it will be a delightful place to live.

[**Editor's Note:** As of this printing, the spa facilities have been completed and the social clubhouse is under construction.]

There's one really interesting, perhaps unique, thing about this project. I've lived in, and been to, a lot of communities around the world. Sometimes you like your neighbors, sometimes you don't. It's the luck of the draw. In Aspen, the chances are that I wouldn't like them; these days it's just drawing the wrong crowd, from my point of view. But I like all the folks I've met who've bought lots at Cafayate and are planning to spend time there. It's a generally laissez-faire, smart, get-along and go-along crowd, drawn from 14 different countries. It's really becoming a Galt's Gulch.

It's been a pain, having to build it myself, but there was simply no existing place in the world that I knew of that had everything or even just most of what I wanted.

One sign of how real this is, is that many of those who've bought lots at Estancia de Cafayate are Argentines—which shows that the pricing is right.

L: And they pay cash.

Doug: Everyone pays cash in Argentina. That's why land prices are real and so low—they are not inflated by borrowed money. There simply is no money to be borrowed for real estate in Argentina. None.

L: And you say Argentina has a very European flavor?

Doug: Yes, at this point, Argentina is more European than Europe is. You know what they say: an Argentine is an Italian who speaks Spanish, thinks he's British, and lives in a French house. That last refers to the gilded age buildings, of which there are thousands. Apartment buildings in La Recoleta generally have 14-foot ceilings and walls two feet thick, because that's how they were made, back in the day.

You know, I talk about how bureaucratic and stupid the government is, but I think there's a chance that the place will reform for the better, much the way New Zealand did in the mid-1980s. In other words, you can be so stupid, for so long, that eventually you have to throw in the towel and try being less stupid. There are several candidates running in the next presidential election who are reasonably market-oriented. If the same thing happens in Argentina as happened in New Zealand in the 1980s, it will boom.

L: With clear consequences for Argentine real estate.

Doug: Exactly, although the place has always had wild fluctuations in prices. When I was first there, BA was more expensive than London. Before the last crisis, it was about like New York. Argentina suits me as a speculator, it suits me as a freedom-lover, and it suits me as a place to live. All things considered, of all the countries in the world, I honestly just can't think of a better one.

And if you want to live there, they are very mellow about it. You don't need some sort of residence permit. For years, the practice has been to let anyone in for three months, and if you overstayed your tourist visa, even by a couple of years, you only pay a fifty-peso fine. And you can come right back in again. Try that in the US and see what happens…

L: What if I wanted to stay more than three months?

Doug: You just take a boat over to Montevideo, get your passport stamped, and come back. Or maybe drive up to Bolivia, or across the mountains into Chile, or maybe Paraguay for a weekend trip. This can be done indefinitely, with no problem. Cafayate actually isn't a bad place from which to get to know the southern half of the continent. But I don't like to leave once I'm there.

L: Okay, so it's no problem to prolong a tourist status, but if for some reason, I wanted to acquire a more permanent residency status, would it be difficult or expensive?

Doug: No, but you'd be wiser to do it in Uruguay. As an Uruguayan, you can cross over to Argentina with much more ease than even Canadians used to be able to cross over into the United States. They are both Mercosur countries, and residents of those countries can move between them freely. You can become a passport holder of Uruguay after only two years—it's not as good a passport to travel on as an Argentine one, but that's the way to do it.

I should also remind our readers that they don't want to keep any money in a bank account in Argentina. It's not a good place for that, but bank accounts and real estate are two totally different things.

L: Anything else? More investment implications?

Doug: I think what's going to happen, given the demographics we spoke of in Europe, is that thousands and thousands of Europeans are going to come to Argentina. Not poor ones, the kind who immigrated a hundred years ago, but wealthy ones. They'll see that the lifestyle is better in Argentina. It's less crowded and vastly cheaper—maybe 20%, or less, of the cost of living in Europe. And they can live there tax-free. As more and more Europeans discover this, you're going to have a lot more of them piling in. This is going to happen with Americans too, though they won't gain the same tax advantages. The IRS will still want to tax them; nevertheless, I think we'll see more of them moving down there. It's very popular with Canadians as well.

With the good things happening in Colombia, Brazil having finally turned the corner, and the problems clowns like Chavez in Venezuela are running into, there's a chance that South America, in general, could be the next sleeper that may soon awake to its day in the sun.

So, it's a place with a future. And any person who does not diversify his or her assets and physical presence, geographically and politically, in today's world is a fool. If they see what we see and don't take action, they'll get what they deserve.

It's especially important for US persons to do this now, before we see foreign exchange controls in the US, making it impossible, or very costly, to get your wealth out of the country.

L: Okay, thanks for the insight and encouragement. 'Til next week.

Doug Casey: Education of a Speculator, Part One

May 26, 2010

L: Doug, a lot of our readers have asked for you to tell some war stories—what were some of your biggest wins and losses, and what were the lessons learned?

Doug: Well, it may not all fit neatly under the rubric of "Lessons Learned," but I can tell you about some of the specific experiences that have shaped my career. There have certainly been some great deals and terrible deals that I've been in—and just as many of both that I've failed to get in.

L: It's all part of what Victor Niederhoffer would call *The Education of a Speculator*[1].

Doug: Vic's an old friend of mine, and his book by that title has some important insights. Although he's mainly a short-term trader. I prefer to only buy things I can hold on to for a few months, if not a couple of years. It gives you enough time to be right. And doesn't clutter your mind up with random noise and fluctuations.

L: Indeed; let the trend be your friend. Okay then, where do we start?

Doug: We've already told the story about my Ferrari business, in our conversation on cars, but that was my first business deal.

L: So, when you got out of the hospital, did you dive right into another deal?

Doug: Actually, I decided to start really educating myself at that point. Among other things, I read Harry Browne's seminal book, *How You Can Profit from the Coming Devaluation*[2], and that led directly to my first big score in the market. I read that book in 1970, and I bought gold coins. More important, as it turned out, is that I bought gold stocks and had a wild ride from 1971 to 1974. I made a *lot* of money, in percentage terms at least, since I was just out of school and had almost no capital to start with.

I then launched my second business venture—

---

1. www.totallyincorrectbook.com/go/274
2. www.totallyincorrectbook.com/go/275

L: Wait, wait… There was a big slump in gold in the mid-'70s. Are you saying you bought early, before Nixon closed the gold window, and then sold at the top of that first surge, realizing gains before the slump?

Doug: Yes, I did. But it's not as heroic as it sounds—I had no crystal ball. I sold near that interim top to invest in my second business, which was a company to market precious metals to the public. I have to say that I learned more painful lessons on that deal than I did crashing the Ferrari. Not only did I lose all the money I had built up, but I lost a bunch of money I didn't have. It took me years to dig myself out of that hole. I never declared bankruptcy, but I had significant negative net worth for some time.

L: That brings up an interesting point. You're a libertarian, and libertarians believe in the sanctity of the contract. That being the case, are there any moral grounds under which a libertarian *can* declare bankruptcy? There were times in my past when I was pretty deep in the red as well, and I couldn't bring myself to file for bankruptcy, even though it would have taken a great pressure off me. I'd made promises, and I just couldn't break them.

Doug: I completely agree with that, and that's why I didn't declare bankruptcy. I've always considered bankruptcy to be the act of hiding behind the state for the purpose of defrauding your creditors. It may be legal, but it's unethical (there's increasingly only an accidental overlap between what's legal and what's ethical). But most debt today is owed to banks. I have to wonder, with the banks increasingly becoming creatures of the state, if the ethics involved haven't become inverted in today's world.

L: It could be ethical to borrow money from the government and then declare bankruptcy to help hasten the state's own demise?

Doug: Could be. Inflation is well known to corrupt a society's morals in many ways. It's a dangerous thing, a slippery slope, to start rationalizing why one needn't make good on debts. But that's what's happening all over the US, with people walking away from their mortgages and their credit card debt, and declaring bankruptcy in record numbers. It's a trend that's going to end very, very badly.

What the state has done by increasingly insinuating its tentacles into every aspect of life is to completely corrupt society. Both the intended and unintended consequences are going to be ugly, because it blurs the ethics of daily life. It's entirely perverse that defaulting on debts can even be considered as a good thing, and inversions like this are proliferating.

L: We should do a conversation devoted to ethics—someone sure needs to. But let's go back to the '70s. What happened next?

Doug: Well, I had to dig myself out of that hole, so I redoubled my efforts to earn money. One of the things I did to earn money at the time was to write my first book, _The International Man_[3].

L: And thus was born a guru...

Doug: Well, it was _Crisis Investing_[4], a couple years later, that really put me on the talk show circuit. The other thing I did back in the mid-'70s was to become a stock broker. Have I told you the story of how I managed to buy precisely at the very bottom of the mid-'70s market trough?

L: No, please do.

Doug: I became a stock broker in 1976, which was fortuitous timing for someone who liked gold stocks. So, I was sitting there at my office in Washington DC, and I got a call from a guy—his name was Elmer—who impressed me as being one of these rich good old boys. I talked to him about what I thought would be good investments for him, and he said, "I'll come into town and put a little bit of money with you." The way he talked, I thought "a little bit of money" was going to be several hundred thousand dollars, at least.

When he came in, it turned out that he was an average Joe who rode in on a bus and really didn't have any money to speak of. But I put a portfolio together for him, worth about $2,500, which included a thousand shares of a stock called Grootvlei, a thousand shares of Bracken, and several hundred shares of Anglo American Corporation of South Africa. Because gold had fallen almost 50%, from $200 at the end of December 1974, Grootvlei and Bracken were penny stocks—substantial producers, but with high cost and short-life mines—that were each yielding indicated dividends of about 50 to 75 percent. Even Anglo was yielding something like 15%.

L: Those are pretty amazing dividends.

Doug: It's incredible what you can get in dividends alone when a market is at a bottom—something people seem to have totally forgotten about today.

At any rate, the day Elmer came in happened to be the day that gold hit its absolute bottom for that cycle—$103.50, if I recall correctly—and also happened to be the very same day there were big riots in Soweto that made headlines in the US.

So, Elmer gets hit with these two things at the same time, calls me back up and says he wants to cancel his order. I said: "Elmer, this isn't Woolworth's. You can't really take the merchandise back." But rather than paying me for what he ordered, he hung up the phone on me.

---

3. www.totallyincorrectbook.com/go/276
4. www.totallyincorrectbook.com/go/277

Having entered the orders for the stocks the previous day, I had to ask my-self what I would do about it. It was something of a revelation to me—it was clear that I was dealing with a very unsophisticated member of the broad public, a representative of a certain mindset. I figured he must be the perfect contrary indicator. In today's terms, I had to ask myself if I was just talking the talk or if I was willing to walk the walk.

So, I journaled those stocks I bought for Elmer into my account and held them until I sold in 1980 or thereabouts. By then, I was getting several times, annually, what I paid for them in dividends alone. It was a fantastic hit, at least in percentage terms.

L: So it was an accident?

Doug: Yes, completely. I didn't know it was the bottom. I just knew the stocks were really cheap. I believed what I had told Elmer about those stocks, and I figured it was more intellectually honest to keep them.

It turns out that I was right. People didn't want stocks that were off 90% and yielding 60%—they figured there had to be something wrong. They'd rather buy something that's gone up ten times, proving it has a good "track record." Track records are the best way to judge people, but the worst way to judge stocks.

L: I don't think I've ever heard of anyone picking the exact bottom of that cycle.

Doug: I got lucky, but it's a perfect example of why it's essential for a speculator to be a contrarian. You've got to believe in your thinking enough to buy when everyone else is selling, even with frightening images on TV, like the riots in Soweto. That's why it's critical to have an understanding of economics, politics, and the technical details of various businesses; only then can you hope to be immune from the blather you'll hear on TV and read in the popular press.

And when it came to gold, few people had a clue. I remember one politi-cally connected investment guru of the day—Eliot Janeway—saying, that if the US government didn't support the price of gold at $35, it would fall to $8. He didn't have a clue. But he influenced scads of people.

L: That's a great story. What a pity for good old Elmer.

Doug: Yes. I have no idea what happened to him after he hung up on me, but I thank him for appearing at the right time. Elmer was completely ignorant of economics and the markets, but he nonetheless taught me a more valuable lesson than any teacher in four years of college.

L: So what happened next?

Doug: The late seventies were very good to me, despite the fact it was the worst time for the economy since the Great Depression—high unemployment, high inflation, and skyrocketing interest rates. I was making great money in my regular business, royalties from *The International Man*, fees from speeches and occasional articles—and putting all my savings into mining stocks and gold, which was on its way to $800.

I wrote *Crisis Investing* in 1978. It was published in 1979 and hit #1 for many weeks on the *New York Times* Best-Seller list in 1980. Then, in 1982, I wrote *Strategic Investing,* which was more focused on the stock market, Dow Jones-type stuff. I got a very large advance, $800,000, from Simon & Schuster. That's a lot of money today, but was a lot more money back then, and it confronted me with the question of what I would do with the cash.

I can't say that I thought gold was done then, but the gold stocks didn't seem cheap, so I bought things like Treasury bonds, which were yielding 12 to 13 percent, and electric utilities, which were also selling for 12-15 percent yields, and other things I recommended in the book. It's an excellent book, <u>still worth reading today</u>[5]. I was dead right about the markets, even though I foolishly remained bearish on the economy—the markets and the economy are not at all the same thing.

L. That was at the beginning of the 20-year bull market for Wall Street.

Doug: Yes, it was my next big hit in the market. At the time, the DJIA was less than 1,000, and I said it was going to 3,000—which was an outlandish and outrageous prediction. Unfortunately, I didn't keep the things I bought long enough—I didn't think the bull market in stocks or bonds would go on anywhere near as long as it did.

I was gone by the time it hit 3,000. That was one of the biggest mistakes of my career. I didn't foresee interest rates dropping as long and as far as they did, eventually driving stocks and real estate to manic heights. I could have held on and done almost nothing else for the next 20 years, but I didn't. Nonetheless, I bought pretty close to the bottom and held on for a good, long run.

L: So what did you do after cashing in, in the '80s?

---

5. www.totallyincorrectbook.com/go/278

Doug Casey: Education of a Speculator, Part Two

June 2, 2010

[**Ed. Note**: When we left our intrepid hero last week, he was hanging off the edge of a golden cliff...]

Doug: That's when I started getting into the mining stocks you now cover. I liked their incredible volatility. But it took me quite a while to really understand the way the game was played. Even though the third thing I wanted to be when I was a kid was a geologist, it took me years to get geologically active, so to speak. But no regrets. It was a great time to get into the field, because there were some fantastic gold stock runs in the '80s, right up to the Bre-X scandal in 1996.

I went out into the field, as you do now, building first-hand understanding for the fundamentals of the business. That's as opposed to treating these things strictly like trading sardines—which, of course, most of them are. But even so, you can trade them much more effectively if you have a solid grasp of the technical areas of the business. And there's no book for learning this; there's really no way to learn how to sort the wheat from the chaff, other than to get out there and apply boot leather, spend a lot of time talking to geos, learn the psychology of the players, and watch the economics of mining companies as they develop.

The '80s were really a period of learning for me, playing around with wins and losses, all of which prepared me to profit from the bull market of the '90s. It's been a wild ride, with resource stocks cyclically going up 1,000%, and then falling 95%—again and again.

L: Heh. You didn't have the advantage I had of a Doug Casey who'd done it before and could teach me the ropes—and whose experience I can now draw upon at any time.

Doug: Yes, it really would have been helpful if I'd had a mentor... but I can't think of anyone back then who could have taught me what I needed to know. If there had been, I sure as hell would have sat at his knee and saved myself a lot of money and aggravation. But all that effort at self-education did prepare me for the 1993–1996 bull market, which was a wonderful, fantastic time to be in the junior mining sector. That was the time when I had the three biggest wins of my career.

L: Ah yes, the famous "accident, scam, and psychotic break." We mentioned those before, in our <u>conversation on winning speculations</u>[1], but you didn't really tell the stories.

Doug: Well, the scam was Bre-X, of course. I was introduced to that by my friend Rick Rule, who also introduced me to Silver Standard Resources and several other huge wins I've had in my career. The company was coming out with fantastic results from its drilling in the orangutan pastures of Indonesia. At the time, the stock was trading for about a buck, and there weren't too many shares out. I started buying, and the story just kept getting better, so I started buying with both hands. Who could have guessed that someone was salting the drill core?

I ended up with a very large position, and as I said before, I finally came to the realization, when the stock was trading over $100, that this exploration play had a market capitalization greater than that of Freeport McMoRan, which had already put billions of dollars into its Ertsberg and Grasberg mines, and was paying dividends, to boot. I asked myself what the point of holding on was, couldn't think of one, and sold on that basis. As you know, the whole thing was exposed as a fraud, and $4 billion of value disappeared.

The accident was Diamond Fields, of which I was a founding shareholder, simply because I was a friend of Robert Friedland's. I did a second private placement in it later, based strictly on the diamond assets. That was an offshore Namibian diamond play that looked great, as so many of these things often do, but didn't work out.

The only reason that Diamond Fields went to over $100 instead of near zero is because a couple geologists on a helicopter ride in Labrador, where the company was closing up shop, saw something out the window that looked interesting. They landed on the discoloration, sampled it, and that led to the world-class Voisey's Bay nickel discovery. It was pure luck those two geos were flying over that place and happened to look down at that time.

The psychotic break was Nevsun, which is still around today and is still active in Africa, as it was back in those days. I did private placements in that stock at $1.00 and $2.00, with full warrants, and rode it all the way up to $20.00,

---

1. www.totallyincorrectbook.com/go/279

when I sold. I call it a psychotic break because there was a broker in Chicago, now deceased, who, for some reason, went wild and decided to put 100% of his clients' money into that stock. He personally took it to $20.00, after which it slid all the way back to becoming a penny stock, before this cycle breathed some new life into it.

This all just goes to show that even armed with the best intentions and expert knowledge, sometimes it's extraneous events that can make all the difference.

L: Which underscores the importance of sticking close to the action, so you're not "out of the room, out of the deal."

Doug: Just so. Ted Turner supposedly attributes a lot of his success to just going where the action is and letting the law of large numbers work for him. It's true. You've got to be out there. Just running on the 9-to-5 treadmill is unlikely to result in anything other than mediocrity. It also helps not to be too risk averse, not to be intimidated by volatility, to have a contrarian nature, and to be inclined to go places others aren't interested in.

L: So, since we've recorded your three biggest wins for history, it would only be fair to record some of your biggest losses. Care to let one of those out of the bag?

Doug: It's funny—I tend to forget about those, actually. It's painful reliving them. Let's say I try to forget the incidents, while remembering the lesson.

L: It's just human psychology. You might think we'd want to remember our most painful experiences so as to never make the same mistakes again, but there also seems to be a tendency to push painful things from our minds, to enable us to continue functioning at all. If so, the unfortunate consequence is that people often repeat their worst mistakes.

Doug: That might explain why I've lost so much money on private deals. When you put money into a company at its founding, while it's still private, and it never goes public, you never get an exit, not even at a loss; the money just dies and goes to money heaven. At least if it was good money.

There are companies I bought decades ago that are, to this day, still not public. For all I know, they never will go public. I won't name names, but for all practical purposes, this is dead money. So I'm extremely reluctant to buy into private deals, although I can't help but look at them and still take the plunge occasionally. Some of these things that were deposited with brokers still show up on my monthly statements. Seeing them there is like getting poked in the eye anew every time, so I recently told the brokers just to delete them—the ones I know are bankrupt anyway.

There's a lot that can go wrong before a private company gains a listing on a stock market. As well as after…

L: But you still do it. I've seen you do it this year.

Doug: You're right, but the price was really, really cheap, and I knew the people involved. If I have high confidence that the people involved will do what they say they'll do, that helps—but it still needs to be at fire-sale prices.

L: Words to the wise, duly noted.

Doug: I'll tell you my best "woulda, coulda, shoulda" story. The stupidest failure to act in my career. A sin of omission, not commission.

L: Okay, shoot.

Doug: One of the largest publishing companies in the US was started by a friend of mine in 1979. At the time, I was just starting to publish my newsletter, the predecessor of the *International Speculator* you now run. He said he'd like to publish it, and I said: "Great, because I'm not a publisher and I don't want to be one." He said he'd sell me 10% of his new company for $10,000, with the idea in mind that that would be the seed capital for publishing the newsletter. I passed on the deal, thinking I was being a shrewd businessman. [Deep sigh.]

Today, I estimate that my 10% share of the dividends would have added up to $3 to $4 million over the years, plus my 10% stake would be worth $5 to $10 million.

L: Wow. But... if you knew your $10,000 was going to be seed capital for the publication of your own newsletter, why on earth didn't you take the deal?

Doug: Well, I had other offers from other publishers, and they seemed more experienced and stable; they didn't need capital to get the job done. My friend's company was private, with no experience in the newsletter publishing business, and I just didn't think it would work. I was simply, totally, dead wrong about it.

It's still a private company, but it would be one of the most productive pieces of my portfolio today, had I not been so clever back then.

And I've got to tell you that another of my best deals was, and still is, a private company. Believe it or not, it was a placer deal in Alaska—

L: You're kidding!

Doug: No. Talk about all the things you shouldn't do in investing: it was private, a placer deal, and with people I didn't know well.

L: Why is it that when you hear of a mining scam, it's so often a placer deal?

[**Ed. Note**: Placer mining is the dredging of rivers, sifting of sand-bars, etc., for gold that has accumulated in dirt, gravel, sand and other "alluvial" matter.]

Doug: The same reason that so few are in public companies—there are just too many X factors. The first thing that happens is that when you get going, your workers see nice nuggets of gold, and those nuggets somehow manage to disappear. More technically, it's really difficult to estimate mining reserves in a placer setting; the flakes and nuggets are inconsistently dispersed into pods. On the other hand, it tends not to be very capital intensive, and values are easy to recover by simple gravity separation. But that also means most of them have already been played out by prospectors. Placer mining is fun to mess around with during your summer vacation, but typically is not commercially viable.

L: So… *Why'd you do it?*

Doug: It seemed like a good idea at the time… famous last words. Actually an old friend, who did know the people, urged me to. And—not that this is an excuse for doing something goofy—it wasn't much money. Sometimes it's better to be lucky than smart, although that's no way to invest.

Anyway, I got into this deal for $20,000, back in the early '80s. That $20K got me 200 ounces of gold over the years, which is still on deposit with a major broker to whom they shipped it. They stopped producing in 2001 at the bottom of the market, when it was just uneconomic, but it's going back into production soon, so I may still get even more gold without putting another penny into the deal.

L: That's more than ten to one on just the gold they've dividended to you so far.

Doug: Yes. The $20k was tax deductible, since it went directly into expenses. And the gold is tax free until I sell it—which I have no intention of doing until there's a better place for the capital. Perhaps US stocks when dividends are in the 6-8% range.

But actually there's another one, an opportunity brought to me by Jim Gibbons, a longtime subscriber who started a company called Seattle Shellfish. In spite of the fact that I'd grown to hate private deals, Jim's project looked good, so I invested some money. It's still private, but it's paying me about 30% per year in dividends, and they've been increasing.

L: Sounds like a love-hate relationship you have with private companies. How does one even start to make a rational decision in that environment?

Doug: Well, they could start with my friend Arthur Lipper's book, *The Guide for Venture Investing Angels: Financing and Investing in Private Companies*[2].

I've had a lot more losers than winners investing in private companies, but almost everybody does. You just hope that the occasional winner is big enough to make up for the losses, plus give you a worthwhile risk-adjusted return. What that means is trying to go only for deals that, in your subjective opinion, have 10-1 potential. Better yet, try to negotiate for some type of security, to reduce your downside risk. A study of Arthur's books, and he's got several, is a cheap education.

L: Sounds like one I need to read, with so many students sending me business plans. Any other painful lessons learned to share?

---

2. www.totallyincorrectbook.com/go/280

Doug: Like I said, I seem to have pushed most from my mind… But maybe I should also say that some of my biggest winners have been outside of the world of gold stocks and mining, and in the world of real estate.

Spain was a good example. I bought real estate in southern Spain before Spain joined the EU—and I recommended doing so in the newsletter. That worked out very well indeed, not just because of the influx of tourists and money from Northern Europe, but because the dollar was much higher back then, making it cheaper to buy all kinds of things for giveaway prices. All of Europe was relatively cheap at the time. I also bought in Hong Kong during a China crisis. Same in Argentina—but crises there come quite often.

L: I'd guess any trend-watcher who was paying attention could have guessed that after Generalissimo Franco took his long-overdue exit from our weary world stage, things must have been at or near a bottom for Spain.

Doug: That's right. Another "woulda-shoulda-coulda" story in real estate is that I was in South Africa looking at beachfront property back in about 2000. It was very cheap at the time because the rand was about twelve to one against the dollar (because the price of gold and other metals was down). Had I done that, I could have made ten-to-one on some of those beachfront properties during the following boom.

L: So why didn't you?

Doug: I didn't want to live in South Africa. The problem with many foreign real estate deals is that if you're not going to be there and watch over things, you just don't know what is going to happen. You get squatters, you get rapacious town councils, and so forth. It's always messy, but it gets out of hand if you're not there, or frequently there. Anyway, gold and gold stocks were so cheap, I thought that was a better place to be. So, there are a lot of big ones like this that got away…

L: Like that castle you could have bought in Rhodesia during the war for $85,000—you told that story in our <u>conversation on real estate</u>[3].

Doug: Sure, but things can go wrong just as easily as they can go well, if not easier. Twenty years ago, I was talking with John Templeton, at his office in Lyford Cay, about real estate, and he told me about how he bought some land in Costa Rica back in the early '70s. That was a smart move on his part, because Costa Rica was very cheap back in those days. But his lawyer, who was an ex-vice president of the country, managed to defraud Templeton. The master at this game lost $200,000, which was a lot of money back in those days—incidentally,

---

3. www.totallyincorrectbook.com/go/281

I'd even met the guy who took the money. So you just have to be very careful about making long-distance investments in real estate, especially if you're not going to use them personally or stay close to them yourself.

L: Hm. Speaking of real estate, I heard a story about you that perhaps you can verify for me. I heard that when you started speculating in mining stocks, you'd actually been wiped out, or had very little cash. So you took out a second mortgage on a house you had in Vancouver, and that became the seed capital for your current fortune.

Doug: I forgot about that—it's true. I bought that house in West Van, which had 900 feet of really beautiful waterfront, for just under a million Canadian, when the Canadian dollar was about 65 cents US. I sold it at the beginning of the 1993 bull market, because I was really tight after the late '80s bear market, and I just really needed the cash more than I needed a big fourth house. So I sold it for C$2.3 million, when the Canadian dollar was at about 83 cents. Today, the house would go for about C$15 million, with the Canadian dollar at near parity. At this point I definitely would urge its owner to hit the bid—whether he needs the money or not. Vancouver property is riding for a fall.

L: That explains a lot. I always wondered about that story, because you always say that people should never risk money they can't afford to lose on mining stocks—"the most volatile stocks on earth." So it seemed strange that you would have gone deep into hock to gamble in the market. But you didn't; you liquidated a non-core asset and remobilized your gains. You missed out on more gains on the house, but that move provided the capital for the three biggest wins in your career, which you just told us about. Sounds like a great move to me.

Doug: Another lesson this brings to mind is that whenever I've made big gains in the market, I've made it a habit to invest the profits I've scraped back off the table into something that can't dry up and blow away.

L: Hence the emphasis on real estate.

Doug: Yes, though real property has carrying costs, and it's illiquid. That's the bad news. The good news is that it—usually—stays where you leave it. That's another advantage of salting away gold coins; you don't tend to liquidate them.

L: So noted. Any more lessons learned?

Doug: Well, I don't regret much in life, but the things I really regret the most, even more than the big losses I've taken, are the opportunities I've let slip through my fingers. It happens to everyone, and you shouldn't regret it too much, but they sure do smart. In most areas of life—not just investments—it's not the things you did that you regret, but the things you failed to do.

340 | TOTALLY INCORRECT

But investment-wise, for example, some friends of mine were founders of Digital Switch some 30 years ago. I didn't really understand the implications of the switch, no pun intended, from electro-mechanical to purely digital switching, so I passed on what could have been a *huge* amount of money.

The founder of AOL was also a friend of mine—I actually used to work for him at one point, when I was in the brokerage business. He made a billion dollars on AOL, another boat I missed. Coming close but no cigar hurts sometimes.

L: So what's the lesson to be learned from that? I bet there are even more deals you were quite right to pass up.

Doug: Lots and lots of bad deals I didn't get in on, for sure. Which re-emphasizes the necessity of looking at hundreds of deals—just so you can afford to walk away from 99% of them.

One more thing, I don't think it's possible to overemphasize the importance of having a voracious mind, of letting your curiosity run wild, into every subject and to every part of the world. To be a good speculator, you should have the broadest and deepest range of knowledge possible. If I had known more, I wouldn't have missed Digital Switch or AOL—it was my own ignorance that cost me those opportunities.

I said before that it's good to be lucky—but luck favors the well-prepared. For speculators, that means having the widest range of experience and knowledge possible, so you can see an opportunity for what it is when it comes knocking.

L: Hence our company motto: "Intensely Curious, Focused on Facts." Great stories, Doug, thanks for sharing them.

Doug: My pleasure. My guess is that this decade is going to feature some of the most volatile markets in history. That's a very good thing for those who are prepared and know what to look for.

End Note

Since you've made it all the way to the end of this longish book, I suspect that what has held your attention is what held mine when I began selecting material from the now vast library of *Conversations With Casey*. What gives the reader the sense that he's found something exceptional is Doug's instinctive affection for the truth. He follows the truth wherever it leads, with no need for reassurance from the opinions of others. And whatever he finds, he reports without compromise and with no tipping of the hat to conventional niceties.

There's nothing in this book that was weighed for acceptability, and nothing was omitted or trimmed to avoid bruising anyone's cherished beliefs. That can be a costly policy. It loses potential readers. It even sends some away angry or disgusted. But if it delivered to you even one idea that you suspected might be true but had never before seen properly saluted, it's the right policy.

Doug, as you know, is an enthusiastic and extraordinarily successful investor. I've met just a few others in the same class, and what they all have in common is that truth thing. It's a conviction that what is true is true regardless of anyone's opinion—or regardless of everyone's opinion if everyone is wrong. That conviction is what arms them to go against the crowd whenever they find that conventional wisdom isn't adding up.

There are more *Conversations* that you might enjoy, and they are waiting for you at http://www.totallyincorrectbook.com. There you can follow all the links that are indicated in this printed book. I hope you'll drop by for a double dose.

—*Terry Coxon*

Index